The Combat Service Support & Deployment

MW00379599

SMARTbook

**Doctrinal Guide to Combat Service Support,
RSO&I and Unit Movement Operations**

The Lightning Press
Norman M. Wade

The Lightning Press

2227 Arrowhead Blvd
Lakeland, FL 33813
24-hour Voicemail/Fax/Order: 1-800-997-8827
E-mail: SMARTbooks@TheLightningPress.com
www.TheLightningPress.com

The Combat Service Support & Deployment SMARTbook

Doctrinal Guide to Combat Service Support, RSO&I and Unit Movement Operations

Compiled, Edited, and Illustrated by Norman M. Wade
Copyright © 2005 Norman M. Wade
ISBN: 0-9742486-3-0

The publisher would like to extend recognition to Tony Gasbarre for his research and assistance with Chapter 4 of this book. Thanks Tony!

Printed and bound in the United States of America.

Preface

The fundamental purpose of the Army is to provide to joint force commanders the sustained and decisive land forces necessary to fight and win the Nation's wars. Combat Service Support (CSS) is an enabling operation that provides the means for the Army to conduct full spectrum operations. To support full spectrum operations, CSS must provide support to all possible mixes of offensive, defensive, stability, and support operations. In some operations, especially support operations, CSS may be the decisive operation. CSS is an integral component of all military operations.

The purpose of this SMARTbook is to provide an outline of the authoritative doctrine by which the Army's combat service support (CSS), as part of the national-theater CSS system, supports joint and full spectrum operations.

This SMARTbook is written from the tactical logistician's perspective, concentrating at the operational and tactical level. The information was collected from various current U.S. Army and joint force CSS doctrine and designed to supplement current logistics publications.

The intended audiences for this SMARTbook include:

- CSS commanders, staffs, and activities at all levels to provide a universal doctrinal understanding of how CSS is organized and functions to support Army, joint, and multinational forces
- Military students at all levels and within all branches of the Army and Services to provide a broad knowledge of CSS and how it works

Over the last decade, the Army relied on the Army of Excellence (AOE) construct for organization and operational doctrine. As the best-trained, best-equipped force in the world, the AOE served as one of the major linchpins in our national security strategy, not only by serving as a strong deterrent but also by physically enforcing peace in various trouble spots throughout the world.

The Force XXI concepts and organizational structures highlighted in this SMARTbook reflect a paradigm shift from a supply-based combat service support system in the AOE to an advanced distribution-based CSS structure.

Eventually, the Army will mature to a complete Force XXI divisional structure to include CSS. The Force XXI division represents a leap forward into the realm of 21st century technology. The smaller Force XXI division is more lethal and mobile, and has real-time situational awareness. Situational awareness enables Force XXI commanders to quickly amass forces allowing this division to defeat a larger but less technologically advanced enemy.

A note about our SMARTbooks...

Chapters and sections are organized in the same fashion as the source manuals where possible. For example, chapter one from a reference equates to section one in this SMARTbook; chapter two is section two, etc. Furthermore, the text is as close to the original source text as possible to replicate approved doctrinal publications and procedures.

SMARTregister for Updates

Keep your SMARTbooks up-to-date! The Lightning Press provides e-mail notification of updates, revisions and changes to our SMARTbooks through it's SMARTnews mailing list. Readers can register for the SMARTnews e-mail list online at www.TheLightningPress.com. Updates and their prices will be announced by e-mail as significant changes or revised editions are published.

References

The following list represents the primary references used to compile The Combat Service Support SMARTbook. All references are open source, available to the general public and designated as "approved for public release; distribution is unlimited." This SMARTbook does not contain classified or sensitive information restricted from public release.

Field Manuals

FM 4-0	Combat Service Support, 29 Aug 2003, SS FM 100-10
FM 4-01.011	Unit Movement Operations, 31 Oct 2002, SS FM 55-65 & FM 55-9
FM 4-01.30	Movement Control, 01 Sep 2003, SS FM 55-10
FM 4-30.3	Maintenance Operations And Procedures, 01 Sep 2000, SS FM 9-43-1
FM 4-93.4	Theater Support Command, 15 Apr 2003, SS FM 63-4
FM 4-93.50	Tactics, Techniques, And Procedures For The Forward Support Battalion (Digitized), 02 May 2002
FM 4-93.51	Tactics, Techniques, And Procedures For The Division Support Battalion (Digitized), 26 MaY 2002
FM 4-93.52	Tactics, Techniques, And Procedures For The Division Support Command (Digitized), 02 May 2002
FM 4-93.53	Tactics, Techniques, And Procedures For The Division Aviation Support Battalion (Digitized), 02 May 2002
FM 10-27-4	Organizational Supply And Services For Unit Ldrs, 14 Apr 2000
FM 55-1	Transportation Operations, 03 Oct 1995
FM 63-2	Division Support Command, Armored, Infantry, And Mechanized Infantry Divisions, 20 May 1991
FM 63-11	Logistics Support Element Tactics, Techniques, And Procedures, 08 Oct 1996
FM 63-20	Forward Support Battalion, 26 Feb 1990, SS FM 63-20, 17 May 85
FM 63-21	Main Support Battalion, 07 Aug 1990
FM 100-10-1	Theater Distribution, 01 Oct 1999
FM 100-17-3	Reception, Staging, Onward Movement, And Integration, 17 Mar 1999
FM 100-17-5	Redeployment, 29 Sep 1999

Other Publications

JP 4-0	Logistics Support for Joint Operations. 6 April 2000
CGSC ST 63-1	Brigade, Division and Corps Combat Service Support, Jul 2004
CGSC ST 101-6	Combat Service Support Battle Book, Jul 2004

Table of Contents

Combat Service Support (FM 4-0)

Chap 2

Logistics Support to Joint Operations

(FXXI) Tactical-Level CSS Operations

Chap 3

Combat Service Support Planning

(FM 4-01.011) Unit Movement Operations

I. Fundamentals of Army Combat Service Support

Ref: FM 4-0 Combat Service Support, chap. 1.

Though global developments and changing security relationships have changed the specific nature of threats, the role of the Army endures. It is the strategic land combat force that provides the nation with the capability to conduct decisive full spectrum operations on land. Combat service support (CSS) capabilities enable Army forces to initiate and sustain full spectrum operations. The fundamental purpose of the Army is to provide the land component of the joint forces that fight and win the Nation's wars, when and where required. Army CSS must always be capable of supporting this mission. It must also be able to support all possible mixes of offensive, defensive, stability, and support operations. In some operations, especially support operations, CSS may be the decisive force of the operation. Operations and CSS are inextricably linked. The purpose of CSS is to generate and sustain combat power and expand the commander's operational reach.

I. CSS in Support of Army Mission Essential Task List (METL)

FM 3-0 introduces and discusses the Army mission essential task list (METL). The Army METL lists the essential and enduring capabilities of the Army. While the tasks are not necessarily unique to the Army, they define its fundamental contributions to the Nation's security. CSS plays an important role in each task of the Army METL.

CSS in Support of Army METL

A Shape the security environment

B Promptly respond to crisis

C Mobilize the Army

D Conduct forcible entry operations

E Dominate land operations

F Provide support to civil authorities

Ref: FM 4-0, chap. 1.

A. Shape the Security Environment

Through peacetime military engagement, Army forces significantly contribute to promoting regional stability, reducing potential conflicts and threats, and deterring aggression and coercion. In support operations, such as humanitarian assistance or disaster relief, CSS forces make up a large part of the effort. CSS in support of such operations helps promote goodwill toward the Nation and its ideals. CSS may be obtained through such activities as contracting support for field services, maintenance, and storage facilities that help foster economic prosperity in some nations. Through many day-to-day interactions, CSS forces bolster and strengthen multinational partnerships and foster the development of democratic institutions.

B. Respond Promptly to Crisis

Army forces respond to crises in any environment. They are strategically responsive and versatile enough to support the nature and circumstances of any situation. Responsiveness is the ability to increase force presence, to increase the magnitude of the enemy's dilemma, and to act decisively. CSS is an integral part of the Army's rapid response. A distribution-based CSS system gives commanders increased management control and visibility of supplies, equipment, and personnel moving to and within the theater. The modular design of CSS organizations and their capability to conduct split-based operations give the force commander flexibility in tailoring CSS to meet the immediate need while minimizing lift requirements and the CSS footprint. Additionally, other CSS reach operations enhance responsiveness by using in-theater resources, such as host-nation support (HNS) and theater support contractors, to provide or augment services for deployed forces.

C. Mobilize the Army

The Army can mobilize Reserve Component forces necessary to meet the contingent needs of combatant commanders or the requirements of war or national emergencies. CSS is a critical part of the mobilization process. As units transition from peacetime to crisis or war, United States (U.S.) Army forces must be quickly brought to wartime readiness in equipment, personnel, supply, maintenance, legal, and medical areas. CSS organizations man and operate mobilization stations and aerial and seaports of embarkation. They also track unit movements. CSS organizations accomplish such tasks while simultaneously mobilizing their own forces. Currently, 70 percent of the CSS forces are in the Reserve Component. The Army trains and equips these organizations to mobilize and deploy forces, as demonstrated during Operation Desert Shield. During this operation, Reserve Component CSS forces were quickly mobilized and integrated with the active component forces.

D. Conduct Forcible Entry Operations

Army forces gain access to contested areas from the air, land, and sea. Army forces make it possible to seize areas previously denied by the enemy force. CSS supports forcible entry operations by aerial delivery, logistics over-the-shore operations, and ground transportation capabilities. The versatility of CSS organizations make it possible for CSS forces to support forcible entry operations and quickly convert to sustainment operations, when terrain is secured. The modular aspect of CSS organizations allows them to be tailored as rapidly deployable and tailorable early entry modules. This capability enhances their ability to support forcible entry operations.

E. Dominate Land Operations

Army forces today are the preeminent land forces in the world. That preeminence translates into the ability to dominate land operations—the decisive complement to air, sea, and space operations. The threat or use of Army forces to close with and destroy enemy forces through maneuver and precision, direct and indirect, fires is the ultimate means of imposing will and achieving a decisive outcome. The commander generates and sustains combat power to accomplish his mission by effectively and efficiently providing CSS. The Army CSS system, as a part of the joint personnel and logistics system, provides personnel, equipment, munitions, fuel, transportation support, and other services required to bring combat operations to a decisive conclusion.

Sustained land operations establish the long-term conditions required by the United States to support National objectives. Army forces are inherently durable, self-sustaining, and self-replenishing. Robust CSS makes sustained land operations possible. CSS consists of a network of people, organizations, and agencies from the continental United States (CONUS) to the area of operations (AO).

F. Provide Support to Civil Authorities

Army forces adapt and tailor their warfighting capabilities to complement and support civil authorities and agencies at home and abroad. Prompt Army assistance to civil authorities is often a critical and decisive element in disaster relief and crisis resolution.

II. CSS Characteristics

The fundamental characteristics of effective and efficient CSS discussed in FM 3-0 apply throughout full spectrum operations. They are consistent and align with the seven logistics principles in JP 4-0. However, an eighth characteristic, integration, is critical to the Army. These characteristics are not a checklist; they are guides to analytical thinking and prudent planning.

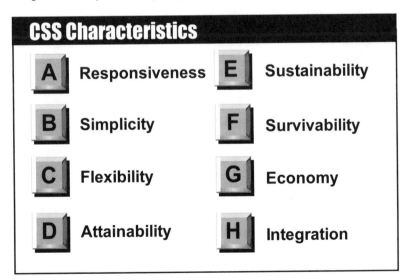

CSS Characteristics

A. Responsiveness   E. Sustainability

B. Simplicity   F. Survivability

C. Flexibility   G. Economy

D. Attainability   H. Integration

Ref: FM 4-0, chap. 1.

A. Responsiveness

Responsiveness is providing the right support in the right place at the right time. It includes the ability to foresee operational requirements. Responsiveness involves identifying, accumulating, and maintaining the minimum assets, capabilities, and information necessary to meet support requirements. It is the crucial characteristic of CSS; responsiveness involves the ability to meet changing requirements on short notice. Anticipating those requirements is critical to providing responsive CSS.

Anticipation

Anticipation is being able to foresee future operations and identify, accumulate, and maintain the right mix, capabilities, and information required to support to the force. Anticipation also enables CSS planners to provide input on the Army CSS forces the joint/multinational support force requires, so the commander can properly sequence them in the time-phased force and deployment data (TPFDD) process. Accurate forecasts of potential operations are necessary to develop a force that is strategically responsive, deployable, and fully capable of performing missions it is likely to receive. Many current CSS initiatives focus on improving the force capability to forecast requirements then execute or act on those forecasts. However, no planner can fully predict the course of the future. A dynamic global society places shifting strategic requirements on the military. Operations often evolve in unexpected directions as commanders constantly seek to exploit fleeting opportunities. Therefore, responsiveness rests on anticipation as well as flexibility. CSS units and personnel continually stay abreast of operations plans and remain flexible and ready to tailor available capabilities rapidly to meet changing requirements.

B. Simplicity

Simplicity means avoiding unnecessary complexity in conducting (planning, preparing, executing and assessing) CSS operations. It fosters efficiency in National and theater CSS operations. Mission orders, drills, rehearsals, and standardized procedures contribute to simplicity. Emerging CSS information systems can be highly efficient tools to help with such tasks as establishing clear support priorities and allotting supplies and services.

C. Flexibility

Flexibility is the ability to adapt CSS structures and procedures to changing situations, missions, and concepts of operations. CSS plans, operations, and organizations must be flexible enough to achieve both responsiveness and economy. The CSS force provides support in any environment throughout the spectrum of conflict and adapts as operations evolve. Flexibility may require improvisation (inventing, arranging, or fabricating what is needed from what is on hand). When established procedures do not provide the required support, CSS personnel seek innovative solutions, rapidly devise new procedures, or take extraordinary measures to adapt to the situation.

D. Attainability

Attainability is generating the minimum essential supplies and services necessary to begin operations. Before an operation begins, the focus of the CSS effort is on generating combat power. The commander sets the minimum level of combat power he needs before an operation begins. This requires integrating operations and CSS planning. It involves the ability to identify and accumulate the critical resources required at the start of an operation.

E. Sustainability

Sustainability is the ability to maintain continuous support during all phases of campaigns and major operations. One of the characteristics of land combat is duration. CSS personnel must work with operations planners to anticipate requirements over the duration of the operation and with CSS operators to synchronize provision of required supplies and services throughout. CSS personnel must effectively perform their roles to attain the minimum combat power, then be able to follow on with additional resources to sustain operations for as long as required.

F. Survivability

Survivability is the ability to protect support functions from destruction or degradation. CSS survivability is a function of force protection, which consists of those actions to prevent or mitigate hostile actions against personnel, resources, facilities, and critical information. Integrating CSS with operation plans and force protection plans is critical to CSS survivability. Economy, through such methods as CSS reach operations contributes to protecting capabilities by limiting the CSS resources that require protection. Dispersion and decentralization of CSS operations may also enhance survivability. The commander may have to balance survivability with economy in considering redundant capabilities and alternative support plans.

G. Economy

Economy means providing the most efficient support to accomplish the mission. Resources are always limited. The commander achieves economy by prioritizing and allocating resources. Economy reflects the reality of resource shortfalls, while recognizing the inevitable friction and uncertainty of military operations. Many CSS developments focus on the ability of the CSS commander to provide required support with the minimum expenditure of resources. Modular forces, split-based operations, and joint and multinational support coordination are some of the methods used to meet these goals. Emerging information technology with modern software packages continue to enhance economy of CSS resources.

H. Integration

Integration consists of synchronizing CSS operations with all aspects of Army, joint, interagency, and multinational operations. First, it involves total integration of Army CSS with the operations (plan-prepare-execute-assess) process. Support of the commander's plan is the goal of all CSS efforts. Effective support requires a thorough understanding of the commander's intent and synchronizing CSS plans with the concept of operations. Army forces conduct operations as part of joint, multinational, and interagency teams in unified actions. Therefore, Army forces integrate their CSS operations with other components of the joint force to:

- Take advantage of each service component's competencies
- Allow efficiencies through economies of scale
- Ensure the highest priorities of the joint force are met first
- Avoid duplicating effort and wasteful competition for the same scarce strategic lift as well as in-theater resources

III. CSS Functions

Ref: FM 4-0, chap. 1.

CSS consists of 11 interrelated functions. CSS commanders must carefully plan, manage, and synchronize these functions.

1. Supply
Supply is the acquiring, managing, receiving, storing, and issuing all classes of supply, except Class VIII, required to equip and sustain Army forces.

2. Field services
Field services are essential services to enhance a soldier's quality of life. They consist of clothing exchange, laundry and shower support, textile repair, mortuary affairs, preparation for aerial delivery, food services, billeting, and sanitation.

3. Transportation
Transportation is moving and transferring units, personnel, equipment, and supplies to support the concept of operations.

4. Maintenance
Maintenance entails actions taken to keep materiel in a serviceable, operational condition, returning it to service, and updating and upgrading its capability.

5. Explosive Ordnance Disposal Support
Explosive ordnance disposal (EOD) is the detection, identification, on-site evaluation, rendering safe, recovery, and final disposal of unexploded explosive ordnance.

6. Health Service Support (HSS)
Health service support (HSS) consists of all services performed, provided, or arranged to promote, improve, conserve, or restore the mental or physical well-being of personnel in the Army and, as directed, for other services, agencies, and organizations.

7. Human Resource Support (HRS)
Human resource support (HRS) provides all activities and functions to sustain personnel manning of the force and personnel service support to service members, their families, Department of the Army civilians, and contractors.

8. Financial Management Operations (FMO)
Financial management operations (FMO) encompasses the two core processes of resource management and finance operations.

9. Legal Support
Legal support is the provision of operational law support in all legal disciplines (including military justice, international law, administrative law, civil law, claims, and legal assistance) to support the command, control, and sustainment of operations.

10. Religious Support
Religious support is the provision and performance of operations for the commander to protect the free exercise of religion for soldiers, family members, and authorized civilians.

11. Band Support
Army band support is the provision of music to instill in soldiers the will to fight and win, foster the support of citizens, and promote National interests at home and abroad.

IV. Engineering Support to CSS Operations

Engineering support, though not a CSS function, plays a critical role in delivering CSS by enhancing its capacities. The ability of CSS elements to support Army operations depends on the capacities of the existing theater infrastructure (such as, force reception/bed down and storage facilities, road and rail networks, and ports and airfields) and environmental considerations. Engineer units, normally in a direct support (DS) relationship to CSS headquarters, are responsible for constructing, maintaining, and rehabilitating the theater distribution system. Their responsibilities include support to other services, agencies, and multinational forces. The numbers and types of engineer units involved in such operations depend on mission, enemy, terrain and weather, troops and support available, time available, civil considerations (METT-TC) factors. Of particular importance are the size of the support bases required, existing host nation (HN) infrastructure, and the perceived threat.

V. CSS Force Agility

The changing nature of modern warfare requires Army forces to be strategically responsive to a wide range of threats, while economically maximizing the Army's effectiveness. FM 3-0 describes an agile Army force. Agile forces are mentally and physically able to transition within or between types of operations with minimal augmentation, no break in contact, and no significant additional training. Responsiveness, flexibility, and economy are key CSS characteristics that enable CSS forces to support an agile combat force and execute operations more swiftly than their opponents. They help get the force what it needs to initiate, sustain, and extend operations. Agile CSS forces allow combat forces to adapt quickly to full spectrum operations and missions, while expending as few resources as possible and minimizing the CSS footprint.

Agile Army CSS requires planning and development within the context of unified action—operations that involve joint, multinational, and interagency organizations. Department of Defense (DOD) executive agent directives, combatant commander lead-service designations, interservice support agreements, contracted support arrangements, and multinational support agreements help commanders tailor the deployment of Army CSS organizations and make overall support as effective, yet as economical as possible.

Another aspect of an agile CSS force is the growing seamless nature of the Army's CSS structure. Elements of the strategic base, such as the U.S. Army Materiel Command (USAMC) logistics support element (LSE) and U.S. Army Medical Research and Materiel Command (USAMRMC) elements, deploy to AOs. Commanders integrate them into the overall CSS force. They provide support at the operational level and, in certain scenarios, the tactical level.

Other aspects of an agile CSS force are modular designs, the ability to tailor CSS organization for the supporting mission, and the ability to conduct split-based operations.

1. Modular Designs

Selected CSS units are structured as modular organizations. This involves company-level force structure designs in which each major company subelement has a cross-section of the company's total capabilities. This allows commanders to employ individual modules to provide a support function, while the rest of the unit remains operational. This lower-level force tailoring enhances responsiveness.

2. CSS Force Tailoring

CSS force tailoring refers to determining and deploying the right mix of CSS units to support the force or mission. CSS commanders must deploy the right type of CSS unit to maximize effectiveness and efficiency, and to minimize the CSS footprint.

3. Split-Based Operations

Split-based operations refer to performing certain CSS administrative and management functions outside the joint operations area (JOA), whether in a secure location in the communications zone (COMMZ), at an intermediate staging base (ISB), or at home station. Soldiers and civilians can perform personnel, materiel, and distribution management functions without deploying to the JOA if the information systems are adequate. This helps minimize strategic lift requirements, reduce the CSS footprint in theater, and still meet support requirements.

VI. Distribution-Based CSS

The Army has begun the challenging transition from a supply-based to a distribution-based CSS system. Distribution-based CSS replaces bulk and redundancy with velocity and control. During this transition, some units may not be able to execute all operations 100 percent according to distribution doctrine. However, only an agile distribution-based CSS system will allow Army forces to be strategically responsive and operationally effective across the full range of military operations. Distribution includes all the actions performed to deliver required resources (units, materiel, personnel, and services) to, from, and within a theater. Distribution-based CSS includes visibility, management, and transportation of resources flowing to supported forces, as well as the information systems, communications, and physical and resource networks of the distribution system. Chapter 5 discusses distribution-based logistics. FM 100-10-1 details the Army's role in theater distribution. JP 4-01.4 covers theater distribution. The following are critical aspects of a distribution-based system.

1. Centralized Management

Distribution management centers /elements (DMC/Es) are being added to support commands. DMC/Es manage the Army's role in theater distribution. Critical to the central management functions of the DMC/E is having integrated, end-to-end visibility and control of the Army's piece of the distribution system capacity and distribution pipeline flow to maximize its efficiency.

2. Maximum Use of Throughput

Throughput is the flow of sustainability assets in support of military operations, at all levels of war, from point of origin to point of use. It involves the movement of personnel and materiel over lines of communications using established pipelines and distribution systems. Throughput distribution bypasses one or more echelons in the system to minimize handling and speed delivery forward. Distribution-based CSS emphasizes using containerization, to include palletization and packaging (within materiel-handling equipment constraints), to accommodate support and improve velocity. Velocity is achieved by throughput of resources from the sustaining base directly to tactical-level support organizations as much as possible.

3. Configured Loads

A configured load is a single or multicommodity load of supplies built to the anticipated or actual needs of a consuming unit, thereby, facilitating throughput to the lowest possible echelon. Configured loads leverage the efficiencies of containerization and capabilities of containerized roll-on/off platforms (CROPs) when possible. The two types of configured loads are mission-configured loads (MCLs) and unit-configured loads (UCLs).

- **Mission-Configured Loads (MCLs).** MCLs are built inside a theater of operations for a specific mission, unit, or purpose. Resources (personnel, equipment, and supplies) in a hub in the COMMZ/ISB or corps area are normally configured as MCLs.
- **Unit-Configured Loads (UCLs).** UCL is a configured load built to the known requirements of a consuming unit. These loads are normally built in the corps AO to be delivered directly to the consuming unit.

4. Scheduled Delivery

Scheduled delivery involves moving resources from the supporting organization to the supported units at agreed-on time intervals. Distribution managers at each echelon coordinate with the supported unit to establish scheduled delivery times for routine replenishment. Generally, this includes items such as bulk fuel, ammunition, and operational rations.

5. Time-Definite Delivery (TDD)

Time-definite delivery (TDD) is a commitment between the CSS manager and the supported commander and specifies order-ship times (OSTs) within which specified commodities requested by the supported unit must be delivered. The commander responsible for both the supporting and supported organizations establishes the TDD as part of the distribution plan. TDD parameters are normally expressed in terms of hours or days for each major commodity. Establishing OSTs involves making trade-offs between responsiveness and the length of lines of communication (LOC). If the commander wants to establish shorter TDD schedules, he has to accept larger stockage levels forward on the battlefield, shorter LOC, or both, with an accompanying loss of flexibility and agility.

VII. Velocity Management (VM)

Effective distribution depends on the movement control principle of maximum use of carrying capacity. This principle involves more than loading each transport vehicle to its maximum cubic carrying capacity. It also means using all available transport capability in the most efficient manner. While allowing for adequate equipment maintenance and personnel rest, transportation operators should keep transportation assets loaded and moving as much as the situation permits. Adhering to the principles of velocity management may conflict with this principle. Delivering a shipment rapidly may require transporting it in a less-than-truckload shipment. Individual commanders and logisticians must consider the ramifications of maximizing the carrying capacity or transporting in less-than-truckload shipment when developing the distribution plan.

Velocity management (VM) is an Army-wide total quality management, process-improvement program. VM strives to provide world-class logistics support while providing a hedge against unforeseen interruptions in the logistics pipeline by leveraging information technologies and optimizing its processes. The overarching objective is to get supplies into the hands of the warfighter in days or hours, not weeks. VM optimizes the Army's entire logistics process by using a simple three-step methodology: define, measure, and improve. VM's objective is to find and eliminate non-value processes, thereby enhancing the responsiveness of the distribution system.

VIII. Situational Understanding

A factor that enables an agile CSS force to focus a distribution-based system to respond to and meet the needs of the operational commander is situational understanding (SU). Situational understanding is the product of applying analysis and judgment to the common operational picture to determine the relationships among the factors of METT-TC (FM 3-0). For the CSS planner SU is enhanced through the use of advanced, seamless information technology, as exemplified by the capability of the combat service support control system (CSSCS) coupled with the future capability of GCSS-A. A discussion of the key elements of SU follows. These elements are in various stages of development.

1. Common Operational Picture (COP)

An operational picture is a single display of relevant information within a commander's area of interest (FM 3-0). A common operational picture is an operational picture tailored to the user's requirements, based on common data and information shared by more than one command (FM 3-0). The COP portrays the same CSS and operational data, the threat, and the environment at all echelons in near real-time to provide commanders and CSS managers the identical battlefield picture. Commanders and managers require this picture to ensure unity of command and integrate operations and CSS. A seamless information network combined with asset visibility and GCSS-A, the new standard Army management information system (STAMIS) for CSS, will ultimately provide a COP that is comprehensive and synchronized with the information from CSSCS.

2. Seamless Information Network

A seamless information network will provide the ability to autonomously exchange large volumes of information across data platforms, such as GCSS-A and CSSCS, and among multiple echelons of command, from the tactical to the strategic level. It will include the capability to determine the actual status of selected weapon systems via assessing the system maintenance and supply (ammunition and fuel) postures directly and feeding the information into the CSS network. It will fuse operational and CSS data to make distribution-based CSS and split-based operations possible. It will also enhance the security of CSS assets by providing a COP.

3. Total Asset Visibility (TAV)

Timely and accurate visibility is necessary to distribute assets on time. Visibility begins at the point where materiel starts its movement to the theater—be that a depot, commercial vendor, or a storage facility—and continues until it reaches the requestor/user. The information is digitized and entered into CSS information systems. Critical to visibility is the capability to update that source data dynamically with the near-real-time status of resources from subsequent CSS systems until they arrive at their ultimate destinations.

4. Integrated STAMIS

An integrated STAMIS is one that incorporates multiple types of functionality within a single system and shares database information between functionalities. GCSS-A is an example of an integrated STAMIS. It will interface with other CSS information systems to provide users access to the maximum amount of information with the minimum amount of data entry. Ultimately, full integration of data and CSS systems will eliminate the need for an application interface.

II. CSS in Unified Action

Ref: FM 4-0 Combat Service Support, chap. 2.

As emphasized throughout FM 4-0, the Army does not operate alone. In today's world, the U.S. military conducts joint operations and often participates in multinational and interagency operations. Therefore, a great degree of coordination, cooperation, integration, and unity of effort in combat service support (CSS) operations is imperative for success.

I. The Army Role in Joint Logistics and Personnel Operations

The Army Service Component Commander (ASCC) exercises administrative control (ADCON) over all Army forces within the combatant commander's AOR. The ASCC commander is responsible for preparing, training, equipping, administering, and providing CSS to Army forces assigned to combatant commands. The ASCC commander is responsible for providing ARFOR to subordinate joint forces, including CSS forces and support resources to support those subordinate joint forces. The ASCC commander is also responsible for meeting any CUL requirements within a particular joint force and tailors the ARFOR accordingly.

The ASCC is responsible for all Title 10 functions within the combatant commander's AOR.

CSS & Joint Logistics Relationships

Joint Logistic Functions	Combat Service Support Functions
▪ Supply ▪ Services ▪ Maintenance ▪ Transportation Health Services Support ▪ General Engineering	▪ Supply ▪ Field Services ▪ Maintenance ▪ Transportation ▪ Health Service Support ▪ Explosive Ordnance Disposal
Joint Personnel Functions	▪ Human Resource Support ▪ Legal Support
▪ Personnel Support ▪ Legal Support ▪ Religious Ministry ▪ Financial Management	▪ Religious Support ▪ Financial Management ▪ Band Support

Ref: FM 4-0, chap. 2, fig. 2-1.

Note: Joint Force Logistics is covered in greater detail in Chap. 2, Logistics Support to Joint Operations.

II. ASCC Title 10 Functions

Subject to the authority, direction, and control of the Secretary of Defense and subject to the provisions of chapter 6 of this title, the Secretary of the Army is responsible for, and has the authority necessary to conduct, all affairs of the Department of the Army, including the following functions:

- Recruiting
- Organizing
- Supplying
- Equipping (including research and development)
- Training
- Servicing
- Mobilizing
- Demobilizing
- Administering (including the morale and welfare of personnel)
- Maintaining
- Construction, outfitting, and repair of military equipment
- Construction, maintenance, repairs of buildings and structures, utilities, acquisition of real property and interests in real property necessary to carry out the responsibilities specified in this section.

Ref: FM 4-0, chap. 2, 10 USC.

The ASCC commander's principal CSS focus is on operational-level CSS. Operational-level CSS focuses on theater support involving force generation and force sustainment. Chapter 4 discusses functions associated with operational-level CSS.

Support stems from a variety of sources, including contractors, DA/DOD civilians, U.S. and allied military organizations, and host-nation support (HNS) resources.

The ASCC commander focuses on generating and moving forces and materiel into theater as well as sustaining these forces during campaigns and other joint operations. In all joint operations, coordinating and executing CSS operations is a service responsibility unless otherwise directed by executive agent directives, combatant commander lead service designations, or ISSAs. The ASCCs, in concert with their associated geographic combatant commanders, are responsible for identifying CSS requirements, coordinating resource distribution from the strategic base, allocating necessary CSS capabilities, and establishing requisite Army CSS command and control (C2) relationships within the theater. Furthermore, the ASCC commander is responsible for properly executing all Army lead service or ISSA-related CUL requirements within the theater.

An ARFOR is designated whenever Army forces are involved in an operation. Even if separate Army forces are conducting independent operations within a joint operations area (JOA), there is only one ARFOR headquarters in that JOA. ASCCs, numbered Army, and corps headquarters (with augmentation) are capable of serving as ARFOR headquarters. In certain small-scale contingencies, a division headquarters may be designated as ARFOR headquarters; however, a division headquarters requires extensive augmentation for this mission.

III. ARFOR Operational/Tactical-Level Ops

Within the context of the JFC's plan, the ARFOR headquarters conducts both the operational and tactical-level sustaining operations to include:

- Support of reception, staging, onward movement, and integration (RSO&I) operations
- Tactical-level CSS
- Distribution management operations, to include synchronization of materiel management and movement control
- Support to reconstitution of Army units
- Execution of CUL support responsibilities
- Security of CSS, maintenance of the lines of communication (LOC), and C2 of tactical combat forces (TCFs)

Ref: FM 4-0, chap. 2.

Within the JFC's framework of responsibilities, the ARFOR headquarters carries out planning responsibilities associated with CSS, as well as assigned lead service support to other services and organizations. The support structure starts with a nucleus of minimum essential support functions and capabilities focused on force generation within the theater. As the deployed force grows, the support structure gains required capabilities. The theater support structure must provide support to the engaged forces; to units in (or passing through) the communications zone (COMMZ); and to other units, activities, forces, and individuals as the JFC directs.

ARFOR include the tactical-level CSS organizations (discussed in chapter 4) that provide support to tactical forces. The ASCC commander tailors an ARFOR to its mission, providing any EAC-level support organizations it requires. These may be the multifunctional TSC as well as specialized engineer, finance, medical, personnel, and transportation EAC-level commands. Each of these Army EAC support units is structured to deploy tailorable, early-entry, functional modules during the early stages of force projection operations. These tailored organizations give the ARFOR commander the requisite CSS functional expertise and C2 capabilities to execute operational-level support missions assigned to the ARFOR. Furthermore, these modular organizations may expand as necessary to provide the proper level of support for each operation or phase. Additionally, the DLA and the U.S. Army Materiel Command (USAMC) may provide support teams that expand the functional expertise and service capabilities of the ARFOR. When tailoring an ARFOR, the ASCC commander balances the ARFOR's tactical and operational requirements against other support requirements, such as CUL.

The ASCC commander ensures that the ARFOR not only has adequate operational-level CSS capability to meet both Army Title 10 and lead service requirements, but also has adequate C2 and staff capabilities to plan, prepare for, execute, and assess operations to meet them. This is especially significant when a tactical-level unit, such as a division or corps, is the foundation of the ARFOR. In these situations, the ASCC/ARFOR commander may choose to establish a single operational-level support headquarters to assist in planning and executing Army Title 10 and CUL functions. The TSC, in many cases, is the preferred building block for such a headquarters.

IV. Army Lead Responsibilities for Support to Other Services & Agencies

Ref: FM 4-0, chap. 2, table 2-1.

The following lists tasking documents and responsibilities assigned to the Army on a relatively permanent basis. However, the support responsibilities of the Army vary for each of these. In addition, despite these guidelines, the geographic combatant commander retains the authority to assign lead responsibility for a specific operation to the service or agency to best meet the operational requirements.

Tasking Document   Support Responsibility

Tasking Document	Support Responsibility
SECDEF Memo	Veterinary Support including food inspection
DOD Memo	Mortuary Affairs
DODD 1315.6	Troop Construction Support to OCONUS USAF
DODD 2310.1	Executive Agent for DOD Enemy Prisoner of War Detainee Program
DODD 4500.9	Common-User Land Transportation in Overseas Areas
DODD 4500.9	Intermodal Container Management
DODD 4500.9	Overseas Ocean Terminal Operations
DODD 4525.6	Management of Military Postal Services
DODD 4705.1	Executive Agent for Land-Based Water Resources
DODD 5030.49	Executive Agent for the Customs Inspection Program
DODD 5160.65	Management of Conventional Ammunition
DODI 4140.50	Locomotive Management
DODD 4140.25	Management of Bulk Petroleum Products, Natural Gas, and Coal
SECDEF Memo	Executive Agent for the Joint Mortuary Affairs Program

A combatant commander may designate a service, usually the dominant user or most capable service/agency, to provide other common item/service support (see JP 4-07). ARFOR CUL functions may include:

- In-theater receipt, storage, and issue Class I, II, III (B), IV, VIII and IX, and water during wartime
- Medical evacuation (ground and rotary-wing aircraft) on the battlefield
- Transportation engineering for highway movements
- Finance, banking, and currency support
- Processing and settlement of claims by (or against) the United States, as designated in DODD 5515.8
- Settlement of Federal tort claims by employees
- Unexploded ordnance (UXO) disposal
- Controlled disposal of waste explosives and munitions
- Mortuary affairs support
- Providing airdrop equipment and systems
- Billeting, medical, and food service support for transient personnel during other-than-unit moves
- Handling of hazardous materials (HAZMAT)

III. CSS in Full Spectrum Ops

Ref: FM 4-0 Combat Service Support, chap. 3.

FM 3-0 describes the doctrine of full spectrum operations as offensive, defensive, stability, and support operations. This section discusses combat service support (CSS) to full sprectum operations. It discusses the four types of Army operations and how CSS influences these operations through its effect on operational reach and sustainability. Finally, it discusses force projection as the responsive means of getting Army forces employed in full spectrum operations. It also includes a discussion of how CSS reach operations support the force while minimizing the Army CSS footprint in the area of operations.

I. CSS To Offensive, Defensive, Stability and Support Operations

Note: See also p. 4-14, CSS Considerations in the Offense and Defense.

CSS planning to support offensive, defensive, stability, and support operations requires a thorough mission analysis, careful identification of the supported force, and an understanding of the commander's intent and concept of operations. CSS planners must consider all specified and implied requirements and be aware of resources available, including those of other U.S. services, the host nation, and theater support contracting capabilities.

A. CSS In Offensive Operations

CSS in the offense is characterized by high-intensity operations that require anticipatory support as far forward as possible. Commanders and staffs ensure adequate support for continuing the momentum of the operation as they plan and synchronize offensive operations. Plans should include agile and flexible CSS capabilities to follow exploiting forces and continue support. Commanders and staffs plan for increased quantities of fuel and selected other classes of supply, as well as for maintenance and recovery of damaged equipment. Planners consider casualty rates and preposition medical treatment and evacuation capabilities forward to clear the battlefield efficiently. The biggest challenge to plans for supporting a rapidly moving force may be the lengthening lines of communication (LOC). Transportation support must be closely coordinated to deliver essential support to the right place at the right time. CSS assets must follow exploiting forces to ensure continuity of support. Plans for all offensive phases must enable CSS elements to react quickly to changing needs, just as total asset visibility (TAV) helps commanders quickly reprioritize assets as situations dictate.

During offensive operations, critical needs present great challenges. The most important materiel is typically Class III and Class V. Service support plans direct the movement of Class III and Class V resupply to meet predicted requirements. As advancing combat formations extend control of the area of operations (AO), personnel elements face similar challenges to reconcile and report command strength information, report casualty information, and conduct replacement operations.

Offensive operations put a high demand on maintenance elements. To continue momentum, task-organized maintenance support teams may operate with forward elements. Similarly, widely dispersed forces and longer LOC require all transportation resources, including aerial delivery assets, to deliver supplies well forward. Movement control personnel manage movement priorities in accordance with the commander's priorities.

The higher casualty rates associated with offensive operations increase the burden on medical resources. Combat support hospitals may move forward to prepare for offensive operations. If the increased numbers of casualties overwhelm medical resources, nonmedical transportation assets may be needed for evacuation. Following an offensive operation, combat stress casualties may be more prevalent and require moving combat stress teams forward.

Plans should also provide for religious support, which may become critical during offensive operations. Chaplain support through counseling and appropriate worship can help reduce combat stress, increasing unit cohesion and productivity.

Using contractors in offensive operations entails great risks. However, the force commander may be willing to accept risk and use contractors in forward areas. Contractor support outside of AOs may help minimize Army CSS force structure at locations such as intermediate staging bases.

B. CSS In Defensive Operations

The commander positions CSS assets to support the forces in the defense and survive. CSS requirements in the defense depend on the type of defense. For example, increased quantities of ammunition and decreased quantities of fuel characterize most area defensive operations. However, in a mobile defense, fuel usage may be a critical part of support. Barrier and fortification materiel to support the defense often has to move forward, placing increased demands on the transportation system. The maintenance effort focuses on returning primary weapon systems and critical equipment to mission capable status. Defensive operations may allow CSS assets to field services and refit degraded units. CSS planners and operators also prepare to resume support to the offensive operations projected to follow the defense.

CSS managers direct routine resupply of forecasted requirements to designated units, as stated in the service support plan. They should push Class IV directly to battle positions, when possible, and give Class V the highest priority. The increased expenditures of ammunition significantly impact transportation assets. Throughput of supplies from the echelons above division (EAD) to the lowest-level supply support activity (SSA) expedites deliveries.

The task of medical units is to triage casualties, treat and return to duty, or resuscitate and stabilize for evacuation to the next higher echelon of medical care or out of the theater of operations. Medical treatment facilities should locate away from points of possible hostile actions.

Using contractors in forward areas during defensive operations may entail unacceptable risk. If not, they may provide support in rear areas of forward deployed units.

C. CSS In Stability Operations

CSS in stability operations involves supporting U.S. and multinational forces in a wide range of missions. Stability operations range from long-term CSS-focused operations in humanitarian and civic assistance (HCA) missions to major short-notice peace enforcement missions. Some stability operations may involve combat. Tailoring CSS to the requirements of a stability operation is key to success of the overall mission. In stability operations, small task-organized CSS forces may operate far from traditional chains of command and support agencies that cannot sustain themselves. Stability operations also include large-scale operations that support peacekeeping and peace enforcement. These operations may or may not involve direct hostile action to U.S. forces and may have nearly the same CSS requirements as offensive or defensive operations. Contracted services and support may significantly augment Army CSS capabilities in major stability operations.

In addition to the movement control challenges typically presented by joint and multinational operations, large numbers of nongovernmental organizations (NGOs) sharing the same LOC and node facilities usually complicate movement control in stability operations. As in any major multinational operation, forces may establish a multinational movement control center to prioritize usage.

Maintenance units often have to support civilian assets as well as those of other military forces. In United Nations (UN) operations, the UN may purchase U.S. equipment for other multinational forces. In such cases, those forces may not have the capability to service the equipment. U.S. units may provide support or identify support packages. Also, the desired end state may require that maintenance support for stability operations include reestablishing or upgrading the infrastructure maintenance capabilities. This may entail providing tools and equipment.

For medical personnel, stability operations often result in more frequent and direct contact with the local population. Planners consider the mix of care-provider skills, instrument sizes, drugs, and supplies to support pediatric, geriatric, and obstetric missions. Human resource support activities (such as postal and morale, welfare, and recreation [MWR]) may have a higher priority and be a more immediate requirement during long-term stability missions than during offensive and defensive missions; long-term stability missions operate at a reduced tempo. These morale-related services become a major focus to both commanders and soldiers. Using contracted services and support may augment some CSS units. (See FM 3-07.)

D. CSS In Support Operations

CSS is often the primary focus of a support operation. Army forces often provide assistance to civil authorities and respond to national and international crises that include significant humanitarian assistance requirements best met with CSS capabilities. In many support operations, Army CSS units conduct the decisive operation. The ability of Army forces to move large amounts of equipment and supplies under adverse conditions and provide small tailored forces on short notice makes Army CSS forces a valuable asset in both domestic support operations and foreign humanitarian assistance missions. Distributing food, water, supplies, field services, and medical support is often the primary emphasis of support operations; the Army has trained personnel and deployable assets to provide such support. Transportation, supply, and medical units are often most in demand.

The key to success in many support operations is interagency coordination. Only in the most extreme situations does the U.S. military provide relief directly to those in need. In most support operations, the U.S. military assists NGOs in providing the required support. Multinational support, host nation support, and support from NGOs may reduce the demands on transportation, medical, food, water, and housing resources. (See FM 3-07.)

II. Operational Reach and Sustainability

Operational reach is the distance over which military power can be employed decisively (FM 3-0). The goal of the CSS effort is to enable the commander to initiate and sustain operations over time as well as extend the operational reach of the force. Operational reach relates to distance; sustainability relates to the ability of the force to conduct operations over time. The following is a discussion about how CSS influences both.

If military operations extend beyond a commander's operational reach, they reach the culminating point. In the offense, the culminating point is that point in time and space where the attacker's effective combat power no longer exceeds the defender's or the attacker's momentum is no longer sustainable, or both. In the defense, the culminating point is that instant at which the defender must withdraw to preserve the force. (See FM 3-0 for a discussion of culminating point.) To avoid this, the commander may choose an intentional operational pause or a reduction in tempo. Commanders can extend operational reach by moving forces, repositioning CSS assets, and securing LOC forward.

Factors that Affect Operational Reach and Sustainability

Several of the interrelated CSS factors that affect operational reach and sustainability are the scope of support, distribution networks, sources of support, and availability of materiel. The commander may adjust any of these factors to extend operational reach or enhance sustainability, but incurs additional risk by doing so. He must do a rigorous risk analysis before adjusting factors.

1. Scope of Support

The scope of support refers to the types and levels of support to provide to the force. The commander decides whether to provide all the CSS functions (and all subfunctions) or to defer certain types of support early in an operation or perform support functions at a reduced level. For example, he may defer food preparation, laundry support, and MWR in the early stages of an operation. However, the phase of the operation is just one consideration in determining what support to provide and to what standard. Other considerations include the type of operation, level of hostility, time available to prepare, expected duration of the operation, and resources available in the AO.

Adjusting the scope of support can extend operational reach and remove the need to move support assets forward. However, it has an associated risk. Deferring some functions (such as laundry or MWR) may simply result in reduced morale. However, deferring or reducing other functions (such as maintenance) has significant impacts, and the commander must carefully manage the associated risk.

2. Distribution Network

The distribution network consists of the information system and physical and resource networks. It has critical effects on operational reach and sustainability. The information system network provides the means to achieve asset visibility through the flow of information among the CSS elements at all levels. The physical network consists of the capabilities of fixed structures and established facilities. It includes factories, warehouses, airfields, seaports, roads, railroads, inland waterways, pipelines, terminals, bridges and tunnels, and buildings. The capacity of the physical network defines the point of diminishing returns of resources (people and machines), influences the feasibility of courses of action, and characterizes the risk inherent in the network. For example, in seaport operations, the capacity of the port is defined in short tons that can move through the port per day. The resource network consists of the people, materiel, and machines operating within and over the physical network. It includes a mix of military and civilian organizations and equipment.

A key element of distribution management is managing the capacity of the distribution system. Enhancing its capacity can extend operational reach or sustainability. The force can employ information systems in theater to enhance those networks. Engineers to repair or construct facilities to increase the capacity of the physical network may be critically important.

The commander can deploy CSS units to the AO to operate support facilities as part of the resource network. Though each of these may extend operational reach or enhance sustainability, they also carry risks. The primary risk is a potentially larger Army CSS footprint, to the detriment of combat force capabilities. However, the risk analysis associated with this decision is complex. (See FM 100-14.) On one hand, deploying CSS assets required to enhance the distribution system causes an additional burden on strategic lift as well as adding to the overall CSS requirements in theater. On the other hand, if the distribution system cannot provide responsive distribution support, the commander must accept other mitigating actions or increased risk. (For example, he may have to increase supply stocks in the AO to compensate for decreased ability to move supplies to the AO quickly; or he may choose to accept the risk of operating without robust supply stocks or a responsive distribution system.) In any case, the operational commander has to weigh his options carefully.

3. Sources of Support

The sources of support can also influence operational reach and sustainability. CSS may come from a myriad of DOD, Army, joint, multinational, contracted, and host nation support sources. Integrating CSS from all available sources maximizes the efficiency and effectiveness of the overall CSS effort. CSS personnel should always exploit all available sources based on a valid risk assessment and mission, enemy, troops, terrain and weather, time available, civil considerations (METT-TC). (FM 100-14 discusses risk assessment. When published, FM 6-0 will discuss the factors of METT-TC.)

However, adjusting sources of support through expanding contracted support also has risks. FM 3-100.21 discusses the risks associated with using contractors to provide support. Risk factors include exposing contract personnel to imminent danger in hostile environments and a possible lack of flexibility in support. Risks with relying on interagency or multinational sources may include lower reliability or varying standards of support. Solid, in-place support contracts and support agreements are critical when using contractors and multinational support.

4. Availability of Material

Availability of materiel is directly related to all three of the other factors. Materiel is available to a force through accompanying stocks and resupply. Internal constraints on a force's accompanying stocks include the upload capacity of its troops and equipment, the storage capacity for materiel not uploaded, and the transportation assets available to move supplies from stockpiles to their point of employment. Enhancing resupply by improving distribution networks or capitalizing on host-nation or locally contracted support and materiel can lessen the need to deploy and establish large stockpiles in theater. Also, increasing its unit basic load (UBL) may extend a unit's operational reach and sustainability, but this may prove impractical due to limited unit storage and transportation capabilities. Normally, if a unit's UBL is increased, it needs transportation augmentation to maintain agility. The commander has to balance unit agility with the threat of disruptions in the distribution system.

III. CSS in Force Projection

The Army's ability to project power with the most capable forces at the decisive time and place relies on focused CSS that is responsive, flexible, and precise. Distribution-based CSS provides rapid crisis response, tracks and redirects assets en route, and delivers tailored CSS packages directly to strategic, operational, and tactical levels. It must be fully adaptive to the needs of the Army's dispersed, mobile forces and provide support in hours or days versus weeks. It enables joint forces to be mobile, versatile, and deployable from anywhere in the world.

Since many CSS enablers are not yet fielded, not all facets of distribution-based CSS are currently executable. Distribution and other CSS functions and organizations are being modernized to incorporate information technologies that will allow Army forces to transition from the rigid vertical organizations of the past to more flexible, precise CSS structures. Modular and specifically tailored CSS packages are evolving in response to wide-ranging contingency requirements.

A. Force Projection Processes

JP 3-35 lays out the five interrelated processes involved in force projection: mobilization, deployment, employment, sustainment, and redeployment. CSS elements are involved in all five processes providing support to the force projected, and as part of that force.

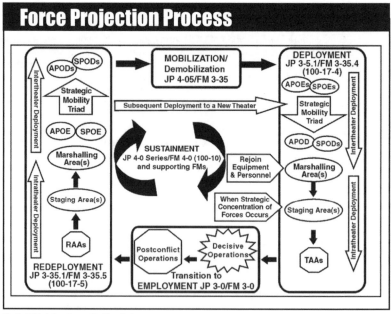

Ref: FM 4-0, chap. 3, fig. 3-1.

Identifying and planning theater infrastructure requirements during mission analysis are essential to establishing the support base and enhancing the responsiveness and sustainability of the force. The time required to establish a support base depends greatly on the extent and nature of the civil and military infrastructure in theater before operations begin. When there are ports, airfields, roads, depots, repair facilities, supplies, and transportation facilities, CSS operations can begin quickly without having to establish a new support base.

B. Force Projection Characteristics

Ref: FM 4-0, chap. 3.

Current world situations require the Army to deploy a first-rate force effectively and efficiently, perform complex and difficult missions, and redeploy it as quickly and efficiently as it deployed. To accomplish this, Army forces require four characteristics of force projection: precision, synchronization, speed, and relevant information.

1. Precision

Precision applies to every activity and each piece of data within force projection. Its effect is far-reaching; the payoff is speed. Precise deployment equipment lists, for example, ensure that CSS staff can quickly assign correct lift assets against the requirement. Precision in loading increases departure speed and safety. Precision in meeting the joint force commander's timeline supports his concept of employment. Current doctrine, realistic training, adequate support structure, and enablers provide the framework for precision. Such current and future CSS efforts as configured loads and modular, rapidly tailorable CSS units enhance precision.

2. Synchronization

Synchronization is a critical force projection characteristic. Just as a commander arranges activities in time and space to gain the desired effect during employment, he should also synchronize deployment activities to close the force successfully. Resources (such as lift assets, technical enablers, time, and information) are scarce. However, effectively synchronizing resources produces maximum use of every resource. Synchronization normally requires explicit coordination among the deploying forces and staffs, supporting units and staffs, a variety of civilian agencies, and other services. Synchronization is best achieved when supported with situational understanding based on timely and accurate data from information technologies that create a common operational picture (COP) and are enhanced with automated optimization, scheduling, and decision aids.

3. Speed

Speed is more than miles per hour; it is the sustained momentum achieved with the complete complement of joint lift assets. The bulk steadily delivered by ship can often outpace the pieces delivered by air. Speed is also the velocity of the entire force projection process, from planning to force closure. In deployment, speed of force projection should be directed to the timely arrival of throughput enablers; maintaining unit integrity; and delivering capability, not just individual units. Factors such as efficient planning tools, agile ports, submission of accurate information, safe and efficient loading, and trained unit movement officers are instrumental elements contributing to deployment speed.

4. Relevant Information

Relevant information is all information of importance to commanders and staffs in the exercise of command and control (FM 3-0). Successful force projection requires commanders to combine knowledge of the deployment process, judgment, and relevant information. Relevant information is the basis on which the commander makes decisions. The deploying commander must make crucial decisions on employment in a short period of time; these decisions set the tone for the remainder of the deployment. Many of the decisions are irretrievable or very hard to change. For example, understanding the time-phased force and deployment data (TPFDD) is imperative to making decisions on high-priority items, sequencing, use of time, and prioritization. Also, knowledge of the theater throughput allows the commander to manage deployment to enable employment.

A. Force Projection Processes

Ref: FM 4-0, chap. 3.

JP 3-35 lays out the five interrelated processes involved in force projection: mobilization, deployment, employment, sustainment, and redeployment. CSS elements are involved in all five processes.

I. Mobilization

Mobilization is the process by which the armed forces or part of them are brought to a state of readiness for war or other national emergency. This includes activating all or part of the Reserve Components and assembling and organizing personnel, supplies, and materiel. (See JP 1-02 for a complete definition. JP 4-05 and JP 4-05.1 provide the joint doctrine for mobilization. FM 100-17 establishes Army doctrine.)

As the TPFDD is developed, the geographic combatant commander and U.S. Transportation Command (USTRANSCOM) allocate transportation assets to ports of embarkation (POEs) and coordinate load planning/uploading of personnel, equipment, and initial sustainment stocks (such as ammunition basic loads [ABLs], UBLs, combat prescribed loads, authorized stockage lists [ASLs] and operational loads).

Graduated Response (GR)

A flexible decisionmaking process referred to as a graduated response (GR) controls the pace and extent of mobilization. GR triggers readiness and response actions incrementally to provide timely, yet reversible, steps that increase the U.S. national security emergency preparedness posture. The levels of mobilization response include selective mobilization, Presidential selected Reserve call-up, partial mobilization, full mobilization, and total mobilization.

II. Deployment

Deployment operations support the initial projection of forces and, once deployed, link the deployed forces with their home station and the strategic-level sustainment base. Ready supplies are available for issue pending additional procurement or expansion of the industrial base to support anticipated requirements. Deployment is the relocation of forces and materiel to desired operational areas. Deployment encompasses all activities from origin or home station through destination, specifically including intracontinental United States, intertheater, and intratheater movement legs, staging, and holding areas (JP 4-0). The deployment process includes all planning, preparation, execution, and assessment activities beginning with a mission requiring deployment of U.S. forces. Deployment is characterized by four phases:

1. Predeployment Activities

Predeployment activities are actions taken to prepare forces for deployment. They are essentially constant and on-going activities performed at home station before and continuing after warning or alert notification. Predeployment activities include training validation; deployment planning, to include force protection plans (see detailed discussion in paragraph 3-52); task organization; equipment maintenance; and soldier readiness processing (SRP). During normal peacetime operations, pre-deployment activities involve preparation for crisis response and force projection missions, always considering the operational requirements of the supported force commander.

2. Fort to Port

Activities at POEs focus on staging, marshaling, and loading personnel, units, equipment, and supplies on designated transportation assets prior to movement to ports of debarkation (PODs). Load planning is driven by the deployment concept and lift assets supporting deployment, the anticipated operational environment, and the anticipated situation at the POD to receive, offload, and reassemble mission capable organizations.The TPFDD synchronizes arriving personnel, equipment, and supplies with mission needs during deployment, and echelons, configures, and schedules units for movement. Time phasing allows for rapid theater reception and onward movement of arriving personnel, equipment, and supplies.

3. Port to Port

Movement to PODs can be conducted using common-user and organic or assigned/attached lift assets. PODs include seaports of debarkation (SPODs) and aerial ports of debarkation (APODs). USTRANSCOM conducts movement to PODs on common-user transportation in consultation with the supported and supporting combatant commanders. USTRANSCOM's primary responsibility is ensuring operational effectiveness in support of the JFC's deployment requirements while striving to attain the most efficient use of transportation resources. Alternatively, movement to PODs on organic or assigned/attached lift is the responsibility of the deploying unit commander in response to mission guidance from the supported JFC.

4. Port to Destination

The last phase of deployment (joint reception, staging, onward movement, and integration (JRSOI]) is the responsibility of the supported combatant commander and subordinate JFC. Joint Reception Staging Onward movement and Integration comprises the essential processes required to transition arriving personnel, equipment, and materiel into forces capable of meeting operational requirements (JP 4-01.8). The Army refers to these same processes as RSO&I. Deployment is not complete until the deploying unit is a functioning part of the in-theater force.

RSO&I

Note: See chap. 6 for more detail on RSO&I operations.

RSO&I is the critical link between deploying and employing forces in the AO. The RSO&I objective is to create a seamless flow of personnel, equipment, and materiel from offload at PODs through employment as reassembled, mission-capable forces. The time between the initial arrival of the deploying unit and its operational employment is potentially the period of its greatest vulnerability.

III/IV. Employment/Sustainment

The CSS force package tailored for each contingency is streamlined, strategically mobile, and focused on the demands dictated by the contingency. Early-entry forces should exploit regionally available assets to include joint, multinational, HNS, and theater support contracting resources for transport, supply, and services to the maximum extent possible within the associated risk. Initial CSS in the theater relies on a combination of UBLs and critical sustainment stocks, either from prepositioned stocks (ashore or afloat) or stocks designated to arrive early in a force projection operation. Early in an operation, CSS is conducted by a theater force opening package (TFOP).

V. Redeployment

Redeployment is the transfer of forces and materiel to support another joint force commander's operational requirements, or to return personnel, equipment, and materiel to the home and/or demobilization stations for reintegration and/or out-processing (JP 3-35). The commander must conduct redeployment in a way that facilitates using redeploying forces and sustainment equipment and supplies to meet new missions. Therefore, if redeployment is not a retrograde operation, it is, in fact, a new deployment in which the current AO becomes a power projection platform. The same operational phases, planning, and coordination actions required for deployment are required for redeployment. See FM 100-17-5 for details covering redeployment.

IV. CSS Reach Operations

Critical to supporting full spectrum operations is minimizing the Army CSS footprint in the theater, thereby reducing strategic lift requirements and enhancing the strategic responsiveness of Army forces. A key to achieving this objective is CSS reach operations. Combat Service Support reach operations involve the operational positioning and efficient use of all available CSS assets and capabilities, from the industrial base to the soldier in the field (FM 3-0). CSS reach operations refer to deploying the minimum essential Army CSS elements to the AO and establishing links to, and fully exploiting all available sources of, support. CSS reach operations include using normal support relationships and reaching in all directions to acquire available support from contractors, HNS, other services, multinational partners, and NGOs.

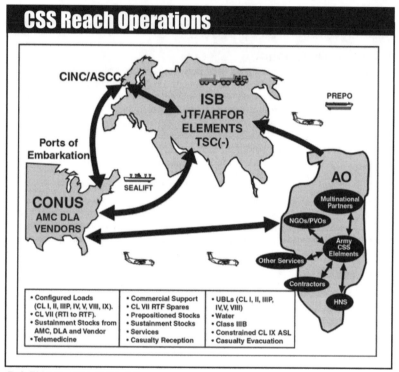

CSS Reach Operations

Ref: FM 4-0, chap. 3, fig. 3-2.

Sources of support available to Army CSS elements in the AO include:

- Strategic-level CSS provider contingency elements
- CSS management and technical support from nondeployed elements of Army CSS organizations and strategic-level CSS providers in the AO
- Prepositioned equipment and supplies
- HNS
- Theater support contractors
- Other service components
- Allies and coalition partners.

Deployed elements of the TSC and other CSS organizations integrate support with deployed elements of several strategic providers. For example, DLA sends a DLA contingency support team and USAMC sends an LSE to an AO, as required.

Deployed Army elements also reach back to elements of their organizations that do not deploy. A prime example is split-based operations. Split-based operations involve deploying only minimal essential CSS management cells to AOs with links back to home station (or in some cases an intermediate staging base [ISB]). With proper information system links, deployed elements may receive support from some strategic-level providers. Telemedicine is an example of technical support available outside of the AO. The COSCOM and TSC MMCs are also capable of performing some materiel management functions from home station, but again, robust and reliable information systems are essential to make split-based operations work.

Another aspect of CSS reach operations involves deliberate positioning of stocks and units/capabilities dedicated for a specific operation. The commander may position these stocks and/or units at home station, an ISB, or another location within or near the theater of operations or joint operations area (JOA). For example, minimal explosive ordnance disposal, personnel, or legal resources could deploy to an AO, with other assets positioned at an ISB for rapid insertion into the AO, if required. This minimizes the CSS footprint in the AO while still providing a relatively high level of responsiveness.

Reliance on HNS and theater support contractors are another facet of reaching to available sources and minimizing the deployment of Army CSS units into the AO. (Chapter 5 covers these sources of support.)

Finally, Army CSS elements integrate support from joint and multinational sources available in the AO. Commanders weigh the risk of joint and, especially, multinational support; this support may not be as reliable or responsive as organic Army support.

V. Intermediate Staging Base (ISB)

An intermediate staging base is a secure staging base usually established near to, but not in, the area of operations (FM 3-0). While not a requirement in all situations, the ISB may provide a secure, high-throughput facility when circumstances warrant. The commander may use an ISB as a temporary staging area en route to a joint operation or as a long-term secure forward support base. An ISB may serve as a secure transportation node that allows the switch from strategic to intratheater modes of transportation and provides a staging area where units can redistribute and finalize their accompanying loads. When possible, an ISB takes advantage of existing, sophisticated capabilities, serving as an efficient transfer point from high-volume commercial carriers to a range of tactical, intratheater transport means that may serve smaller, more austere ports.

The ISB may enhance the strategic responsiveness of the deploying force by providing continuous and wide-ranging capabilities. Army forces may use an ISB in conjunction with the other joint force elements to preposition selected CSS capabilities for rapid deployment into the JOA. ISB personnel may perform limited CSS functions (such as materiel management and selected maintenance support routinely performed in the communications zone [COMMZ]). ISBs may also serve as secure staging areas for redeploying units, noncombatant evacuation operations (NEO), and redeployment or evacuation of other individuals and units, until strategic lift is available to final destinations. Using ISBs when operationally feasible may allow joint forces to minimize the CSS footprint in an AO, thus enhancing the combatant commander's ability to meet operational requirements rapidly.

Decision on Using an ISB

Using an ISB is operationally dependent on, and must support, the combatant commander's campaign plan. It is normally located within the theater of operations and outside the AO. The JFC determines the feasibility of using an ISB, its location, and when it should be established and disestablished. This determination is based on the availability, length, and security of the LOC (water, air, and rail) between the ISB and the JOA, and on the criticality of a specific support function. However, there are disadvantages inherent in using ISBs. An ISB is a transshipment point, so it may add extra time and handling to the deployment or CSS process. Further, additional infrastructure (personnel and equipment) is required to operate the ISB.

In an ideal situation, secure bases are available within the AO for RSO&I operations and continued support of the deployed force, lessening the need for an ISB. Unfortunately, the very situation that results in deploying forces may negate the advantages of basing within the AO.

VI. CSS to Special Operations Forces

Most SOF units locate in CONUS and operate in a force-projection mode. The U.S. Army Special Operations Command (USASOC) has aligned its Special Operations Support Command (SOSCOM) and SOF CSS organizations and activities with the U.S. Army's concept of force projection. This change allows SOF to integrate organic CSS elements within the theater support structure for continuous and responsive sustainment to deployed Army special operations forces (ARSOF).

In a mature theater, the theater base is established, prepositioned stocks and operational stocks are in place, and support agreements exist. When operating in a fully developed CONUS or overseas base, ARSOF operate as part of, or collocated with, a conventional force. They receive support from three primary sources:

- Army Title 10 support through Army CSS units

- CUL lead service units (in most cases Army CSS units)

- SOF channels for SOF-peculiar items that are beyond normal CSS element capabilities

In a developing theater, ARSOF units bring enough resources to survive and operate until the United States sets up a bare-base support system or arranges for HNS. The bare-base support system may function from CONUS, stocks afloat, or from a third country. Until this system becomes operational, the joint force special operations component commander (JFSOCC) may authorize SOF units to request items through their parent units or directly from the CONUS wholesale CSS system. ARSOF units may request CSS for SOF-peculiar and conventional items through the special operations theater support elements (SOTSEs). The SOTSEs are forward deployed, regionally oriented elements from the SOSCOM with the mission to coordinate ARSOF CSS support. (See FM 100-25.)

The nature of special operations frequently imposes stringent operations security (OPSEC) requirements on the CSS system. Certain special operations are extremely sensitive and require compartmentalization of their support to avoid compromise. Supporting CSS commanders ensure OPSEC within their own activities.

SOF units are comparatively small and, except for special operations aviation, consume few critical combat supplies (Class I, bulk Class III, and Class V). However, they use special operations-peculiar and low-density items of standard and nonstandard configuration. The solution to SOF CSS requirements is theater-specific and situation-dependent.

IV. Roles & Responsibilities

Ref: FM 4-0 Combat Service Support, chap. 4.

This section frames combat service support (CSS) organization roles and responsibilities in the context of the levels of war.

I. Strategic-Level Roles

The strategic level deals with attaining national objectives. It involves the integrated efforts of the President and Secretary of Defense (SECDEF), the Joint Chiefs of Staff, and several National agencies, including the Department of Defense (DOD). However, many of the agencies discussed in this chapter may perform functions associated with the strategic, operational, and tactical levels, either through split-based operations or by deploying elements to the AO.

Strategic-level support links the global economic base (people, resources, and industry) to military operations in theater. At this level, the joint staff, military departments, U.S. Transportation Command (USTRANSCOM), Defense Logistics Agency (DLA) , and other DOD agencies focus on force readiness and supporting force projection operations.

A. Industrial Base

The Army depends primarily on private industry as the foundation for military materiel production. Therefore, the defense industrial base has a significant impact on the conduct of wars due to the long lead times required to build up the industrial base. Active plants and production lines have some capability to surge. Repair parts manufacturers may be able to surge production for items that sustain deployed weapon systems. Active end-item production lines obtain urgent critical parts and subsystems.

B. Department of Defense and Defense Agencies

The SECDEF is the principal assistant to the President in all matters relating to the DOD. DOD performs its functions under the SECDEF's authority, direction, and control. Of particular note in CSS, the SECDEF issues directives, instructions, and memoranda delineating DOD Executive Agency responsibilities under the authority of 10 USC 165(c). The Chairman of the Joint Chiefs of Staff (CJCS) is assigned specific supervisory and joint operation planning responsibilities in the areas of strategic direction, strategic planning, and joint operation planning. JP 0-2 outlines the responsibilities of the DOD and Joint Chiefs of Staff.

1. Defense Logistics Agency (DLA)

The DLA is DOD's major logistics agency. Controlled and directed by the Under Secretary of Defense for Acquisition, Logistics, and Technology, DLA functions as an integral element of the DOD military logistics system. It provides worldwide distribution support to the military departments and the combatant commands, and to other DOD components, Federal agencies, foreign governments, and international organizations. DLA is responsible for providing consumable items of common supplies and services within DOD. Its responsibilities include worldwide integrated management of subsistence, petroleum, and property disposal operations. DLA manages or distributes more than 80 percent of existing stocks of defense materiel, including service-owned stocks and nearly all of the fuel and petroleum products for military use. It is the lead DOD organization for automated identification technology (AIT).

2. Defense Contract Management Agency (DCMA)

The Defense Contract Management Agency (DCMA) is the DOD contract manager. Controlled and directed by the Under Secretary of Defense for Acquisition Logistics and Technology, DCMA supervises and administers contracts with over 20,000 suppliers who deliver goods and services to DOD. DCMA functions as an integral element of the DOD acquisition system by providing worldwide contract administration services to the military departments and the combatant commands, as well as to other DOD components, Federal agencies, foreign governments, and international organizations.

3. Defense Finance and Accounting Service (DFAS)

As the DOD executive agent for finance and accounting, the Defense Finance and Accounting Service (DFAS) plays a critical role in supporting joint operations. However, the services retain tactical finance personnel to provide the finance and limited accounting support required for their deployed forces during operations. DFAS is responsible for DOD finance and accounting policies, procedures, standards, systems, and operations to support combatant commanders and the services. (See JP 1-06.)

4. Defense Security Cooperation Agency (DSCA)

The Defense Security Cooperation Agency (DSCA), under the authority, direction, and control of the Assistant Secretary of Defense for International Security Affairs, serves as the DOD focal point and clearinghouse for developing and implementing security assistance plans and programs. DSCA monitors major weapon sales and technology transfer issues, budgetary and financial arrangements, legislative initiatives and activities, and policy and other security assistance matters. It also supports developing cooperative programs with industrialized nations. DSCA's Office of Humanitarian Assistance and Demining is responsible for managing the overseas humanitarian, disaster, and civic aid appropriation; oversight of the combatant commander's operational demining and humanitarian and civic assistance (HCA) programs; and the DOD humanitarian assistance program (HAP). HAP provides excess, nonlethal property to authorized recipients; arranges funding and space-available transportation for NGOs to deliver humanitarian goods to countries in need; coordinates foreign disaster relief missions; and procures, manages, and arranges for delivery of humanitarian daily rations (HDR) to those in need. JP 4-07 and JP 4-09 provide a detailed discussion of the DSCA.

5. Defense Information Systems Agency (DISA)

The Defense Information Systems Agency (DISA) is responsible for planning, developing, and supporting command, control, communications, computer, and intelligence (C4I) systems that serve the needs of the SECDEF. It provides guidance and support on technical and operational C4I issues affecting the office of the SECDEF, the military departments, the CJCS and the joint staff, the combatant commands, and the defense agencies. DISA ensures the interoperability of the global command and control system—Army (GCCS-A), the global combat service support system-Army (GCSS-A), and the other CSS command and control, asset visibility, and transportation systems.

C. Dept of the Army & Strategic-Level Commands

The Secretary of the Army is responsible for the administration and support of all Army forces. The Secretary of the Army fulfills these responsibilities by exercising administrative control (ADCON) through the commanders of the ASCCs of the combatant commands. (FM 3-0 discusses ADCON.) The military departments exercise authority and responsibilities codified under U.S. law, DOD directives, and joint doctrine that describe the command relationships between combatant and component commanders. A number of strategic-level CSS commands and agencies provide vital support to Army and other supported forces.

The Levels of War

Ref: FM 3-0.

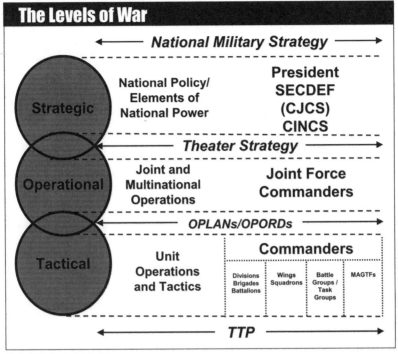

The Levels of War

	National Military Strategy →
Strategic	National Policy/ Elements of National Power	**President SECDEF (CJCS) CINCS**
	← Theater Strategy →
Operational	Joint and Multinational Operations	**Joint Force Commanders**
	OPLANs/OPORDs →
Tactical	Unit Operations and Tactics	**Commanders** Divisions Brigades Battalions / Wings Squadrons / Battle Groups / Task Groups / MAGTFs
	← TTP →

Ref: JP 3-0, pp. II-2 to II-3.

I. The Strategic Level

The strategic level is that level at which a nation, often as one of a group of nations, determines national and multinational security objectives and guidance, and develops and uses national resources to accomplish them. The geographic combatant commander has a strategic perspective with respect to his area of responsibility and is responsible for unified actions that integrate joint, multinational, and interagency activities. The theater strategy relates to both U.S. National strategy and operational activities within the theater.

II. The Operational Level

The operational level is the level at which campaigns and major operations are conducted and sustained to accomplish strategic objectives within theaters or areas of operations (AOs). The operational level links the tactical employment of forces to strategic objectives.

III. The Tactical Level

The tactical level is the realm of close combat, where friendly forces are in immediate contact and use direct and indirect fires to defeat or destroy enemy forces and to seize or retain ground. Tactics is the employment of units in combat. It includes the ordered arrangement and maneuver of units in relation to each other, the terrain, and the enemy to translate potential combat power into victorious battles and engagements.

1. U.S. Army Materiel Command (USAMC)

U.S. Army Materiel Command (USAMC) performs assigned materiel and related functions for research, development, test and evaluation; acquisition, logistics support, and technical assistance for materiel systems; and other materiel-acquisition management functions. It provides Army national-level maintenance support and serves as the DOD single manager for conventional ammunition. USAMC missions include:

- Providing equipment and services to other nations through the Security Assistance Program
- Developing and acquiring nonmajor systems and equipment
- Providing development and acquisition support to program managers
- Maintaining the industrial mobilization capabilities necessary to support the Army
- Managing Army prepositioned stocks (APS), less Class VIII, worldwide
- Managing the LOGCAP

USAMC also manages operational policies, programs, objectives, and resources associated with operational projects worldwide. All of the above functions and capabilities are available to the ASCC/ARFOR through the USAMC logistics support element (LSE). See FM 63-11 for information on the LSE.

USAMC is the Army's single stock fund (SSF) manager and serves as the single national manager with sole obligation power for the Army Working Capital Fund, Supply Management Army (AWCF-SMA). In this capacity, USAMC consolidates management of current wholesale, theater, corps/installation, and division authorized stockage list (ASL) inventories into a seamless logistics and financial system and creates an integrated supply and maintenance operation in the ACWF-SMA business area. Non-Army managed items (NAMIs) (such as fuel, subsistence, clothing, engineer supplies, and medical items not included in the SSF) bypass the SSF and are transmitted directly to DLA. USAMC is also the national maintenance manager (NMM) and oversees the national maintenance program (NMP).

2. U.S. Army Medical Research and Materiel Command (USAMRMC)

The U.S. Army Medical Research and Materiel Command (USAMRMC) is a major subordinate command of the U.S. Army Medical Command (USAMEDCOM). It is responsible for the life-cycle management of medical materiel from basic laboratory research through advanced development, prototyping, procurement, delivery to units, maintenance, and disposal. This command operates six medical research laboratories and institutes within CONUS that make up the core science and technology capability of the command. Further, this command operates subordinate units exclusively focused on medical materiel development, contracting, medical logistics management, health facility planning, and information management and technology.

3. U.S. Total Army Personnel Command (USTAPERSCOM)

The U.S. Total Army Personnel Command (USTAPERSCOM) integrates, manages, monitors, and coordinates military personnel systems to develop and optimize the Army human resources in peace and war. The commander of USTAPERSCOM is the Army functional proponent for the military personnel management system within the objectives set by the Deputy Chief of Staff for Personnel. USTAPERSCOM major functions include the following:

- Carry out the nine major functional categories of the Army personnel life cycle: force structure, acquisition, individual training and development, distribution, deployment, sustainment, professional development, compensation, and transition.
- Man the force, and provide personnel support and personnel services to soldiers, their families, and organizations.
- Synchronize all military personnel activities to achieve efficient and cost effective execution of all military personnel processes on an Army-wide basis to ensure current and future personnel requirements are defined.
- Interact with personnel organizations in the field, including U.S. Army training centers, U.S. Army garrisons, divisions and corps, installations, and forward deployed bases to ensure policy, procedures, and service delivery systems support operational requirements at all levels.

4. USTRANSCOM and Transportation Component Commands

USTRANSCOM provides air, land, and sea transportation and common-user port management at air/seaports of embarkation and debarkation for DOD. The commander, USTRANSCOM serves as the DOD single worldwide manager for common-user ports of embarkation and debarkation. The single port manager concept ensures the seamless transfer of cargo and equipment in any given theater. Supported combatant commanders determine movement requirements and required delivery dates. The commander, USTRANSCOM is the supporting commander who, with the transportation component commands, provides a complete movement system from origin to initial theater destination. The USTRANSCOM component commands operate the Defense Transportation System (DTS). JP 4-01 covers DTS-specific operations.

- **The Military Traffic Management Command (MTMC)**, a major U.S. Army command, is the transportation component command of USTRANSCOM responsible for surface transportation management. MTMC provides common-user ocean terminal and traffic management services to deploy, employ, sustain, and redeploy U.S. forces on a global basis. MTMC conducts transportation engineering to ensure deployability and feasibility of present and future deployment assets. Additionally, MTMC is the worldwide seaport manager under the single port manager concept for all common-user seaports of embarkation (SPOEs) and seaports of debarkation (SPODs). When designated, MTMC may also serve as the port operator, using stevedoring, services contracts, or HNS.
- **The Air Mobility Command (AMC)** is a major U.S. Air Force command. As a transportation component command of USTRANSCOM, AMC provides common-user airlift, air refueling, and strategic aeromedical evacuation transportation services to deploy, employ, sustain, and redeploy U.S. forces on a global basis. Additionally, AMC is the single aerial port manager and, where designated, operator of common-user aerial ports of embarkation (APOEs) and aerial ports of debarkation (APODs).
- **The Military Sealift Command (MSC)** is a major command of the U.S. Navy. As a transportation component command of USTRANSCOM, MSC provides common-user and exclusive-use sealift transportation services to deploy, employ, sustain, and redeploy U.S. forces on a global basis.

5. Army and Air Force Exchange Service (AAFES)

Army and Air Force Exchange Service (AAFES) mobile field exchanges are deployable truck- or tent-based resale outlets that provide health and comfort merchandise support to deployed forces. AAFES civilian employees operate these nonappropriated fund activities. Merchandise originates from AAFES system stock.

E. Supported Geographic Combatant Commands

Geographic combatant commanders are responsible for developing joint plans and orders in response to mission taskings in their areas of responsibility (AORs).

The combatant commander delegates to service component commanders directive authority for logistics (DAL) for specific, common-item support. Overall authority for CSS remains with each of the service component commanders. Delegated common item support authority—accomplished through either temporary CUL lead or long-term SITLM responsibilities—must be clearly delineated in, and executed in accordance with, combatant commanders' OPLANs/OPORDs or directives.

F. Subordinate Joint Force Commands

The subordinate joint force commander (JFC), normally a subordinate unified command or JTF, works for a combatant commander who has overall responsibility for conducting CSS for joint operations. However, the JFC establishes a man-power and personnel directorate (J1) and logistics directorate (J4) that coordinate personnel and logistics support through the combatant commander. They also coordinate with any subordinate JTFs, service components, and agency J1 and J4s or equivalent staff officers. While each service is responsible for the CSS of its own forces, the service components will use the common distribution network and other combatant commander-directed CUL support to execute the overall CSS mission. The subordinate JFC plays a major role in optimizing resources and synchronizing support to the assigned forces. See JP 4-07.

II. Operational-Level Roles

Operational CSS includes the support required to conduct campaigns and major operations. A campaign is a related series of military ops aimed at accomplishing a strategic or operational objective within a given time and space (JP 1-02).

The combatant commander's concept for the campaign or major operation is the basis for support planning. Like strategic-level CSS, operational-level CSS is usually a joint effort and often a multinational effort. Army support at this level is integrated into the total support system required to conduct joint/multinational campaigns and other military activities. The combatant commander's strategic logistics concept will focus on the ability to generate and move forces and materiel in the theater base and to desired operating locations, where operational-level logistics concepts are employed. Key Army functions associated with operational-level CSS include the following (numbers refer to Universal Joint Task List tasks):

- Coordinating supply of arms, munitions, and equipment (OP 4.1)
- Synchronizing supply of fuel (OP 4.2)
- Maintaining equipment and stocks that support the supply system (OP 4.3)
- Coordinating support of forces (OP 4.4); including, human resources (OP 4.4.1.1), field services (OP 4.4.1), health services (4.4.3), religious (OP 4.4.6), financial (OP 4.4.2), and legal (OP 4.4.7)
- Managing materiel (OP 4.5), controlling movement (OP 4.5.1), and managing distribution (OP 4.5)
- Providing lead service CUL to other services, multinational partners, and civilian agencies (OP 4.5)
- Establishing, managing, and maintaining sustainment facilities, including storage areas (OP 4.6) and medical facilities (OP 4.4.3.3)
- Planning, coordinating, managing, and supervising the positioning (OP 1.2) and security (OP 6.2) of CSS activities
- Acquiring, managing, and distributing funds to conduct in-theater contracting to acquire supplies and services to support the mission (OP 4.8)

Federal Agencies and Organizations

Ref: FM 4-0, chap. 4.

Numerous Federal agencies play a role in CSS operations. This section briefly summarizes the CSS role of several key agencies.

1. Department of State (DOS)

The Department of State (DOS) is the lead agency for coordinating and distributing Class X items that support nonmilitary programs (such as, economic and agricultural development, civic action, and various relief and education programs).

2. Department of Transportation (DOT)

Under the National Plan for Emergency Preparedness (Executive Order 12656), the Secretary of Transportation leads the Federal transportation community. During National defense emergencies and in periods of crisis, the Secretary of Transportation has a wide range of delegated responsibilities, including executive management of the Nation's transportation resources. See JP 4-01.

3. Federal Emergency Management Agency (FEMA)

The Federal Emergency Management Agency (FEMA) coordinates the emergency preparedness actions of all Federal agencies, including distributing military support to civil authority missions. As the key agency for emergency assistance to civil authorities, it coordinates all military support directly with the Director of Military Support (DOMS). Close coordination with FEMA is essential in most domestic support operations (DSO).

4. U.S. Customs Service

The U.S. Customs Service is a Department of the Treasury bureau responsible for enforcing U.S. laws concerning carriers, cargo, and persons entering and departing the United States. Its responsibilities include assessing and collecting duties; detecting and intercepting contraband, including drugs; and ensuring that imported material meets the requirements for legal entry. All forces and materiel redeploying to CONUS require U.S. customs clearance.

5. U.S. Postal Service (USPS)

The U.S. Postal Service (USPS) is part of the global distribution network that supports joint force operations by moving DOD mail, including material shipped via parcel post. The military postal system is an official extension of USPS outside continental United States (OCONUS). The Military Postal Service Agency (MPSA), a joint service staff headquarters under the executive direction of Department of the Army, is the DOD single military mail manager and point of contact with USPS. MPSA conducts DOD contingency planning and provides postal support to combatant commanders. Transporting official and personal mail to and from forces OCONUS is a MPSA responsibility.

6. General Services Administration (GSA)

The General Services Administration (GSA) provides common-use items to DOD through a network of customer service centers and distribution centers. GSA is a major source for general commodities (such as office supplies and paper products, tools, furniture, paints, and chemicals). GSA also provides vehicle acquisition and leasing service and is the Federal contracting agency for the government purchase card program and domestic express small-package delivery service.

A. Army Service Component Command (ASCC)

At the combatant command level, the ASCC consists of the Army service component commander and all the Army forces assigned to the combatant command or
further assigned/attached to a subordinate unified command or JTF. The ASCC has
responsibilities that derive from Title 10. These Title-10 responsibilities include
planning, preparing, training, equipping, administering, and providing CSS to Army
forces assigned to combatant commands. The ASCC may be required to support
the geographic combatant commander by conducting land operations to support or
attain the combatant commander's objectives. These land operations often are
conducted by a subordinate ARFOR headquarters, such as an augmented corps
or division, as part of a JTF. Even in operations where the ASCC commander is not
exercising operational control over Army forces, he remains responsible for
providing the necessary capabilities, including CSS.

B. Multifunctional and Specialized Commands

A number of Army commands habitually operate at the operational level. In some
situations, especially at the lower end of the spectrum of conflict, tactical-level
CSS organizations may perform operational-level support missions. If so, they
require augmentation, typically from the EAC organizations.

The support structure starts with a nucleus of minimum essential support functions
and capabilities focused on force generation. As the deployed force grows, the
support structure gains required capabilities. The theater support structure must
provide support to engaged forces; to units in or passing through the JRA; and to
other units, activities, forces, and individuals as the JFC directs. FM 4-93.4
describes an operational-level theater force opening package and possible build-
up of operational-level CSS forces.

1. Theater Support Command (TSC)
Note: See pp. 3-57 to 3-64 for additional information on the TSC.
This multifunctional logistics command provides area support to designated
elements in the JRA and sustainment support to tactical forces. The TSC provides
C2 of EAC logistics organizations and other organizations, as directed by the
ASCC. FM 4-93.4 details the build-up of a TSC in a force-projection operation.

2. Area Support Group (ASG)
Area support groups (ASGs) are subordinate units assigned to the TSC. They are
responsible for area support in an AO and may provide support to corps or other
forces. The mission of the ASG is to provide direct support (DS) logistics support
to designated units and elements within its AO. This support typically includes DS
supply (less ammunition, classified map supply, and medical supply and support),
DS maintenance, and field services, as well as other support directed by the
ARFOR commander through the TSC. ASGs can also provide GS supply and
sustainment maintenance support to TSC and DS supply organizations, and
sustainment maintenance to support the theater. If an operational-level ammunition
group is not established, specialized battalions assigned to the ASG provide
ammunition support. ASGs can support ISB and RSO&I operations. Early entry
modules (EEMs) of specialized units may be attached to an ASG headquarters EEM
during initial stages of an operation. FM 54-40 contains additional details on the
composition and capabilities of ASGs.

3. Transportation Command (TRANSCOM)
Through subordinate transportation units, the Army TRANSCOM provides transportation support to Army, joint, and multinational forces as directed by the JFC/ASCC
commander. It provides policy and technical guidance to all Army transportation
units in theater and directs allocation of Army transportation resources in coordination with the ASCC/ARFOR headquarters and the theater joint transportation board.
FM 55-1 and FM 4-93.4 have more information on the Army TRANSCOM.

4. Medical Command (MEDCOM)

The Medical Command (MEDCOM) directs health service support to designated elements in theater. It provides policy and technical guidance to in-theater Army medical units and maintains technical links to the ASCC/ARFOR staff surgeon and to strategic-level medical activities. The MEDCOM provides a wide range of medical capabilities; develops policies, plans, procedures, and programs; and supervises training and administrative support of medical brigades. FM 4-02, FM 8-42, and FM 8-55 describe these and other functions.

5. Personnel Command (PERSCOM)

The theater personnel command (PERSCOM) maintains and reports on personnel readiness of theater forces, conducts theater sustainment operations necessary to man the force, and provides personnel services and support. It exercises C2 over assigned and attached theater-level Army personnel units. FM 12-6 covers the units, operations, and relationships involved in providing personnel support at this level.

6. Finance Command (FINCOM)

The Finance Command (FINCOM) conducts operational-level finance operations. In coordination with the ASCC/ARFOR Deputy Chief of Staff for Resource Management, it provides staff advice on financial management matters and provides financial management policies and procedures for Army financial management activities in the theater. It may also exercise C2 over finance battalions not assigned to finance groups. FM 14-100 contains details on the FINCOM and other finance organizations that operate within the theater.

7. Engineer Command (ENCOM)

Engineer command (ENCOM) C2 engineer units provide the full spectrum of engineering support. This includes general engineering, topographic support, and operational-level mobility/ countermobility/survivability support to Army, joint, and multinational forces. The ENCOM and subordinate EAC engineer units normally provide either general support or direct support to the TSC and other CSS units. Technical engineering services include construction design/management, real estate acquisition and management, real property maintenance activities (RPMA), electric-power generation/distribution, troop construction, facility rehabilitation and repair, environmental engineering support, and transportation engineering support. ENCOMs typically push the engineer work lines of EAC engineer assets forward into the combat zone to facilitate the forward focus of corps engineer assets and to accomplish tasks beyond the corps engineer's capabilities. Examples of such tasks are constructing/maintaining main supply routes (MSRs) (with specific emphasis on LOC bridges), inland petroleum distribution systems (IPDS), forward landing strips, and forward-positioned medical facilities. (See FM 5-116.)

III. Tactical-Level Roles

The goal of CSS at all levels is to generate and sustain combat power at the tactical level. CSS at the tactical level includes all functions necessary to support battles and engagements. (FM 3-0 and FM 3-90 discuss battles and engagements.) The focus of tactical-level CSS is to provide the CSS necessary to meet the commander's intent and concept of operations, and to maximize his freedom of action. It involves synchronizing all CSS functions. Tactical-level CSS is more immediate than operational-level CSS.

Note: See chap. 3, (FXXI) Tactical-Level CSS Operations, for additonal information on tactical-level units, operations, roles and responsibilities.

CSS Staff Responsibilities

Ref: FM 4-0, chap. 4.

At the tactical level, some CSS functions are performed by the commander's staff.

Coordinating Staff Officers

• **Assistant Chief of Staff, G1/AG (S1) Personnel.** The G1/AG (S1) is the principal staff officer for all matters concerning human resources (military and civilian), including personnel readiness, personnel services, personnel support, and headquarters management.

• **Assistant Chief of Staff, G4/(S4) Logistics.** The G4 (S4) is the principal staff office for coordinating the integration of supply, maintenance, transportation, and services for the command. The G4 (S4) is the link between the support unit and commander and the rest of the staff.

Special Staff Officers

Every staff has special staff officers who are responsible for CSS functions.

• **Resource Manager or Comptroller.** The resource manager or comptroller is responsible for budget preparation and resource management analysis and implementation. Resource managers or comptrollers are normally located at corps and division.

• **Finance Officer.** The finance officer is responsible for coordinating and providing finance services to the command.

• **Surgeon.** The surgeon is responsible for coordinating health assets and operations within the command. A surgeon is authorized on all staffs from bn through corps.

• **Veterinary Officer.** The veterinary officer is responsible for coordinating assets and activities concerning veterinary service within the command. A veterinary corps officer is authorized at corps level.

• **Explosive Ordnance Disposal (EOD) Officer.** The EOD officer is responsible for coordinating the detection, identification, recovery, evaluation, rendering safe, and final disposal of explosive ordnance. An EOD officer is authorized at corps and division levels. He normally serves as the EOD group, bn, or company commander.

Personal Staff Officers

Personal staff officers work under the immediate control of the commander and have direct access to him. The commander establishes guidelines or gives specific guidance when the personal staff officer should inform, or coordinate with, the chief of staff or other members of the staff.

Most personal staff officers also perform duties as special staff officers working with a coordinating staff officer. They do this case-by-case, depending on the guidance of the commander or the nature of the task. Personal staff officers may also work under the supervision of the chief of staff.

• **Chaplain (Coordinating Staff Responsibility, ACofS, G1/AG (S1)**, when required). The chaplain is responsible for coordinating the religious assets and operations within the command. A chaplain is located at every echelon of command from battalion through corps.

• **Staff Judge Advocate (SJA) (Coordinating Staff Responsibility, ACofS, G1/AG (S1)**, when required). The SJA is the commander's personal legal advisor on all matters affecting the morale, good order, and discipline of the command. The SJA provides legal support to the members of the command and community. A SJA is located at corps, division, and major support command levels. A legal support element, including at least a judge advocate, deploys in direct support of each brigade-level task force.

Ref: FM 4-0 Combat Service Support, chap. 5.

Combat service support (CSS), like the other battlefield operating systems, is the commander's business. The purpose of Army CSS is to generate Army combat power, extend operational reach, and sustain the force. Achieving this purpose requires commanders at all levels to orchestrate effective CSS to Army forces by planning, preparing, executing and assessing CSS operations. CSS involves working with operations planners to determine requirements, acquire resources and distribute them.

I. CSS Command and Control

Command and control is the exercise of authority and direction, by a properly designated commander, over assigned and attached forces in the accomplishment of the mission. C2 functions are performed through an arrangement of personnel, equipment, communications, facilities, and procedures employed by a commander in planning, directing, coordinating, and controlling forces and operations in the accomplishment of the mission (FM 3-0).

A. CSS Commander

The CSS commander is responsible for planning, preparing, executing, and assessing the CSS mission in coordination and in conjunction with the combatant commander's operations plan (OPLAN)/operations order (OPORD). Like the combat commander, the CSS commander must execute the leadership aspects of visualizing, describing, and directing CSS operations (see FM 3-0).

Visualize

Upon receipt of a mission, CSS commanders conduct a mission analysis to develop their initial vision, which they continually confirm or modify. To visualize the desired outcome, CSS commanders must clearly understand the mission, enemy, troops, terrain and weather, time, civilian considerations (METT-TC) in the battlespace.

This framing of the battlespace takes place during mission analysis (see FM 101-5) and continues with battle tracking during execution of the combat operation. This facilitates posturing for the most effective and efficient method of providing uninterrupted sustainment and building of combat power.

Describe

Unless subordinate commanders and staffs understand the commander's visualization, there is no unifying design. The commander must communicate his visualization by describing it in doctrinal terms. Commanders describe their visualization through the commander's intent, planning guidance, and commander's critical information requirements (CCIR), using terms suited to the nature of the mission and their experience. Commanders may also describe their visualizations graphically using doctrinal graphics for easier communication. Describing is not a one-time event. As the commander confirms or modifies his visualization, he continues to describe his visualization to his staff and subordinates so they may better support his decisionmaking. Better effort in describing leads to better comprehension by subordinates of the context of his decision. It also enables better decisions on subordinates part when exercising individual initiative.

Direct

CSS forces do not respond to a decision until directed to do so. To effect execution or adjustment decisions, the commander must direct the action. Subordinate CSS forces then perform their own decisionmaking and direct actions by their forces. After the commander makes an execution or adjustment decision, the staff must synchronize the operation. This involves synchronizing the operation in time, space and purpose across all battlefield operating systems (BOS) to seize, retain, or exploit the initiative.

B. CSS Command and Control System

The C2 system is the arrangement of personnel, information management, procedures, and equipment and facilities essential to the commander to plan, prepare for, execute, and assess operations (FM 6-0). A commander cannot exercise C2 alone except in the simplest and smallest of units. Even at the lowest levels, a commander needs support to exercise C2 effectively.

C. Army Battle Command System (ABCS)

The Army battle command system (ABCS) is the Army's C2 information system. ABCS comprises seven separate systems to support key C2 functions of maneuver, fire support, air defense, intelligence, air support, battle command, and CSS. ABCS allow commanders to provide information to subordinates to guide the exercise of disciplined initiative within the commander's intent. This information provides subordinates with a common operational picture (COP) to facilitate their own situational understanding and conveys their superior cdr's perspective.

Combat Service Support Control System (CSSCS)

Combat service support control system (CSSCS) is the CSS node of the ABCS. It is an automated CSS C2 tool for the commander. CSSCS provides information collection and processing capabilities that support maneuver sustainment operations. CSSCS maintains the maneuver sustainment status of all assigned units, tracks the CSS commander's sustainment posture, and meets the combat commander's requirements for CSS information that affect the command's combat power. CSSCS maintains a database of personnel, military specialties, equipment, ammunition, blood, repair parts, and other supply items. The commander identifies items within CSSCS he considers critical to the operation and forms a commander's tracked item list (CTIL).

Force XXI Battle Command, Brigade and Below System (FBCB2)

Force XXI battle command, brigade and below system (FBCB2) is a digitized battle command information system that provides on-the-move battle command information to tactical combat, combat support, and CSS commanders. FBCB2 is a key component of the ABCS and integrates with ABCS at the brigade and below level. It also interfaces with CSSCS. The CSS functions of FBCB2 include logistics situation reports, personnel situation reports, call for support, and logistics task order and task management.

II. CSS Planning

Note: See chap. 4, Combat Service Support Planning, for additional information.

CSS is vital to executing operations successfully. CSS planning, preparation, execution, and assessment must be versatile; they complement combat plans and operations, thus enhancing the ability of the supported commander to accomplish his mission. Commanders must anticipate their unit mission requirements and provide responsive support. They assess what resources and capabilities are

Civilian Personnel

Ref: FM 4-0, chap. 5.

Civilian personnel provide essential CSS for military operations in peacetime as well as during operations. Identifying requirements for civilian personnel (governmental or nongovernmental agency civilians and contractors) and identifying qualified personnel to fill those requirements are essential when planning for operations. For more detailed information on contractors, see JP 4-0, FM 100-10-2, and FM 3-100.21.

A. DA Civilians

Civilian personnel who provide essential CS and CSS roles in a theater are a key part of the Army. Fifteen hundred DA civilians in more than 100 different occupational specialties deployed from commands throughout the world to Southwest Asia during Operation Desert Shield and Operation Desert Storm. The functional proponent for Army personnel support to DA civilians (appropriated and nonappropriated fund [NAF] employees) is Headquarters, Department of the Army, G1. Contracting activities and contracting officers provide contractual oversight for contract civilians. The Army and Air Force Exchange Service (AAFES) performs NAF civilian personnel management for AAFES personnel.

B. Contractors

Contracted support is an effective force multiplier. It can bridge gaps before military support resources arrive and when host-nation support is not available. It also augments existing support capabilities. Theater support contracts may provide effective support thus allowing the combatant commander to better operate within the limits of strategic lift or military force caps realities, particularly in stability operations and support operations.

Types of Contractors

There are three types of contractors. They are characterized by the general type of support provided and by the source of their contract authority.

- **Theater Support Contractors**. Theater support contractors support deployed operational forces under prearranged contracts, or contracts awarded from the AO, by contracting officers serving under the direct contracting authority of the theater principal assistant responsible for contracting (PARC). Theater support contractors provide goods, services, and minor construction, usually from the local vendor base, to meet the immediate needs of operational commanders.

- **External Support Contractors**. External support contractors provide for deployed forces support, separate and distinct from either theater support or system contractors. They may be associated with prearranged contracts or contracts awarded during the contingency. Contracting officers who award and administer external support contracts retain distinct contracting authority to organizations other than the theater PARC.

- **System Contractors**. System contractors support deployed forces under prearranged contracts awarded by program executive officers (PEOs), program managers (PMs), and the USAMC to provide specific support to materiel systems throughout their life cycles, during both peacetime and contingency operations. These systems include, but are not limited to, vehicles, weapon systems, aircraft, and information systems infrastructure and equipment. Contracting officers working for the PMs and USAMC subordinate commands administer their system contractor functions and operations via their contracts.

available in theater and tailor follow-on forces accordingly. They ensure deploying/ deployed units are sustainable in the theater of operations until establishing lines of communication (LOC) or providing other support from within the area of operations (AO) (for example, through contracted support or host nation support [HNS]).

The combatant commander bases his CSS plan on the overall campaign plan. As he develops his strategic concept of operations, he concurrently develops, in coordination with his Army service component command (ASCC) and other service component commanders, a concept of support.

Logistics Prep of the Theater (LPT)

Logistics preparation of the theater (LPT) is a key conceptual tool available to personnel in building a flexible strategic/operational support plan. Logistics preparation of the theater consists of the actions taken by combat service support personnel at all echelons to optimize means (force structure, resources, and strategic lift) of supporting the joint force commander's plan. A detailed estimate of requirements, tempered with logistics preparation of the theater, allows support personnel to advise the JTF/ASCC/ARFOR cdr of the most effective method of providing adequate, responsive support while minimizing the CSS footprint.

Note: See. pp. 4-7 to 4-14, Logistics Preparation of the Theater/Battlefield.

III. Acquisition of Resources

The LPT ties support requirements and acquisition support together at the operational level. The LPT process ensures CSS personnel have considered all possible sources of support. The LPT provides the details in the CSS reach consideration of such sources as joint and multinational capabilities, HNS, and contractors.

The acquisition of resources refers to the activity at all levels to gain access to the support resources identified in the requirements determination aspect of planning. The process of acquiring resources is closely related to force tailoring in two ways: the commander aims to attain the resources identified during the planning process, and barriers to acquisition may influence support requirements. The acquisition of CSS resources is also associated with distribution. Acquisition of resources to support military operations involves such varied activities as:

- Contracting materiel and services
- Negotiating ISSAs and ACSAs at the National level
- Arranging LOGCAP and HNS agreements
- Utilizing private voluntary and nongovernmental organizations
- Recruiting military and civilian personnel
- Conducting mobilization activities

IV. Distribution

Distribution is the process of synchronizing all elements of the CSS system to deliver the right things to the right place at the right time to support the commander. The distribution system is a complex of networks tailored to meet the requirements of the force across the range of operations. These networks are overlaid on existing infrastructure that the host-nation and military, civilian, and multinational forces participating in the same operation must share. Combinations of U.S. military, host nation, multinational, and contractor organizations operate the nodes and modes that distribute the forces and sustainment resources. These organizations collect and report data to a network of operational and CSS headquarters responsible for processing the data into information and issuing instructions to the node and mode operators. This process enables the JFC and subordinate ARFOR commander to carry out CSS effectively and efficiently.

Theater Distribution

Ref: FM 4-0, chap. 5.

The theater portion of distribution is the responsibility of the geographic combatant commander, but a subordinate JTF normally executes this responsibility. Theater distribution occurs in the distribution pipeline extending from the port of debarkation (POD) to the user. Distribution resources within the theater are finite, and regardless of the commodity distributed or the operational phase, the distribution system competes for resources. The theater distribution manager must possess total visibility over all distribution capabilities, service requirements, and common-item supply resources flow within the theater distribution system. This maximizes distribution flexibility and combines the overall system capacity. JP 4-01.4, which is currently under development, will be the joint reference for theater distribution.

The Army Role

Ongoing developments in CSS activities support the Army role in theater distribution as it moves to distribution-based CSS. These include establishing distribution management centers/elements (DMC/E), developments in information systems, advancements in configured loads, emphasis on maximizing throughput, and enhancing capabilities to operate intermodal terminals.

To facilitate distribution management, the Army is creating distribution DMC/Es within theater, corps, and division support commands. For Army forces, the key link to the theater system is the TSC DMC. It develops the ASCC's piece of the distribution plan in coordination with the ASCC G4. See FM 4-93.4 for more information.

Total Asset Visibility (TAV) - Information Systems

Distribution managers require timely and accurate TAV information to manage the distribution pipeline efficiently and effectively to build and sustain combat power. This includes information about warfighter requirements, tactical operations and the overall situational awareness from the ABCS (such as CSSCS) and the on-hand, in-transit and in-maintenance TAV information. The ability to receive the logistics portion of the COP in the form of TAV enables CSS operations to build and sustain combat power efficiently and effectively for the warfighter. TAV has three primary components: asset visibility, in-transit visibility, and in-maintenance visibility.

1. Asset Visibility

Asset visibility involves the ability to see what is on-hand and on-order. In-theater asset visibility begins at the SSA for cargo and at replacement centers for personnel. The SSA and DMC track cargo receipt, storage, and issue functions using GCSS-A and radio frequency data collection (RFDC). Information from RF tags required for receipt, storage, and issue processing passes to the GCSS-A management module. The replacement centers and DMC track personnel using SIDPERS and smart cards.

2. In-Transit Visibility (ITV)

In-transit visibility is the ability to see what is moving in the distribution pipeline. In-theater in-transit visibility begins at the POD during RSO&I.

3. In-Maintenance Visibility (IMV)

In-maintenance visibility refers to the ability to see what is being repaired. In-maintenance, visibility begins with current shop status of equipment at direct support maintenance locations in the AO. Maintenance status information passes through GCSS-A to the GCSS management module. RF data collection bar code scanners are receipts of parts for maintenance operations. Future uses of RF technology include tracking internal maintenance shop workload and equipment history.

Army Prepositioned Stocks

Ref: FM 4-0, chap. 5.

Army prepositioned stocks are supplies located at or near the point of planned use or at other designated locations to reduce reaction time and to ensure resupply (FM 100-17-2). These reserves are intended to provide support essential to sustain operations until resupply can be expected.

Automated Battlebook System (ABS)

The Automated Battlebook System (ABS) contains details on each APS program. G3 planners and unit movement officers use ABS to identify equipment in the categories to accompany troops (TAT) and not authorized for prepositioning (NAP). ABS also provides a consolidated list of all APS stockpile inventories. ABS supports deployment planning by providing the deploying unit with a contingency-updated database for all APS equipment and selected supplies in prepositioned locations. Forces Command (FORSCOM) is the proponent for ABS. The FM 3-35-series manuals provide detailed discussions on APS. There are four APS categories:

1. Prepositioned Sets

Unit sets consist of prepositioned organizational equipment (end items, supplies, and secondary items) stored in unit configurations to reduce force deployment response time. Equipment is configured into brigade sets, division units, and corps/echelon above corps (EAC) units. Materiel is positioned ashore and afloat.

2. Army Operational Project Stocks

Operational project stocks are materiel above normal table of organization and equipment (TOE), table of distribution and allowances (TDA), and common table of allowance (CTA) authorizations, tailored to key strategic capabilities essential to the Army ability to execute force projection. They are primarily positioned in continental United States (CONUS), with tailored packages prepositioned overseas and afloat.

3. War Reserve Sustainment Stocks

War reserve stocks are acquired in peacetime to meet increased wartime require-ments. They provide minimum essential support to operations and post-mobilization training beyond the capabilities of peacetime stocks, industry, and HNS. Sustainment stocks are prepositioned in or near a theater of operations to last until resupply at wartime rates or emergency rates are established.

4. War Reserve Stocks for Allies

War reserve stocks for allies (WRSA) is an Office of the Secretary of Defense (OSD)–directed program that ensures U.S. preparedness to assist designated allies in case of war. The United States owns and finances WRSA assets, and prepositions them in the appropriate theater. The United States positions APSs as follows:

- **APS-1 (CONUS)**. Operational project stocks and war reserve sustainment stocks

- **APS-2 (Europe)**. Prepositioned sets, operational project stocks, and limited war reserve sustainment stocks

- **APS-3 (Army prepositioned afloat)**. Prepositioned sets, operational project stocks, and war reserve sustainment stocks

- **APS-4 (Pacific)**. Prepositioned sets, operational project stocks, war reserve sustainment stocks, and war reserve stocks for Allies-Korea (WRSA-K)

- **APS-5 (Southwest Asia [SWA])**. Prepositioned sets, operational project stocks, and war reserve sustainment stocks

VI. Supply & Field Services

Ref: FM 4-0 Combat Service Support, chap. 6.

See also pp. 3-41 to 3-52, (FXXI Tactical-Level CSS Ops) Sustaining the Force.

Supply and services consist of wide-ranging functions that extend from determining requirements at the strategic level to delivering items and services to the user at the tactical level. Supply involves acquiring, managing, receiving, storing, and issuing all classes of supply except class VIII. Field services involve feeding, clothing, and providing personnel services to soldiers. It consists of clothing exchange, laundry and shower support, textile repair, mortuary affairs, preparation for aerial delivery, food services, billeting, and sanitation.

I. The Supply System

The supply system spans all levels of war. The following is a discussion of the considerations at each level.

A. Strategic Considerations

At the strategic level, supply activity focuses on determining realistic, supportable resource requirements; acquiring, packaging, managing, and positioning supplies; and coordinating moving materiel into the theater base and staging areas. Effective supply and field services planning and execution supports strategic and operational commanders in planning campaigns and, subsequently, ensuring operational and tactical commanders are able to execute their warfighting mission with confidence that the combat service support (CSS) community can support them.

Strategic planners determine requirements to support the force based on the National Security Strategy (NSS), the National Military Strategy (NMS), the missions the Army can expect to receive to achieve strategic end states, and theater strategies and campaign plans. They consider all potential sources of supplies to reduce the deployment requirements to support Army operations. Sources include host nation support, contracting, and joint and multinational forces. Commodity centers assigned to U.S. Army Materiel Command (USAMC),U.S. Army Medical Materiel Agency (USAMMA), Defense Logistics Agency (DLA), Defense Commissary Agency, and other defense agencies manage supply operations at the strategic level with the assistance of the Army service component command (ASCC) in accordance with the combatant commander's directives and priorities.

Critical considerations include determining stockpiling requirements and supply production capabilities. CSS personnel preposition supplies in overseas regions (primarily where forward-presence forces locate) for initial support. They preposition certain critical supplies as well as unit equipment afloat to provide flexible support to forward-presence, reinforcing, or contingency forces. Some supplies are stored in continental United States (CONUS) military stockpiles. Other supplies, such as construction materiel, are routinely available directly from the Army's economic base, contractor support, or local purchase in theater; the CONUS military system does not stockpile such supplies.

B. Operational Considerations

Supply at the operational level involves requisitioning or acquiring, receipt, storage, protection, maintenance, distribution, and salvage of supplies. Supply planners and managers must understand the joint task force (JTF)/ASCC/ARFOR commander's priorities and the requirements for supporting campaigns and major operations. Requirements include considering the needs of joint and multinational forces.

Supplies are throughput whenever possible from the port of debarkation (POD) or local sources to the appropriate supply support activity (SSA) or receiving unit. Multiple consignee cargo comes to a supply activity for sorting before transshipment to the appropriate SSA or receiving unit.

C. Tactical Considerations

Tactical-level supply focuses on readiness and supports the commander's ability to fight battles and engagements or achieve his stability or support mission. CSS planners work with supporting commanders and materiel managers to ensure required supplies are available when and where the user needs them. Units carry a basic load of supplies with them to support their operations until the system can resupply them. When time and mission constraints require, a push system provides supplies. Under this type of system, planners estimate the supply requirements and arrange to have supplies delivered to supported elements. As the theater matures and stocks become readily available, supply elements convert by commodity to a "pull" system. Requests generated by supported elements are the basis of a "pull" system. FM 10-1 discusses planning considerations and request procedures.

Both operational and tactical supply systems include SSAs operated by GS and DS supply units. These units establish SSAs from the COMMZ as far forward as the brigade support area. On a temporary basis, DS elements may operate even further forward at forward logistics bases to reduce the distances users have to travel to receive support. The support structure at each command level from separate brigade/division up also includes a materiel management organization to manage supply and maintenance operations.

Under a pull supply system, a using unit submits a request to its supporting DS supply element. If stocks are available, the direct support (DS) element fills the request and notifies the materiel manager, who initiates replenishment. If it cannot fill the request, the supply unit passes it to the materiel manager. In that case, the manager directs issue from general support (GS) stocks to the DS unit or passes the requisition to the appropriate MMC or commodity center to meet the requirement.

Retrograde of materiel usually involves supplies and repairable equipment. Repairable items are generally in maintenance facilities and returned to supply channels when restored to serviceable condition. Salvage items are unserviceable and uneconomically repairable. They are evacuated through the supply system, destroyed, or demilitarized based on theater policy and commodity center instructions. FM 10-1 has more details.

II. Classes of Supply

In addition to the general considerations guiding all supply operations, there are specific considerations for each commodity.

This section addresses the considerations that apply to most classes of supply. Section VIII, p. 1-57 covers Class V and Class IX. Section IX, p. 1-65 covers Class VIII. JP 4-07 addresses Class X. FM 100-10-1 explains the flow of each class of supply.

Classes of Supply

Ref: FM 4-0, table 6-1, p. 6-4.

The Army divides supply into ten classes for administrative and management purposes.

Class	Symbol	Description
Class I		Subsistence, gratuitious health and comfort items
Class II		Clothing, individual equipment, tentage, organizational tool sets and kits, hand tools, administrative and housekeeping supplies and equipment
Class III		Petroleum fuels, lubricants, hydraulic and insulating oils, preservatives, liquids & gases, bulk chemical products, coolants, deicer and antifreeze compounds, components and additives of petroleum products, and coal
Class IV		Construction materials including installed equipment, and all fortification and barrier materials
Class V		Ammunition of all types, bombs, explosives, mines, fuzes, detonators, pyrotechnics, missiles, rockets, propellants, and associated items
Class VI		Personal demand items (such as health and hygiene products, soaps, toothpaste, writing material, snacks, beverages, cigarettes, batteries & cameras—nonmilitary sales items).
Class VII		Major end items such as launchers, tanks, mobile machine shops, and vehicles.
Class VIII		Medical material, including repair parts peculiar to medical equipment
Class IX		Repair parts and components to include kits, assemblies, and subassemblies (repairable or non-repairable) required for maintenance support of all equipment.
Class X	CA	Material to support nonmilitary programs such as agriculture and economic development (not included in Classes I through IX).
Misc		Water, maps, salvage, and captured material

Class I

Class I supply directly links to the field service of food preparation. During the initial phase of a conflict, the Class I distribution system pushes rations—typically meals ready-to-eat (MREs)—and, when cooks become available, the unitized group heat and serve rations. Personnel strength, unit locations, type of operations, and feeding capabilities determine the quantities and types of rations ordered and pushed forward. As the AO stabilizes, the Class I distribution system converts to a pull system with limited enhancements (salad, fresh fruit, and pouch bread).

Class II

Class II supplies include a variety of supplies and equipment from clothing and individual equipment to tools and unclassified maps. In most cases, Class II consumption is predictable. Demand history, with anticipated fluctuations, can provide accurate forecasting of needs. Divisions carry limited stock of Class II; such items are bulky and impede mobility. Division supply elements normally carry only critical items. Such items may include chemical defense equipment, helmets, and mechanics' tools. Clothing supply creates a special challenge due to its excessive transportation and storage requirements.

Class III

Today's Army consumes large quantities of petroleum products to support operations and will continue to do so into the near future. Its ability to move and fight depends on its supply of fuel. There are two categories of Class III supplies: bulk fuel and packaged petroleum products.

- **Bulk Fuel.** During peacetime, each service is responsible for planning and preparing for bulk petroleum support to its own forces. This includes managing war reserve and peacetime operating stocks. It also includes operating bulk storage, handling, and distribution facilities. Each service computes its require-ments and submits them to the Defense Energy Support Center for supply and acquisition action. During war (or in specified military operations other than war), the Army is responsible for the inland distribution of bulk fuels. This includes distributing bulk fuels to the Air Force and Marines. This inland distribution responsibility requires the Army to provide the necessary force structure to construct, operate, and maintain overland petroleum pipelines and to distribute bulk fuels via non-pipeline means. (However, the Air Force and Marines remain responsible for the retail distribution of bulk fuels to their units.) Inherent in this responsibility is the requirement to manage the distribution of bulk fuels within the theater. Units pass forecasted requirements up S4/G4 channels to materiel managers who manage distribution in coordination with movement control and GS supply elements. Tankers, rail tank cars, and hose lines move bulk fuels from GS to DS supply elements. Deliveries bypass intermediate storage locations when possible. Details are in FM 10-67-1.

- **Packaged Petroleum Products.** Packaged products include lubricants, greases, hydraulic fluids, compressed gasses, and specialty items that are stored, transported, and issued in containers with a capacity of 55 gallons or less. (Normally, this category does not include fuels.) Managers use the distribu-tion concept associated with Class II supplies to manage packaged petroleum products. These products require intensive management due to quality surveil-lance needs and criticality to combat effectiveness.

Class IV

Class IV items consist of fortification, barrier, and construction materials. Units use barrier and fortification materials to prepare fighting and protective positions as well as field fortifications. Engineers use Class IV materials to prepare fortifications beyond the capabilities of units. They also use them for such functions as:

- Upgrading, maintaining, or building roads, bridges, and bypasses.
- Repairing airfields or building expedient airstrips and landing zones.
- Assembling rafts or bridges for river crossings.
- Upgrading, repairing, or building facilities to support the CSS effort or to enhance the infrastructure of the host nation as part of a stability operation or support operation.

Class V

Section VIII, p. 1-57 covers Class V and Class IX.

Class VI

Class VI supplies are AAFES items for sale to troops and authorized individuals. Class VI supplies may be available through local procurement, through transfer from theater stocks, or through requisitioning from the AAFES in CONUS. Available shipping space dictates Class VI supply to the theater. Class VI supply responsibilities differ significantly from other classes of supply. AAFES has responsibility for worldwide planning and monitoring of all tactical field exchanges (TFE).

Class VII

Class VII supplies consist of major end items such as launchers, tanks, vehicles, and aircraft. A major end item is a final combination of end products that is ready to use. Command channels usually control Class VII items due to their importance to combat readiness and their high costs. If not, the supporting materiel manager controls them. Each echelon intensely manages the requisitioning, distribution, maintenance, and disposal of these items to ensure visibility and operational readiness.

Forces report losses of major items through both supply and command channels. Replacing losses requires careful coordination and management. Managers at each command level work to maximize the number of operational weapon systems. Replacement requires coordination among materiel managers, Class VII supply units, transporters, maintenance elements, and personnel managers.

Supply units at the operational level process weapon systems arriving in theater from storage or transport configuration and make them ready to issue. They install all ancillary equip. and ensure that basic issue items are on board, and fuel equipment.

Class IX

Section VIII, p. 1-57 covers Class V and Class IX.

Class X

JP 4-07 addresses Class X.

Water

Normally, units receive potable water by supply point distribution with only limited unit distribution. Water elements set up water points as close to the using units as practical, given the location of a water source.

The DISCOM operates the water points in the division area. In most areas of the world, the division is self-sufficient in water. In arid regions and unusual circumstances, the division support units require additional water storage and distribution capability. Under these conditions, the division receives water as outlined in this chapter under water purification. Separate brigades and ACR have organic water production capability. Force XXI divisions have water teams, organic to the DISCOM, that can be used to augment division brigades operating in isolated locations.

Echelons above division (EAD) supply companies provide water to nondivisional customers on an area basis. CSS planners may augment Army forces with EAD water production capabilities, when they are operating without division support. FM 10-52-1 provides more detail on water operations and equipment.

III. Field Services

The Army no longer classifies field services as either primary or secondary. Instead, all field services receive the same basic priority. The commander decides which are most important. The ASCC influences priorities through the time-phased force and deployment data.

Locations and Services

Quartermaster corps personnel in a variety of units perform field service functions. During combat operations, military personnel provide most of the field service support in forward areas, with HNS and contractors providing a limited amount. Conversely, HNS and contractors provide much of the support in rear areas.

A. Food Preparation

Food preparation is a basic unit function performed by unit food service personnel. It is one of the most important factors in soldier health, morale, and welfare. Virtually every type of unit in the force structure, divisional and nondivisional, has some organic food service personnel. These personnel support the unit food service program, as directed by the commander.

The field feeding system assumes theater-wide use of the MRE for the first several days following deployment. The theater then begins to transition to prepared group feeding rations. The theater initially transitions from the MREs to UGRs. Then, as the operational situation permits, logisticians attempt to introduce the A-ration (fresh foods) into theater. This requires extensive logistics expansion, since it requires refrigerated storage and distribution equipment and a capability to make or acquire ice for unit storage. The feeding standard is to provide soldiers at all echelons three quality meals per day. The meals fed depend on the prevailing conditions. Disposing of garbage is important to avoid leaving signature trails and maintain field sanitation standards. See FM 10-1 for more details.

B. Water Purification

Water is an essential commodity. It is necessary for sanitation, food preparation, construction, and decontamination. Support activities (such as helicopter maintenance and operation of medical facilities) consume large volumes of water. Water is critical to the individual soldier. Classification of the water function is somewhat different from other commodities; it is both a field service and a supply function. Water purification is a field service. Quartermaster supply units normally perform purification in conjunction with storage and distribution of potable water—a supply function. GS and DS water units do not store or distribute non-potable water. Therefore, non-potable water requirements (for example, water for construction, laundry, and showers) are the responsibility of the user.

Water supply units perform routine testing. However, monitoring water quality is primarily the responsibility of the preventive medicine personnel of the medical command or corps. The command surgeon performs tests associated with water source approval, monitors potable water, and interprets the water testing results. Each service provides its own water resource support. However, the Army or another service, as directed by the JFC, provides support beyond a service capability in a joint operation. AR 700-136 details the responsibilities of Army elements for water support.

Engineers play a major role in providing water to Army forces. The engineers, through the Topographical Engineering Center, develop and maintain an automated database for rapidly retrieving water source-related data. The engineers are also responsible for finding subsurface water; drilling wells, and constructing (including doing major repair and maintenance) permanent and semipermanent water facilities. In addition, they assist water units with site preparation, when required.

C. Mortuary Affairs

Each service has the responsibility for returning remains and personal effects to CONUS. The Army is designated as the executive agent for the Joint Mortuary Affairs Program. It maintains a Central Joint Mortuary Affairs Office (CJMAO) and provides general support to other services when their requirements exceed their capabilities. The Mortuary Affairs Program is divided into three subprograms:

- The current death program operates around the world in peacetime and outside of AOs during military operations. It may also continue in AOs depending on the CSS and tactical situation. It provides mortuary supplies and associated services for permanently disposing remains and personal effects of persons for whom the Army is or becomes responsible.

- The Graves Registration Program provides search, recovery, initial identification, and temporary burial of deceased personnel in temporary burial sites. Temporary burials are a last resort, and the geographic combatant commander must authorize them. It also provides for the care and maintenance of burial sites and for the handling and disposing of personal effects.

- The concurrent return program is a combination of the current death and Graves Registration Programs. This program provides the search, recovery, and evacuation of remains to collection points and further evacuation to a mortuary. It provides for identification and preparation of remains in a mortuary and shipment to a final destination, as directed by the next of kin.

All commanders are responsible for the search, recovery, tentative identification, care, and evacuation of remains to the nearest collection point or mortuary. Each division has a small mortuary affairs element (two to three personnel) organic to the DISCOM. They train division personnel to perform initial search, recovery, identification, and evacuation of human remains and personal effects. During hostilities, the mortuary affairs personnel organic to the division operate collection points. This procedure continues until the division receives additional mortuary affairs personnel or a mortuary affairs unit. A mortuary affairs unit assigned to the corps support command supports nondivisional units on an area basis. This unit operates collection points throughout the corps, division, and brigade areas. These points receive remains from units, assist and conduct search and recovery operations, and arrange for the evacuation of remains to a mortuary or temporary burial site.

Mortuary affairs units operate theater collection points, evacuation points, and personal effects depots. Mortuary affairs personnel initially process remains in theater. Then, they arrange to evacuate remains and personal effects, usually by air, to a CONUS POD mortuary. CONUS POD mortuaries positively identify the remains and prepare them for release, in accordance with the desires of the next of kin. Recent wars and military operations other than war (MOOTW) have shown this procedure is quite effective.

JP 4-06 and FM 10-64 have more information on decontamination of remains and mortuary affairs in general.

D. Aerial Delivery

Supporting aerial delivery equipment and systems includes parachute packing, air item maintenance, and rigging of supplies and equipment. This function supports both airborne insertions and airdrop/airland resupply. Airborne insertions involve the delivery of an airborne fighting force and its supplies and equipment to an objective area, by parachute. FM 10-500-1 covers airborne insertions in detail. Airdrop resupply operations apply to all Army forces. The airdrop function supports the movement of personnel, equipment, and supplies. It is a vital link in the distribution system; it provides the capability of supplying the force even when land lines of communication (LOC) have been disrupted and adds flexibility to the distribution system.

USAMC manages most airdrop equipment and systems (ADES) at the strategic level. It maintains the national inventory control point (NICP) and national maintenance point for ADES. At the operational level, there are two types of airdrop support units. A heavy airdrop supply company provides reinforcing support to corps-level airdrop supply companies. In addition, an airdrop equipment repair and supply company provides supply and maintenance support to airdrop supply companies in the corps (other than the airborne corps) and at EAC.

A light airdrop supply company provides airdrop/airland resupply support to the corps. In addition, it provides personnel parachute support to units such as long range surveillance units. If the corps cannot support an airdrop request, it passes the request to the airdrop supply company at EAC. Most of the supplies used for rigging by the airdrop supply company come directly from the strategic level, bypassing the airdrop equipment repair and supply company at EAC. The EAC ADES repair and supply company provides ADES maintenance support for the corps light airdrop supply company. The airborne corps has an organic airdrop capability. If it cannot meet the airdrop resupply requirement, it forwards the requirement to the supporting airdrop unit at EAC.

E. Laundry, Shower, Clothing & Light Textile Repair

Clean, serviceable clothing and showers are essential for hygiene and morale purposes. During peacetime, fixed facilities or field expedient methods normally provide shower, laundry, and clothing repair for short-duration exercises. During operations, they are provided as far forward as the brigade area. The goal is to provide soldiers with one shower and up to 15 pounds of laundered clothing each week. Soldiers receive their own clothing from a tactical laundry within 24 hours. Responsibilities at the strategic level are those involving provisioning. For information on clothing replacement, see Class II under supply.

Forces receive support from a combination of units, HNS, and contractors. In low levels of hostilities, HNS and contractors may provide much of this support. LOGCAP offers considerable capability during the early deployment stages.

A field service company provides direct support at the tactical level. The company has the modular capability of sending small teams as far forward as desired by the supported commander. The unit provides one shower for each soldier each week. Other sources (such as field expediency methods, small-unit shower equipment, HNS, or contract services) could be used to increase showers from one to two per soldier per week.

F. Force Provider

The Army's Force Provider is a modular system, principally designed to provide the front-line soldier with a brief respite from the rigors of a combat environment. Each of 36 modules provides life support for up to 550 soldiers. It includes environmentally controlled billeting; modern containerized latrines, showers and laundry; an all electric kitchen; and space for MWR activities. Additionally, the module infrastructure incorporates a complete water distribution/disposal system and power grid. Six modules can provide contiguous support to a brigade-sized force. The cadre for operating Force Provider modules consists of one Force Provider company, which has six platoons that operate one module each, and five reserve companies that require significant augmentation to effectively operate up to six modules each. A LOGCAP contractor can set up and operate these modules.

VII. Transportation Support

Ref: FM 4-0 Combat Service Support, chap. 7.

See also pp. 3-35 to 3-40, (FXXI Tactical-Level CSS Ops) Moving the Force.

Army transportation operates as a partner in the Defense Transportation System (DTS) to deploy, sustain, and redeploy forces in all military operations. Transportation provides vital support to the Army and joint forces across the strategic, operational, and tactical levels of war. It is a seamless system that unites the levels of war with synchronized movement control, terminal operations, and mode operations. Army transportation incorporates military, commercial, and host nation capabilities. It involves the total Army (active and Reserve Components). More detailed information on Army transportation is in the FM 4-01-series of manuals.

I. Strategic Transportation

At the strategic level, the U.S. Transportation Command (USTRANSCOM) provides air, land, and sea transportation and common-user port management at seaports of embarkation (SPOEs) as well as seaports of debarkation (SPODs). USTRANSCOM controls strategic movements through its transportation component commands (TCC), Military Traffic Management Command (MTMC), Air Mobility Command (AMC), and Military Sealift Command (MSC).

USTRANSCOM schedules strategic deployment according to the supported commander's priorities. The time-phased force deployment data (TPFDD) is the commander's expression of his priorities. Both MTMC and USAMC generate port call messages based on the TPFDD. These messages specify when units and equipment must be at a POE. Port call messages set in motion the movement from the installation or depot. The Army service component command (ASCC) commander ensures units and equipment arrive at the POE as directed.

Military Traffic Management Command (MTMC)

MTMC is a major command of the U.S. Army and transportation TCC of USTRANSCOM. MTMC's mission is to provide global surface transportation to meet national security objectives, in peace and war, by being the continental United States (CONUS) land transportation manager and providing worldwide common-user ocean terminal services to deploy, employ, sustain, and redeploy U.S. forces. MTMC handles peacetime and war time responsibilities through its single port manager role for all common-user SPOEs and SPODs, responsive planning, crisis response actions, traffic management, terminal operations, global intermodal management, and provision of in-transit visibility, information management, and deployability transportation engineering.

Air Mobility Command (AMC)

The AMC is a major command of the U.S. Air Force and a TCC of USTRANSCOM. AMC provides common-user airlift, air refueling, and strategic aeromedical evacuation transportation services to deploy, employ, sustain, and redeploy U.S. forces on a global basis.

Military Sealift Command (MSC)

The MSC is a major command of the U.S. Navy and a TCC of USTRANSCOM. MSC provides government-owned and government-chartered sealift transportation services to deploy, employ, sustain, and redeploy U.S. forces on a global basis.

Installation Transportation Offices (ITOs)

In CONUS, installation transportation offices (ITOs), with movement officers at each echelon, coordinate movement to the POE. The defense movement coordinator in each state movement control center plans and routes CONUS surface movements, in accordance with port calls issued by MTMC. Outside CONUS, the ASCC has movement control units that perform functions similar to the ITO. Deployable movement control units and personnel organic to Army units at operational and tactical levels of war also play an active role in preparing their forces for deployment. However, their focus is on early deployment to develop the operational- and tactical-level theater transportation capability.

Strategic transportation also includes redeployment through movements back to home station. In CONUS, it may include transportation associated with demobilization. The FM 3-35-series manuals has additional information on force projection.

II. Operational and Tactical Transportation

The variety and complexity of military operations require the Army to establish a transportation system that is expandable and tailorable. The objective is to select and tailor required transportation capabilities at the operational and tactical levels to achieve total integration of the system. These capabilities include movement control, terminal operations, and mode operations. At the theater strategic and operational levels, sufficient force structure deploys early to conduct reception, staging, and onward movements, which includes opening ports, establishing inland LOC, and providing C2 for movements. An important facet of building combat power during the reception, staging, and onward movement phase of the operation is receiving the force and sustainment supplies at the POE. This same transportation force structure is required to redeploy the force when operations conclude. Ports, terminals, and inland LOC are critical nodes in the distribution system. At the theater strategic and operational levels, transportation supports the reception of units, personnel, supplies, and equipment at PODs and provides for their movement as far forward as required.

Theater transportation requirements largely depend on mission, enemy, troops, terrain and weather, time, civilian considerations (METT-TC). The logistics preparation of the theater discussed in chapter 5 is essential in determining requirements. Additionally, the Army provides transportation support to other services and multinational partners when directed by the combatant commander or JFC. Establishing communications links to other than Army forces is a challenge; however, transportation planners must integrate all requirements and support considerations into movement plans and programs. At the tactical level, transportation weights the battle through the same functions as at the operational level. However, the commander directs force structure and focus to forward support.

III. Movement Control

Movement control is the linchpin of the transportation system. Movement control units and staffs plan, route, schedule, and control common user assets, and maintain in-transit visibility (ITV) of personnel, units, equipment, and supplies moving over lines of communication. They are the using unit point of contact for transportation support.

Movement Control Team (MCT)

Units request transportation assets from the servicing movement control team (MCT) in their area. The MCT commits (tasks) allocated transportation modes and terminals to provide support in an integrated movement program according to command priorities. Movement control remains responsive to changes in METT-TC, which require adjustments to the plan. A responsive theater distribution system, operating over extended distances, requires centralized control of transportation platforms and synchronized movement management allowing commanders to shift limited transportation resources to move assets forward to influence the tactical situation. Effective movement control requires access to information systems to determine what to move as well as, when, where, and how. It also provides visibility of what is moving, how it is moving, and how well it is moving.

Distribution Management Centers/Elements (DMC/Es)

Transportation staff planners and movement managers at each echelon perform movement control activities. Movement control is integral to distribution management centers/elements (DMC/Es) at each echelon. They coordinate the efforts of the movement control units and the materiel managers.

Joint Transportation Board (JTB)/Joint Movement Center [JMC]

In addition to synchronizing movements with other Army elements, movement control personnel coordinate movements with other services and countries when operating as part of a joint or multinational force. The JFC may create a fully integrated joint board or center (such as a joint transportation board [JTB] or a joint movement center [JMC]) to exercise directive authority for movement control. The JTB organizations consist of representatives from the service component movement control activities and the U.S. operations directorate (J3) and logistics directorate (J4). The JMC plans future operations and monitors overall theater transportation performance. It performs the planning tasks by continually monitoring the balance between forecasted requirements and current capabilities of all modes. A service movement control organization may create a JMC. It should act as the movement C2 cell for the deployment process of an operation. The Army theater transportation command provides movement controllers that normally form the nucleus of the JMC. Similarly, a multinational force commander may form a multinational movement control agency. JP 4-01.3 discusses joint movement control.

At the operational level, the senior movement control organization looks forward to activities within the AO, as well as rearward to the sustaining base. Movement control personnel coordinate with materiel managers for efficient distribution of materiel. They develop movement plans that take into account all movement requirements, the transportation system capabilities, and the commander's priorities. Movement control elements use these factors when tasking transportation units to meet movement requirements. FM 55-10 has more information on movement control.

IV. Information Systems

This discussion covers only those transportation systems essential to transportation operations in a theater of operations.

1. Transportation Coordinators' Automated Information for Movement System II (TC-AIMS II)

TC-AIMS II will be used by the installation transportation office (ITO) to support day-to-day installation-level transportation operations. It provides the functionality essential for moving all inbound and outbound cargo and personnel. TC-AIMS II facilitates the movement of units deploying from home station, the daily non-unit transportation-related activities for outbound shipments, and the deploying of units back to home station. TC-AIMS II also provides accurate shipment location information by employing automatic identification technology devices to create, collect, and transmit movement data.

V. Terminal Operations

Ref: FM 4-0, chap. 7.

A terminal operation is the staging, loading, discharge, transfer handling, and documentation of cargo and manifesting of personnel among various transport modes. Terminals are key nodes in the distribution system that supports the commander's concept of operation. When linked by modes of transport, they define the transportation structure for the operation. Force projection missions require early identification and establishment of terminals. A well-conceived plan assures that terminals can support the deployment, reception, and onward movement of the force and its sustainment. Crucial to executing the operation is assigning the right personnel, cargo, and materiel-handling equipment at each terminal.

MTMC is USTRANSCOM's global single port manager (SPM) for DOD. The SPM integrates the commercial transportation industry, MTMC's commercial business practices, and military force structure. MTMC information systems are linked, through the Worldwide Port System (WPS), to the Global Transportation Network that provides the combatant commanders visibility over ocean cargo.

A. Ocean-Water Terminals

Ocean-water terminals include major port facilities, unimproved port facilities, and bare-beach facilities. Major port facilities are improved networks of cargo-handling facilities, specifically designed for transferring ocean-going freight, vessel-discharge operations, and port clearance. They normally have roll-on/roll-off service and container-handling capability. Unimproved port facilities are not as fully developed as major ports. They may require support from terminal units and shallow-draft lighterage to discharge vessels. Lack of fixed-terminal facilities at bare-beach locations requires that lighterage deliver cargo across the beach. Ports may be degraded by enemy action such as sinking vessels or damaging cranes or piers. Such activities can quickly turn a major port into the equivalent of an unimproved port.

B. Inland Terminals

Army transportation units establish inland terminals where required, throughout the theater to transship, load, and unload cargo. They operate motor transport terminals and trailer transfer points at both ends, and at intermediate points along line-haul routes. These terminals link local-haul and line-haul service and assist in changing the carrier or transportation mode, when required.

C. Intermodal Terminals

Forces establish an intermodal terminal early in the AO to provide cargo transfer and mode operations functions. As the scope of the operation enlarges, the commander adds additional sections/companies to meet the demand flow. While the operations may differ slightly, the essential units and command and control structure of the hub remain constant. Cargo transfer operations at the intermodal terminal assist in the throughput of supplies and materiel, configure multiple consignee shipments into single consignee shipments, and process frustrated cargo. In a mature theater, contracted U.S. or host nation civilians may perform intermodal terminal functions.

D. Intermediate Transfer Points

In addition to intermodal terminals, Army cargo transfer units perform transfer functions at intermediate transfer points on inland waterway systems. Army cargo transfer units clear Army cargo and personnel from air terminals served by the AMC or from theater airlift aircraft. They may also provide such assistance at forward landing fields that are not regularly scheduled stops for theater airlift aircraft. FM 55-17 has more information on terminal operations.

VI. Mode Operations

Ref: FM 4-0, chap. 7.

The Army can move personnel, cargo, and equipment by motor, rail, air, and water with organic, host nation, or contract assets. While each situation may not be conducive to using a particular mode, the Army must prepare to operate, or supervise, the operation of all these modes of transport. Mode platforms include trucks, trains, containers, flatracks, watercraft, aircraft and commercial delivery, when permitted by METT-TC. Mode operations include intratheater air (C-130 and CH-47); local and linehaul motor transport; heavy equipment transport; and rail, coastal and inland waterway transport. Mode operations and movement control elements working together match up the correct asset capability, cargo characteristics, and required delivery time.

A. Motor

Tactical vehicles are the backbone of the support structure. They are mobile, flexible, and reliable. The motor transportation unit and equipment mix for an operation depend on METT-TC. Planning factors include the planned flow of personnel and materiel and the availability and quality of the road networks. Motor transport provides the connecting links between the PODs and the receiving units. The right tactical trucks, in the right place, at the right time are essential to the success of any military operation.

FM 55-10 has detailed information on motor transport units and operations.

B. Rail

Rail is potentially the most efficient method of hauling large tonnages of materiel by ground transportation; the Army normally depends on the host nation to provide this mode of transportation. The Army has limited railway operating, construction, and repair capability. These Army assets augment host nation support or provide those capabilities in theaters where host nation support is not available, or is not capable or reliable. Information on rail transport units and operations is in FM 55-20.

C. Air

Air is the most flexible transportation mode. While wide-ranging CSS needs within a theater require U.S. Air Force and Army airlift assets to support forces, commanders normally employ Army aviation in a combat support role. However, the ALOC becomes increasingly important as the intensity, depth, and duration of operations increase. Air Force and Army airlift assets provide airlift within a theater. Army cargo and utility helicopters provide support at the operational and tactical levels through movement control channels in response to mission requirements and the commander's priorities. Likewise, the U.S. Air Force provides theater airlift support to all services within a theater through a process of allocating sorties on a routine basis or providing immediate support to operational requirements. While airlift is the preferred method of delivery, airdrop is a field service that can provide flexibility to the transportation system by extending ALOC.

D. Water

Army watercraft is an essential component of theater transportation. They may augment capabilities of other modes when integrated with appropriate terminal operations. Army watercraft move materiel and equipment along inland waterways, along theater coastlines, and within water terminals. Their primary role is to support cargo discharge and onward movement from the SPOD to inland terminals or to retrograde from inland terminals. Army watercrafts have a role in joint operations along with Navy and Marine Corps lighterage, or in conjunction with HNS assets. FM 55-80 has details on Army watercraft units and operations.

The unit move module of TC-AIMS II has four basic functional areas.

- It stores unit personnel and equipment information.
- It maintains deployment information, and plans and schedules deployments.
- It manipulates/updates information for convoys, rail, and air load planning, and personnel manifesting. Other transportation systems share unit movement information.
- It allows units to update their operational equipment list (OEL) and unit deployment list (UDL) and electronically send the updates through the chain of command to the ITO.

2. Global Transportation Network (GTN)

GTN is an information system used for collecting transportation information from selected systems. It provides automated support for planning, providing, and controlling common-user airlift, surface, and terminal services to deploying forces. It provides the user with the ability to track the status, identity, and location of units, non-unit cargo and passengers, medical patients, and personal property from origin to destination.

3. Movement Tracking System (MTS)

The movement tracking system (MTS) provides the capability to identify position, track progress, and communicate with the operators of tactical wheeled vehicles. With positioning and communication satellites, transportation movement control and mode operators can locate and communicate with tactical wheeled vehicle (TWV) anywhere.

The MTS is a satellite-based tracking/communication system consisting of a mobile unit mounted in the vehicle and a base unit controlled/monitored by movement elements control and mode operators. The MTS includes—

- Global positioning system capability.
- Capability to send messages between base and mobile units.
- Capability to locate/track a vehicle position on a map background using personal computer-based software.

4. Radio Frequency Indentification (RFID)

Radio frequency identification (RFID) uses radio wave transmission and reception to identify, locate, and track objects. Information is stored on a radio frequency (RF) tag with media storage capability similar to a computer floppy disk. Antennas, commonly called interrogators, read and pass information contained on the RF tag attached to vehicles, containers, or pallets. This information passes to a central database. Units attach a RF tag to all major shipments in theater. RF interrogators are located at key transportation nodes to provide visibility of the shipments en route to final destination. MTS integrates RFID technology to provide total visibility of in-transit cargo.

5. Worldwide Port System (WPS)

The Worldwide Port System (WPS) is the primary source system for ITV and total asset visibility of surface cargo movement in the DTS. WPS provides timely and accurate information to the supporting and supported combatant commands through the GTN.

VIII. Maint/Ordnance Support

Ref: FM 4-0 Combat Service Support, chap. 8.

See also pp. 3-27 to 3-34, (FXXI Tactical-Level CSS Ops) Fixing the Force.

Success on today's battlefield demands that forces maintain, recover, repair, or replace equipment as quickly as possible. Good maintenance practices, forward positioning of maintenance units, effective repair parts and equipment replacement systems, and clear priorities for recovery and repair are vital. Likewise, sound theater policies on repair and evacuation and sufficient sustainment repair and replacement facilities greatly contribute to battlefield success. This section covers the entire spectrum of ordnance support to include maintenance, explosive ordnance disposal (EOD), and ammunition support.

I. Maintenance Across the Levels of War

Maintenance support includes activities at all levels of war. The following is a brief discussion of each level of war.

A. Strategic Support

The strategic base is the backbone of the National maintenance program and the sustainment maintenance system. At this level, maintenance supports the supply system by repairing or overhauling components or end items not available or too costly to procure. Maintenance management concentrates on identifying the needs of the Army supply system and developing programs to meet them. Strategic support also includes maintaining prepositioned equipment.

B. Operational Support

The goal of the overall maintenance plan is to support the operations plans and objectives of the commander. Its primary purpose is to provide field maintenance, and maximize the number of operational combat systems available to support the tactical battle. The maintenance-supply interface at the operational level is the fusion point between the field and sustainment maintenance management echelons. Maintenance managers in operational headquarters support the tactical battle by ensuring that the maintenance system supports campaigns and sustains theater forces.

The operational support plan ties tactical unit requirements together with the capabilities of the strategic base. The maintenance system drives and supports the supply system. DS (field) maintenance units meet tactical requirements through close support, while general support (GS) (sustainment) maintenance units/ activities alleviate maintenance and supply shortfalls. Surge maintenance capabilities from all sources, including the industrial base, meet unexpected demands.

C. Tactical Support

The nature of the modern battlefield demands that the maintenance system repair equipment quickly and at, or as near as possible to, the point of failure or damage. This requirement implies a forward thrust of maintenance into division and brigade areas. There the battle is more violent and the damage greater. Maintenance assets move as far forward as the tactical situation permits to repair inoperable and damaged equipment and to return it to the battle as quickly as possible.

The structure of maintenance units includes highly mobile maintenance support teams (MSTs). MSTs provide support forward on the battlefield as directed by the DS (field) maintenance company commander and maintenance control officer. They send people; parts; test, measurement, and diagnostic equipment (TMDE); and tools to forward areas, as required, and redistribute assets when no longer needed.

Battle damage assessment and repair (BDAR) may be critical at this level. BDAR is the procedure used to return disabled equipment rapidly to the battle by expeditiously fixing, bypassing, or jury-rigging components. It restores the minimum essential combat capabilities necessary to support a specific combat mission or to enable the equipment to self-recover. Crews, unit maintenance teams, MSTs, and recovery teams perform BDAR.

II. The Maintenance System

The current Army maintenance program is a flexible, four-level system. The levels are operator/unit, DS, GS, and depot. Each level has certain capabilities based on the skills of the assigned personnel and the availability of tools and test equipment. Force XXI and Stryker brigade employ new maintenance concepts that consolidate levels of maintenance. The thrust of this redesign effort is to position the Army to adopt a two-level maintenance system. In the new system, unit and DS maintenance comprise the first of the two maintenance echelons known as field maintenance. Field maintenance focuses on repairing and returning major end items and components for immediate use by the supported force. The second maintenance echelon is sustainment maintenance. Sustainment maintenance includes GS and depot levels. Sustainment maintenance focuses on repairing major end items and components to support the supply system. (Army aviation maintenance has three levels.) When properly integrated, the levels serve as a logistics multiplier, adding an extra dimension to the commander's plan.

Materiel Management Center (MMC)

The materiel management center (MMC) is the maintenance manager for deployed Army forces. It is the link between the deployed forces and the support base. The MMC maintains a close working relationship with the logistics support element (LSE). The NMM through the LSE directs the theater-level GS (sustainment) maintenance mission. In addition, these activities may support equipment of other services or multinational forces. The commander of the LSE maintains a coordination relationship with USAMC and other organizations providing assets to the LSE. The NMM distributes the total national maintenance workload across all sustainment maintenance providers, based on the overall national needs. This coordination ensures receiving timely support from the theater or continental United States (CONUS) base maintenance operations.

Maintenance Support Levels

There are two basic levels of maintenance support: field maintenance and sustainment maintenance.

A. Field Maintenance Support

Field maintenance support includes operator/unit, DS, and component repair capability designed to repair components and end items for customer units versus the supply system. The multicapable maintainer will be the cornerstone of field maintenance support. This individual performs both unit and DS tasks to improve system readiness and reduce repair cycle time.

1. Operator/Unit Maintenance

Preventive maintenance checks and services (PMCS) initiate most maintenance actions. PMCS is the care, servicing, inspection, detection, and correction of minor faults before these faults cause serious damage, failure, or injury. Command

III. Maintenance Principles

Ref: FM 4-0, chap. 8.

Maintenance is central to any mission operational success. A viable maintenance system is agile and synchronized to the combat scheme of fire and maneuver. It anticipates force requirements. A commander who has 65 percent of his tanks operational may wisely delay an attack if he can realistically expect the repair process to have 90 percent ready within 24 hours. Alternatively, he can weight the battle by allocating replacement systems. The guiding maintenance principles are:

1. To replace forward and repair rear

Maintenance activities, with a forward focus on system replacement, task and use the distribution and evacuation channels to push components and end items to the sustainment level for repair.

2. To anticipate maintenance requirements

To maximize the number of combat systems available, maintenance leaders and managers anticipate the requirements for support by using on-board sensors integrated into equipment design and linked by a distributive communication system. The diagnostic data helps anticipate future reliability and provide maintenance managers the ability to preposition repair parts and maintenance personnel.

3. Maintenance is a combat multiplier

When opposing forces have relative parity in numbers and quality of equipment, the force that combines skillful use of equipment with an effective maintenance system has a decided advantage. That force has an initial advantage if it enters battle with equipment that is operational and likely to remain operational. It has a subsequent advantage if it can quickly return damaged and disabled equipment to the battle. Securing this advantage is the purpose of a maintenance system.

4. Elements at all levels work together to ensure attaining the strategic goals and objectives

They must have the proper personnel, equipment, tools, and replacement parts. Personnel must be well trained in maintenance theory and maintenance principles of all systems and capable of diagnosing and correcting faults. Additionally, they must have immediate access to high-usage repair parts.

5. The type and location of maintenance units that best support the commander's requirements are a prime concern of the theater logistician

A viable maintenance system complements the capabilities of the supply system. When equipment is in short supply or otherwise unavailable to support require-ments, commanders use the maintenance system to offset the shortfall. As equipment becomes more technically complicated, it is easier to meet surge requirements by redirecting the maintenance effort than by influencing the supply effort. Therefore, the job of maintenance managers at all levels is to ensure the proper mix (type and location) of maintenance units that best supports the tactical and operational commanders' requirements. In addition, early arrival of essential maintenance capabilities is important in force projection operations to ensure deployed and prepositioned equipment is operational.

emphasis is vital to ensure an effective PMCS program. This program requires trained operator/crews and routine supervisory and implementing procedures. Ineffective command emphasis can lead to cursory PMCS programs that fail to correct deteriorating effects before they adversely affect readiness and combat capability, and unnecessarily burden technical maintenance systems.

Unit maintenance efforts concentrate on returning equipment to the user quickly enough to influence the outcome of a given task or mission. The operator or crew identifies malfunctions using on-board sensors and visual inspections. Personnel make quick repairs by using on-board spares and tools to perform on system maintenance.

2. Direct Support (DS) Maintenance

DS (field) maintenance organizations consist of a base maintenance company augmented with commodity-specific modules that allow tailored support for supported units. The composition of the supported units determines the type and number of teams assigned or attached to the base company. These teams directly support units on an area basis or dedicated basis. Those that support units on a dedicated basis accompany the supported unit as it moves around the AO. They receive repair parts and backup maintenance support through the nearest DS (field) maintenance company.

DS (field) maintenance units and maintenance teams expected to operate in forward areas must be as mobile as the supported customer. Maintainers in these units focus on repair by replacement. If these units cannot repair equipment due to lack of time, or specialized tools, and/or test equipment, supporting teams from a higher maintenance echelon repair the equipment on site or evacuate it. As with unit maintenance elements, maintainers in DS (field) maintenance units may repair selected components to eliminate higher echelon backlogs and maintain technical skills when mission, enemy, troops, terrain and weather, time, civilian considerations (METT-TC) permits.

B. Sustainment Maintenance Support

Sustainment maintenance support includes maintenance performed by depots, directorate of logistics (DOL) assets, special repair activities (SRAs), and forward repair activities (FRAs). There are also a limited number of specialized GS units that provide missile and signal-unique support.

GS and depot repair activities locate where they can best support the theater operations plan. They support the theater supply system through table of organization and equipment (TOE)/table of distribution and allowances (TDA) units, host nation support, and contracted personnel. These activities generally move into available fixed or semi-fixed facilities in the theater. They remain there for the duration of operations. While they are able to displace forward, it is a very time-consuming, labor- and equipment-intensive process. However, they can deploy platoons, sections, or teams as far forward as required to support the tactical situation. When deployed forward, the elements are attached to the nearest maintenance company, and all requirements pass through that headquarters.

1. General Support (GS) Maintenance

The primary mission of GS repair activities is repairing components to support the supply system. Managers set priorities on anticipated consumption rates of components. Sustainment maintenance managers determine consumption rates. GS maintenance activities, placed in a theater, perform component repair when no other assets are available or when the supply pipeline is insufficiently viable to accept the disruption in operations. GS maintenance activities also serve as training bases to develop specialized maintainers.

2. Depot Maintenance

Depot maintenance supports the strategic level of war. USAMC depots or activities, contractors, and host nation support personnel perform this level of maintenance to support the supply system. Normally, elements perform depot maintenance where it is most appropriate to support the force. This may be in CONUS, in the AO, at an ISB, or in a third country. Production-line operations characterize this support. Such operations support the national maintenance program (NMP) and the overall DA inventory management program. They are an alternative or supplement to new procurement as a source of serviceable assets to meet DA materiel requirements.

Headquarters, Department of the Army approves and USAMC controls programs for depot maintenance. Army arsenals and depot maintenance facilities execute some approved programs. In other cases, the depot maintenance and interservicing (DMI) program plays an important role in depot maintenance.

IV. Specific Maintenance Considerations

Aviation, watercraft, signal, and information systems and maintenance in an NBC environment have special maintenance considerations.

A. Aviation Maintenance

The objective of Army aviation maintenance is to ensure maximum availability of fully mission-capable aircraft to the commander. Aviation maintenance elements accomplish this by performing maintenance on all aviation items, including avionics and weapon systems, as far forward as possible.

The aircraft maintenance system consists of three levels: aviation unit maintenance (AVUM), aviation intermediate maintenance (AVIM), and depot maintenance.

1. Aviation Unit Maintenance (AVUM)

The aircraft crew chiefs and AVUM unit comprise the first line of aircraft maintenance. AVUM units are organic to aviation battalions and squadrons. They provide support as far forward as possible. Forward support teams perform on-aircraft maintenance tasks that require minimal aircraft downtime. AVUM elements also perform more extensive recurring scheduled maintenance tasks in rear areas. AVUM tasks include replacing components; performing minor repairs; making adjustments; and cleaning, lubricating, and servicing the aircraft.

2. Aviation Intermediate Maintenance (AVIM)

The AVIM, or second-level maintenance element provides one-stop intermediate maintenance support and backup AVUM support. It performs on-aircraft system repair and off-aircraft subsystems repair. AVIM units also provide aviation repair parts to supported units. AVIM tasks normally require more time, more complex tools and test equipment, and higher skilled personnel than the AVUM element has available.

3. Depot Maintenance

Depot maintenance is the third level of maintenance. Depot maintenance includes very detailed and time-consuming functions. It requires sophisticated equipment and special tools, special facilities, and maintenance skills. Typical depot tasks include aircraft overhaul, major repair, conversion or modifications, special manufacturing, analytical testing, and painting. FM 3-04.500 has details on aviation maintenance.

V. Repair Parts Support

Class IX items (repair parts) consist of any part, subassembly, assembly, or component required for installation in maintaining an end item, subassembly, or component. They support maintenance and repair functions performed throughout the Army on all materiel except medical materiel. They range from small items of common hardware to large, complex line replaceable units.

1. Strategic Level

Managing repair parts at the national strategic level normally depends on the general classification of the item rather than its end item use. In these instances, requisitions to support a unit maintenance mission go to more than one national inventory control point (NICP) or commodity command. When the end item is a major system (for example, an M1A1 tank), a program manager ensures that the CSS for that end item is effective and efficient. Therefore, units experiencing problems have a single point of contact to handle their concerns. At the national level, supply requirements may drive the NICP manager to use, through the NMM, sustainment maintenance to repair unserviceable assets to support supply requirements.

2. Operational Level

The operational level of supply focuses on providing repair parts and a level of stockage for items not sent to the theater by aerial lines of communication (ALOC). Easing these supply requirements are serviceable assets generated by the sustainment maintenance of line replaceable units. These items become theater-generated assets that can offset a requirement to provide support from the strategic level of supply.

3. Tactical Level

Repair parts at the tactical level support unit and DS (field) maintenance missions. Organizations can stock a limited number of items on the prescribed load list (PLL) to support their maintenance mission. Normally, the number of lines is restricted to 150; however, they should be demand supported and combat essential. The commander has some latitude to accommodate expected requirements and for other justifiable reasons. Mobility of PLL items is also a consideration. The PLL should be 100 percent mobile on unit transportation. Unique maintenance elements that support strategic signal, air traffic control, and missile systems maintain authorized stockage list (ASL) items for their supported customer units.

GS maintenance units maintain shop stocks to support authorized maintenance tasks. They requisition replenishment stocks through their supporting MMCs and do not maintain ASLs. This does not apply to AVIM units.

Cannibalization/Controlled Exchange

The commander who owns unserviceable equipment decides whether to perform cannibalization or controlled exchange. Cannibalization is the authorized removal, under specific conditions, of serviceable and unserviceable repair parts, components, and assemblies from unserviceable, uneconomically reparable, or excess end-items authorized for local disposal. Controlled exchange is removing serviceable parts, components, assemblies and subassemblies from unserviceable, economically repairable equipment for immediate use in restoring a like item of equipment to a combat mission-capable condition. Commanders may use supervised battlefield cannibalization and controlled exchange when parts are not available from the supply system.

VI. Explosive Ordnance Disposal (EOD)

EOD elements participate in security and advisory assistance, antiterrorism, counterdrug operations, training, ordnance disposal, arms control, treaty verification, and support to domestic civil authorities, and other stability operations and support operations.

During war, preserving the commander's combat power becomes more challenging for EOD because of the increasingly complex and lethal battlefield. EOD integration into staff planning must be sufficiently explicit to provide for battle synchronization, yet flexible enough to respond to change or to capitalize on fleeting opportunities. For detailed information on EOD support, see FM 9-15.

VII. Ammunition

See also pp. 3-19 to 3-24, (FXXI Tactical-Level CSS Ops) Arming the Force.

Due to limited quantities of modern munitions and weapon systems, commanders must manage munitions to ensure availability and enhance combat readiness. Most major military operations are joint and multinational and based on unexpected contingencies. These operations require the munitions logistics system to be modular, tailorable, and easily deployed. Ammunition units deploy based on operational needs and are essential to moving Class V.

Planning logistics munitions support must be coordinated and synchronized across the levels of war. The mission at every level of war is to ensure munitions arrive in the right quantities and proper types at the decisive time and place. Having munitions in the right quantity, type, and place enhances the Army's ability to engage the enemy decisively and sustain the operations culminating with the successful accomplishments of objectives.

A. The Ammunition System

The ammunition logistics system provides to the force the right type and quantity of ammunition in any contingency. The challenge is to move required amounts of ammunition into a theater from the CONUS sustaining base and other prepositioned sources in a timely manner to support an operation. The system must be flexible enough to meet changing ammunition requirements in simultaneous operations around the world. The objective of the system is to provide configured Class V support forward to the force as economically and responsively as possible to minimize handling or reconfiguring; quickly adapt to changes in potential threat; introduce new/improved weapons and ammunition; and be more responsive in getting the product to the forces. The unique characteristics of ammunition complicate the system. These factors include its size, weight, and hazardous nature. It requires special handling, storage, accountability, surveillance, and security.

B. Ammunition Management

The management process begins during peacetime planning. Combatant commands, ASCCs, ARFOR, and service/readiness commands determine Class V requirements for possible contingencies. They consider the concepts of operation and task organization including the projected force deployment sequences, the availability of stocks, storage locations, deployability into various theaters, and the responsiveness of the production base to meet shortfalls. It is unlikely that future conflicts will require the massive volumes of stocks needed to support the cold war forces of the 1980s.

Ammunition Support Activities

Ref: FM 4-0, chap. 8.

Combat forces initially deploy into theater with their ammunition basic loads. Commanders estimate their Class V needs (required supply rates) in accordance with combat priorities to weight the battle. The ARFOR commander determines the controlled supply rate (CSR) by comparing the total unrestricted ammunition requirements against the total ammunition assets on hand or due in. Forces receive resupply in the forward areas from tactical ammunition support activities (ASAs).

The three types of ASAs in the theater are: theater storage areas (TSAs), corps storage areas (CSAs), and ammunition supply points (ASPs). See FM 4-30.

1. Theater Storage Area (TSA)

The TSA encompasses the storage facilities located in the COMMZ. This is where the bulk of the theater reserve ammunition stocks are located. Modular ammunition companies, with a mixture of heavy- and medium-lift platoons, operate and maintain TSAs. Besides shipping ammunition to CSAs, the TSA provides area ammunition support to units operating in the COMMZ. The ASCC determines the TSA stockage objective. AR 710-2 contains basic days of supply (DOS) policy for Class V. The TSC ammunition group must keep the TSC materiel management center (MMC) informed of storage limitations or shortages in each TSA.

2. Corps Storage Area (CSA)

The CSA is the primary source of high-tonnage ammunition for the division and corps. Modular ammunition companies, with a mixture of heavy- and medium-lift platoons, operate the CSA. The number of units assigned to operate a CSA depends on the corps authorized ammunition stockage level. CSAs receive 50 percent of their ammunition from the POD and 50 percent from the TSA. At a minimum, each corps identifies an ASA to meet these requirements. The COSCOM establishes stockage objectives for the CSA and bases them on projected theater combat rates. Initially, the stockage objective of a CSA should be 10 to 15 days of supply. After the initial combat draw down, the CSA should maintain 7 to 10 days of supply. When a CSA wartime stockage objective exceeds 25k short-tons, the cdr should establish a second CSA.

3. Ammunition Supply Point (ASP)

ASPs are another source of ammunition for a division. ASPs receive, store, issue, and maintain a one- to three-day supply of ammunition. ASP stockage levels are based on tactical plans, availability of ammunition, and the threat to the resupply operation. ASPs are located in the division rear. Normally, three ASPs support a division and provide manning for the division rear ATP. A modular ammunition company, with one or more medium-lift modular ammunition platoons, normally operates one large ASP behind each brigade. By doctrine, Class V containers go only as far as the CSA.

ASPs provide 25 percent of each ATP ammunition requirement in the form of MCLs. Besides supporting ATPs, ASPs provide ammunition to units operating in the division rear area. These nondivisional and corps units normally receive support from the closest ASA.

4. Ammunition Transfer Point (ATP)

ATPs are the most mobile and responsive of the munitions supply activities. CSAs and ASPs deliver ammunition to the ATP using corps transportation assets. This ammunition is kept loaded on semitrailers, containerized roll-on/off platforms (CROPs), or PLS flatracks until ATP personnel transload it to using unit vehicles. If the situation demands, personnel can transfer ammunition immediately to using unit tactical vehicles.

IX. Health Service Support

Ref: FM 4-0 Combat Service Support, chap. 9.

See also pp. 3-35 to 3-40, (FXXI Tactical-Level CSS Ops) Class VIII Resupply at Echelons I & II.

Health service support (HSS) is a single, integrated system. It consists of all services performed, provided, or arranged to promote, improve, conserve, or restore the mental and physical well-being of personnel in the Army and, as directed, for other services, agencies, and organizations. It is a continuum of care and support from the point of injury or wounding through successive levels to the continental United States (CONUS) base. This system encompasses the ten functional areas of medical treatment: area support, medical evacuation, medical regulating, hospitalization, preventive medicine, health service logistics, dental, veterinary, combat operational stress control services, and medical laboratory support. Health service support involves delineation of support responsibility by geographical area.

I. HSS Across the Levels of War

Health service support (HSS) includes activities across all levels of war. The following are considerations for HSS across the levels of war.

A. Strategic Health Service Support

Strategic HSS and supporting services include activities under the control of the Department of the Army (DA), Department of Defense (DOD), and Secretary of Defense (SECDEF). These include the U.S. depots, arsenals, data banks, plants, research laboratories, and factories associated with the U.S. Army Medical Materiel and Research Command (USAMRMC) (including the U.S. Army Medical Materiel Agency [USAMMA]), and disease and nonbattle injury (DNBI) surveillance centers (such as the Centers for Health Promotion and Preventive Medicine [USACHPPM]), the DLA, national inventory control point (NICP), military health systems, and Veterans Administration and civilian hospital systems of the National Disaster Medical System (NDMS). Strategic HSS focuses on:

- Supporting force deployment by ensuring soldier medical readiness
- Medical surveillance and occupational and environmental (OEH) health surveillance
- Early employment/deployment of preventive medicine (PVNTMED) and veterinary services
- Medical laboratory services for in-theater confirmatory identification of suspect NBC samples/specimens
- Mobilizing the industrial base
- Determining requirements and acquiring medical equipment, supplies, blood, and pharmaceuticals to support force projection
- Stockpiling and prepositioning medical materiel
- Supporting the host nation
- Medical evacuating, medical regulating, and hospitalization
- Mobilizing
- Preserving the force by returning injured soldiers to full health
- Demobilizing

B. Operational Health Service Support

Operational HSS encompasses all of the medical activities to support the force employed in offensive, defensive, stability, and support operations. Operational HSS focuses on:

- Supporting deployment and reception, staging, onward movement, and integration (RSO&I) operations
- PVNTMED, veterinary services, and COSC
- Medical facilities in the theater
- Managing distribution of medical materiel and blood
- Supporting forward deployed forces
- Reconstituting medical units in theater
- Supporting redeployment operations

At the operational level, managers balance current requirements with the need to extend capabilities along the lines of communication (LOC) and build up support services for subsequent major operations.

C. Tactical Health Service Support

Tactical planning is proactive rather than reactive. HSS must be thoroughly integrated with tactical plans and orders. Commanders reallocate medical resources as tactical situations change. HSS commanders tailor medical units to adapt to the flow of battle and to meet reinforcement or reconstitution requirements. Elements to reconstitute medical units normally come from the next higher level of HSS. Due to the massive destructive and disabling capabilities of modern conventional and NBC weapons, medical units can anticipate large numbers of casualties in a shorter period. Medical units are flexible. They alter their normal scope of operations to provide the greatest good for the greatest number. However, these mass casualty situations usually exceed the capabilities of local medical units. Key factors for effective mass casualty management are:

- On-site triage
- Emergency resuscitative care
- Early surgical intervention
- Reliable communications
- Skillful evacuation by air and ground resources

Medical personnel may also have to defend themselves and their patients within their limitations. Medical personnel are only authorized the use of small arms for the protection of themselves and the patients in their care. In certain situations, HSS units in rear areas must be able to defend against level I threats and to survive NBC strikes while continuing to support the operation. Medical personnel are not required to perform perimeter defense duties for nonmedical units. Due to the protections afforded medical personnel under the provisions of the Geneva Conventions, medical personnel must be exclusively engaged in their humanitarian duties and can, therefore, only defend medical unit areas.

III. Levels of Medical Care
Ref: FM 4-0, chap. 9.

Health service support is arranged in levels of medical care. They extend rearward throughout the theater to the CONUS support-base. Each level reflects an increase in capability, with the functions of each lower level being within the capabilities of higher level.

Level I
The first medical care a soldier receives occurs at Level I. It is provided by the trauma specialist/special operations forces combat medics (assisted by self-aid, buddy aid, and combat lifesaver skills, and at the battalion aid station [BAS] by the physician and physician assistant). This level of care includes immediate lifesaving measures, prevention of DNBI, COSC preventive measures, patient collection, and medical evacuation to supported medical treatment elements.

Level II
Medical companies and troops of brigades, divisions, separate brigades, armored cavalry regiments, and area support medical battalions (ASMBs) render care at Level II. They examine and evaluate the casualty's wounds and general status to determine treatment and evacuation precedence. This level of care duplicates Level I and expands services available by adding limited dental, laboratory, optometry, preventive medicine, health service logistics, COSC/mental health services, and patient-holding capabilities. When required to provide far-forward surgical intervention, the medical company may be augmented with a forward surgical team (FST) to provide initial wound surgery. The FST is organic to airborne and air assault divisions.

Level III
Level III is the first level of care with hospital facilities. Within the combat zone, the combat support hospital (CSH) provides resuscitation, initial wound surgery, and postoperative treatment. At the CSH, personnel treat patients for return to duty (RTD) or stabilize patients for continued evacuation. Those patients expected to RTD within the theater evacuation policy are regulated to an echelon above corps (EAC) CSH.

Level IV
At Level IV, the patient is treated at an EAC CSH. Those patients not expected to RTD within the theater evacuation policy are stabilized and evacuated to a Level V facility.

Level V
Definitive care to all categories of patients characterizes Level V (primarily CONUS-based) care. The Department of Defense (DOD) and Department of Veteran's Affairs (VA) hospitals provide this care. During mobilization, the National Disaster Medical System (NDMS) may be activated. Under this system, civilian hospitals care for patients beyond the capabilities of the DOD and VA hospitals.

III. Principles of Health Service Support

Providing HSS is guided by six principles consistent with JP 4-02:

- Health service support conforms to the tactical commander's operation plan (OPLAN). By taking part in developing the OPLAN, the HSS planner can determine support requirements and plan for the support needed to prevent DNBI and to effectively clear the battlefield of the ill, injured, and wounded.
- Technical control and staff supervision of HSS resources must remain with the appropriate command-level surgeon.
- The HSS staff must maintain continuity of care since an interruption of treatment may cause an increase in morbidity and mortality. No patient is evacuated farther to the rear than his medical condition or the tactical situation dictate.
- The proximity of HSS assets to the supported forces is dictated by the tactical situation (mission, enemy, troops, terrain and weather, time, civilian considerations [METT-TC]).
- The HSS plan must be flexible to enhance the capability of shifting HSS resources to meet changing requirements. Changes in the tactical situation or OPLAN make flexibility essential.
- Mobility is required to ensure that HSS assets remain close enough to combat operations to support combat forces. The mobility of medical units must be equal to the forces supported.

IV. Functional Areas

There are ten functional areas within the Army Medical Department (AMEDD).

A. Medical Evacuation and Medical Regulating

Medical evacuation is the timely, efficient movement and provision of en route medical care of sick, injured, or ill persons from the battlefield or other locations to medical treatment facilities (MTFs). It is the responsibility of the gaining level HSS to evacuate or coordinate the evacuation from the lower level. The health care provider attending the patient determines the mode and precedence of evacuation. Air evacuation is the primary means of medical evacuation for urgent and priority casualties. In the combat zone, ground ambulance squads organic to medical sections, platoons, and companies evacuate patients within their AOs. Medical evacuation battalions evacuate patients from Level II MTFs to Level III hospitals. The battalion also evacuates patients laterally from hospital to hospital within the corps area, and from hospitals to U.S. Air Force (USAF) staging areas for evacuation out of the combat zone.

Strategic evacuation is a function of the USAF aeromedical evacuation system. The theater surgeon recommends a theater evacuation policy through the combatant commander and Joint Chiefs of Staff for approval by the SECDEF. The policy establishes the number of days an injured or ill soldier may remain in the theater to return to duty. Soldiers who will not return to full health within the established time are evacuated to definitive care facilities in CONUS or other designated locations. FM 8-10-6 has more details on evacuation.

Medical regulating is the coordinated movement of patients to MTFs that are best able to provide timely and required care. The corps medical command (MEDCOM), medical brigade medical regulating office (MRO) and, if established, joint patient movement requirements center (JPMRC) provide medical regulating in the combat zone. In the COMMZ, the theater MEDCOM/EAC medical brigade MROs and the theater patient movement requirements center (TPMRC) provide support. The TPMRC provides both intratheater and intertheater medical regulating.

B. Hospitialization

Hospitalization, provided by the CSH, is part of the theater-wide system for managing sick, injured, and wounded patients. The CSH capabilities include triage/emergency care, outpatient services, in-patient care, pharmacy, laboratory, blood banking, radiology, physical therapy, medical logistics, emergency/essential dental care, nutrition care, and patient administration services. See FM 4-02.10.

C. Health Service Logistics (HSL)

The health service logistics (HSL) system encompasses planning and executing medical supply operations, medical equipment maintenance and repair, blood storage and distribution, and optical fabrication and repair. It also includes contracting services, medical hazardous waste management and disposal, production and distribution of medical gases, and blood banking services for Army, joint, multinational, and interagency operations. The theater HSL system consists of the following organizations:

- Medical logistics management center (MLMC)
- HHD, MEDLOG battalion
- Logistics support company
- Medical logistics company
- Blood support detachment (BSD)
- Medical logistics support team (MLST)

D. Dental Services

Within the theater of operations, there are three levels of dental support: unit, hospital, and area. These levels are defined primarily by the relationship of the dental assets supporting the patient population within each level.

Unit-level dental care consists of those services provided by a dental module organic to divisional and nondivisional medical companies and all special forces groups. This module provides emergency dental treatment to soldiers during tactical operations.

Hospital-level dental care consists of those services provided by the hospital dental staff to minimize loss of life and disability resulting from oral and maxillofacial injuries and wounds. The hospital dental staff provides operational dental care, which consists of emergency and essential dental support to all injured or wounded soldiers as well as the hospital staff.

Dental service companies provide dental support on an area support basis. These dental units provide operational care. The dental companies are composed of modular dental teams capable of operating separate dental treatment facilities (DTFs) or of consolidating units and operating one large facility, depending on the METT-TC. Other teams provide far-forward emergency and essential dental care.

E. Veterinary Support

The U.S. Army Veterinary Service is the executive agent for veterinary support to all services and other U.S. agencies in theater. Services include sanitary surveillance for food source and storage facilities, procurement, and surveillance and examination of foodstuffs for safety and quality. The veterinary unit is responsible for publishing a directory of approved food sources for the theater/AO. Veterinary preventive medicine provides an effective combat multiplier through monitoring endemic zoonotic (animal) disease threats of military significance. The animal medical care mission provides complete medical care to all government-owned animals, especially military working dogs (MWDs), in the AO. See FM 8-10-18.

F. Preventive Medicine (PVNTMED)

In past conflicts, DNBI rendered more soldiers combat ineffective than combat action. Preventive medicine services to counter the medical threat and prevent DNBI are the most effective, least expensive means of providing commanders with the maximum number of healthy soldiers. The Armed Forces Medical Intelligence Center conducts area studies on diseases for all regions. Medical companies of brigade and divisional support battalions, area support medical battalions, separate brigade support battalions, and medical troops of ACR support squadrons provide preventive medicine services. See FM 4-02.17 for more details.

G. Combat Operational Stress Control (COSC)

Combat operational stress control (COSC) conserves the fighting strength by minimizing losses due to battle fatigue and neuropsychiatric disorders. The focus of Army COSC is on:

- Promoting positive mission-oriented motivation
- Preventing stress-related casualties
- Treating and the early detection of soldiers suffering from battle fatigue
- Preventing harmful combat stress reactions, such as misconduct stress behaviors and post-traumatic stress disorders

FM 22-51, FM 8-51, and FM 6-22.5 discuss COSC programs and activities.

H. Area Medical Support

Medical companies of divisions, separate brigades, and ACR, and the corps/EAC ASMB provide area medical support. These companies provide Levels I and II medical care throughout the division, corps, and EAC areas. They employ medical treatment squads/teams to establish Levels I and II MTFs and to reinforce medical treatment elements (BAS) of maneuver battalions. The ground ambulance platoons of these companies provide medical evacuation support on an area support basis from Level I MTFs and supported units to Level II MTFs.

I. Medical Laboratory Support

The theater MEDCOM area medical laboratory includes capabilities in endemic diseases, OEH hazards, and NBC. Its focus is the total health environment of the theater, not individual patient care. Its facility conducts studies in pest identification, the efficacy of pesticides, frequency of infectious agents, monitoring immune response, and transmission of zoonotic diseases, and in-theater confirmatory identification of suspect NBC samples/ specimens. Its personnel also function as consultants to hospital clinical laboratory services within the theater. It may task-organize teams and employ them forward to troubleshoot a particular problem. All Level II MTFs provide basic laboratory services within the theater. They perform basic procedures in hematology, urinalysis, microbiology, and serology. Level II MTFs receive, maintain, and transfuse blood products. Levels III and IV MTFs (CSH) perform procedures in biochemistry, hematology, urinalysis, microbiology, and serology. These hospitals also provide blood-banking services.

J. Medical Information Systems

Medical information systems facilitate the proper management of medical information that is critical to providing HSS. Decisions, such as those on where to treat casualties and when to evacuate to hospitals, depend on knowing what medical resources are available at all times. An effective medical management information system supports theater HSS operations by providing the capability to track resources, requirements, and patients.

X. Human Resource Support

Ref: FM 4-0 Combat Service Support, chap. 10.

See also pp. 3-53 to 3-56, (FXXI Tactical-Level CSS Ops) Manning the Force.

Human resource support (HRS) encompasses the following functions: manning the force, personnel support, and personnel services. These activities include personnel accounting, casualty management, essential services, postal operations, and morale, welfare, and recreation. They are provided to service members, their families, DA civilians, and contractors.

I. HRS Across the Levels of War

HRS covers all levels of war. Human resource (HR) considerations for each level or war include the following.

A. Strategic Support

Strategic HRS involves the national-level capability to plan, resource, manage, and control the HR life cycle functions for the Army. It involves integrating HR functions and activities across the Army staff, among the respective Army components, and among the services. At the strategic level, the DA Deputy Chief of Staff for Personnel (Army G1) provides HRS to all active component Army forces. The Army G1 develops Army policy for all systems and functions in HRS, while the assistant Secretary of the Army (Manpower and Reserve Affairs) is responsible for civilian personnel policy and operations. The U.S. Total Army Personnel Command (USTA PERSCOM) applies and implements these policies for military personnel. The assistant Chief of Staff for Installation Management (ACSIM), the U.S. Army Community and Family Support Center, and the Military Postal Service Agency also provide strategic support to the force for morale, welfare, and recreation services, and postal operations. The Chief, Army Reserve and the Director of the National Guard Bureau provide strategic HRS for the Army Reserves and National Guard elements respectively.

B. Operational and Tactical Support

Policies and procedures translate into action at the operational and tactical levels. Theater PERSCOMs, MACOM DCSPERs, corps and division G1/AGs, and brigade and battalion S1s provide the operational and tactical level HR life cycle support to service members, their families, civilians, and contractors. They are responsible for executing each of the following HR functions. HR providers at all levels are responsible for successfully implementing the human dimension of soldiering.

II. Manning the Force

Manning the force consists of personnel readiness management, personnel accounting, personnel information management, and replacement operations management. The manning challenge is getting the right soldier to the right place at the right time with the right capabilities. Manning combines anticipation, movement, and skillful positioning of personnel assets. It relies on the secure, robust, and survivable communications and digital information systems of emerging technologies that provide common operational picture, asset visibility, predictive modeling, and exception reporting. This constitutes a significant reduction of forward-deployed personnel assets that manage the deployed forces.

A. Personnel Readiness Management

The purpose of the personnel readiness management system is to distribute soldiers to units based on documented requirements or authorizations to maximize mission preparedness and provide the manpower needed to support full spectrum operations. This process involves analyzing personnel strength data to determine current mission capabilities and project future requirements. It compares an organization personnel strength to its requirements, and results in a personnel readiness assessment and allocation decision. This system depends on personnel asset visibility from the foxhole to strategic national provider level.

B. Replacement Operations Management

Replacement operations management moves personnel from designated points of origin to ultimate destinations. There are two parts to replacement operations management: replacement management and replacement support. Replacement management relates to accounting and processing while replacement support is the physical reception, support, and delivery of military and civilian personnel. This includes replacements and return-to-duty (RTD) soldiers. The system provides primarily for individual replacements and groupings of individuals up through squad, crew, or team level, as required by operations. Replacement management requires real-time access to information about all replacements, movement status from the point of selection, and personnel readiness management information to determine the final destination of replacements and RTD soldiers.

C. Personnel Accounting

Personnel accounting is the system for recording by-name data on soldiers when they arrive in, and depart from, units; when their duty status changes (for example from duty to hospital); and when their grade changes. Strength reporting is a numerical end product of the accounting process. It starts with strength-related transactions submitted at unit level and ends with a database update through all echelons to the total Army personnel database. Standard reports available from the personnel accounting system include the following:

- Battle roster
- Personnel summary
- Personnel requirements report
- Command and control task force personnel summary

Personnel accounting will be accomplished primarily through the application of a corporate database and web enabled processes that facilitate personnel support from home station, thus reducing the personnel footprint on the battlefield.

D. Personnel Information Management

Personnel information management encompasses the collecting, processing, storing, displaying, and disseminating of relevant information about soldiers, units, and civilians. Personnel readiness managers, casualty managers, and replacement managers all use a personnel information database when performing their missions. The Defense Integrated Military Human Resource System (DIMHRS) operates as a centralized database of all military personnel. Personnel readiness, casualty, and replacement managers access DIMHRS for the real-time information needed to perform their mission.

During split-based operations, the personnel information processing activity of the personnel services battalion (PSB) element or military personnel division at the home station provides continued support to deployed forces. The rear personnel information system element performs sustaining base personnel information management. A forward deployed personnel detachment or a forward area support team provides only essential services in contingency operations. The forward element synchronizes databases in the theater, and transmits, updates, and receives them from the rear element.

III. Personnnel Services

Personnel services are integral to unit readiness as well as the human dimension of the force. Personnel services encompass casualty operations management, essential personnel services, and military pay.

A. Casualty Operations Management

The casualty operations management system includes the recording, reporting, verifying, and processing of information from unit level to Headquarters, Department of the Army. It also involves notifying appropriate individuals and assisting family members. The system involves collecting casualty information from a number of sources, collating it, and analyzing it to determine the appropriate action. Accuracy and timeliness are critical components of casualty management, and depend on satellite communications and reliable access to personnel information.

Casualties can occur on the first day of an operation. Thus, casualty managers from each echelon of command may need to deploy early. Units report all casualties found to include civilians, contract personnel, and military personnel from other U.S. Army units, other services, and multinational forces. Reports go to the PSB as well as through G1/S1 channels. The future digital information exchange, through the management module of GCSS-A, provides an interface between medical facilities, mortuary affairs collection points, and personnel operators. Casualty liaison teams currently provide an interface between medical facilities, mortuary affairs collection points, and the personnel group.

Casualty operations require 100 percent personnel accounting reconciliation. The unit verifies casualty information against the database and emergency data in an individual's deployment packet. Initial and updated reports move through channels to the USTAPERSCOM. USTAPERSCOM verifies information in the casualty report against available information systems. It then directs and coordinates notification actions through the appropriate casualty area commander. The casualty area commander (usually a commander of an active duty installation in CONUS) makes the notification to next of kin and provides casualty assistance.

B. Essential Personnel Services

Essential personnel services include:

- Awards and decorations
- Noncommissioned officer and officer evaluations
- Enlisted promotions and reductions
- Officer promotions
- Enlisted and officer transfers and discharges
- Identification documents
- Leaves and passes
- Line of duty investigations
- Officer procurement
- Band support

There is a possibility that during combat operations, the current S1 structure can provide only critical wartime personnel support and essential personnel services, limiting and delaying other services throughout the operation.

C. Military Pay

Military pay input transactions are an integrated and embedded process within the personnel system architecture. They capitalize on information systems and seamless processes to maintain the critical links between personnel actions and activities that impact pay entitlements.

IV. Personnel Support

Personnel support activities encompass the elements of postal operations management; morale, welfare, and recreation; and band operations.

A. Postal Operations Management

The postal operations management system provides a network to process mail and provides postal services within a theater of operations. Processing mail involves receiving, separating, sorting, dispatching, and redirecting ordinary and accountable mail, conducting international mail exchange, and handling casualty, contaminated, and enemy prisoner of war mail. Postal services involve selling stamps; cashing and selling money orders; providing registered (including classified up to secret), insured, and certified mail services; and processing postal claims and inquiries.

Official mail moves through the postal system until it reaches the postal services platoon of the unit addressed. FM 12-6 and AR 25-51 address official mail.

B. Morale, Welfare, and Recreation (MWR) and Community Support

This system enables commanders to provide soldiers and civilians with recreational and fitness activities and goods and services not available through appropriated funds. For contingency operations, the MWR network provides unit recreation and sports programs and rest areas for brigade-size and larger units. MWR personnel provide these services and facilities.

Community Support

Community support programs include the American Red Cross (ARC), family support, and the exchange system. During mobilization and deployment, the ARC provides emergency communication and case management services to support the health, welfare, and morale of the armed forces and their families. ARC provides forward-deployed units a direct link to their families during family emergencies. The mission of family support programs is to foster total Army family readiness. Mission accomplishment for forward-deployed units depends on soldiers' confidence that their families are safe and capable of carrying on during their absence. AAFES, through its exchange system, provides basic health, hygiene, and personal care items to soldiers and deployed civilians.

The MWR System

The MWR system becomes an immediate outlet for soldiers to combat stress, which is critical to sustaining the readiness of the force, as the speed and intensity of operations escalate. The MWR system relies on Force Provider packages, DA civilians, and contract recreation specialists. It capitalizes on using cellular, e-mail, and video-teleconference (VTC) technologies to provide links between soldiers and their families. Soldiers are entertained through the latest in visual and audio entertainment over satellite, worldwide web, and virtual reality technologies.

(FM 4-0) Combat Service Support

XI. Financial Mgmt Ops

Ref: FM 4-0 Combat Service Support, chap. 10.

Financial management operations sustain Army, joint, and multinational forces. The two core processes, finance operations and resource management operations, provide funding for procuring goods and services that are critical in austere theaters. FM 14-100 fully describes financial management operations.

Financial management and accountability requirements are not service unique. Therefore, while the Army sustains deployed civilian and military personnel from other services and nations, many non-tactical responsibilities lie with the Department of Defense. The Defense Finance and Accounting Service (DFAS) performs core fiduciary activities for all services—standard finance and accounting policies, procedures, systems, and oversight. Real-time financial management information, accounting, and payment services emanate from DFAS with two exceptions: tactical operations and classified activities. Army financial managers provide finance and resource management services within the tactical arena.

I. Finance Operations

Modular finance force structure design allows units to task-organize, even in rapidly changing situations. Units can tailor financial management support to operational task forces from platoon to corps-size. Finance elements deploy with the advance tactical force and immediately coordinate with procurement and host nation elements for contracting support, commercial vendor payment procedures, banking and currency support, and conversion rates. Finance units support local procurement of supplies, equipment, and services by both combat service support (CSS) elements and operational forces.

There are four types of support provided by finance operations: contract support, banking support, currency support, and disbursing.

Finance Operations

 A Contract Support

 B Banking and Currency Support

 C Disbursing

Ref: FM 4-0, chap. 11.

A. Contract Support

Contract support pays for laundry and shower operations, transportation assets and facilities, all classes of supply, and maintenance services obtained through formal contracting procedures. Commercial vendor services support is for the immediate needs of the force that Army CSS elements cannot reasonably or economically satisfy. The force makes cash payments for day-laborer wages, Class I supplements, and purchasing construction materials.

B. Banking and Currency Support

To provide banking and currency support, finance elements coordinate with embassies, DFAS, and/or the Treasury Department to set up in-country banking facilities. They link with the host-nation banking industry officials to establish local depository (LD) accounts and coordinate an established exchange rate. Finance personnel provide U.S. currency, foreign currencies, and U.S. Treasury checks to all U.S. Army finance units and other U.S. services. Requisite pay support benefits military, civilian, and foreign national personnel, and includes advice and assistance to enemy prisoners of war (EPW) camp commanders in the payment of EPWs and civilian internees. Pay support for civilians in theater may include technical guidance, leave and payroll data, pay inquiries, and pay actions.

C. Disbursing

Disbursing officers disburse and collect currency; they are personally and legally accountable for all funds. Disbursing is essential to all deployments, and is particularly critical in underdeveloped areas and in early stages of all deployments. Finance personnel:

- Disburse funds by treasury check, cash, and electronic funds transfer (EFT) on properly certified vouchers
- Receive, collect, and control currencies
- Exchange currencies (on limited bases)
- Maintain accountable records
- Fund paying agents
- Cash personal checks and similar negotiable instruments for military, civilian, and contractor personnel

Disbursing officers make solatium payments to alleviate grief, suffering, or anxiety over injury and personal or property loss, and to meet cultural expectations. They also support noncombatant evacuation operations (NEO) and bounty programs. This disbursement is made through finance units operating in the AO. In all cases, accounting is accomplished to rigid standards.

II. Resource Management Operations

Resource management operations involve the execution of the resource management mission, which includes providing advice and guidance to the commander, developing command resource requirements, identifying sources of funding, determining cost, acquiring funds, distributing and controlling funds, tracking costs and obligations, cost capturing and reimbursement procedures, and establishing a management control process (JP 1-02). Resource management helps maintain peacetime readiness, and is a key to success in full spectrum operations. Resource management functions relate to acquiring, distributing, controlling, executing, and reporting funds. Resource managers advise commanders on time phasing and actions, and provide support on fund controls and reporting requirements.

XII. Legal Support

Ref: FM 4-0 Combat Service Support, chap. 12.

Legal support to operations encompasses all legal services provided by judge advocates and other legal personnel in support of units, commanders, and soldiers in an area of operation (AO) and throughout full spectrum operations. Legal support to operations falls into three functional areas: command and control, sustainment, and personnel service support (referred to as support). For more information, see FM 27-100.

Command and staff functions to commanders, staffs, and soldiers include:

* Interpreting, drafting, and training commanders, staffs, and soldiers on rules of engagement
* Participating in targeting cells
* Participating in the military decisionmaking process
* Participating in information operations
* Applying the Law of War (LOW)
* Advising commanders on policies regarding jurisdictional alignment, convening authority structure, and authority to issue general orders

Legal support to operations must include operational law (OPLAW) and each core legal discipline (military justice, international law, administrative law, civil law, claims, and legal assistance).

Legal Support to Operations

A Operational law

B Military justice

C International law

D Administrative law

E Civil law

F Claims

G Legal Assistance

Ref: FM 4-0, chap. 12.

A. Operational Law

OPLAW is domestic, foreign, and international law that directly affects the conduct of operations. OPLAW supports the command and control of military operations, to include the military decisionmaking process and the execution of operations. OPLAW supports the military decisionmaking process by performing mission analysis, preparing legal estimates, designing the operational legal support architecture, wargaming, writing legal annexes, assisting in developing and training the rules of engagement (ROE), and reviewing plans and orders. OPLAW supports the execution of operations by maintaining a common operational picture, and advising and assisting with targeting, ROE implementation, and information operations. OPLAW also involves the provision of core legal disciplines that sustain the force.

SJAs normally provide OPLAW support at each brigade headquarters (main command post [CP]), and at each key operational cell at every higher level of command (tactical CP, main CP, rear CP, G3 plans, G3 operations, information operations cell, and targeting cell). OPLAW supports each joint and multinational headquarters. Some missions also require OPLAW support at battalion level, or in specialized units or operational cells. This is increasingly the case in peace operations and disaster relief.

B. Military Justice

Military justice is administering the Uniform Code of Military Justice (UCMJ), and disposing alleged violations by judicial (courts-martial) or nonjudicial (Article 15, UCMJ) means. The purpose of military justice, as a part of military law, is to promote justice, to assist in maintaining good order and discipline in the armed forces, to promote efficiency and effectiveness in the military establishment and, thereby, to strengthen the National security of the United States (MCM, Part I, para 3).

The Judge Advocate General (TJAG) is "responsible for the overall supervision and administration of military justice within the Army." (AR 27-10). The commander is responsible for administering military justice in the unit, and must communicate directly with the SJA about military justice matters.

There are three components of military justice, each with its distinct functions.

1. Military Justice Advice and Services to the Command

First, the SJA is responsible for military justice advice and services to the command. The SJA advises commanders concerning the administration of justice, the disposition of alleged offenses, appeals of nonjudicial punishment, and action on court-martial findings and sentences. The SJA supervises the administration and prosecution of courts-martial, prepares records of trial, and manages the victim-witness assistance program and military justice training.

2. Defense Counsel Services

Second, the Chief, U.S. Army Trial Defense Service supervises, controls, and directs defense counsel services. Judge advocates assigned to the trial defense service advise soldiers and represent soldiers before courts-martial. These judge advocates also represent soldiers in adverse administrative hearings.

3. Military Judges

Third, the Chief Trial Judge, U.S. Army Trial Judiciary provides military judges for general and special courts-martial, supervises military judges, promulgates rules of court, and supervises the military magistrate program. Military judges assigned to the Trial Judiciary preside over courts-martial, exercise judicial independence in conducting courts martial, conduct training sessions for trial and defense counsel, and perform or supervise military magistrate functions. Military magistrate functions include reviewing pretrial confinement and confinement pending the outcome of foreign criminal charges, and issuance of search, seizure, or apprehension authorizations.

C. International Law

International law includes applying international agreements, international customary practices, and the general principles of law recognized by civilized nations relating to military operations and activities. Within the Army, the practice of international law also includes foreign law, comparative law, martial law, and domestic law affecting overseas, intelligence, security assistance, and counterdrug and civil assistance activities.

D. Administrative Law

Administrative law is the body of law containing the statutes, regulations, and judicial decisions that govern the establishment, functioning, and command of military organizations.

Administrative law support is usually provided at brigade headquarters, main and rear command posts in Army of Excellence divisions and corps, rear command posts in Force XXI divisions, COSCOM headquarters, and at each higher Army, joint, and multinational headquarters. Because of the vast scope of issues they face, administrative law attorneys, especially, must be capable of conducting specific technical legal research and writing.

E. Civil Law

Civil law is the body of law containing the statutes, regulations, and judicial decisions that govern the rights and duties of military organizations and installations regarding civil authorities. The practice of civil law includes contract law, fiscal law, environmental law, and many other specialized areas of law.

1. Contract Law

Contract law is applying domestic and international law to acquire goods, services, and construction. The practice of contract law includes battlefield acquisition, contingency contracting, bid protests and contract dispute litigation, procurement fraud oversight, commercial activities, and acquisition and cross-servicing agreements.

2. Fiscal Law

Fiscal law is applying domestic statutes and regulations to funding military operations, and supporting non-Federal agencies and organizations. The SJA's fiscal law responsibilities include providing legal advice on the proper use and expenditure of funds, interagency agreements for logistics support, security assistance, and support to non-Federal agencies and organizations.

3. Environmental Law

Environmental law is the body of law containing the statutes, regulations, and judicial decisions relating to Army activities affecting the environment to include navigable waters, near-shore and open waters, and any other surface water, groundwater, drinking water supply, land surface or subsurface area, ambient air, vegetation, wildlife, and humans. Overseas, host nation law may also affect Army operations.

F. Claims

The Army claims program investigates processes, adjudicates, and settles claims on behalf of, and against, the United States worldwide. The claims program supports commanders by preventing distractions to the operation from claimants, promoting the morale of Army personnel by compensating them for property damage suffered incident to service, and promoting good will with the local population by providing compensation for personal injury or property damage caused by Army or personnel. Categories of claims include claims for property damage of soldiers and other employees arising incident to service, torts alleged against Army or personnel acting within the scope of employment, and claims by the United States against individuals who injure Army personnel or damage Army property.

The Secretary of the Army (SA) heads the Army Claims System. TJAG supervises the Army Claims Program and settles claims in accordance with delegated authority from the SA. The U.S. Army Claims Service (USARCS) administers the Army claims program and designates area claims offices, claims processing offices, and claims attorneys. SJAs, or other supervisory judge advocates, operate each command's claims program and supervise the ACO or CPO designated by USARCS for the command. ACOs and CPOs are the normal claims offices at Army installations that investigate, process, adjudicate, and settle claims against the United States. They also identify, investigate, and assert claims on behalf of the U.S. claims attorneys at each level, settle claims within delegated authority and forward claims exceeding that authority to the appropriate settlement authority.

G. Legal Assistance

Legal assistance is providing personal civil legal services to soldiers, their family members, and other eligible personnel. The Army Legal Assistance Program promotes morale and discipline and, thereby, contributes directly to mission accomplishment.

Legal assistance attorneys and legal staffs working under their supervision, provide legal assistance in a variety of settings. This includes:

- Combat readiness exercises, premobilization legal preparation (PLP), soldier readiness program processing (SRP), demobilization briefings, noncombatant evacuation operations
- Client interviews, informal requests for assistance
- Federal and state income tax assistance
- Preventive law programs

They also provide extensive legal services:

- Ministerial and notary services
- Legal counseling, legal correspondence, negotiation, legal document preparation and filing, limited in-court representation, legal referrals, and mediation
- Handle a variety of cases such as family law, estates, real property, personal property, economic matters, civilian and military administrative matters, torts, taxes, and civilian criminal matters

Legal assistance is provided at the ASCC headquarters, TSC headquarters, main and rear command posts in Army of Excellence divisions and corps, and main command posts in Force XXI divisions and, as required, at brigade or lower echelons. While each service and each troop contributing nation is responsible to provide legal assistance for its personnel, some legal assistance may be required at joint or multinational headquarters.

XIII. Religious Support

Ref: FM 4-0 Combat Service Support, chap. 13.

Chaplains, on behalf of the commander, provide and perform religious support (RS) in the Army to ensure the free exercise of religion. Chaplains are obligated to provide for those religious services or practices that they cannot personally perform. Chaplains perform religious support when their actions are in accordance with the tenets or beliefs of their faith group. Chaplain assistants assist the chaplain in providing or performing this religious support.

The First Amendment guarantees every American the right to the free exercise of religion. Title 10 requires the military to ensure that right to military personnel. The Army implements this requirement in AR 165-1. Religious support operations ensure those rights of free exercise of religion to the soldier, family members, and authorized civilians. This includes religious services, rites, sacraments, ordinances, pastoral care, religious education, family life ministry, institutional ministry, professional support to the command and staff, management and administration, religious/humanitarian support, religious support planning/operations and religious support training. Religious support also includes advice to the command on matters of religion, morals, morale, and the coordination with nongovernmental organizations (NGOs) and private voluntary organizations (PVOs), as appropriate. FM 1-05 and JP 1-05 provide detailed discussions of religious support.

Unit Religious Support

 ### Unit Support

Support provided to the unit to which the UMT is assigned or attached. The team normally gives first priority to this mission.

 ### Area Support

Support provided to soldiers, members of other services, and authorized civilians who are not a part of the team's unit, but operate within the supporting unit area of operations (AO).

 ### Denominational Support

Support given to soldiers and other authorized persons of the chaplain's denomination or distinctive faith group. Limited assets affect the availability of denominational support.

Ref: FM 4-0, chap. 13.

I. Religious Support Functions

Comprehensive religious support includes the following three major functions.

1. Nurture the Living

In preparation for missions that span the full spectrum of operations, unit ministry teams (UMTs) develop and provide religious support activities to strengthen and sustain the spiritual resilience of soldiers and family members. During the battle UMTs bring hope and strength to those who have been wounded and traumatized in body, mind, and spirit assisting the healing process.

2. Care for the Dying

UMTs provide religious support, spiritual care, comfort, and hope to the dying. This focus of religious support affirms the sanctity of life, which is at the heart of the chaplaincy. Through prayer and presence the UMT provides the soldier with courage and comfort in the face of death.

3. Honor the Dead

Our nation reveres those who have died in military service. Religious support honors the dead. Funerals, memorial services, and ceremonies reflect the emphasis our American people place on the worth and value of the individual. Chaplains conduct these services and ceremonies fulfilling a vital role in rendering tribute to America's sons and daughters who paid the ultimate price for their nation.

II. Religious Support Across the Levels of War

A. Strategic-Level Religious Support

Religious support planning and management at the strategic level considers force-tailoring UMTs to perform and provide religious support for all types and sizes of forces in all contingencies. The senior Army chaplain in theater provides staff supervision over all Army religious support in the theater and is responsible for recommending religious support policy to the commander of the Army service component command (ASCC). Installation chaplains and their staffs provide seamless religious support across all levels of war via information systems.

B. Operational-Level Religious Support

The ARFOR chaplain supports the ARFOR commander's operational-level responsibilities and roles by:

- Establishing links with joint, multinational, interagency, NGOs, PVOs, and religious leaders of the host nation
- Planning and executing religious support for corps operations
- Monitoring religious support in major subordinate commands
- Executing support operations to sustain subordinate Army forces

Religious support is tailored to the operation when the division is designated as an ARFOR or as part of a joint task force (JTF)

C. Tactical-Level Religious Support

The UMT is embedded within and provides religious support to combat, CS, and CSS units at the battalion, squadron, brigade, regiment, and division; this includes specialized and special operations units like the Rangers and special forces.

(FM 4-0) Combat Service Support

XIV. Band Support

Ref: FM 4-0 Combat Service Support, chap. 14.

Army Bands are a powerful commander's tool to promote goodwill and good relations to members of a local population. Army Bands entertain soldiers and citizens of the United States, its allies, and host nations in both garrison and battlefield environments. Details on Army bands are covered in FM 12-50 and AR 220-90.

I. Types of Army Band Support

Army bands are capable of a wide variety of musical support. Bands perform indoors and outdoors in most climatic conditions. See AR 220-90 for regulatory guidance on use of Army bands. A band's committing authority is normally the G1/AG.

Army Band Support

A Ceremonial Support

B Civic Support

C Recruiting Support

D Other Support

Ref: FM 4-0, chap. 14.

A. Ceremonial Support

Army bands perform music that is connected to American heritage, military history, unit lineage, and individual honors. Among soldiers, ceremonial music helps build enthusiasm, maintain motivation, and increase devotion to the unit, the Army, and the United States. Army band participation in a ceremony adds dignity, solemnity, tradition, and honor. Music creates an emotional bond that leaders can use to draw a unit closer together, to show honor and devotion to a leader, and to remind them of friends and family back home. Music highlights history and draws attention to sacrifices and hardships as well as victory and heroism.

Army bands can be used to enhance ceremonial events and are not limited to reviews, military honor guards and cordons, and funerals.

B. Civic Support

The Army band supports and participates in public events because the Army belongs to the American people. A successful community relations program enhances the community's perception of the Army and fosters an appreciation and spirit of cooperation for the military installation, the soldiers and their families, and civilians who are part of the installation. Civic events that may be appropriate for Army band participation include parades, holiday and community concerts, sporting events, dedications, cultural events, and ribbon cutting ceremonies.

C. Recruiting Support

Army bands are an important tool for use in recruiting. Bands highlight the Army and support local recruiting activities. Musical selections may be drawn from many styles ranging from patriotic to popular music in a single performance. All Army bands in continental United States (CONUS) are directly charged to support recruiting efforts.

D. Other Support

In addition to the types of support mentioned previously, Army bands may participate in most events not prohibited by AR 360-1 and AR 220-90. These regulations and DODD 5500.7, govern off duty participation in unofficial events.

II. Types of Army Bands

Army bands are organized into three distinct types.

A. Special Bands

Special bands have no tactical equipment or capability. There are four special bands: the U.S. Army Band (Pershing's Own), the Old Guard Fife and Drum Corps, the U.S. Army Field Band, and the U.S. Military Academy Band

Special bands provide—

- Musical support to the Military District of Washington (MDW) and its tenant and supported activities, national U.S. Army recruiting operations and, as directed, by Headquarters, Department of the Army
- National and international musical support to strengthen the ties between the Army and the civilian community for the Office, Chief of Public Affairs and, as directed, by Headquarters, Department of the Army
- Musical support for the U.S. Military Academy, its tenant and support activities and, as directed, by Headquarters, Department of the Army

B. General Support Bands

General support (GS) bands are assigned to a major command (FORSCOM, TRADOC, and USAREUR) and are so designated by table of organization and equipment (TOE). They provide both CONUS and OCONUS support.

GS bands provide support to information operations and should be integrated into public affairs (PA), CMO, and psychological operations (PSYOP) plans. GS bands are capable of providing augmentation for local security forces.

C. Direct Support Bands

Direct support (DS) bands are units that are not a special or GS band, and are assigned to a corps, division, TRADOC branch qualifying schools, or other activity of the U.S. Army, and are normally OPCON to the G1/AG, or equivalent.

I. Logistics Overview

JP 4-0

Ref: JP 4-0 Logistics Support of Joint Operations, chap I.

I. Levels of Logistic Support

Joint doctrine states that there are three interrelated levels of war — strategic, operational, and tactical. These same levels apply to operations in war and peace. The Joint Staff and Service staffs concentrate on strategic logistics matters. Serving as supported commanders, the geographic combatant commanders as well as supporting commands and agencies link strategic and operational level logistics to support their assigned missions. Subordinate commanders blend operational logistic and tactical support to accomplish tasks assigned by the commander of a combatant command (CINC).

Major Logisitic Areas

Material	Personnel	Services	Facilities
▪ Design and Development ▪ Acquisition ▪ Storage ▪ Movement ▪ Distribution ▪ Maintenance ▪ Evacuation ▪ Dispostion ▪ Contracting	▪ Movement ▪ Evacuation ▪ Hospitilization	▪ Contracting ▪ Furnishing	▪ Contracting ▪ Construction ▪ Maintenance ▪ Operation ▪ Disposition

Ref: JP 4-0, fig. I-1, p. I-1.

Logistics is the science of planning and carrying out the movement and maintenance of forces. In its most comprehensive sense, those aspects of military operations which deal with:

- Design and development, acquisition, storage, movement, distribution, maintenance, evacuation, and disposition of materiel
- Movement, evacuation, and hospitalization of personnel
- Acquisition or construction, maintenance, operation, and disposition of facilities
- Acquisition or furnishing of services

The science of logistics concerns integration of the strategic, operational, and tactical sustainment efforts, while scheduling the mobilization and deployment of units, personnel, equipment, and supplies in support of the employment concept of a geographic combatant commander. The relative combat power that military forces can bring to bear against an enemy is enabled by a nation's capability to plan for, gain access to, and deliver forces and materiel to the required points of application across the range of military operations. A nation's capability to deliver logistic resources has historically been a major factor in military operations.

II. Logistics Functions

Logistic support requirements involve six broad functional areas: supply, maintenance, transportation, civil engineering, health services, and other services.

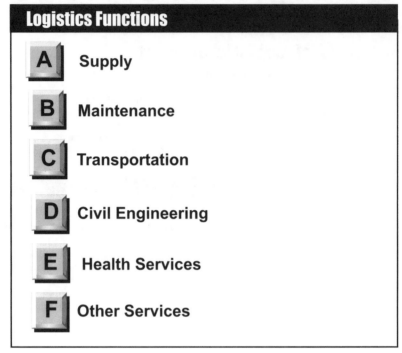

Logistics Functions

A Supply

B Maintenance

C Transportation

D Civil Engineering

E Health Services

F Other Services

Ref: JP 4-0, fig. I-3, p. I-3.

A. Supply

Supply includes actions to acquire, manage, receive, store, and issue the materiel required by the operating forces to equip and sustain the force from deployment through combat operations and their redeployment.

B. Maintenance

Maintenance includes actions taken to keep materiel and equipment in a serviceable condition, to return it to service, or to update and upgrade its capability.

C. Transportation

Transportation is the movement of units, personnel, equipment, and supplies from the point of origin to the final destination and redeployment upon completion of the mission or as directed. This includes the expeditious retrograde of reparable materiel for repair.

D. Civil Engineering

Civil engineering provides construction, damage repair, operation, and maintenance of roads and facilities, and logistics enhancements required by the CINC in order to sustain military operations. Examples of civil engineering products include: shelter, warehouses, supply routes, terminals, hospitals, water, electric power, sewage treatment, and water and fuel storage and distribution. Within Service limitations, civil engineers may also conduct environmental support operations, provide fire protection, and conduct explosive ordnance disposal, provide water purification and disposal, conduct engineer reconnaissance, and provide force protection construction support.

E. Health Services

Health services include patient movement, primary care, hospitalization, medical logistics, medical laboratory services, blood management, vector control, force health protection services, veterinary services, dental services, preventive health care, and the required command, control, and communications.

F. Other Services

Other services are associated with nonmaterial support activities and consist of various functions and tasks provided by Service personnel and the logistic community that are essential to the technical management and support of a force. Included in this category of support are: food service, billeting, textile repair and clothing exchange, laundry and shower, postal, finance, personnel administration, religious, and mortuary affairs. The Marine Corps categorizes laundry and shower as "engineering" and light textile repair as "maintenance."

III. Joint Support Responsibilities and Requirements

CINCs exercise combatant command (command authority) (COCOM) over assigned forces. COCOM includes directive authority for logistics, giving the CINC the unique ability to shift logistic resources within the theater. COCOM gives the supported or supporting CINC the statutory authority, whether over assigned forces or forces designated by the Secretary of Defense, to direct all aspects of logistics necessary in order to accomplish a mission. Normally, this authority is exercised through subordinate joint force commanders (JFCs) and Service component commanders. A CINC's authority does not diminish the Services' responsibilities to provide support to their own forces. While a CINC's authority is generally confined to the theater, logistic support beyond the theater is usually a Service responsibility. In war the CINC may direct, when circumstances dictate, that materiel or equipment be transferred between Service components. This transfer will normally be accomplished on a reimbursement basis, but the reimbursement process will not delay directed transfers. The CINC's directive authority for logistics underscores the need for accurate and well coordinated prior planning between the supported command, Services, supporting agencies, and allies. Support, which often involves logistics, is the action of a force that aids, protects, complements, or sustains another force and may involve the provision of services, resources, and combat power, but does not involve the transfer of forces or units. Support is characterized as mutual support, general support, direct support, and close support.

- Logistic resources necessary to generate combat forces and sustain their operations
- The procurement process to ensure the availability of logistic resources in a timely manner
- The process of allocating available logistic resources among subordinate commands
- The distribution system necessary to achieve optimum mission effectiveness

Ref: JP 4-0, fig. I-4, p. I-6.

IV. Unique Aspects of Multinational (Allied and Coalition) Logistics

CINCs cannot enter into multinational relationships that are contrary to US policy without National Command Authorities (NCA) direction. US participation in future multinational operations will vary considerably in terms of missions, leadership, command and control (C2), mutual support, contract, and funding arrangements.

Detailed consideration of the effect of these differing characteristics is provided in JP 4-08, "Joint Doctrine for Logistic Support of Multinational Operations.

II. Logistics Principles

Ref: JP 4-0 Logistics Support of Joint Operations, chap II.

The principles of logistics complement the principles of war. To support the national military strategy, logistics must be responsive in and capable of meeting military personnel, equipment, mobility, medical readiness, infrastructure, and sustainment requirements of the Armed Forces of the United States across the full range of military operations. Logistics must integrate the national and theater effort to mobilize, deploy, employ, sustain, reconstitute, redeploy, and demobilize the forces assigned and attached to a combatant commander. Identifying those principles that have priority in a specific situation is essential to establishing effective support. The application of these principles to a specific mission and situation dictates the concept of logistic support. The principles of logistic support are not a checklist, but rather a guide for analytical thinking and prudent planning.

I. Principles of Logistics

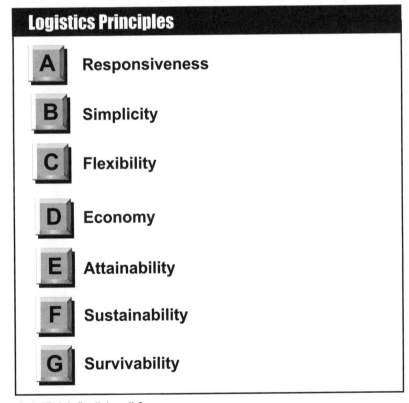

Logistics Principles

A Responsiveness

B Simplicity

C Flexibility

D Economy

E Attainability

F Sustainability

G Survivability

Ref: JP 4-0, fig. II-1, p. II-2.

A. Responsiveness

Responsiveness is the right support in the right quantity in the right place at the right time. Among the logistic principles, responsiveness is the keystone; all else becomes irrelevant if the logistic system cannot support the concept of operations of the supported commander.

B. Simplicity

Simplicity reflects the need to reduce complexity and often fosters efficiency in both the planning and execution of national and theater logistic operations. Mission-type orders and standardized, interoperable procedures contribute to simplicity. Establishment of priorities and pre-allocation of supplies and services by the supported unit may simplify logistic support operations.

C. Flexibility

Flexibility is the ability to adapt logistic structures and procedures to changing situations, missions, and concepts of operation. Logistic plans and operations must be flexible in order to achieve both responsiveness and economy. The commander must retain positive C2 over subordinate organizations to maintain flexibility. The principle of flexibility also includes the concepts of alternative planning, anticipation, reserve assets, redundancy, forward support of phased logistics, and centralized control with decentralized operations. This principle is a guide for strategic thinking and forms the template for synchronized and coordinated joint logistic planning.

D. Economy

Logistic economy is achieved when effective support is provided using the fewest resources at the least cost, and within acceptable levels of risk. At some level and to some degree, resources are always limited. When prioritizing and allocating resources, the CINC must continuously consider economy and optimize use of resources to ensure effectiveness and mission success while supporting every effort toward achieving efficiency.

E. Attainability

Attainability (or adequacy) is the ability to provide the minimum essential supplies and services required to begin combat operations. The commander's logistic staff develops the concept of logistic support, completes the logistic estimate, and initiates resource identification based on the supported commander's requirements, priorities, and apportionment. An operation should not begin until actions are taken to mitigate risk and minimum essential levels of support are on hand.

F. Sustainability

Sustainability is a measure of the ability to maintain logistic support to all users throughout the theater for the duration of the operation. Sustainability focuses the supporting commander's attention on long-term objectives and capabilities of the supported forces. Long-term support is the greatest challenge for the logistician, who must not only attain the minimum essential materiel levels to initiate combat operations (readiness) but must also sustain those operations.

G. Survivability

Survivability is the capacity of the organization to prevail in the face of potential destruction. Examples of military objectives selected for their effect on logistics and subsequent theater operational capability include industrial centers, airfields, seaports, railheads, supply points and depots, line of communications (LOC), shipping, rail and road bridges, and intersections. Logistic units & installations are also high-value targets that must be safeguarded by active & passive measures.

1. Active Measures

Active measures must include a defense plan for logistics with provisions for reinforcement and fire support.

2. Passive Measures

Passive measures include dispersion, physical protection of personnel and equipment, deception, and limiting the size of an installation to what is essential for the mission.

II. Logistic Considerations

A. Employment Planning Considerations Directly Impact the Projection or Deployment of Forces

From employment planning decisions, the CINC identifies: force requirements; intent for the deployment operation; the time-phased arrival of unit personnel, equipment, and materiel in-theater; sustainment requirements; and the closure of forces required to execute decisive operations. Equally important to the successful conclusion of joint operations will be effective reconstitution and redeployment planning performed to either return a unit to home station or deploy it to another mission area.

B. Logistics as a Factor in Determining Objectives

Depending on the theater operations and logistic concepts that a geographic combatant commander employs in a campaign, logistic factors will almost always affect a theater campaign and exert different constraints. Logistics is a positive enabler to the execution of successful operations. Good logistic synchronization is a combat multiplier.

Strategically, logistic capabilities may limit the deployment, concentration, and employment options available to the NCA, Chairman of the Joint Chiefs of Staff, or CINCs. Operationally, theater logistic constraints may dictate the rate of strategic buildup or theater onward movement, overall composition of the combat force, and the depth, tempo, and duration of combat operations. Tactically, the logistic initiatives at the strategic and operational levels must be focused on ensuring that the engaged mission forces have the right support at the right place at the right time.

C. Coordination of Logistic Planning with Operation Planning

Operations and logistics are inseparable facets of war. Although logistic plans are derived from operational goals, neither can claim primacy; each is integral to the other. Integration of the operations and logistic planners' efforts is necessary throughout the planning and execution phases. Although obvious, such integration does not occur automatically. Command emphasis at all levels is essential. It is imperative that logistic support and operations planning occur simultaneously for multinational (allied and coalition) operations. Nations are often reluctant to (and sometimes prohibited from) sharing national OPLANs with potential allies or coalition partners because of their highly sensitive nature. Nonetheless, the effort should be made to share integrated operations and logistic support plans during the plan development stage and rapidly adjust them as required during execution.

D. Forward Impetus

Forward impetus derived from the synergy of information and logistic resources is required to provide rapid, continuous, and responsive support to the CINC. This includes delivery, tracking, and shifting of units, personnel, equipment, and supplies (even while en route) in order to optimize support to the warfighter.

E. Balance Between Combat Forces and Logistic Forces

The aim of any military organization is to produce the greatest possible combat power in a combat environment with the resources available. CINCs must determine the proper balance of combat forces and logistic forces based on the differences between various logistic and operations concepts. Efforts to enhance combat power by arbitrarily shifting logistic manpower into combat units may achieve the opposite result. Each campaign or operation demands its own analysis of the proper balance between combat and logistic forces. The requisite strength of logistic elements depends on many factors such as the gross requirements for logistic resources and where and when they are needed, the adequacy of available transportation networks and assets, the length of the LOC, the availability of local labor, and the types of operations being supported. Caution should especially be exercised when assuming local labor will provide augmentation during operations.

The balance between logistics and combat forces at the beginning of hostilities is important. Overall, planning must be based on the mission ranging from major theater war to military operations other than war (MOOTW) and the CINC's intent. Fully trained and equipped logistic elements must be available and deployed in adequate numbers to render immediate sustained support to the combat troops. A combat force without logistic support is not sustainable and may not be fully capable of mission success. For sustained combat, CINCs should give serious consideration to the availability, capability, state of organization, and limitations of logistic forces allocated to them for wartime operations. This is critical when the US logistic force structure has been reduced in anticipation of the availability of HN assets.

F. Command and Control of Logistics

Unity of command is essential to coordinate national and theater logistic operations. Logistics is a function of command. This principle is met through the CINC's directive authority for logistics, which gives the CINC authority to direct logistic actions and resources necessary to meet mission and operational taskings assigned to the command. To exercise control at the strategic, operational, and tactical levels of war, subordinate joint force and theater level Service component commanders must also exercise control over their respective logistic resources subject to the directive authority of the CINC.

In multinational operations, unity of command may be more difficult to achieve because of the reluctance of nations to relinquish control over their logistic resources and national legal restrictions regarding the use or transfer of logistic resources to other nations. During the operational planning phase, every effort should be made to clarify the C2 of logistic resources. If established, the roles, responsibilities, and authorities of an overall logistic support coordinator and/or command should be clearly defined.

See JP 4-08, "Joint Doctrine for Logistic Support of Multinational Operations," for the unique considerations associated with planning logistic support for multinational operations.

G. Apportionment and Allocations

Apportionment involves distribution for planning of limited resources among competing requirements, whereas allocation involves distribution of limited resources among competing requirements for employment. The senior commander will usually attain the best results by apportioning and allocating reasonably expected and available resources among subordinate commanders based on the concept of operations and the subordinate commanders' stated requirements. Allocations may be less than the amounts requested by, or apportioned to, some of the subordinate commanders, due to the limited availability of logistic assets. Threat distribution and phase duration are useful tools for determining the allocation of resources.

H. Accommodation for Wartime Requirements

The ideal logistic organization within the nation's economy and the military does not require a fundamental change to manage the transition from peace to war in order to meet an emergency. Although civilian and military leaders may be prevented from attaining the ideal, they should strive to come as close to it as possible. If they do not create and train an organization in peacetime that will work in war, the leadership will be burdened with urgent reorganization and training requirements at a time when they should be free to focus on the employment of that organization.

I. Logistic Discipline

Logistic resources should be optimized. At the strategic theater level, there may be limitations such as fiscal constraints or the unavailability of materiel, industrial facilities, and skilled labor and long lead times for mobilization and deployment that may affect the strategic concentration of forces and supplies within the theater. At the operational and tactical levels, common limitations are attributed to: inadequate transportation means, port capacities, and throughput capabilities; insufficient quantities of certain munitions, equipment, and critical spare parts; the lack of trained logistic personnel; and the failure to plan for adequate, interoperable C4 systems. Unwise use of logistic resources may result in combat forces being deprived of adequate manpower, equipment, supplies, and training, and constitutes a disregard for economy of force.

True economy of supply requires the careful planning and buildup of levels to provide those resources and combat facilities (based on threat distribution and phase duration) that are essential to initiate and sustain combat operations. At the same time, planners should avoid building too large a stockpile. Excess stocks waste resources, decrease flexibility, drain transportation resources from other priorities, and deny sustainment to other areas.

J. Movement Control

Deployment planning begins when situation awareness prompts COA planning. Deployment execution is directed and/or specified in appropriate orders. The supported commander is responsible for movement control into and through the geographical AOR. USTRANSCOM monitors and provides movement summaries of AMC, MSC, and MTMC assets from departure to arrival in the theater. USTRANSCOM also maintains the transportation portion of the JOPES data base and provides analysis to the Joint Staff, supported combatant command, and others. This analysis includes progress reports, status, problems, port workloads, daily movement statistics, and resolution of force closure problems encountered in the common-user transportation system. In transportation operations, force closure is the process of a unit arriving at a specific location. It begins when the first element arrives at a designated location (e.g., POE or POD), intermediate stops, or final destination and ends when the last element does likewise.

Deployment and Redeployment

In deployment and redeployment operations, force closure is when the CINC determines that the deploying force has completed movement to the specified operational area with sufficient resources and is ready to conduct its assigned mission. It normally coincides with the integration phase of JRSOI. JOPES and the Joint Planning and Execution Community provide the CINC with a capability to change or delete requirements during main force deployment. The geographic combatant commander is responsible for the integration of the required intratheater movement and the strategic concentration of forces and logistics. Inadequate control of movement, whether into or within the theater, results in waste, reduced logistic effectiveness and efficiency and, consequently, a loss of potential combat power.

K. Deployment Information Flow

Accurate, up-to-date information is vital to effective logistic planning, coordinating unit movements, and sustainment operations. It is as important to know where units and supplies are as it is to have them physically present. OPLANs are published in JOPES format. JOPES is used to monitor, plan, and execute mobilization, deployment, employment, sustainment, and redeployment activities. JOPES supports national, theater-level, and supporting structures in peacetime and wartime. JOPES and GTN are currently the tools used by the Joint Chiefs of Staff, supported and supporting CINCs, and the Services to monitor and update deployment information. Access to JOPES via GCCS is critical to deploying and supporting forces. During planning and execution, the supported and supporting CINCs will, in most cases, make decisions concerning priority of forces and allocation of scarce airlift and sealift based on the situation they are facing and information available through multiple systems that include GCCS, JOPES, GTN, and JTAV.

L. Logistic Reserves

Logistics may be a pacing factor at the operational level of war when it determines how quickly a campaign can proceed. Just as strategic and operational reserves are necessary to exploit tactical or operational success or respond to unanticipated contingencies, it is necessary to establish reserves of logistic resources that can be committed only by the geographic combatant commander.

M. Pre-positioning

CINCs and Service component commanders planning for combat operations and MOOTW in undeveloped theaters of operations must give adequate consideration to available pre-positioned equipment and sustainment within their operational areas.. The Services have established both afloat and shore-based pr-epositioning of unit equipment and sustainment to meet force closure requirements and offset the competing demand for strategic lift by the early deploying joint force.

N. Industrial Base Requirements

CINCs, Service component commanders, and their staff planners must factor in administrative lead time, production time, and distribution time when determining logistic response time for the industrial base. Definite DOD plans to support a combatant command, with appropriate investment strategies and offsets, must be in place prior to the start of any contingency to ensure timely response from the Services, DLA, and industry. Although the greatest demand occurs within the first 30 to 60 days of a contingency, industrial surge to meet demands requires significant time to build to maximum output. The Department of Defense will frequently compete with private sector customers for a manufacturer's industrial capacity and inventories. To ensure appropriate industrial surge planning for troop support items and spares, critical items must be identified and communicated through the appropriate inventory control point and DLA to the industrial base.

O. Contracting for Supplies and Services

There are basically three sources of supplies and services for US forces deployed in a contingency operation. They are: US force structure, HNS, and contracting.

III. Logistics Planning

JP 4-0

Ref: JP 4-0 Logistics Support of Joint Operations, chap III.

Note: See chap. 4, pp. 4-1 to 4-22 for additional information on CSS planning.

Joint logistics is a complex, interdependent concept that may apply leverage (plus or minus) to a CINC's combat power. An understanding of the CINC's concept of operations and early involvement by the logistic staff will ensure that national and theater deployment and sustainment requirements are balanced with logistic capabilities. Logistic planning considerations aid the CINC in providing guidance to staff planners and assessing the adequacy and feasibility of campaign and operation plans. JP 5-0, "Doctrine for Planning Joint Operations," discusses sustainment planning that is directed toward providing and maintaining levels of personnel, materiel, and consumables required to sustain the planned levels of activity for the estimated duration and at the desired level of intensity. Special considerations must be made for operations in less developed countries where infrastructure support (communications, transportation, port facilities, aircraft materials handling equipment [MHE] and industrial capability) are limited. An advanced party should visit these locations prior to deployment in order to determine availability of adequate infrastructure to support operations.

Special Logistics Planning Considerations

- Demands of an expanding force
- Critical items
- Constraints
- Movement control
- Balancing push versus pull resupply
- Logistic outsourcing
- Noncombatant evacuation operations (NEO)

Ref: JP 4-0, fig. III-2, p. III-5.

Integrating Logistic Plans

Logistic plans must be integrated with a CINC's OPLAN annexes and with plans of other commands and organizations within the Department of Defense. Additionally, external departments and agencies and HNs that will be supporting the CINCs should be considered and included.

I. Levels of Logistic Planning

Logistic planning must be done at the strategic, operational, and tactical levels. The supported commander ensures that strategic, operational, and tactical logistic planning are integrated and complementary to ensure effective support and optimize efficiency to the extent possible.

A. Strategic and Operational Logistic Support Concepts

The CINC's strategic logistic concept will focus on the ability to generate and move forces and materiel into the theater base and on to desired operating locations, where operational logistic concepts are employed. With the transportation and distribution systems in mind, planners must determine the basic but broad mobilization, deployment, sustainment, and retrograde requirements of the CINC's concept of operations. The combatant commander and staff must plan to optimize the use of JRSOI, theater distribution, and common-user logistic operations.

B. Tactical Logistic Support Concepts

This planning is done primarily by the Service components. It includes line-item planning and involves the detailed application of the best planning factors available from historical usage data, analysis, or exercise experience. Also, planners determine the size and precise location of logistic facilities and units. CINCs and their staffs should examine the Service components' methods, assumptions, and factors to determine their validity and to guard against duplication of effort and any tendency to establish unnecessarily high safety margins or standards of living.

II. Theater Organization

The area organization that evolves from the geographic combatant commander's concept of logistic spt will influence subordinate theater-level logistic decisions.

Area Organization Influence on Logistics

- Responsibilities for providing common or joint service for maintenance, medical, salvage, transportation and mortuary affairs
- Locations and functions suitable fo contractor support
- Contingency plans to respond to destruction or damage to theater infrastructure
- Requirements for long lead-time special projects
- Requirements for wartime host-nation support
- Items suitable for common supply in specific areas: subsistence; selected petroleum, oils, and lubricants; selected munitions; Class IV (field fortification and construction material); Class VI (personnel support items); Class VIIIA/B (medical supplies and blood); and selected Class IX (repair parts).

Ref: JP 4-0, fig. III-1, p. III-4.

A. Organization of an Operational Area

When warranted, geographic combatant commanders may designate theaters of war and, perhaps, subordinate theaters of operations for each major threat. In time of war, the NCA or geographic combatant commander may elect to define a theater of war within the CINC's AOR. The theater of war is that area of air, land, and water that is or may become directly involved in the conduct of war. A theater of operation is defined as that area required to conduct or support specific combat operations within the theater of war. Different theaters of operations within the same theater of war will normally be geographically separated and focused on different enemy forces. To assist in the coordination and deconfliction of joint action, the CINC may define operational areas or joint areas. For operations somewhat limited in scope and duration, CINCs may designate the following operational areas: JOA, joint special operations area, joint rear area, amphibious objective area, area of operation, and area of interest.

B. Communications Zone

CINCs may establish combat zones and communications zones (COMMZs). The combat zone is an area required by forces to conduct large-scale combat operations. It normally extends forward from the land force rear boundary. The COMMZ contains those theater LOCs, organizations, and other agencies required to support and sustain combat forces. The COMMZ usually includes the rear portions of the theaters of operations and theater of war and reaches back to the CONUS base or a supporting CINC's AOR. The COMMZ includes air and sea ports that support the flow of forces and logistics into the operational area. It is usually contiguous to the combat zone, but may be connected only by fragile LOC.

C. Logistic Base

In smaller-scale operations or MOOTW, the JFC may establish a logistic base from which operations are projected and supported. The logistic base will provide support tailored to fit the mission and situation. Most, if not all, of the support capability located in the COMMZ of largescale operations will be found with a reduced footprint at the logistic base. Similarly, a logistic base may be established in large-scale operations when support forward of the COMMZ is required.

III. Special Planning Considerations

A. Demands of an Expanding Force

Execution of an operation order (OPORD) or campaign plan or response to a crisis may be accompanied by general expansion of the Armed Forces of the United States. Historically, demand for items increases faster than the supply system can provide, and special management actions might become necessary. To anticipate campaign priorities, planners must: provide instructions or guidance for redistributing assets from low- to high-priority organizations within the command; obtain assets from external sources with lower priority needs; control the allocation of new assets in short supply; and provide efficient means to retrograde, repair, and then reissue critical items.

B. Critical Items

Critical supplies and materiel must be identified early in the planning process. Critical items are supplies vital to the support of operations that are in short supply or are expected to be in short supply. Critical items may also be selected mission-essential items that are available but require intense management to ensure rapid resupply for mission success.

C. Constraints

Logistic planners must understand the constraining factors affecting all phases of the deployment, sustainment, and retrograde plans. Intra-CONUS, inter-theater, and intra-theater movements may encounter constraints that limit or degrade the ability to support a campaign or operation plan. Identifying constraints en route to or within the theater is the first step in coordinating activities to avoid overloading LOCs. Traditionally, limited unloading capacities at ports and airfields, lack of asset visibility, and limited inland transportation have constrained the operational reach of combat forces. Logistic planners must anticipate congestion and seek solutions to constraints. Finally, if multinational operations are planned, the impact of multinational land, naval, and air forces competing for real estate, ship berthing and unloading facilities, transportation, labor, and construction materials on US force deployment and employment plans must be assessed. Planners must evaluate the impact of using SPODs, APODs, and/or JLOTS when preparing for operations.

D. Movement Control

Movement control must coordinate transportation assets of all modes — terminals, services, commands, and HNs — to support the CINCs' concept of operations. As the Department of Defense's single manager for common-user transportation, USCINCTRANS will provide for proper liaison with the CINC for movement of personnel and materiel into the theater during peacetime and Historically, demand for items increases faster than the supply system can provide, and special management actions might become necessary. To anticipate campaign priorities, planners must: provide guidance for redistributing assets from low- to high-priority organizations within the command; obtain assets from external sources with lower priority needs; control the allocation of new assets in short supply; and provide efficient means to retrograde, repair, and then reissue critical items.

E. Balancing Push and Pull Resupply

Automatic (push) resupply works best for commodities and classes of materiel with valid usage rates. It is particularly useful for establishing and maintaining the stocks of common-user items, which may then be distributed within the theater. Requisitioning (pull) is preferable for variable usage rate requirements. Properly used and regulated, a combination of push and pull resupply will minimize transportation requirements and the logistic footprint in-theater. Current logistic initiatives are designed to further reduce the logistic footprint, increase the velocity and visibility of resupply, and emphasize pull resupply for maximum efficiency. In this regard, planners must realize that for certain commodities such as repair parts and major end-items, the Services have oriented their logistic system to a pull system, heavily reliant on information systems and a rapid, time-definite distribution system.

F. Logistic Outsourcing

Planning should identify sources of supplies and services from civilian sources and integrate them with operational requirements. The types of support provided by contracted logistics include: construction and maintenance of facilities; receiving, storing, issuing, and inventory of supplies; food service; transportation; maintenance; sewage and waste removal; water production; and shower and laundry.

G. Noncombatant Evacuation Operations

Conducting NEO in conjunction with combat operations may place unexpected demands against the supply and services and transportation capabilities of the CINC. NEO requirements must be identified early in the planning process and included in overall assessments of plan feasibility.

(JP 4-0) Logistics Support to Joint Operations

IV. Theater Logistics

Ref: JP 4-0 Logistics Support of Joint Operations, chap IV.

Joint theater logistics applies logistic resources to generate and support theater combat power. This chapter focuses on the CINC's theater logistic concepts, including balancing objectives, scheme of maneuver, and operations timing. It discusses the concept of extending operational reach and concludes with a number of specific logistic applications that apply to the theater. CINCs must ensure that their campaign plans fully integrate operational and logistic capabilities. The CINCs must maintain an interrelationship between operations and logistics by insisting on close cooperation and early-on understanding of the missions assigned to subordinate commanders. The influence of the CINC is essential in bridging any operational-logistic gap.

I. Combatant Commander's Logistic Concept

Although the Service component commanders provide logistic resources, combatant commanders are responsible for ensuring that the overall plan for using these resources supports their theater concept of operations.

A. The Logistic System

A critical element of a theater logistic system is timely integration of inter-theater and intra-theater transportation of personnel, equipment, and materiel in the theater distribution system. The means to move people and equipment forward and to evacuate them to the rear is fundamental to successful theater operations.

Key Elements of the Logistic System

- **Lines of Communication (LOCs)**

  LOCs consists of all the routes (land, water and air) that connect an operating military force with a theater base of operations and along which supplies and military forces move.

- **Theater Transportation Network**

  The ports, bases, airports, rail heads, pipeline terminals, and trailer transfer points that serve as the reception and transshipment points for the LOC.

- **Host Nation, Allied and Coalition Support**

  Desired civil and military assistance from allies that include: en route support, reception, onward movement, and sustainment of deploying U.S. forces.

- **Contingency Contracting**

  Contracting personnel in support of a contingency in an overseas location pursuant to the policies and procedures of the Federal Acquisition Regulatory system. Contractor support may be provided in areas of facilities, supplies, services, maintenance, transportation and quality of life support.

Ref: JP 4-0, fig. IV-1, p. IV-2.

Considerations in developing a logistic system are as follows:

Considerations in Developing a Logistic System

1. Geography
2. Transportation
3. Logistic Capability
4. Logistic Enhancements
5. Logistic Infrastructure Protection
6. Echelon of Support
7. Assignment of Responsibility
8. Availability of Host-Nation and Multinational Support

Ref: JP 4-0, fig. IV-2, p. IV-3.

1. Geography

The planner must examine the impact of topography, climate, and external factors affecting the logistic system, especially the impact on the various segments of the transportation system, including all waterways, rail systems, roads, pipelines (petroleum, natural gas, water), and airways.

2. Transportation

Many factors influence the time-phased selection of transportation modes to meet operational requirements. For example, sealift is by far the most efficient mode for bulk tonnage; however, airlift is often the most expedient for people or for rapid movement of essential equipment and supplies when time is critical. This is particularly important when considering transportation requirements for rapid, time-definite delivery of critical high priority items. On land, rail (for bulk tonnage) and pipeline (for bulk liquids) are more efficient than trucks.

3. Logistic Capability

In today's environment of smaller inventories, the logistic capability must be considered from the manufacturer (the industrial base) down to the DLA, Services, and combatant command infrastructure. The logistic planner must know to what level supply production may surge during a crisis, what avenues are available to fulfill the initial demands, what the transportation system can support, how retrograde will be handled, and what special requirements or procedures need to be put in place. The ability of the theater infrastructure to receive, warehouse, and issue logistic resources must also be understood.

4. Logistic Enhancements

Plans must include or consider means to reduce the impact of logistic constraints. Some examples are opening or gaining access to high-capacity ports, expanding airfield parking aprons, additional MHE, and expedient airfield matting. Improved use of commercial International Organization for Standardization containers vice breakbulk may also aid in port clearance and theater distribution of sustainment. Planners should recognize that container distribution operations will require handling equipment, particularly in many austere port and inland transshipment points. Asset visibility also provides the opportunity to divert forces and sustainment around constraints.

5. Logistic Infrastructure Protection

Provisions must be made for security of the logistic system because it is integral in the sustainment of any mission.

6. Echelon of Support

The logistic system must be responsive to the needs of the most forward combat forces. It must start from CONUS and extend to the forward operational areas, providing supplies and services when and where they are needed.

7. Assignment of Responsibility

In coordination with USCINCTRANS, CINCs should assign responsibility for operating the seaports, bases, and airports to the Service components (or HNs, if applicable).

8. Availability of Host-Nation and Multinational Support

The level of assistance in terms of transportation resources, labor, facilities, and materiel that may be provided by host, allied, and coalition nations affects the amount of airlift and sealift that may be devoted to initial movement of combat forces or sustainment. ACSA and implementing arrangement (IA) to DCAs are a simplified method of receiving or providing resources and services in a multinational environment.

B. Theater Concept of Logistic Support

The concept of logistic support must be derived from the estimate of logistic supportability of one or more COAs developed during the commander's estimate phase of planning. The CINC's J-4 prepares these estimates for each alternative COA proposed. The estimate of logistic supportability for the selected COA, along with the logistic system framework considerations outlined above, may be refined into the concept of logistic support for an operation or campaign.

The concept of logistic support is the envisioned manner in which the capabilities and resources of the combatant command Service components will be employed to provide supply and services, maintenance, transportation, engineering, and health services. It is the organization of capabilities and resources into an overall theater support concept.

The concept of logistic support needs to specify how operations will be supported. It should give special attention to the major LOC to be developed, as well as support to be provided by each allied nation. If here is to be a COMMZ to support air or land operations or a network of intermediate and advanced bases to support naval operations within a theater, the general organization and functions should be laid out.

II. Extending Operational Reach

Operational reach is the distance over which military power can be concentrated and employed decisively. At the strategic level, the CINCs focus primarily on defeating the enemy's strategy and will, and on gaining strategic depth, initiative, and advantage by proper strategic concentration of forces and logistics. The CINCs direct the operating forces to accomplish these tasks. The operating forces' view of operational reach centers on the range at which commanders may mass and employ forces decisively for war or MOOTW. It goes beyond merely conducting reconnaissance or strike operations at a distance.

Operational reach is influenced by the length, efficiency, and security of the distribution system and LOCs. Operational reach also depends on the ability to phase reserves and materiel forward. Finally, it must include the operating ranges and endurance of combat forces and sustainment. The CINC may seek to extend operational reach (with associated increase in risk) by deploying combat forces ahead of support forces ahead of support forces. The logistician must use all available assets to provide a sufficient level of sustainment to the deployed forces. Operational reach may be improved by establishing advanced bases or depots and by improving the security and efficiency of the distribution system and LOCs.

Joint Logistics References

Ref: JP 4-0, fig. IV-3, p. IV-5.

JP 3-05	Special Operations Logistic Support
JP 3-17	Theater Airlift Operations
JP 3-35	Joint Deployment/Redeployment Operations
JP 4-01	Mobility Systems
JP 4-01.1	Airlift Support
JP 4-01.2	Sealift Support
JP 4-01.3	Movement Control
JP 4-01.4	JointTheater Distribution
JP 4-01.5	Terminal Operations
JP 4-01.6	Joint Logistics Over-the-Shore
JP 4-01.8	Joint Reception, Staging, Onward Movement, and Integration
DODD 6480 series	Blood Program
DODD 6480 series and JP 4-02	Medical Services
DODD 4140 series and JP 4-03	Petroleum Support
JP 4-04	Engineer Support
JP 4-05	Mobilization Planning
JP 4-06	Mortuary Services
JP 4-07	Common User Logistics Planning Joint Operations
JP 4-08	Joint Doctrine for Logistic Support of Multinational Operations
JP 4-09	Global Distribution
DOD 5000	Contracting

(JP 4-0) Logistics Support to Joint Operations

V. JTF J-4 Logistics

Ref: JP 5-00.2 Joint Task Force Planning Guidance and Procedures, chap. VIII.

Logistics, like intelligence, will play a key role in JTF operations from the earliest stage of planning through the final stage of redeployment of forces.

Logistics provides the foundation of combat power. Logistics is the process of planning and executing the movement and sustainment of operating forces in execution of military strategy and operations. Joint logistics should use existing individual Service policies and procedures whenever possible. If this is not possible, the differences should be identified to the supported combatant commander as early as possible for resolution.

I. JTF Logistics Organization

Organizing factors include but are not limited to the nature of anticipated operations, composition of JTF forces, geographical and seasonal conditions, operational environment, existing logistics arrangements, and quality and quantity of potential host-nation support (HNS) and acquisition cross-service agreements (ACSAs). JTF J-4 should consider forming a JTF logistics readiness center (LRC) and a joint movement center (JMC).

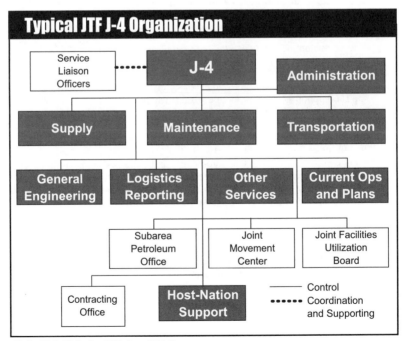

Typical JTF J-4 Organization

Ref: JP 5-00.2, fig. VIII-1, p. VIII-3.

Logistics responsibilities follow single-Service command channels; therefore, it is recommended that the JTF J-4 staff have representatives or liaison personnel from each Service involved in the JTF. Since SOF relies on conventional Service counterparts for support, it also is recommended that the special operations components or JSOTF, if activated, have representatives involved as well.

It is recommended that the CJTF establish an LRC to provide the following logistics control and coordination functions:

- Monitor current and evolving JTF logistics capabilities
- Coordinate logistic support and maintain total assets visibility
- Advise the CJTF on supportability of proposed operations or COA
- Determine logistics sustainment requirements for planning and execution
- Coordinate with the supported combatant commander's LRC and act as the JTF agent and advocate for logistic support
- Provide a central point for logistic-srelated boards, offices, and centers

II. Logistics Authority

A combatant commander exercises directive authority for logistics and may delegate authority for a common support capability to the CJTF within the JOA. It is critical that the JTF J-4 determine what, if any, logistics directive authority for a common support capability the combatant commander has delegated to the CJTF and if the scope of the authority meets the JTF requirements. The joint theater logistics management concept, described in Joint Pub 4-0, "Doctrine for Logistic Support of Joint Operations," should be used in order to optimize resources by synchronizing all materiel support efforts in-theater with the objectives to provide the assets required for joint force mission accomplishment in a timely manner.

Service Responsibilities for Logistics

The combatant commander's logistics directive authority does not negate the individual Service's responsibility for logistic support or discourage coordination by consultation and agreement, nor is it meant to disrupt effective procedures or efficient use of facilities or organizations. Each Service is responsible for the logistic support of its own forces, except when logistic support is otherwise provided for by agreement with national agencies, multinational partners, or by assignments to common, joint, or cross-servicing. The supported combatant command may determine that common serving would be beneficial within the theater or designated area. In addition, the applicability of Standard NATO Agreements, Foreign Military Sales, agreements under the NATO Mutual Support Act, other bilateral and multinational agreements, and international programs vary from nation to nation, and the distinction between programs is often unclear. Determinations must often be made on a case-by-case basis.

UN Operations

Authority over logistics under multinational and UN operations is different and situationally-dependent. Areas which must be clarified include funding, cross-servicing, and mutual support agreements.

III. JTF J-4 Responsibilities

Ref: JP 5-00.2, pp. VIII-8 to VIII-9.

1. Coordinate the overall logistics functions and requirements of the JTF.

2. Advise the CJTF on logistics matters that affect the accomplishment of the mission.

3. Formulate JTF logistics policies.

4. Develop Annex D (Logistics) to CJTF's OPLANs, OPORDs, or campaign plans. Develop appropriate sections of paragraph 4 of the Basic Plan and Commander in Chief's Strategic Concept.

5. Coordinate common item supply support in accordance with tasking assigned in Annex D (Logistics) to the OPLAN or OPORD.

6. Coordinate agreements for inter-Service supply and support, local procurement and controls, and allocate indigenous facilities and logistics resources available at staging bases and in the JOA.

7. Monitor critical classes of supply support capabilities for the purpose of mission tasking and economy of resources and apportioning critical resources.

8. Arrange for and monitor transportation movement requirements; assess capabilities and limitations of assigned forces, supporting cmds, agencies, and in-country assets.

9. Identify and coordinate JTF HNS requirements with the CMOC. During disaster relief and/or FHA, the J-4 can play an important supporting role to the CMOC in meeting NGO and/or PVO requests for assistance and aiding them in coordinating all aspects of providing assistance with limited resources.

10. Arrange HNS with the appropriate agency in the JOA.

11. Coordinate the operation of beaches, airports, and seaports within the JOA.

12. Exercise staff supervision or cognizance over applicable military engineering matters (e.g., construction, maintenance, and base development).

13. Coordinate maintenance, recovery, and salvage operations to ensure economy of inter-Service and HN resources, even though these are primarily a Service vice J-4 responsibility.

14. Assist the JTF surgeon in developing the logistics of the JTF's HSS system.

15. Coordinate joint mortuary affairs, including return of remains.

16. With the J-1 and PM, coordinate support for returning EPW, civilian internees, displaced civilians, and other detained persons.

17. Refine logistics OPSEC planning guidance, ensure logistics-related activities are conducted to eliminate OPSEC vulnerabilities, and support military deception initiatives.

18. Maintain liaison with the other JTF staff agencies, subordinate task forces, and component commands.

19. Identify requirements for contracting and request contracting officers with the appropriate warrants. Additionally, identify resources available to advise the contracting officers on such contract, acquisition, and fiscal law questions as may arise.

20. Coordinate agreements, transactions, and implementing instructions for US and multinational mutual support logistics exchange issues with the appropriate component and multinational points of contact.

IV. Logistics Considerations

Ref: JP 5-00.2, pp. VIII-4 to VIII-7.

1. Logistics As A Factor In Determining Objectives

Strategically, logistics capabilities may limit the deployment, concentration, and employment options. Operationally, theater logistics constraints may dictate the rate of strategic buildup or theater onward movement, overall size of the combat force, the depth of any attack, or the speed of advance.

2. Coordinate Log Planning With Operational Planning

Operations and logistics are inseparable. J-4 must coordinate closely with current operations, future operations, and future plans to be effective.

3. Forward Impetus

JTF requirements should be reviewed periodically and refined if required. Service component cdrs can help determine the best method of continuous replenishment.

4. Balance Between Combat Forces And Logistics Forces

The aim of any military organization is to produce the greatest possible combat power with the resources available. Commanders must determine the proper balance based on differences between various logistics and operation concepts. The balance at the beginning of hostilities is especially important. Fully trained and equipped combat support elements must be available and deployed early enough and in adequate numbers to render immediate sustained support to combat troops.

5. Logistics Command and Control

Unity of command requires coordination not only between Services, but among government departments and agencies, NGOs, PVOs, and multinational forces.

6. Apportionment and Allocation

Apportionment is distribution for planning of limited resources, whereas allocation is distribution of limited resources among competing requirements.

7. Accommodation for Requirements

JTF J-4 organization should be set up to meet all the JTF requirements. An effective J-4 organization will be able to meet the JTF logistics needs without a reorganization should a change in the JTF missions and responsibilities occur.

8. Logistics Discipline

True economy of supply requires the careful planning and buildup of levels to provide those resources required. Excess stock or unwise use of priorities decreases flexibility and drains transportation, facilities, and logistics resources.

9. Movement Control

Accurate, up-to-date information is vital to effective operations. A JTF needs the capability to monitor and track movement of forces, equipment, and supplies coming into and within the JOA. Radio frequency tags may be used for monitoring and tracking the movement of supplies throughout the operational area.

10. Deployment Information Flow

Accurate, up-to-date information flow is vital. It is almost as important to know where units and supplies are as it is to have them physically present.

11. Logistics Reserves

Logistics can be a pacing factor at the operational level of war when it determines how quickly a campaign can proceed. It is necessary to establish the requirement for logistics reserves with the supported combatant commander.

12. Industrial Base Requirements

Planners must identify the items that must come directly from the industrial base vice existing stocks.

V. Logistics Boards, Offices and Centers

While not all of the below-listed joint boards, offices, or centers may be required, each should be evaluated based on the projected operations.

The following theater-level organizations may be established by the supported combatant commander to assist the JTF in coordinating logistics efforts:

1. Joint Transportation Board (JTB)

A JTB establishes priorities and allocates common-user transportation resources within theater.

2. Joint Petroleum (JPO)

The JPO coordinates POL planning and execution, as well as the supply of common bulk petroleum products. Normally, the supported combatant commander's JPO provides wholesale bulk petroleum management.

3. Joint Civil-Military Engineering Board (JCMEB)

The JCMEB, a temporary board, establishes policies, procedures, priorities, and overall direction for civil-military construction and engineering requirements in the JOA.

4. Joint Facilities Utilization Board (JFUB)

The JFUB evaluates and reconciles requests for real estate, facilities, inter-Service support, and construction in compliance with JCMEB priorities.

5. CINC Logistic Procurement Support Board (CLPSB)

The CLPSB coordinates contracting operations with US embassies and HN for acquisition of supplies and services to arrange for single-Service contracting.

6. Joint Materiel Priorities and Allocation Board

This board modifies and recommends priorities for allocation of materiel assets for both US and multinational forces.

7. The Joint Movement Center

The Joint Movement Center implements the CJTF's taskings and priorities for movement. The JMC tracks strategic movements to ensure that they meet the JTF commander's expected flow of force capabilities into the operational area, maximizing the use of available in-transit visibility automation tools. Additionally, the JTF's JMC coordinates the employment of all transportation assets, including multinational and HN, within the JOA.

8. The Sub-area Petroleum Office

When tactical operations warrant extensive management of wholesale bulk POL in theater, a Sub-area Petroleum office is established by the JPO to coordinate, plan, and execute common bulk petroleum products for the JTF.

9. The Joint Facilities Utilization Board

This board evaluates and reconciles requests for real estate, facilities, inter-Service support, and construction at the JTF level. JFUB actions will be guided by the provisions of Joint Pub 4-04, "Joint Doctrine for Civil Engineering Support."

10. The JTF Contracting Office

The JTF Contracting Office, working with the CLPSB, is established (with warranted contracting officers) to coordinate contracting requirements for and assisting in the acquisition of local facilities, supplies, services, and support.

A complete description of the functions and responsibilities for boards, centers, and offices can be found under Appendix B to JP 4-0, "Doctrine for Logistic Support of Joint Operations."

VI. Host-Nation Support

HNS can be a significant force multiplier. Whenever possible, available and suitable HNS should be considered as an alternative to deploying logistic support from CONUS. HNS may increase dramatically the timeliness of response to a developing situation and reduce the strategic airlift and sealift requirements necessary to deploy forces to the JOA.

Countries without a government infrastructure may not be able to provide logistics assistance; however, limited support may be obtained through local contractors. To maximize the JTF logistics effort, HNS functions (i.e., identification of require- ments and procurement) should be centralized and coordinated within the J-4. CA personnel assigned to the JTF are trained to identify and coordinate HN support resources and can provide valuable assistance to the J-4 staff.

The HN agreement should include the authority for the CJTF to coordinate directly with the HN for support, acquisition, and use of facilities and real estate. Every effort should be made to obtain language support for negotiations with local nationals. The most effective negotiations occur when military members show competence in local language and customs. The J-2 may assist in obtaining personnel for use in negotiations.

A JTF legal advisor should be involved in the development process for HN agreements. It is critical to determine a lead agency (UN, Service, component, or other agency) for contracting and negotiating for support. Authority for negotia- tions must be obtained through the supported combatant commander, Joint Staff, Office of the Secretary of Defense (OSD), and the Department of State (DOS) channels.

Host-Nation Areas of Support

- Transportation
- Supplies
- Rear Area Protection
- Petroleum, Oils and Lubricants
- Telecommunications

- Facilities
- Acquisition of Equipment
- Civilian Labor
- Health Services Support
- Contracting
- Services

Ref: JP 5-00.2, fig. VIII-3, p. VIII-13.

Chap 3

I. Force XXI CSS Overview

Ref: FM 4-93.52 Tactics, Techniques, and Procedures for the Division Support Command (Digitized), chap. 1.

The Army's Force Division (FXXI) represents a leap forward into the realm of 21st Century technology. The Division possesses greater lethality, quicker mobility as well as the combat service support (CSS) imperative of situational understanding (SA). Real time "situational understanding" means a complete, common operating picture (COP) of the battlefield for every commander. This information enables commanders to quickly mass forces, allowing this division to defeat a larger, but less technologically advanced enemy.

The CSS structure's capability to project, receive, and support this force will directly impact the effectiveness of future military operations. The battlefield imposes new challenges on support functions and leaders. Logistics will require new organization, new doctrine, as well as advanced distribution equipment and information technology.

The concept and organizational structures found in the FM 4-93 series of CSS doctrine reflect a paradigm shift from a supply-based CSS system in Army of Excellence (AOE) to an advanced distribution-based CSS system for Force XXI. Technology enhances this capability.

CSS Ops

I. Force XXI CSS Imperatives and Principles

Force XXI CSS imperatives and principles meet Force XXI challenges by incorporating advanced information and transportation technology, streamlined CSS organizations, and a shift from the AOE supply-based CSS system to a distribution-based system. Force XXI CSS principles hinge on four integrated imperatives:

FXXI CSS Imperatives

| A | Unity of Command |

| B | Increased Velocity |

| C | An Agile CSS Force Structure |

| D | Situational Understanding |

Ref: FM 4-93.52, p. 1-8.

A. Unity of Command

The first CSS imperative is unity of command. It is one of the nine principles of war described in FM 3-0 (100-5) as "directing and coordinating the action of all forces toward a common goal, or objective".

1. Single CSS Operator

The single CSS element at each echelon serving as the focal point for CSS; providing unity of command and effort; and providing centralized distribution management for CSS operations.The single CSS operator provides centralized distribution management and the CSS assets required supporting its designated maneuver unit. This single CSS operator is responsible for establishing unity of effort; providing and/or coordinating CSS surge capability where required to support the maneuver commander's intent. The single CSS operators are:

CSS Operators

Echelon	Single CSS Operator
Maneuver Battalion	Forward Support Company (FSC)
Maneuver Brigade	Forward Support Battalion (FSB)
Division	Division Support Command (DISCOM)
Corps	Corps Support Command (COSCOM)
Theater	Theater Support Command (TSC)*

* Army Theater CDR's decision

Ref: FM 4-93.52, p. 1-9.

2. Surge Capability

The capability to mass CSS resources at a point and time on the battlefield to weight the battle logistically by maximizing combat power at the decisive point as determined by the supported commander. Surge capability is enabled by flexible, modular organizational capabilities and by fused CSS and operational information.

3. Centralized Distribution Management

A single distribution manager at each echelon that leverages information technology to coordinate, prioritize, and synchronize materiel management and movement control operations to maximize the distribution pipeline's capability to throughput units and follow-on sustainment.

B. Increased Velocity

Increased velocity refers to the time required to move supplies, equipment, and capability from the strategic base through the distribution system to the end user. Time is critical for a force projection Army. Increased velocity has made reductions in the CSS battlefield footprint, in terms of personnel, equipment and supplies possible. The increased velocity concept relies on effective command and control provided by unity of command coupled with situational understanding.

Distribution-based CSS

A distribution-based CSS system leverages advanced planning and optimization (APO) tools to forecast requirements, plan and control distribution operations, obtain visibility of intransit stocks, combined with limited stocks at storage locations, and velocity and speed of distribution to support and sustain Army operations.

II. FXXI Distribution-Based CSS System

Ref: FM 4-93.52 pp. 1-1 to 1-3.

The concept and organizational structures found in the FM 4-93 series of CSS doctrine reflect a paradigm shift from a supply-based CSS system in Army of excellence (AOE) to an advanced distribution-based CSS system for Force XXI. Technology enhances this capability. Distribution-based CSS leverages information, force structure designs, technological enablers, and C2 relationships to move the Army away from its traditional dependence upon echeloned stockpiles to a system capable of delivering the "right stuff, at the right time, to the right location".

1. Throughput to Forward Areas

Leveraging configured loads, containerization, information, force structure design, technological enablers, and C2 relationships to deliver sustainment from the operational level directly to the customer or its direct support unit; bypassing intermediate, general or direct support units.

2. Minimize Load Handling

Leveraging configured loads, containerization, information, force structure design, technological enablers, and C2 relationships in order to reduce the number of times sustainment is handled by multiple echelons and support units between the strategic provider and the ultimate customer. New transportation technology such as the palletized loading system (PLS), load handling system (LHS), container roll-in, roll-out platforms (CROP), and the "slip sheet" significantly reduce handling requirements.

3. Configured Loads

A configured load is a single or multi-commodity load of supplies built to the anticipated or actual needs of a consuming unit thereby facilitating throughput to the lowest echelon, METT-TC dependent.

- **Strategic Configured Load**: A configured load built outside of the theater of operations in CONUS, or sanctuary, to anticipated rqmts of a consuming unit.

- **Mission Configured Load**: A configured load with all of the characteristics of a SCL except that it is built inside a theater of operations for a specific mission, unit or other purpose (e.g. an artillery raid, emergency resupply, etc.). A MCL will normally be configured using resources (personnel, equipment and supplies) found in a hub in the corps or theater area.

- **Unit Configured Load**: A configured load built to the known requirements of a consuming unit. Typically, a UCL will form the basis of a scheduled delivery LOGPAC that may consist of some combination of SCLs, UCLs and the UCL.

4. Scheduled Delivery

A fundamental distribution planning parameter established as a component of each echelon's distribution plan. Scheduled delivery involves the movement of sustainment from the supporting organization to the supported unit at agreed upon time intervals.

5. Time Definite Delivery (TDD)

A fundamental distribution planning parameter, established as a component of each echelon's distribution plan, TDD establishes order ship times (OST) within which specified commodities requested by the supported unit must be delivered. Additionally, it deals with the consistency the distribution system delivers given resources within established OST, and serves as the metric to measure the distribution system's performance.

C. An Agile CSS Force Structure

An agile CSS force structure is one that has a relatively small footprint, and does not encumber the maneuver commander with large stockpiles of supplies or large numbers of combat service support personnel on the ground.

1. Modular Design

A force structure design parameter used by TRADOC force designers to create company level force structure designs wherein each major company sub-element possesses a cross section of the total company's capabilities, thus enhancing the commander's ability to tailor CSS force structure to the mission and requirements.

2. Tailorable Force Packages

An operational planning consideration where CSS organizations and units are customized through the use of modular units and sub-units (platoon, team, or section) to produce the required CSS capabilities without adding unnecessary, redundant, or non-value adding units, sub-units, or elements to the task org.

3. Split-Based Operations

Leveraging force structure designs, advanced automation, information, and communications capabilities to enable a unit to perform its management and C2 mission in support of the warfighter with a small forward element deployed to the theater of operations, while the balance of the unit remains outside of the theater of operations in a sanctuary area.

4. Contractors on the Battlefield

Leveraging contractors to bridge the gap between required capabilities and actual force structure availability within the theater of operations. Lessons learned from military operations throughout our history indicate that contracting and outsourcing can be effective force multipliers. Contracted capability can extend existing Army capabilities and provide alternative sources of supplies and services.

5. Replace Forward/Fix Rear

Replacing line replaceable units (LRUs) or modules instead of attempting to repair the LRUs or modules by leveraging advanced prognostic and diagnostic tools, support equipment, and training. The LRUs or modules are then retrograded to higher levels of maintenance for repair and return to the distribution system.

6. Multi-Capable Maintainer (MCM)

A mechanic trained to perform organizational and direct support level maintenance on the M1 Abrams tank and the M2/3 Bradley fighting vehicle system (BFVS). This mechanic has a broad, but shallow range of skills designed to enable him to replace LRUs or modules to rapidly return a vehicle to mission capable status. This supports the concept combining organizational and direct support maintenance by providing maintainers capable of performing both the organizational level tasks as well as the on-board direct support level tasks on the M1 and the M2/3 BFVS.

7. Combination of Organizational/DS Maintenance

Unifying organizational and direct support (DS) level maintenance responsibilities and capabilities into one organization, the Division XXI FSC, to focus maintenance leadership, management, technical expertise, and assets under a single CSS operator ensuring maintenance can be planned, allocated, and swiftly executed when and where needed to satisfy the commander's requirements.

D. Situational Understanding

Situational understanding refers to the logistician's complete picture of the friendly situation, the enemy situation, and the CSS situation through the use of advanced, seamless information technology.

III. Situational Understanding

Ref: FM 4-93.52 pp. 1-1 to 1-3.

Situational understanding refers to the logistician's complete picture of the friendly situation, the enemy situation, and the CSS situation through the use of advanced, seamless information technology. The following key Force XXI principles relate directly to situational understanding:

1. Common Operating Picture

Ability to view the same CSS and operational data at all echelons in near real time to provide commanders and CSS managers the identical battlefield picture.Leveraging force structure designs, advanced automation, information, and communications capabilities to fuse operational and CSS data to create a common operating picture of the battlefield, both tactically and logistically, for commanders and logisticians at all echelons from the tactical to the strategic level, which in turn facilitates optimal logistical operations.

2. In-Transit Visibility (ITV)

Leveraging advanced automation, information, and communications capabilities to track cargo and personnel while enroute from origin to destination. Visibility is the most essential component of distribution management. Timely and accurate visibility information provides logisticians necessary information to distribute assets on time thus maintaining high confidence levels. Visibility is based on a continuum of CSS data from the sustainment base into and through the distribution processes of the distribution system (factory to foxhole). Visibility must begin at the point where materiel starts its movement to the theater of operations, be that a depot or commercial vendor or a storage facility in another theater or war reserve stockpile. The information must be digitized and subsequently entered into the necessary CSS information systems. The next critical element to visibility is the capability to dynamically update that source data with updates from subsequent CSS systems as to the transport, storage, maintenance, or supply status of that particular item/shipment until it is received at the ultimate consumer location.

3. Integrated STAMIS

The consolidation of previously separate, such as stovepiped, functional information systems into a single common operating environment (COE) that allows common usage of information between functions. An integrated STAMIS is defined as one that incorporates multiple types of functionality within a single system and can share database information between functionalities.

4. Seamless Information Network

The ability to autonomously exchange large volumes of information across data platforms such as GCSS-Army and CSSCS, and between multiple echelons of command from the tactical to the strategic level. A seamless information network provides the common operating picture and intransit visibility (ITV) that makes distribution-based CSS operations and split-based operations possible.

5. Near Real Time (NRT) Information

The ability to autonomously exchange large volumes of information within an information network as the data is created at the point of origination. Near real time refers to the ability to capture events in the information network as they are happening; providing the logistician the capability to act almost immediately to the changing situation.

Force XXI Operations - FM 4-93 Series

Ref: FM 4-93.52 Tactics, Techniques, and Procedures for the Division Support Command (Digitized), preface and chap. 1.

The 4-93 series of field manuals provides information on the structure and operations of the division support command (DISCOM) digitized and it's various components (FSB, DSB, DASB). The series of manuals is directed toward the commander and battle staff of the DISCOM and his supporting and supported units organized under the division redesign and the Force XXI division concept for combat service support (CSS) operations.

FM 4-93.4	Theater Support Command (SS FM 63-4); 15 APR 2003
FM 4-93.50	Tactics, Techniques, and Procedures for the Forward Support Battalion (Digitized); 02 MAY 2002
FM 4-93.51	Tactics, Techniques, and Procedures for the Division Support Battalion (Digitized); 26 MAY 2002
FM 4-93.52	Tactics, Techniques, and Procedures for the Division Support Command (Digitized); 02 MAY 2002
FM 4-93.53	Tactics, Techniques, and Procedures for the Division Aviation Support Battalion (Digitized); 02 MAY 2002

One of the nine principles of war described in FM 3-0 as "...directing and coordinating the action of all forces toward a common goal or objective" is unity of command. Although "...coordination may be achieved by cooperation; it is best achieved... by vesting a single commander with the requisite authority to direct and to coordinate all forces employed in the pursuit of a common goal", such as combat service support.

The FM 4-93 series is based on doctrine in FM 3-0 (100-5), FM 4-0 (100-10), FM 3-100.71 (71-100), FM 3-91.3 (71-3), FM 4-02 (8-10), FM 4-02.55 (8-55) and tactics, techniques, and procedures developed in ST 63-2. FM 3-0 (100-5) Operations is the Army's capstone doctrinal manual and outlines how the Army will conduct operations. FM 4-0 (previously 100-10) is the Army's main CSS doctrinal manual and provides an overview of the CSS system for supporting the Army in the field.

The creation of multi-functional logistics companies within the FSB consolidates CSS organizational elements currently embedded within the maneuver battalion with the direct support (DS) capability currently in the FSB. Personnel and other soldier related support functions including manning, sustaining soldiers through religious, legal, command information support, and funding through finance and resource management support are generally unaffected.

The FM 63 series of manuals outline Army of Excellence (AOE) organizations and operations:

FM 63-2	Division Support Command, Armored, Infantry, and Mechanized Infantry Divisions; 20 MAY 1991
FM 63-11	Logistics Support Element Tactics, Techniques, and Procedures; 08 OCT 1996
FM 63-20	Forward Support Battalion (SS FM 63-20, 17 May 85); 26 FEB 1990
FM 63-21	Main Support Battalion; 07 AUG 1990
FM 63-23	Aviation Support Battalion; 06 JUN 1996

II. CSS Support Structure

Ref: FM 4-93.52 Tactics, Techniques, and Procedures for the Division Support Command (Digitized), chap. 1.

Note: See pp. 1-27 to 1-35 for information on strategic- and operational-level CSS organizations and activities.

The Army's Force XXI Division represents a leap forward into the realm of 21st Century technology. The smaller Force XXI Division possesses greater lethality, quicker mobility as well as the combat service support (CSS) imperative of situational understanding (SA). Real time "situational understanding" means a complete, common relevant picture (CRP) of the battlefield for every commander. This information enables Force XXI commanders to quickly mass forces, allowing this division to defeat a larger, but less technologically advanced enemy.

I. Corps Support Command (COSCOM)

The corps support command (COSCOM) and division support command (DISCOM) function as the major subordinate commands responsible for directing and managing logistics (less medical) support within their supported unit AOs. They coordinate and supervise the implementation of policies and directives relative to supporting current and future operations. They develop plans and orders in concert with operations planners to ensure continuous support operations. The fluidity of battle demands constant changes to these support plans.

As the logistics support command assigned to the corps, the COSCOM executes an extensive portion of the corps CSS plan. The COSCOM provides logistics support to the corps and other units, services, or multinational partners as directed. It coordinates logistics elements to support corps forces and, when required, coordinates with joint, multinational and interagency forces/agencies. It organizes different types of logistics units into support packages to meet the mission requirements of supported forces. (See FM 4-93.4.) Depending on mission, enemy, troops, terrain and weather, time, civilian considerations (METT-TC), the COSCOM units perform the following missions.

- **Supply Support**. In general, COSCOM units provide DS and GS supply support to nondivision units. They provide GS supplies to the divisions, separate brigades, and armored cavalry regiments (ACRs).

- **Field Services Support**. The COSCOM provides mortuary affairs support; shower, laundry, and clothing repair support; and tactical post exchange, with or without AAFES augmentation.

- **Maintenance Support**. The COSCOM maintenance support mission includes maintenance management; DS maintenance and aviation intermediate maintenance (AVIM) to nondivisional units; reinforcing DS maintenance and AVIM to the divisions, separate brigades, and ACRs; missile/rocket maintenance; and calibration support.

- **Transportation Support**. The COSCOM corps-wide transportation support functions consist of movement control; mode operations; cargo transfer operations; terminal operations (to include water terminals when augmented by EAC); and aerial delivery support.

- **Explosive Ordnance Disposal**. EOD companies provide support to corps. These companies are normally collocated with a CSB. The companies provide GS to the corps on an area basis and can be DS to a specific maneuver unit, normally a division.

Non-Divisional CSS Inside FXXI Divisional Battlespace

Ref: FM 4-93.52, fig. 5-2, p. 5-2.

Non-Divisional CSS Inside Force XXI Divisional Battlespace (METT-TC Dependent)

Command and Support Relationships May Vary Based on METT-TC, as well as Availability of EAD CSS Capability

In Support of the Division

MST	+Air MEDEVAC
F&E Rpr	+Gnd Ambulance
Allied Trades	+FST
DS Reinf Trk&Whl	+Cbt Stress Ctrl Tm
	+ Conttiingency K Tm
Wtr Purif Det/Tm	+AMC-LSE//LAO Tm
ASP	+CA Tm
MCT	

In Support of the Div in Brigade Battlespace

Commel Repair
Wtr Purif Dett/Tm
MA Tm

+Air MEDEVAC Element
+Gnd Ambulance Element

In Support of Corps Troops/ Division Area Support

Trailer Transfer Point FDRP	
TMDE/Call Tm	EOD Dett
PSB&Fin Bn elements	Field Svc Co

In Support of Corps Trps in Brigade Battlespace

FLE FA Bde	FLE Engr Bde
Log C2	Log C2
MST	MST
Supply	Supply
Trans	Trans

Log Task Force ACR
Log C2
MST
Supply
Trans

+Air MEDEVAC Element
+Gnd Ambullance Element

In Support of Corps Troops in the Division Rear

CSB HQ/HHC	DS Supplly Co
DS/GS Mt Co	Perishable Sub Plt
Wh/Trk Veh Rpr	DS Ammo Co
Arm/FC Rpr	Trk Co (PLS/POL)
FA/ADA/Msl Rpr	MCT
Pwr Gen Rpr	MA Sectt
Commel/F&E Rpr	
Allied Trades	+Area Spt Med Co
Recovery	+Air MEDEVAC

Note: Med units denoted by + will likely be C2 by Med HQ; CA/AMC by their respective command

Corps Support Group (CSG)

The COSCOM provides both area and corps-wide support. Area support is the most efficient and affordable way to provide support. The COSCOM corps support groups (CSGs) have an area support mission. For CSGs, area support means the location of the units requiring support determine DS supply and maintenance relationships. CSG subordinate DS units provide support on an area basis to units located in, or passing through, their AO. The CSG's support operations section maintains support operations overlays depicting support locations and times of operations. FM 54-30 covers CSGs in detail.

Corps Medical Command

The corps MEDCOM, the major health service support (HSS) command assigned to the corps, in coordination with the COSCOM, executes the HSS portion of the corps CSS plan. The MEDCOM provides HSS to corps forces and to other units, services, or multinational forces as directed. See FM 4-02.

II. Division Support Command (DISCOM)

The DISCOM is a multi-functional organization capable of providing, coordinating, and synchronizing logistical support to the division. The DISCOM's mission of sustaining the division's combat power is more critical than ever. The DISCOM consists of FSBs, a DSB, a DASB, and the headquarters and headquarters company (HHC). The DISCOM provides combat service support for the division. It provides arming through its Class V operations, fueling through Class III operations, fixing through its maintenance operations, transportation through the truck company in the DSB and the supply and transportation sections in the FSBs, sustaining through the provision of rations, individual equipment, and medical support. The personnel sections throughout the division provide the manning function. This chapter will discuss the six tactical logistics functions throughout the DISCOM to give the FSB commander and battle staff an understanding of what and how CSS integrates from higher, DISCOM and EAD, laterally, with the DSB and DASB, and to the lower supported units.

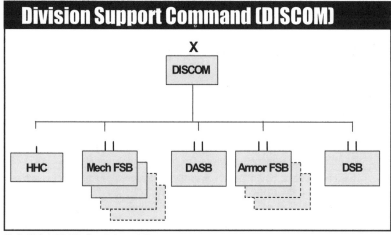

Ref: FM 4-93.52, fig. 1-1, p. 1-3.

III. Division Support Battalion (DSB)

The division support battalion (DSB) is the main CSS unit in the division rear. The DSB provides combat medical support on an area basis to division rear area troops, transportation support to the entire division, as well as direct support (DS) supply and maintenance support to the division headquarters, DSB, division support command (DISCOM) headquarters, division artillery (DIVARTY) headquarters, multiple launch rocket system (MLRS) battalion, air defense artillery (ADA) battalion, military intelligence (MI) battalion, signal battalion, military police (MP) company and designated units in the division rear area. When augmented, it provides field services. The DSB directs and coordinates security of its organic units or units attached to the DSB. The DSB provides limited reinforcing support (Class III bulk and transportation only) to the forward support battalions (FSBs) and division aviation support battalion (DASB).

One DSB is organic to the DISCOM. The command element is responsible for the supervision, direction, and coordination of assigned and attached units that run the support operations in and around the DSA. It also directs and coordinates security of the units.

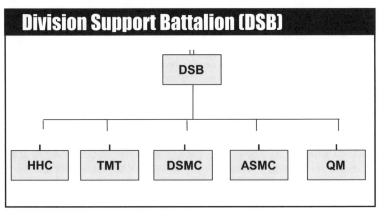

Ref: FM 4-93.52, fig. 1-2, p. 1-4.

IV. Division Aviation Support Bn (DASB)

The multi-functional DASB provides DS to the aviation brigade (AB) and the division cavalry squadron. The DASB may function in a highly dispersed manner, with some DASB elements close to the attack units and others near the brigade rear area. The DASB commander is the aviation brigade commander's single CSS operator. His battle staff manages and monitors sustainment through an array of digital information systems and other technological innovations. The DASB provides, or coordinates for all logistical support, and ties together the entire spectrum of supplies and services for the aviation brigade.

The maneuver commander, however "unencumbered", must be involved in synchronizing the maneuver of the DASB and its subordinate companies and attached elements with inbound shipments from echelons above division and brigade. The use of assured communications, digitization of all CSS echelons, digitization of battlefield distribution (BD) platforms, and lastly modular organization structures, give the DASB commander and brigade S4 the information dominance needed to tailor the CSS support package. Through real-time situational under standing, the brigade battle staff is able to make up-to-the-minute adjustments in its support requirements. The widespread use of enablers on the battlefield allows the DASB battle staff to anticipate changes in requirements and rapidly redirect assets or, if necessary, have a surge capability to provide seamless CSS to all levels of the AB.

The DASB supports the AB and the division cavalry squadron by providing or coordinating all classes of supply and maintenance. The DASB can function in a dispersed manner to support the division cavalry squadron or AB when they are operating forward. The DASB may attach aviation and ground maintenance teams and fueling assets forward to augment the FSB, who then provides area support to the division cavalry squadron. The DASB does not have any combat health support (CHS) capabilities. Based on mission, enemy, terrain, troops, time available, and civilians (METT-TC), combat health support is provided by either the DSB or FSB medical companies to the DASB, AB and division cavalry squadron. The DASB contains a headquarters and supply company (HSC), a ground maintenance company (GMC), and an aviation maintenance company (AMC). The DASB maintains one day of operational fuel requirements for the AB, division cavalry squadron, and the DASB.

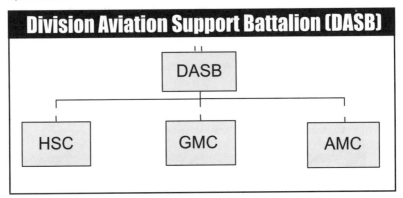

Ref: FM 4-93.52, fig. 1-3, p. 1-6.

The HSC consists of a battalion headquarters and a supply company. The battalion headquarters provides command, control and administration support for all organic and attached DASB units.

The battalion headquarters plans, directs and supervises support for the AB and division cavalry squadron. The supply platoon provides receipt, issue, and limited storage of Class II, III(P), IV, and IX (common and air) items in support of the AB and division cavalry squadron. It also receives and issues Class I and VI at the field ration issue point, and receives and issues Class VII as required. The supply platoon maintains the standard army retail supply system (SARSS-1) or global combat support system-Army (GCSS-Army). The Class III/V platoon provides bulk Class III and Class V support to its customers. It also operates a division rear aircraft refuel point for divisional and medical evacuation (MEDEVAC) aircraft. The company also provides food service support for units organic and attached to the DASB.

The GMC consists of a company headquarters, a battalion maintenance platoon and a direct support maintenance platoon. The GMC provides unit maintenance for all DASB non-air items and direct support maintenance for all AB, DASB and division cavalry squadron non- air items, including track, turret, missile, automotive, communications-electronics, engineer, utility, power generation, and small arms.

The AMC provides aviation intermediate maintenance to the division's aviation brigade, the division cavalry squadron, and corps medical aircraft operating in the division area. The AMC provides intermediate level avionics maintenance support, aircraft airframe, powerplant, armament, and component repair. The AMC's mobile maintenance support teams perform aviation intermediate maintenance (AVIM) forward, and provide forward repair/recovery teams that perform on-site technical assistance, and can also provide backup aircraft recovery, retrograde of repairable aviation equipment by ground, and coordination for air recovery backup and rigging capability for recovery of supported aircraft. The AMC provides maintenance test flight evaluator support to supported aviation unit maintenance (AVUM) units. The AMC will form a collection and classification point for aircraft peculiar materiel and provide fueling and defueling service for supported aircraft while in the AMC. This unit performs unit maintenance on all organic equipment, except communications-electronics (CE) and communications security equipment (COMSEC).

The DASB is dependent for medical support on the area support medical company of the division support battalion or the forward support medical company (FSMC) of the forward support battalion.

V. Forward Support Battalion (FSB)

Ref: FM 4-93.50 Tactics, Techniques, and Procedures for the Forward Support Battalion (Digitized), chap. 1 and 6.

The multi-functional FSB provides DS to the maneuver brigade. The FSB may function in a highly dispersed manner, with some FSB elements close to the maneuver units and others near the brigade rear area. The FSB commander is the brigade commander's battle logistician and serves as the single CSS operator for support to the maneuver brigade. His battle staff monitors and manages sustainment operations through an array of digital information systems and other technological innovations.

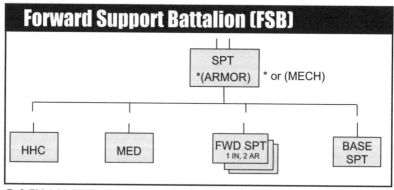

Forward Support Battalion (FSB)

SPT
*(ARMOR)   * or (MECH)

HHC   MED   FWD SPT
1 IN, 2 AR   BASE SPT

Ref: FM 4-93.50, fig. 1-1, p. 1-4.

The FSB provides all logistical support, and ties together the entire spectrum of supplies, maintenance, and services for the maneuver brigade. The maneuver commander, however, while "unencumbered", must be involved in synchronizing the maneuver of the FSB and its subordinate companies with the inbound shipments from EAD. For the Force XXI brigade, all CSS, for maneuver and engineer units, has been consolidated into the new FSB design. The FSB places a single smaller footprint on the battlefield through dispersion and centralization of services and support. This FSB, with centralized distribution management of CSS, frees the maneuver brigade commander from complex logistical support and task organization decisions. This provides him greater flexibility and mobility. The FSB contains forward support companies (FSCs), a brigade support company (BSC), a forward support medical company (FSMC), and a headquarters and distribution company (HDC). The FSC provides multi-functional support, both organizational and DS, directly to a maneuver battalion task force (BN/TF). The BSC provides maintenance support, both organizational and DS, directly to the maneuver brigade. This includes the engineer battalion, brigade HHC, and the brigade cavalry troop (BCT) and DS only maintenance support to the artillery battalion. It also provides limited reinforcing/back-up support to the FSCs. The FSMC provides echelons I and II CHS, to include sick call, advanced trauma management, limited laboratory and x-ray, dental treatment, combat stress control, preventive medicine, patient holding, and medical evaluation within the FSB support area. Corps maintenance plugs may augment the FSB in order to provide back-up support capability forward.

The maneuver brigade S4 identifies the logistics requirements for the brigade maneuver plan and provides them to the FSB commander. The use of assured communications, digitization of all CSS echelons, digitization of battlefield distribution (BD) platforms, and lastly, modular organizational structures, provides the FSB commander and brigade S4 the information dominance and digital tools needed to tailor the CSS package. Through near real-time situational understanding, the brigade battle staff is able to make timely adjustments in its support requirements. The use of enablers on the battlefield allows the FSB battle staff to anticipate changes in requirements and rapidly redirect assets or, if necessary, have a surge capability to provide seamless CSS to all levels of the maneuver brigade.

The FSB provides CSS to the supported maneuver brigade. The FSB's FSCs provide CSS (less medical) to their supported maneuver BN/TF. The FSC commander is the single CSS operator for the BN/TF. The FSC is in DS to the BN/TF, emplaced by the maneuver battalion commander and employed by the FSB commander. Support includes all classes of supply, field feeding and field maintenance (organizational/DS). The maneuver BN/TF provides Echelon I medical support to their supporting FSC. The FSCs locate, based on METT-TC, four to twelve kilometers behind their supported maneuver BN/TF in the task force support area (TFSA). The maneuver unit company supply sergeants are located in the TFSA. They assemble their logistics packages, (LOGPACS) and then move their vehicles forward to the company logistics release point (LRP). The maneuver company first sergeant (1SG) or his representative meets the LOGPAC and guides it to the company resupply point. The FSCs co-locate a support operations cell with the maneuver BN/TF S1/S4 at the Combat Trains Command Post (CTCP) to facilitate coordination, planning, and interface. The CTCP is located one to four kilometers behind the BN/TF in the maneuver BN/TF combat trains. Based on METT-TC, the FSC has the flexibility to locate the Unit Maintenance Collection Point (UMCP), recovery, immediate resupply of Class III and V, and other assets from the TFSA in this FSC forward location. The maneuver battalions will normally collocate their Battalion Aid Stations (BAS) with the FSC forward for force protection. Combat repair teams (CRTs) from the FSCs are placed forward with each maneuver company under the operational control of the maneuver 1SG.

The BSC provides field maintenance to elements within the brigade rear, FSB units in the BSA, the engineer battalion in support of the maneuver brigade, brigade recon troop (BRT), the brigade headquarters, and limited back up and reinforcing support to the FSCs. The HDC provides all classes of supply, minus VIII for brigade units not supported by one of the FSCs. The FSB collocated with the brigade S1/S4 in the administrative and logistics operations center (ALOC) is located in the brigade support area (BSA).

The FSB provides medical (Echelon II), maintenance, supply, and transportation support to the maneuver brigade. In the BSA the FSB includes the HDC, an FSB support operations center, the BSC, and the FSMC. Based on the tactical situation and CSS support requirements, the HDC/BSC may be tasked by the FSB support operations to organize a tailored forward logistics element (FLE) to push critical supplies forward to a designated unit or location, such as the brigade recon troop (BRT) or the brigade tactical operations center (TOC). Another option or tool available to the FSB to support the engineer battalion, brigade TOC, and brigade recon troop is to establish a brigade forward support area (BFSA). This places another logistical node forward of the BSA to employ modular support such as the engineer support element, forward repair platoon elements, M88 recovery capability, and critical assets such as Class III and V closer to support the maneuver brigade. Corps plugs working in the brigade area of operation can also work from the BFSA.

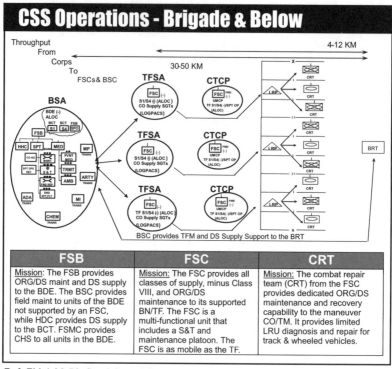

CSS Operations - Brigade & Below

FSB	FSC	CRT
Mission: The FSB provides ORG/DS maint and DS supply to the BDE. The BSC provides field maint to units of the BDE not supported by an FSC, while HDC provides DS supply to the BCT. FSMC provides CHS to all units in the BDE.	**Mission:** The FSC provides all classes of supply, minus Class VIII, and ORG/DS maintenance to its supported BN/TF. The FSC is a multi-functional unit that includes a S&T and maintenance platoon. The FSC is as mobile as the TF.	**Mission:** The combat repair team (CRT) from the FSC provides dedicated ORG/DS maintenance and recovery capability to the maneuver CO/TM. It provides limited LRU diagnosis and repair for track & wheeled vehicles.

Ref: FM 4-93.50, fig. 1-3, p. 1-8.

The FSB TOC, under the supervision of the FSB commander, anticipates, requests, coordinates, and integrates CSS for the tactical mission. The brigade S4 assists the FSB commander and his battle staff by providing in-depth analysis of the maneuver plan and the CSS requirements inherent to that plan. The FSB TOC has the capacity to pass CSS information using Force XXI battle command brigade and below (FBCB2), the movement tracking system (MTS), and the combat service support control system (CSSCS). The FSB TOC will receive information from the brigade TAC; brigade TOC, the BN/TF TOCs, TFSAs, and CTCPs. The CSS functionality on the FBCB2 system gives the war fighter a clear picture of the current CSS situation at his echelon of command and at subordinate levels for operational planning and execution. The FBCB2 also provides the logistician a better overall tactical view and CSS situational understanding throughout the battlefield. The FBCB2 common operating picture of the tactical and logistics picture in near real time allows the FSB to provide synchronized support to the maneuver brigade. The CSS functionality on FBCB2 provides logistical messaging, situational understanding, and task management capabilities.

Battalion-Level Support Trains

Ref: CGSC ST 63-1, pp. 3-19 to 3-22

Trains are any grouping of personnel, vehicles, and equipment organized to provide CSS at company team and battalion level. Trains may be centralized in one location (unit trains), or they may be echeloned in two or more locations. Under AOE doctrine, there are three types of trains—unit trains, combat trains, and field trains.

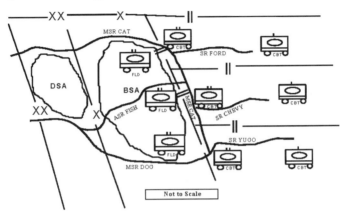

Unit Trains

Unit trains consist of all battalion logistics assets, including company team assets, and any supporting assets from higher HQ. Unit trains are common in assembly areas (AAs) and during extended tactical marches. Once combat operations begin, the battalion commander, based on the tactical situation, will either keep all logistics assets in one location as a unit train or echelon logistics forward.

Combat Trains

Combat trains are organized at company and battalion levels to support combat operations.

- **Company Combat Trains**. The 1SG controls the company combat trains that normally consist of medical and maintenance teams. The rest of the company logistics assets (supply section) will be at either the battalion field trains or combat trains. The company combat trains will normally operate about 500 to 1,000 meters (or one terrain feature) to the company's rear to provide immediate recovery, medical aid, and maintenance.

- **Battalion Combat Trains**. The battalion supply officer (S4) controls the battalion combat trains. They normally consist of a command post (CP), limited amounts of Class III and V (for emergency resupply), medical platoon elements (BASs), and elements of the maintenance platoon at the UMCP. A MST from the FSB may also be located at the UMCP. The battalion combat trains should be close enough to the front lines to be responsive to the forward units but not within range of enemy direct fire. Normally, this distance is 4 to 8 km behind the most forward company.

Battalion Field Trains

Battalion field trains consist of those remaining logistics resources not required for the combat element's immediate or critical support. The HHC commander controls the field trains, and they are usually located in the brigade support area (BSA). This may be 20 - 25 km behind the TF cbt trains in the offense and 20 - 40 km in the defense.

Forward Support Company (FSC)

Ref: FM 4-93.50, chap. 6.

The FSC commander is the single CSS operator for the maneuver BN/TF. The FSC commander is responsible for executing the CSS plan in accordance with maneuver commander's guidance. The FSC commander responds directly to the Bn/TF XO who serves as the Bn/TF CSS integrator and assists the Bn/TF S4 in CSS synchronization and troubleshooting. The FSC is DS to the maneuver BN/TF and must regularly must interface with the FSB in order to provide CSS support to the Bn/TF. The FSC provides field maintenance and all classes of supply, less medical, to its supported BN/TF. The maneuver BN/TF provides Echelon I medical care to its supporting FSC. The FSCs accomplish their core functions through centralization of support. Centralization of support provides an increased efficiency and effectiveness in the flow of support and supplies. Centralized support allows the FSB commander to cross-level between FSCs and weight the battle logistically, or surge, as required. Centralization of support is enhanced through the employment of FBCB2 and CSSCS. The FSC has the capability to command, control, and integrate attached units such as engineer support teams or teams from Corps assets. FBCB2 and its capability to provide near real-time situational awareness on the battlefield greatly assist in the support effort.

Forward Support Company

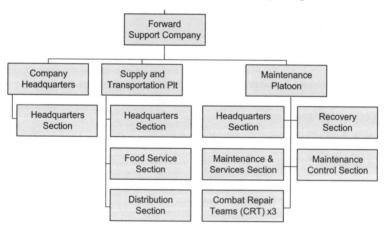

Ref: FM 4-93.50, fig. 6-2, p. 6-3.

The FSC is a multi-functional unit that includes an S&T platoon and a maintenance platoon organized to provide habitual support to a maneuver Bn/TF. The FSC is as mobile as the unit it supports. This mobility provides greater flexibility for the maneuver commander. The FSCs locate, based on METT-TC, four to twelve kilometers behind their supported maneuver BN/TF in the task force support area (TFSA). The maneuver unit company supply sergeants and Bn/TF HHC XO are located in the TFSA. They assemble their logistics packages (LOGPACS) and then move their vehicles forward to the company logistics release point (LRP). The company first sergeant (1SG) or his representative meets the LOGPAC and guides it to the company resupply point. The HHC XO provides operational liaison, support and advice to the FSC commander.

The FSCs co-locate a support operations cell with the maneuver BN/TF S1/S4 at the Combat Trains Command Post (CTCP). The CTCP is located within the FSC forward location, one to four kilometers behind the BN/TF. Based on METT-TC, the FSC has the flexibility to locate the unit maintenance collection point (UMCP), recovery, emergencies re-supply of Class III and V, and other assets from the TFSA in this FSC forward location. The maneuver units will normally locate their Battalion Aid Station (BAS) within the combat trains location for force protection and proximity considerations. Combat repair teams (CRTs) from the FSCs are placed forward with each maneuver company under the control of the maneuver 1SG. The maneuver 1SG also has under his operational control the combat medical team (CMT) with track ambulance capability. Casualties are evacuated by track ambulance to the casualty collection point (CCP), consolidated, and further evacuated back to an ambulance exchange point (AXP).

FSC Doctrinal Template

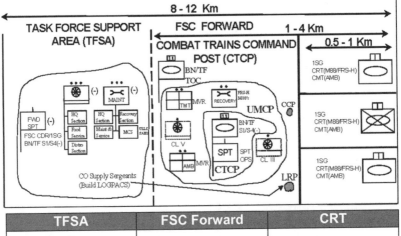

TFSA	FSC Forward	CRT
Mission: The FSC(-) provides all classes of supply, minus Class VIII, and field maintenance (ORG/DS) to its supported BN/TF. The FSC is a multi-functional unit that includes a S&T and maintenance platoon. The FSC is as mobile as the TF.	Mission: The FSC Forward develops logistical forecasts at the CTCP (FSC SPT OPS/BN S4). This management function forward plus situational awareness equals precision logistics. Assets placed forward are tailored based on METT-TC.	Mission: The CRT from the FSC provides field maintenance (ORG/DS) and recovery capability to the CO/TM. It provides limited LRU diagnosis and repair for track & wheeled vehicles. CRT OPCON to the CO/TM 1SG.

Ref: FM 4-93.50, fig. 6-1, p. 6-2.

The FSC depends upon the following (list not all-inclusive):
- The FSB support operations section for situational awareness, integrated materiel management, movement, maintenance, and distribution management direction
- The FSB and/or TF S2 for intelligence
- TF S1/S4 for common tactical picture and supported unit/echelon CSS situational awareness
- The BSC or EAB for resupply assets to maintain the required quantity of materiel for push forward to the supported battalion
- Fuel delivery twice a day; all other supplies are daily or as required (METT-TC)
- The FSMC, FSB, for combat health support and patient evacuation
- The HDC for water distribution to the FSC

CSS Support/Operating Areas

Ref: FM 4-93.52, FM 63-3, FM 63-2 and CGSC ST 63-1.

Communications Zone (COMMZ)

Rear part of theater of operations (behind but continuous to the combat zone) that contains the lines of communications, establishments for supply and evacuation, and other agencies for the immediate support and maintenance of the field forces.

Rear Area

(DOD) For any particular command, the area extending forward from its rear boundary to the rear of the area assigned to the next lower level of command. This area is provided primarily for the performance of support functions. [Note: Army adds, "… and is where the majority of the echelon's sustaining functions occur."]. See also brigade support area; division support area. See FM 3-0.

Division Support Area (DSA)

The division support area is that portion of the division rear occupied by the DISCOM and division rear command posts and many of the units organic and attached to the DISCOM. This area may also contain combat support units and COSCOM elements operating in support of the division. The DISCOM commander is the DSA commander. The division rear CP normally collocates with the DISCOM CP. This is done to help with coordination, share area communication assets, and draw life support and security.

The DSA is normally between the division rear boundary and the BSAs and next to air-landing facilities and the MSR. The precise location of the DSA is contingent on a number of factors. Some of the major factors are the tactical plans, the location of COSCOM installations, and the MSRs. The terrain in the area of operations, security, and access to lines of communication must also be considered.

Brigade Support Area (BSA)

A designated area in which combat service support elements from division support command and corps support command provide logistic support to a brigade. (FMs 3-21.30 and 7-30).

Task Force Support Area (TFSA) and Company Trains Collection Point (CTCP)

Forward Support Company (FSC) operations and support areas are depicted on pp. 3-16 and 3-17. Battalion-level support trains are described on p. 3-15.

Forward Arming and Refueling Point (FARP)

(DOD) – A temporary facility – organized, equipped, and deployed by an aviation commander, and normally located in the main battle area closer to the area where operations are being conducted than the aviation unit's combat service support area – to provide fuel and ammunition necessary for the employment of aviation maneuver units in combat. The forward arming and refueling point permits combat aircraft to rapidly refuel and rearm simultaneously. (FMs 3-04.111 and 1-111).

Rearm, Refuel, and Resupply Point (R3P)

A designated point through which a unit passes where it receives fuel, ammunition, and other necessary supplies to continue operations. (FM 3-09.5/6-50).

Note: Ammunition Support Areas (TSA, CSA, ASP, ATP) can be found on p. 1-64.

Chap 3

(FXXI) Tactical-Level CSS Operations

III. Arming the Force

Ref: The information in this section is derived from ST 101-6, FM 4-30.13, and FM 4-93.52.

Note: See pp. 1-63 to 1-64 for additional information on ordnance ops (FM 4-0).

Providing the required quantity and type of ammunition to the combat user at the time and place it is needed requires a responsive and flexible ammunition supply system. MOADS/PLS provides flexibility through rapidly moving ammunition, fewer ammunition transfers, and using missionconfigured loads (MCLs). MOADS/PLS requires fewer soldiers, less equipment, and allows for ITV of munitions stocks.

In addition to these combat users, other units may receive ammunition support on an area basis from the ammunition supply activity (ASA) [e.g., ammunition supply point (ASP) or corps storage area (CSA)] or ATP closest to the unit. Other units operating in the division rear area receive ammunition support on an area basis from either a DS ammunition company ATP or ASP unless the division directs otherwise. The ASP can support units directly and directly ship selected items to the ATPs. GS companies that operate CSAs in the corps rear provide GS ammunition support.

CSS Ops

I. Ammunition Transfer Point (ATP)

The ATPs act mainly as a temporary distribution point, conveniently located to facilitate rapid issues to users. The Taps are operated by the HDC (FSB) for the maneuver brigades and the HSC (DASB) for the aviation brigade and division cavalry squadron. The rear ATP, when utilized, is located vicinity of the DSA. It is established and operated by the corps DS ammunition company. The rear ATP is responsible for providing Class V support to divisional and non-divisional assets located in the division rear. One DAO representative will be located at each ATP. The ATP will be used when forward deliveries are not required. Units that are directed to pickup ammunition from the ATP will follow the normal request procedures outlined above, and will also prepare a DA Form 581 to be sent to the DAO representative at the ATP. The requesting unit will submit the DA Form 581 through the BN/TF S4 who will approve the request and either forward it to the brigade S4, or have the unit hand carry it to the brigade S4 for approval. The DAO representative will confirm the request through the DAO prior to issue. If the unit has PLS, it will be directed to the appropriate "rack" to be picked up. If the unit requires "break bulk" issue, the ATP section will issue based upon the DA Form 3161 provided by the DAO representative. Coordination on the location, amount, and type of ammunition (MCLs) to be received at the ATP will be made via the FBCB2 free text among the DAO, COSCOM support operations office, and the respective support operations officer based on guidance from the DISCOM commander, division G4, and G3. Ammunition will be delivered on flat racks by corps transportation assets using PLS trucks and trailers. The ATP personnel will interrogate RFID tags of arriving PLS shipments to gain immediate visibility of the shipment and enable it to quickly identify the organization it is to be issued to. Units arrive at the ATP to pick up ammunition, drop off empty or partially empty ammunition flat racks and retrieves fully loaded flat racks. The ATP personnel will interrogate RFID tags of arriving PLS shipments to gain immediate visibility of the shipment and enable it to immediately identify the organization to which it is to be issued. The ATP personnel will assist units PLS in transloading ammunition. The ATP section will reconfigure loads to meet mission requirements on a limited basis only. The flat racks will normally be issued as shipped. If partially empty flat racks are returned and the returned ammunition is required within the brigade, the ATP section may consolidate the ammunition from the partially empty flat racks and make full loads for issue within the brigade. All empty flat racks will be shipped back to the ASP or CSA as soon as possible. The DAO representative will report all issues and turn-ins. The corps transportation assets used to deliver ammunition resupply will pick up the unit turn-ins for immediate retrograde. When time and equipment permits, the DAO representative will attach RFID tags to the retrograde shipments. The MTS will track the ammunition returns as they are retrograded to the rear. The MTS provides the ability to redirect the shipment if needed. The ATP will maintain only those limited ammunition stocks that they can transport.

II. Ammunition Supply Point (ASP)

The ASP is located in the vicinity of the DSA, but is non-organic to the division and is run by corps assets. The ASP is run by the corps DS ammunition company and provides support to the Taps in the division and also serves as an alternative source of Class V to units not supported by an ATP.

III. Division Ammunition Officer (DAO)

The DAO is responsible for ammunition resupply for all units operating in the division AO and represents the DISCOM commander and DMMC on all ammunition-related matters. The DAO has the following five broad missions:

- Consolidating division ammunition requirements
- Preparing plans and procedures for ammunition operations
- Maintaining ammunition stock records and reports using the SAAS-MOD
- Planning, coordinating, and conducting division ammunition operations
- Validating ammunition requests

The DAO operates from the DMMC where he can oversee the division's Class V support missions. The DAO maintains constant communication with the customers, MSC staffs, CMMC, and COSCOM; ASAs supporting the division; and ATPs while coordinating ATP operations/Class V resupply for corps and division units. This communications capability and knowledge of planned and current operations enables the DAO to anticipate supported units' ammunition consumption and then coordinate issues or resupply.

The MSC S4 consolidates requests for ammunition and forwards them to the DAO. Depending on SOP, the maneuver brigade S4 may route the request through the supporting FSB to the DAO. The division G3 informs the DAO of planned operations, unit priorities, and unit RSRs. The DAO then coordinates with the CMMC for the required or allocated ammunition to be shipped to the designated ATP for the using unit to pick up. The DAO notifies the ATP representative and MSC S4s of inbound ammunition shipments. The MSC S4s must notify subordinate units when and where to pick up ammunition. Based on the division commander's concept of the operation, the DAO specifies which units (division, corps, or other) each ATP supports. The DAO also recommends locations for the ATPs to the organizations responsible for their positioning.

In some situations, the DAO may designate an ASP instead of an ATP to provide more responsive ammunition resupply to units operating in the division rear. Upon receiving the issue, the users may configure the ammunition into appropriate LOGPACs for movement forward to combat units. During defensive operations, the DAO will coordinate for the delivery of munitions barrier material (mines and demolition materials) directly to an ESP near the emplacement site.

Class V Control Procedures

Ref: FM 4-30.13.

Ammunition Supply Rates

The procedures used to control ammunition consumption are the required supply rate (RSR) and controlled supply rate (CSR). The Standard Army Ammunition System—Modernization (SAAS-MOD) is the management information system used to support these control procedures.

1. Required Supply Rate (RSR)

The RSR is the amount of ammunition a maneuver commander needs to sustain tactical operations, without restrictions, over a specified time period or for a specific mission. The RSR is expressed as rounds per weapon per day or, for selected items such as mines or demolition materials, as a bulk allotment per day or per mission. As the threat or mission changes, RSRs should change to reflect revised ammunition expenditure estimates. Maneuver commanders develop RSRs and submit them to the next higher HQ through operations channels. Each HQ reviews, adjusts, and consolidates RSRs and forwards them through operations channels. At the HQ that has ammunition management responsibilities, normally at TA/ASCC level, the total ammunition requirements are compared against total ammunition resupply capabilities for that period. If there is a shortfall in capability, a CSR will be established.

2. Controlled Supply Rate (CSR)

The CSR is that amount of ammunition that can be allocated based on the availability of ammunition types or quantities, Class V storage facilities, and transportation assets over a specific time period. The CSR is expressed in the same terms as the RSR. Commanders should use CSRs to allocate or prioritize the ammunition flow to units engaged in combat and to units held in reserve. They could also withhold some ammunition, especially high-lethality, low-density ammunition, to meet unforeseen requirements.

Ammunition Basic Loads (ABLs)

ABLs originate with a tactical force's planned deployment. An ABL is that quantity of ammunition either allocated to or issued to a unit [depending on the MACOM's policy] to sustain its operations in combat until it can be resupplied.

Basic load requirements are based on unit weapon density and mission requirements and are designed to meet a unit's anticipated initial combat needs. Units must be able to transport ABLs in one lift on organic weapon systems, equipment, and unit personnel. An ABL is normally expressed in rounds per weapon but may be expressed IAW MACOM policy as a number of required combat loads (example: battalion loads for artillery systems). The following factors influence ABLs:

- Nature of the enemy threat
- Type of mission
- Intensity of engagement
- Resupply transport availability
- Ammunition availability
- Number and types of weapons in unit

Lift Capability

Ammunition units' capabilities are measured in lift. A lift uses MHE to pick up ammunition and set it down, with each pickup and set down constituting one lift. A lift is measured in short tons (STONs) (2,000 pounds). Ammunition units' expressed lift capabilities are limited by personnel and MHE availability.

Class V / Distribution (FXXI)

Ref: FM 4-93.52, fig. 5-3, p. 5-6.

The division operates four ATPs. These are usually arrayed to support one maneuver brigade each and one to support the aviation brigade and division cavalry squadron. A DAO representative manages each ATP. In addition to the division ATPs, the corps DS ammunition company establishes an ATP, which provides Class V, support to divisional and non-divisional troops in the division area. The corps DS ammunition company also operates an ASP to provide support to the ATPs in the division and as an alternative source of Class V to units not supported by an ATP. Both the ASP and rear ATP are corps assets.

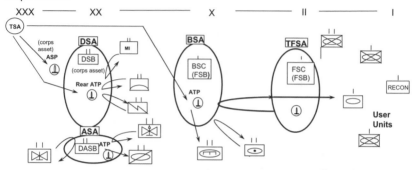

ASP/Rear ATP	ATP	Ammo NCO
Mission: The ASP and the Rear ATP are Corps assets located in or around the division rear. The ATP provides Class V support to units operating in the division rear. The ASP provides support to ATPs in the division and is an alternate source of Class V to units not supported by an ATP.	**Mission:** The ATP in the BSC of the FSB provides Class V support to units in the brigade area/brigade recon. The ATP in the HSC of the DASB provides Class V support to the Div Cav Sqdn and Avn Bde.	**Mission:** One 55B is assigned to each FSC to account for ammo at the site and ensure the correct number of transportation assets are sent to the ATP to pick up ammo.

1. Unit Level Ammunition Status Reporting

Using the LOGSITREP, unit ammunition on-hand status is reported per unit SOP to the 1SG, with information copies going to the company commander. The 1SG consolidates the unit's on-hand quantities and forwards them via the LOGSITREP to the BN/TF S4, with information copies to the BN/TF commander and S3. Company commanders will indicate in their LOGSITREP remarks any critical ammunition shortages or forecasted changes in ammunition requirements. At the discretion of the CO/TM cdr cross leveling on-hand ammunition within platoons or throughout the company is accomplished.

2. Determining/Requesting Battalion Ammununition Requirements

The BN/TF S4 will determine ammunition resupply requirements based on information provided in the LOGSITREP and guidance received from the battalion commander and S3. The BN/TF S4 will consolidate the entire battalion ammunition requirement. He will then submit company roll-ups for ammunition resupply through the LOGSITREP to the brigade S4. The brigade S4 will consolidate the ammunition request and pass that request to the support operations officer located in the supporting FSB.

Units in the division rear submit their requests through the LOGSITREP or LOGSTAT to the support operations officer located in the DSB. The support operations officer for the FSB, DASB and DSB will request the ammunition support from the DAO.

The ATP, operated by the HDC in the FSB, is responsible for supporting all units located in the brigade rear that are assigned, attached, have established a support relationship, or as directed by the DISCOM commander. The rear ATP, operated by corps, is responsible for supporting all divisional and non-divisional units in the division rear.

The ATP is designed to provide the required lift and transload capability associated with high-volume and high tonnage. The support operations officer of the FSBs and DASB, in conjunction with the DAO NCO representative, will coordinate directly with those non-organic units that will be supported by the ATPs. The support operations officer/ DAO representative will consolidate their ammunition requirements, and their request for resupply will be "rolled-up" with the brigade's request. Ammunition and explosives will be accounted for and provided proper physical security at all times.

3. Ammunition Request Validation

The DAO validates the brigade's ammunition requests by comparing the amount of ammunition requested against the CSR and the on-hand stocks in the brigade's ATP, DASB ATP, and the rear ATP. The DAO will take into account the current mission posture, scheduled/future mission posture, and operational guidance. Once all of these factors have been considered, the DAO will either validate the request or adjust it to meet the situation. The DAO will then determine, based on mission enemy, terrain, troops, time available, civilians (METT-TC) and transportation availability, whether the ammunition resupply will be throughput to the unit's combat trains command post (CTCP) location or delivered to an ATP. Ammunition can be throughput to a cache (a storage location where corps transportation drops flatracks loaded with ammunition, the ammunition will be closer to the maneuver unit to reduce transit time) unless the tactical situation does not allow delivery that far forward. "Prep-fire" ammunition will be delivered as close to the batteries as possible to prevent the artillery ammunition carriers from having to up-load after the "prep-fire." The ammunition resupply requests and transportation requests are then sent to the COSCOM support operations office , with information copies to the brigade DAO representatives, and the brigade and battalion S4s. The brigade DAO representatives will notify the HDC ATP (FSBs), HSC ATP (DASB), or rear ATP section (run by corps) of any scheduled ammo deliveries.

4. Ammunition Resupply

The division support operations Class V section, using SAAS-MOD and recommenda- tions from the DAO, then determine whether the ammunition resupply will come from the ASP or the CSA. The DAO will use the CSSCS Class V Taps report to determine the ammunition status of the five Taps in the division. This information will determine if ammunition within the division can be cross-leveled to meet ammunition requirements. If the ammunition is coming from the ASP, the COSCOM support operations office cuts a MRO directing the ammunition shipment. If the ammunition needs to be brought forward from the CSA, the COSCOM support operations office will submit a request for ammunition resupply to the corps G4. Ammunition will arrive in theater in standard configured loads (SCL)s. The supporting activity, either the corps ASP in the division area or the CSA, will reconfigure the SCLs into mission configured loads (MCLs) prior to transportation asset arrival. The COSCOM support operations office will schedule transportation IAW priorities. The ASP is then notified of where and when transporta- tion will arrive by the COSCOM support operations office. After ammunition has been loaded, the RFID tags will be verified along with the correct cargo and destination. All ammunition shipments will be tracked through the movement tracking system (MTS). Delivery coordinates and time will be sent by CSSCS free text message to the receiving unit/activity, with information copies furnished to the DAO, brigade S4, brigade DAO representative, the BN/TF S4, and respective FSB/DASB/DSB support operations. In the event an ammunition shipment needs to be diverted within the brigade, the brigade commander or designated representative will retain the sole authority to do so. Ammunition shipments that need be diverted within the division will be directed by the DISCOM commander or designated representative.

IV. The Corps Materiel Management Center (CMMC)

The CMMC's missile and munitions division interfaces with the DAOs and MSC G4/S4s to coordinate ammunition support within the corps. The CMMC performs the following ammunition support functions:

- Approves stockage objectives for CSAs/ASPs
- Reviews RSRs and recommends CSRs to the corps staff
- Processes unit requisitions
- Directs ammunition distribution in the corps based on stockage levels and unit requisitions
- Coordinates with the corps movement control center (CMCC) to integrate daily ammunition distribution requirements into corps transportation missions
- Coordinates with the theater army MMC (TSCMMC) and/or national inventory control point (NICP) to fill ammunition requirements
- Operates the SAAS-MOD to oversee ammunition assets on hand and in transit, and determines authorized levels for corps CSAs and ASPs

V. Mission-Configured Loads (MCLs)

Mission-configured loads (MCLs) are ammunition configured into complete round mixes/weapon system mixes to meet a specific theater of operations requirement. MCLs simplify planning and coordination for ammunition resupply by specifying a predetermined mix of ammunition designed to fit on a specific vehicle [PLS flatrack or stake and platform (S&P) trailer] and transported as a single load. Units request resupply by type and quantity of MCLs versus individual Department of Defense identification code (DODIC) requests. MCL use simplifies the requesting process and ensures all items necessary for a complete round (i.e., artillery projectile, primer, fuze, and propellant) or weapon system mix (i.e., 120mm HEAT, 120mm APFSDS-T, .50-cal, 7.62mm, and smoke grenades for the M1 tank) arrives at the unit at the same time. MOADS/PLS maximizes MCL use. Using MCLs does not preclude units from requesting resupplies of single DODICs.

MCL planning is done in peacetime to enhance wartime resupply coordination between the customers and the DAO and from the DAO to the CMMC. MSC S4s submit proposed MCL configurations to the DAO based on their type of unit, TF, or weapon system. The DAO reviews MCL submissions and submits a consolidated division MCL listing to the corps. The CMMC, in coordination with the corps staff, reviews all MCL requests and establishes a corps set of standard MCLs to support the corps maneuver units. Corps MCLs are then published in the corps SOP or applicable OPORD to standardize MCLs within the corps.

IV. Fueling the Force

Ref: Derived from ST 101-6 and FM 4-93.52, chap. 5.

Class III(B) is handled by the corps petroleum distribution system, along with 1/2 days of supply (DOS) of reinforcing bulk fuel support to the FSBs and DASB handled by the fuel platoon of the QM company in the DSB. The reinforcing fuel in the DSB provides capability for surge or pursuit and exploitation operations and it also is contingency in case the EAD fuel is interdicted. The Class III(B) and water supply branch of the general supply office in the division support operations controls and manages the supply of bulk fuels to division elements. It determines fuel requirements and recommends priorities, allocations, and other controls for bulk fuels.

The fuel platoon of the QM company (DSB) will provide receipt, limited storage, and issue of Class III(P) to the DSA, and reinforcing support to the FSB's and DASB. The distribution section of the supply and transportation platoon (HDC) is responsible for the receipt, issue, and delivery of Class III(P) to the BSA and FSC's. The distribution section of the supply and transportation platoon (FSC) is responsible for receipt, issue, and delivery of Class III(P) to the BN/TF. The distribution section of the supply platoon of the HSC in the DASB is responsible for receipt, issue and delivery of Class III(B) to the aviation brigade and division cavalry squadron.

Fuel status and requests are initiated at the platoon or company level, and reported daily to the 1SG using the LOGSITREP report in FBCB2. Information copies will be furnished to commanders at each echelon. The 1SG consolidates on-hand quantities and submits the fuel status report via FBCB2 to the BN/TF S4, with information copy to the FSC support operations section. The BN/TF S4 consolidates the fuel status report for the CO/TM and submits by company roll-up on hand quantities via FBCB2 to the brigade S4, with information copy to the FSC support operations. The brigade S4 consolidates the BN/TFs and brigade troops fuel status reports and submits the report to the FSB support operations via FBCB2, with information copy to the division G4 via CSSCS. The FSC and HDC using FBCB2, submits their bulk fuel status report to the FSB support operations section. The FSB support operations section consolidates the bulk fuel status reports for the brigade and slice elements, and submits it to the division support operations section using CSSCS. Units supported by the DSB submit their bulk fuel status reports to the DSB support operations using LOGSITREP or LOGSTAT. The DSB support operations consolidates the bulk fuel status report for the division troops and submits it to the division support operations using CSSCS. The DASB support operations consolidates the bulk fuel status report for the aviation brigade and division cavalry squadron and submits it to the division support operations using CSSCS. The division support operations uses the bulk fuel status reports and requirements from the FSBs, DSB and DASB to compute the Class III(B) requirements for the division. The division support operations submits the consolidated division requirements to the COSCOM support operations office using CSSCS, with information copy to the division G4.

The COSCOM resupplies the division with bulk fuel twice daily. It may be transported into the division by 5,000-gallon tanker, rail, or pipeline. The division support operations, with guidance from the G4, will coordinate the bulk fuel distribution into the division. Throughput will be maximized down to the lowest level. The preferred method of distribution is via logistics release point (LRP) operations as coordinated by the DSB, DASB, and FSB support operations.

Class III(B) Operations

Ref: FM 4-93.52, fig. 5-4, p. 5-10.

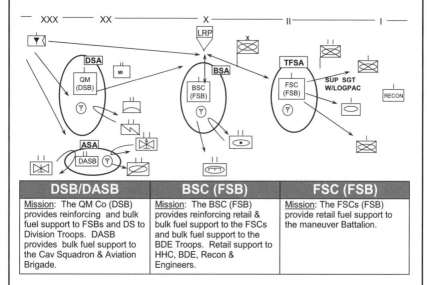

DSB/DASB	BSC (FSB)	FSC (FSB)
Mission: The QM Co (DSB) provides reinforcing and bulk fuel support to FSBs and DS to Division Troops. DASB provides bulk fuel support to the Cav Squadron & Aviation Brigade.	Mission: The BSC (FSB) provides reinforcing retail & bulk fuel support to the FSCs and bulk fuel support to the BDE Troops. Retail support to HHC, BDE, Recon & Engineers.	Mission: The FSCs (FSB) provide retail fuel support to the maneuver Battalion.

The QM company of the DSB provides DS to division troops and reinforcing support to the FSBs and DASB. The QM company provides supply point and unit distribution to the division troops, as determined by fuel consumption/distances/METT-TC. Preferred method of resupply is via LRP operations. The DASB HSC provides bulk refueling to the aviation brigade and the division cavalry squadron. Bulk fuel will be issued based on priorities established by the division G4 with guidance from the division commander. The FSB support operations is responsible for coordinating the resupply of bulk fuel to the FSC's and the HDC. The HDC provides direct support to the brigade troops and backup/reinforcing support to the FSCs. The FSC support operations and the BN/TF S4 will coordinate the refueling site and quantity of issue for the maneuver companies using FBCB2. Fuel HEMTT tankers located in FSC accomplish the tactical refueling operations for the maneuver companies.

Planning Fuel Sustainment Support

To support the movement and momentum of initial clashes, the COSCOM must push fuel forward and deep from the battle's very outset. Petroleum officers will preplan bulk fuel resupply. Plans will need to include uninterrupted fuel flow to joint or combined operational forces. The COSCOM support operations section ensures that the corps Class III(b) distribution plan agrees with the TA inland distribution plan for bulk fuel. The petroleum planner must consider time, space, distance, terrain, existing resources, scope of requirements, and operating environment. More specifically, he must consider:

- Number and types of fuel-consuming equipment that use motor gasoline (MOGAS), diesel, and JP-8
- Subordinate units' availability and capability to provide the required support
- Number and location of distribution points, including throughput distribution
- Transportation mode (pipeline, rail, barge, or truck)
- Type of terrain, time, and distance between units

V. Fixing the Force

Ref: FM 4-30.3 Maintenance Operations and Procedures; FM 4-93.52, chap. 5 and FM 4-93.53.

Note: See pp. 1-57 to 1-62 for additional information on maintenance operations (FM 4-0).

Maintenance is one of the 11 CSS functions that supports soldiers and their systems in the field. It sustains materiel in an operational status, restores it to serviceable condition, or upgrades its functional utility through modification or product improvement. The Army Maintenance System designates the scope of tasks performed by maintenance activities. It provides support planning requirements for maintenance of materiel systems when fielded and after fielding. It also establishes requirements for managing activities that physically perform maintenance.

Maintenance tasks include any action that retains or restores materiel to a fully mission-capable condition. Tasks range from simple preventive maintenance checks and services (PMCS) of equipment to complex depot operations performed in fixed shop facilities. The maintenance allocation chart remains the primary tool for assigning tasks.

Replace Forward

Replace Forward means a soldier performs "on-system" maintenance. "On-system" refers to replacing components or subcomponents at the point of repair, the breakdown site, or the UMCP. Maintainers normally diagnose down to the major component failure. They then replace that component and return the system to operational condition. Based on the METT-TC, the soldier may diagnose and replace subcomponent items depending on the availability of tools, parts, and time. An example of a replace function is the replacement of a full-up power pack (FUPP). If a serviceable FUPP is available, the maintainer replaces the major assembly.

Repair Rear

Repair Rear means that soldiers perform "off-system" maintenance. "Off-system" refers to those actions taken to return components and subcomponents of weapon systems to serviceable condition. These repair actions take place at designated places throughout the battlefield. Corps maintenance units may have the capability to repair certain LRUs or assemblies for major weapons systems they support. Corps component repair companies or special repair activities in the corps or theater area repair other components and assemblies as determined by sustainment maintenance managers (SMMs). An example of a repair function at the corps or theater level is the rebuild of a tank engine or other major assembly.

Anticipating future requirements allows prepositioning of maintenance support capabilities. Anticipation rests on the ability to foresee future operations and to identify, accumulate, and maintain the assets, capabilities, and information required to support them.

Leaders must tailor and position maintenance support to provide quick, mobile responses to changes in units and weapon systems. Maintenance managers must coordinate the best use of available resources to repair and return the maximum number of critical items. They must maintain close, consistent interaction between maintenance organizations and their SSAs to ensure quick access to repair parts. Support elements ust perform maintenance work as far forward as practical within the limitations of the METT-TC and the commander's priorities.

I. DISCOM Maintenance Section

The maintenance section of the division support operations manages maintenance. It designs and manages the maintenance functions that are generally external to DSB, DASB and FSBs. The section monitors unit maintenance throughout the division. It collects, analyzes, and reports maintenance statistics. It keeps records of the status of division equipment. The section also provides disposition instructions on all unserviceable materiel.

II. Division Support Bn (DSB)

The DSB area support maintenance company (ASMC) provides DS maintenance to division troop units not supported by the FSBs or DASB. Except for medical items, airdrop equipment, light textiles, and munitions, this company provides the following:

- Performs field level maintenance for itself and the DISCOM headquarters company
- Performs DS maintenance to all authorized divisional troop units' equipment
- Provides technical assistance to division troop units
- Provides modular DS maintenance teams forward in support of ADA, MI, signal, and FA (MLRS)
- Provides base shop maintenance for all divisional troops land combat and SHORAD missile/gun systems
- Performs quality assurance/quality control inspections
- Conducts technical assistance inspections when requested by user units
- Provides on-site repair for all missile systems not organic to the brigades

All requests for ASMC maintenance support are directed through the division support battalion (DSB) support operations section. The DSB support operations section receives the maintenance calls for support (CFS) then forwards the task orders (TO) to the ASMC MCS. The MCS forwards the task orders to the appropriate section or team who will perform the mission.

The ASMC manages organizational maintenance using ULLS-G. When unit level parts are required, the ASMC checks its PLL. If not available, ULLS-G forwards the request to the SARSS-1 site in the DSB Quartermaster (QM) company where the request is either filled or passed to the SARSS-2A site at the division support operations section. The SARSS-2A site checks divisional SSAs, and either issues the part or forwards the request to the COSCOM support operations office.

When DS level maintenance support is required, the supported unit sends a CFS to the DSB support operation section via FBCB2 or SINCGARS radio. The DSB support operations section sends a task order to the ASMC maintenance control section. The MCS dispatches appropriate maintenance personnel and equipment to link up with the supported unit at the predetermined place and time to diagnose/troubleshoot and repair the piece of equipment. If repairs cannot be made on-site, the inoperable piece of equipment is recovered to the ASMC MCP or other designated location.

The maintenance support team and base maintenance platoon order all required DS level repair parts on a DA Form 2407, maintenance request, which is then inputted into SAMS-1. The MCS issues those shop stock items that are available and orders the remaining parts through the SARSS-1 site in the DSB QM company. The MCS monitors inoperable equipment using its SAMS-1 computer system. In addition, the DSB support operations section and the maintenance section of the DISCOM support operations section use SAMS-2 to assist in both maintenance and readiness management.

Maintenance Levels (less aircraft)

Ref: FM 4-30.4, fig. 5-5, p. 5-20.

Level	Description
Unit	• Foundation of the maintenance system; requires continuous emphasis by commanders. • Repairs made by operator/crew as well as mechanics assigned to organization. • Operator/crew is cornerstone; they perform PMCS IAW applicable operator's series (-10 level) technical manual (TM). • TM 20-series PMCS tables used to perform scheduled PMCS services to sustain and extend combat-capable life of equipment. • Repairs on certain equipment completed by operator/maintainer. Operator performs checks, services, and maintenance prescribed in both -10 and -20 level TMs.
DS	• One-stop service to supported customers. • Highly mobile, weapon-system-oriented maintenance. • Backup support to unit-level maintenance. • Repair and return to the user. • Support provided to dedicated customers or on area basis.
GS	• Commodity-oriented repair of components and end items in support of theater supply system. • Backup maintenance support to DS units. • Job shop/bay or production line operations with capability to task/organize to meet special mission requirements. • Located at echelons above corps (EAC).
Depot	• Maintenance performed by tables of distribution and allowances (TDA) industrial-type activities operated by the Army. • Provides combat-ready materiel to the Army supply system. • Repairs and returns to wholesale supply system at national level or, by exception, to theater of operations. • Provides technical support and backup to DS and GS maintenance units. • In wartime, "warfighter Commander in Chief " (CINC) assumes control of depot-level maintenance operations in theater of operations.

Two-Level Maintenance System (FY06)

It is the Army's intent to transition to a two-level maintenance system beginning in fiscal year (FY) 06. Under a two-level maintenance system the unit and DS levels of maintenance will be combined (and called "field level") and the GS and depot levels will be combined (and be called "sustainment maintenance").

• **Field Maintenance.** Field maintenance actions typically involve replacement of Class IX components, on-system, for repair and return to echelon, and in deployable TOE units. These repairs will generally be performed by uniformed maintenance personnel at least through corps/joint task force (JTF) level.

• **Sustainment Maintenance.** Sustainment maintenance actions typically involve repair of reparable Class IX components, off-system, for return to the supply system. Sustainment maintenance will be performed at echelons above brigade (EAB), and perhaps eventually at echelons above division (EAD). Sustainment maintenance can be performed by uniformed maintenance personnel, Department of the Army (DA) civilians, or contractors. The decision as to whether or not to have sustainment maintenance includes detailed off-system inside-the-box repair of line replaceable units (LRUs) thru shop replacement unit (SRU) repair/replacement, engine/trans rebuilds, and the like.

III. Division Aviation Support Bn (DASB)

A. Aircraft Maintenance

The organization for Army aircraft maintenance consists of three levels:

1. Aviation Unit Maintenance (AVUM)

Units perform AVUM on their assigned aircraft. Company-sized aviation maintenance units perform primarily preventive maintenance tasks, unscheduled maintenance repair, and component/LRU) replacement functions associated with sustaining a high level of aircraft operational readiness. AVUM equates to unit/organizational and limited DS ground maintenance.

2. Aviation Intermediate Maintenance (AVIM)

Heavy DASBs, AVIM battalions, light division AVIM companies, and nondivisional AVIM units support AVUM units. This support includes all maintenance functions authorized at the AVUM level, plus intermediate levels of testing, repairing, and replacing selected items that cannot be accomplished at the AVUM level due to test, measurement, and diagnostic equipment; special tools; facilities; and expertise. AVIM equates to DS and GS ground maintenance. Doctrinal passback maintenance is the percent of the divisional AVIM workload that is "passed back" to the supporting corps AVIM battalion. All divisional TOEs are decremented to compensate for doctrinal maintenance passback, and the corps AVIM battalions are designed to accommodate it.

3. Depot

Depot-level maintenance for aircraft is not designed for field applications. It supports the "repair and return to the supply system" concept and includes maintenance that is above the AVIM level. Most depot-level aviation maintenance is performed in CONUS. There are a number of depot-level special repair activities (SRAs) located outside the continental United States (OCONUS) theaters of operations. These SRAs are limited in their depot capabilities and focus on mission equipment and exceptional items that economy and fleet-readiness dictate in theater depot-level repair. Civilian aerospace service contractors who interface with the corps-level AVIM units for component distribution and workload operate the SRAs.

Aviation Maintenance Company

The aviation maintenance company (AMC) is assigned to the DASB in the DISCOM. The company is structured to support the aircraft assigned to the division, specifically the observation, utility, and attack helicopters. The objective of aircraft maintenance is to ensure maximum availability of mission-capable aircraft. Aircraft maintenance provides maximum mission capability of total weapon systems through the accomplishment of maintenance where it can be most effectively and economically performed.

The AMC provides aviation intermediate maintenance (AVIM), located within the DASB, and performs extensive on-aircraft systems maintenance. This maintenance includes:

- Making structural and airframe repairs
- Repairing components for immediate reinstallation on aircraft or to support its organic reparable exchange program
- Performing scheduled AVIM-level inspections
- Serving as the next-level processing agency for aviation brigade (AB) supply transactions under an automated system

The AMC employs mobile; weapon system-oriented forward repair/recovery teams to perform authorized intermediate maintenance in the forward areas.

B. Ground Maintenance

The ground maintenance company provides unit maintenance for all DASB non-air items and direct support maintenance for aviation brigade/division cavalry squadron non-air items, including automotive, engineer, utility, power generation, C-E equipment, and small arms. Its mission is to provide support as far forward as possible to return ground combat systems to the battle rapidly. Repairing equipment forward saves transportation assets and time. Whenever practical, equipment repair should be done on site. The tactical situation, extent of damage, and availability of resources may require recovery and evacuation.

The cavalry system support team (CSST) is structured to support the division cavalry squadron. This team normally operates out of the cavalry squadron trains area. It is reinforced with other DISCOM elements as required. The teams repair capabilities include: automotive/tracked vehicles, armament/fire control systems, ground support equipment, and communications-electronics.

IV. Forward Support Bn (FSB)

The maintenance mission of the BSC is to provide field maintenance to the brigade HHC, the brigade reconnaissance troop, the FSB forward support medical company (FSMC), the headquarters and distribution company (HDC), and itself. It also provides limited back up maintenance to the forward support companies (FSCs) and divisional units in the brigade area. The BSC also provides direct support maintenance to FA units that are part of the brigade. To provide direct and habitual combat service support to a divisional engineer battalion, less class VIII and medical support. These functions include the following:

- Field maintenance (organizational and DS)
- Management of Class IX spares (PLL & shop stock)
- Providing all classes of supply to an engineer battalion

1. Base Maintenance Platoon, Brigade Support Company

The BSC base maintenance platoon provides field maintenance (organizational and direct support) to the HDC FSB, BSC, FSMC, HHC brigade, and brigade reconnaissance troop. It also provides DS maintenance support to other units operating in the brigade support area. The platoon performs and coordinates backup and reinforcing support to the FSC maintenance platoons and the ESE forward engineer repair teams. The goal of the "replace forward" concept is to repair systems forward on the battlefield returning combat systems to battle as rapidly as possible. The base maintenance platoon consists of the maintenance control section, automotive maintenance section, GSE repair section, and armament repair section

2. Forward Repair Platoon, Brigade Support Company

The forward repair platoon provides field maintenance to brigade and divisional units not supported by FSCs or the DSB on an area basis. The service and recovery section provides welding services and limited recovery/lift support. The missile/electronic maintenance support team provides land combat missile systems (LCMS) and communications/electronic maintenance support either forward on-site, or at the base shop as directed by the MCS. The artillery support section provides on-site DS level maintenance to the artillery battalion in support of the maneuver brigade. The wheel/track section is capable of providing contact (on-site) support to the brigade headquarters, brigade reconnaissance troop, engineer battalion, and reinforcing support to the FSCs as directed and also provides limited reinforcing and back up support to the FSCs.

3. Engineer Support Element (ESE)

The engineer support element (ESE) is a multi-functional unit that includes a food service section, a distribution section, and maintenance sections organized to provide habitual support to divisional engineer battalion. The new engineer support element is as mobile as the unit it supports. It is modular enough to be broken into three multi-functional engineer support teams (EST)s each capable of providing habitual combat service support to an engineer company. These ESTs can co-locate or be attached to maneuver FSCs that are in support of the battalion task force that the supported engineer company is in support of. The ESE can also consolidate all of the ESTs with the ESE headquarters and form a separate engineer task force support area based on METT-TC.

The base support company maintenance control section manages limited combat spares consisting of major assemblies and key combat system components. During combat operations, these combat spares are maintained by the engineer CRT, engineer support element and managed by the MCS.

4. Forward Support Company (FSC)

The FSC commander is the single CSS operator at the maneuver BN/TF level. The FSC provides field maintenance and all classes of supply, minus medical, to its supported BN/TF. The maneuver BN/TF provides level 1 medical support to their supporting FSC. The FSCs accomplish their core functions through centralization of support and new technologies. Centralization of support accomplishes the dual functions of providing the maneuver commander with greater mobility as well as increased efficiency and effectiveness in the flow of support and supplies. Centralized support allows the FSB commander to cross level between FSCs and weight the battle logistically, or surge, as required. Centralization of support is enhanced through employment of maturing technology available to the division logistician. The FBCB2 and its' capability to provide near real time situational understanding to all on the battlefield greatly assist in the support effort.

The FSC is a multi-functional unit that includes an S&T platoon and a maintenance platoon organized to provide habitual support to a maneuver battalion. This new FSC is as mobile as the unit it supports. This mobility provides greater flexibility for the maneuver commander. The FSCs locate, based on METT-TC, four to twelve kilometers behind their supported maneuver BN/TF in the task force support area (TFSA). The maneuver unit company supply sergeants are located in the TFSA. They assemble their logistics packages (LOGPACS) and then move their vehicles forward to the company logistics release point (LRP). The company first sergeant (1SG) or his representative meets the LOGPAC and guides it to the company resupply point.

The FSCs co-locate a support operations cell with the maneuver BN/TF S1/S4 at the combat trains' command post (CTCP). The CTCP is located within the FSC forward location, one to four kilometers behind the BN/TF. Based on METT-TC, the FSC has the flexibility to locate the unit maintenance collection point (UMCP), recovery, emergency re-supply of Class III and V, and other assets from the TFSA in this FSC forward location. The maneuver units will normally locate their treatment and ambulance sections within the FSC forward location for force protection and proximity considerations. Combat repair teams (CRTs) from the FSCs are placed forward with each maneuver company under the operational control of the maneuver 1SG. The maneuver 1SG also has under his operational control the combat medic track ambulance crew. Casualties are evacuated by track ambulance to the casualty collection point CCP consolidated and further evacuated back to the battalion aid station. The FSC is emplaced by the maneuver battalion commander and employed by the FSB commander.

Fix - Division XXI

Ref: FM 4-93.52, fig. 5-5, p. 5-20.

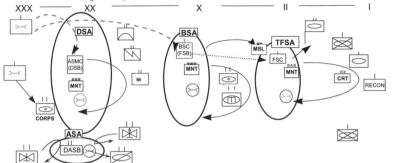

DSB/DASB	BSC (FSB)	FSC (FSB)
Mission: The ASMC (DSB) provides Unit and DS maintenance to itself and DISCOM HQ and DS to the Division Troops. The DASB provides DS/AVIM maintenance to the Cav Squadron and Unit/DS/AVIM maintenance to the Aviation Brigade.	**Mission:** The BSC (FSB) provides Unit and DS maintenance to the Bde HQ, Recon Troop, EN BN and FSB (-); area support to units within the BSA; reinforcing support to the FSCs. Engineer Support Platoon Combat Repair Teams (CRT) to Engineer Bn from BSC.	**Mission:** The FSCs (FSB) provide DS and Unit maintenance to itself and bn/TF; modularized DS and Unit maintenance to 3 COs.

The overarching principle of "replace forward/fix rear" remains unchanged. In the redesigned division some maintenance procedures and doctrinal methods are changed to gain greater effectiveness and efficiencies. Generally speaking, all DS and unit maintenance functions are consolidated in the FSB and are now called field maintenance. This applies to the mechanized and armor maneuver battalions, engineer battalions, brigade headquarters, division headquarters, and brigade reconnaissance troop. The division troops and field artillery retain their unit mainte-nance sections. Division troops are provided DS maintenance from either the base shop of the area support maintenance company of the DSB or maintenance support teams (MST)s organic to the DSB. The only exception is the artillery battalion supporting a maneuver brigade.

Maintenance Operations in the Offense

Offensive operations are characterized by fast movement and rapid changes in the situation. Command, control, and communications for the CSS effort are difficult. Maintenance elements normally operate as part of a larger CSS element, which reduces some of this difficulty.

Maintenance Operations in the Defense

The primary thrust of the maintenance effort in the defense is to maximize the number of combat-ready weapon systems. Once the defensive battle begins, the thrust is to fix the maximum number of inoperable systems and return them to the battle. This requires forward support at, or as near as possible to, the intended AO of the systems.

Recovery and Evacuation

On the Force XXI battlefield, mechanized, armor and engineer battalions will still remain responsible for operator and crew level maintenance. Operators/crews may perform BDAR through the use of onboard BDAR kits and will use self-recovery techniques to greatest extent possible.

CSS Ops

Repair Parts Supply Operations

Ref: FM 4-30.3, chap. 5.

The supply system includes the wholesale level, retail level, and unit level. Wholesale supplies are managed at the strategic management level, retail supplies are managed at the operational and tactical levels, and unit level supplies are managed at the unit level.

Prescribed Load List (PLL)

The PLL is a list of the authorized quantities of supplies required by a unit to do its daily unit maintenance. Units that are authorized personnel, tools, and equipment to perform maintenance maintain a prescribed load of repair parts. Units that regularly support other units without maintenance capabilities include the supported unit's equipment in their PLL computations. A PLL consists of repair parts and other stocks. The unit PLL consists of unit-level maintenance repair parts that are demandsupported (15 DOS), non-demand-supported, and specified initial stockage for newly introduced equipment.

Authorized Stockage List (ASL)

The ASL consists of those parts stocked in DS repair parts supply units for issue to user units and to support DS-level maintenance operations. The MMC, based on priorities established by the commander, will establish the guidelines for issue, ASL design, or distribution. The MMC is the common exit point for requisitions and other supply documents for the division.

Mandatory Parts Lists (MPLs)

MPLs, which are published as DA pamphlets, are used to standardize the combat PLLs. The MPL is the mandatory portion of the standardized combat PLL. Parts on the MPL must be on-hand or on order at all times.

Weapon System Replacement (WSRO)

Weapon System Replacement Operations (WSRO) is a management tool used to supply the Combat Commander with fully operational major weapon systems, including both the required equipment and trained crews. Procedures for issue of weapon systems differ from those for other Class VII items. Weapon systems replacement is managed at each level of command. Two terms often used to describe WSRO are ready-for-issue and ready-to-fight.

Operational Readiness Float (ORF)

ORF is a quantity of selected end items or major components of equipment authorized for stockage at CONUS installations and overseas support maintenance activities, which extends their capability to respond to materiel readiness requirements of supported activities. It is accomplished by providing supported units with serviceable replacements from ORF assets when their like items of equipment cannot be repaired or modified in time to meet operational requirements.

Controlled Exchange

Controlled exchange is the removal of serviceable parts, components, or assemblies from unserviceable, but economically reparable equipment and their immediate reuse in restoring a like item of equipment to combat operable or serviceable condition.

Cannibalzation

Cannibalization is the authorized removal of parts, components, or assemblies from economically non-repairable or disposable end items. Cannibalization supplements and supports the supply operation by providing assets not readily available through the normal supply system.

VI. Moving the Force

Ref: FM 4-01.11, Unit Movement Operations; FM 4-01.30, Movement Control; and FM 4-93.52, chap. 5.

Note: See pp. 1-51 to 1-56 for additional information on transportation support (FM 4-0), specifically terminal and mode operations, and chap. 5 for specific information on unit movement operations.

As the Armed Forces' principal land warfare component, the Army and the role that Army transportation provides is critical to the success of ground military operations. Once Army forces are introduced into an operation, the logistics distribution function significantly increases in importance. At the operational level of war, the senior tactical commander is responsible for distribution system development and, ultimately, for all transportation operations. This is normally the Army service component cdr (ASCC). At the tactical level, all transportation assets are designed to provide mvmt support for personnel and materiel from the operational terminals (SPODs and APODs) to the user level. These transportation ops are normally in DS of committed forces and characterized by habitual support relationships.

Generally within a theater of operation, the corps HQ is the smallest organization with all of its transportation elements organic to its force structure. If a smaller force is deployed, many transportation functions can meld within the senior Army HQ through ad hoc measures.

The transportation system is comprised of three distinct elements: mode operations (highway, rail, water, and air), terminal operations, and movement control. Of these elements, movement control is the most critical component of the system. A movement control system must coordinate the efforts of transportation modes, terminals, services, commands, contractors, and host nations during deployment, sustainment, and redeployment.

Movement Control Operations

Movement control is the planning, routing, scheduling, controlling, coordination, and in-transit visibility of personnel, units, equipment, and supplies moving over Line(s) of Communication (LOC) and the commitment of allocated transportation assets according to command planning directives. It is a continuum that involves synchronizing and integrating logistics efforts with other programs that span the spectrum of military operations.

Movement Control Functions

Movement control involves staff planning and movement regulation:

- Planning
- Allocating
- Routing
- Coordinating
- In-Transit Visibility (ITV)

Ref: FM 4-01.30, fig. 1-3, p. 1-4.

I. Brigade Transportation Operations

The brigade HQ has no separate transportation staff element and technically no transportation assets. Due to having no transportation assets in the FSB, supply point distribution is the normal method of logistics operations within the brigade. Most combat arms battalions' support platoons include an S&T section that has the only trucks and drivers in the brigade who support transportation requirements. This section's mission is to support the battalion's LOGPAC operations, and they are normally not available for additional missions. Other sections and units within the brigade do have organic vehicles they can use to support emergency and ad hoc transportation missions. Normally the unit's operations non-commissioned officer (NCO) or 1SG directly controls these ad hoc missions. Generally, the brigade depends on the DISCOM to provide transportation support other than normal LOGPAC and sustainment operations.

The brigade S4 is responsible for validating transportation requirements, including coordinating times and locations with battalion TF S4s, consolidating all requests, and submitting them to the FSB SPO. The brigade S4 ultimately controls all movement within the brigade rear area.

II. Division Transportation Operations

The DISCOM provides direct support CSS to the division. The foundation of this support is a single CSS operator providing unity of command and centralized distribution management at all echelons to meet the maneuver commander's intent. Under Force XXI operations, this doctrinal premise is dependent upon battlefield distribution, throughput to forward areas, and improved situational understanding through the application of enabling technologies.

Significant changes in division transportation operations under Force XXI operations include: an improved division transportation motor transport company design that replaces the M931 tractors/M871 trailer combinations with palletized load handling systems; merger of movements and materiel management at the DISCOM distribution management center; reliance on corps throughput for sustainment resupply; transportation assets forward in the supply & transportation platoons of the support companies (HDC and FSCs); and movement managers located in the FSB support operations to provide movement control and transportation coordination for the maneuver brigade.

To maximize division transportation capability, planners and operators must employ the Force XXI CSS integrating imperatives discussed below as the basis for all transportation operations.

First Destination Reporting Point (FDRP)

A first destination reporting point (FDRP) is normally established along a MSR at or near the division rear boundary. The FDRP is a point manned by a movement regulating team, a movement control team, or military police that diverts a driver and cargo to an alternate consignee or destination. Basically, FDRPs are logistical information checkpoints. The FDRPs support velocity management and situational understanding.

Even though the division is digitized, a FDRP is routinely required since many echelon above division (EAD) supporting units, host nation support, and/or contractors will be non-digitized. Either the division or an EAD unit can operate the FDRP. Optimally, both the division and supporting EAD headquarters have representatives located at the FDRP continuously. Security arrangements, command and control, and communications support must be addressed prior to FDRP establishment. Further amplification of FDRP operations can be included in unit SOPs.

Movement Control Operations

Ref: FM 4-01.30 Movement Control, chap. 1, 5 and 6.

Transportation Command Element (TCE)

The TCE provides guidance and technical assistance to the corps MCB. The TCE provides movement programs, policies, and procedures established by the Army Service Component Command (ASCC).

Corps Movement Control Battalion (CMCB)

The corps MCB controls the movement of all personnel, units, and materiel in the corps AO. It commands, controls, and supervises movement control teams.

Corps Provost Marshals and Military Police

The corps PMs and MPs integrate movement control and highway regulation plans into the MP battlefield circulation control plan. They provide traffic control on MSRs and enforce highway regulation plans.

Highway Traffic Section (HTS)

The HTS performs highway regulation within the corps area. It coordinates with the TCE, other MCB highway traffic sections, DTOs, and appropriate HN authority, for any mvmts that originate in the corps area, but which terminate outside the corps.

Movement Control Teams (MCTs)

MCTs are attached to MCBs in the theater to decentralize execution of movement responsibilities on an area basis or at essential transportation nodes. The various sizes and capabilities of the MCTs provide flexibility.

- **Area MCTs** perform movement control functions for movement of units, cargo, and personnel (except bulk POL by pipeline) within an assigned geographic area. Area MCTs validate transportation requirements, coordinate transportation support, highway clearance and inbound clearance for moving units, personnel, and cargo. They coordinatetransportation movements, diversions, reconsignments, and transfers of units, cargo and personnel.
- **Port MCTs** expedite, coordinate, and supervise, transportation support of units, cargo, and personnel into, through, and out of air or water ports (except bulk POL by pipeline). This team provides movement control functions at airport of debarkation or seaport of debarkation and small army operated air and sea terminals. The port MCT expedites the port clearance of cargo and personnel arriving or departing by air or sea.

Movement Regulating Teams (MRTs)

MRTs, with MP assistance, ensure that authorized traffic on corps-designated MSRs flows efficiently. MRTs operate at locations such as critical highway points, APODs, SPODs, trailer transfer points (TTPs), terminal transfer locations, first destination reporting points, and railheads. They report to the CMCB/MCT on vehicle and convoy movement along designated routes.

Division and Separate Brigade Transportation Officers

Division and separate brigade TOs coordinate with the corps MCB and the CSGs through the supporting CSG MCT to obtain transportation assets to meet division requirements beyond the division's organic capability. The Force XXI brigade includes a movement control NCO as the link between the brigade transportation mode operators and the brigade users of transportation.

Division Movement Control Officer (MCO)

The MCO is the link between the division transportation mode operators and the division users of transportation. The MCO is normally located with the DISCOM CP.

Some tasks performed at the FDRP include:

- Track location of critical supplies
- Perform movement control functions
- Provide instructions to convoys
- Provide and receive latest intelligence
- Reroute convoys/vehicles
- Provide information on routes and weather
- Establish division "light line" for blackout driving
- Linkup point for armed convoy escort vehicles

III. Corps Transportation Operations

The corps combines the operational and tactical levels of war. The corps will conduct numerous types of movements. The principal types will be unit movements and sustainment. All movements operating concurrently must be coordinated, ensuring a continuous flow of available transportation assets, infrastructure, and lines of communications (LOCs). Movement planning is conducted by the corps G3 and G4 staffs, MCB, and by the COSCOM support operations staff. On the corps coordinating staff, the G3 plans and directs maneuver and recommends corps priorities. The G4 recommends logistical support priorities in coordination with the CTO and COSCOM support operations staff. The CTO receives technical support from the MCB and the COSCOM transportation support branch.

The corps is the smallest Army HQ that has all of the organic transportation units assigned to provide the basic transportation functions of movement control, terminal operations, and mode operations without augmentation. One of the COSCOM's primary missions is to provide for the corps' integrated distribution system that predominately relies on ground LOCs in the form of MSRs with only limited airlift. The COSCOM relies on the CMCB and the transportation group to accomplish these distribution missions. Within the corps, the primary types of movement are unit movements and sustainment convoys. The CMCB provides for centralized movement control, while the transportation group provides for mode and terminal operations.

IV. Flatrack Management Operations

Flatracks offer tactical efficiencies that serve an increased pace of logistical operations and significantly alter the speed at which service support is provided to the warfighters. The key to sustaining these efficiencies and maintaining improved throughput velocity is flatrack employment, management, and retrograde proce-dures at each echelon of support. An increased battlespace depth and a reduction of CSS force structure challenge flatrack management and ultimately sustainment of combat power within the FXXI division area of operations. Flatrack management is a challenge that must be met in order to successfully sustain combat power on the FXXI battlefield.

Flatrack employment, management, and retrograde operations are the responsibility of distribution managers integrated at each echelon of support throughout the division area. Flatracks will be dispersed throughout the distribution pipeline, particularly from the division rear boundary to the combat trains' command post of a maneuver task force. It is imperative that stringent flatrack management procedures be implemented at the tactical level on an area basis.

Move - Division XXI

Ref: FM 4-93.52, fig. 5-6, p. 5-24.

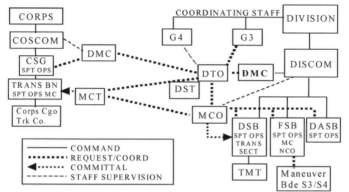

NOTE: DISCOM MCO ALSO COMMITS DIVISION AVIATION ASSETS ALLOCATED FOR CSS AIR MOVEMENT OPERATIONS

CSS Ops

Movement and maneuver of combat forces are normally given priority over other movements, even though CSS traffic is essential to the success of battles. Movements planning and execution in the division are staff responsibilities, rather than being vested in operational units found at corps and above. Transportation mode operators and movement control elements at division level manage the movement of non-committed units in the division area and require close coordination between the division's G3 and G4. The G3 plans and directs maneuver. The G4, through the division transportation officer, DISCOM distribution management center, and DISCOM MCO coordinates and controls division transportation operations.

The division G4 DTO is the primary advisor to the division commander, the coordinating-special-staff for transportation matters, and is the formal link between the division and corps. The DTO plans for movement of the division by all modes based on the division commander's guidance. The DTO develops and coordinates movement control and highway planning with division staff, the corps transportation officer (CTO), and division support movement control team (MCT) habitually supporting from corps. The division G3 prioritizes CSS movement and tactical maneuver missions in support of the division operation and the DTO incorporates these priorities into all movement planning. The DTO participates in the military decision making process as a member of the division planning staff and recommends the allocation of division transportation assets and establishment of MSRs.

The DISCOM MCO supports movement control through planning and controlling the tasking to the TMTC. The TMTC commander provides a current status of fleet availability to the MCO. The FSB, DASB, and DSB support operations sections, as well as separate companies and battalions supported by the DISCOM pass requests for movements to the MCO. The MCO balances the request to the availability of TMTC company assets, then assigns the mission to the TMTC.

The MCO coordinates with subordinate support operations movement/materiel managers to ensure delivery of sustainment resupplies to the correct location and integrates retrograde movement of equipment, flatracks, and personnel. Throughput distribution is the preferred method of delivering commodities and supplies to requesting supply support activities or to the user. Sustainment materiel delivered to the DSB, DASB, and FSB will normally be scheduled deliveries and synchronized with subordinate support operations sections and customer units.

Airlift / Air Resupply Support

Ref: FM 4-93.52, pp. 5-31 to 5-32.

Air Force Airlift/Resupply Support

The tactical commander obtains airlift support from the Air Force using the airlift request system established in the AO. The airlift is usually in the form of C-130 aircraft. Within the corps, three elements participate in this system. They are the corps G3 and the G4 (who use the CTO) and the CMCB. An Air Force liaison officer (LO) supports them. Joint Pub 4-01.1 describes the airlift request process.

Army Airlift/Resupply Support

The primary Army aviation unit is the Aviation Brigade. The Army AB is a versatile organization found at division, corps, and EAC. It may contain observation, attack, utility, and cargo helicopters and a limited number of fixed-wing C2 aircraft. Helicopters move high-priority cargo and personnel into areas not accessible by any other mode of transport. The corps G3 provides the missions and the priority of support for their use. The G3 coordinates with the corps G4 to provide for logistics requirements. The G3 allocates airframes to the COSCOM where the MCB enters them in the movement program. General helicopter CSS mission areas include:

Transition To War
- Self-deploy to area of operations
- Provide early in-theater transport
- Move priority cargo, weapons, ammo, POL and barrier material forward from ports/staging areas to establish supply points

Deep Battle
- Move troops, equipment, weapons systems, ammo, POL, priority supplies from rear to forward staging areas to support deep battle operations
- Deploy reinforcing units; evacuate wounded, recover battle-damaged equipment, and forward repositioning of artillery
- Covering Force And The Main Battle
- Support air assault units with rapid resupply of ammo and POL
- Augment reaction forces into blocking positions to contain enemy

Rear Battle
- Move forces and equipment to counter operations in rear
- Augment reaction forces into blocking positions to contain enemy

Combat Support
- Emplacement, repositioning, resupply of forward area refueling points (FARPs)
- Rapid repositioning of reinforcement troops, equipment, artillery etceteras
- Transport barrier materials, mines, bridging equipment for engineering support

Combat Service Support
- Provide logistical air transport of cargo from rear to as far forward as brigade rear areas meeting time sensitive and surge demands
- Deliver critical loads to areas not accessible by ground or Air Force airlift
- Employed to move priority cargo to overcome congestion and enemy inflicted gaps in transportation system

VII. Sustaining the Force

Ref: FM 10-27, General Supply in Theaters of Operations; FM 54-30, Corps Support Groups; FM 63-3, Corps Support Command; and FM 4-93.52, chap. 4 & 5.

Note: See pp. 1-43 to 1-50 for more information on supply and field service operations (FM 4-0) to include clases of supply.

Supplying the force is one of the major elements in logistically supporting the battle. It is the process of providing all items necessary to equip, maintain, and operate a unit. Supply operations involve storing, distributing, maintaining, and salvaging supplies. Its primary purpose is to sustain soldiers and weapon systems in strategic, operational, and tactical environments on the modern battlefield.

To be successful, supply support must be effective and efficient. Limited resources require that supply operations be efficient. However, efficiency cannot handicap effectiveness. Five logistics characteristics facilitate effective, efficient supply operations. Foremost among these is anticipation. Commanders and logisticians must anticipate requirements, and so must the supply system. They integrate supply concepts and operations with strategic, operational, and tactical plans. Supply operations and systems must be responsive to the commander and provide continuous support to forward-deployed forces. Finally, logisticians must improvise to expedite actions when required.

CSS Ops

The Strategic Level of Supply

At the strategic level, supply is largely the purview of the CONUS industrial and civilian sectors. National political and military leaders, as well as civilian and military suppliers and contractors, effectively combine their efforts to provision the force. This deals with mobilization, acquisition, force projection, mobility, and concentrating supply support in the theater base and the COMMZ. Strategic-level supply is the link between the nation's economic base and the military supply operations in a theater. Strategic and operational levels interface in a theater of operations.

The Operational Level of Supply

Operational-level supply focuses on sustainment, supply unit deployment, and distributing and managing supplies and materiel. Contractors and civilians provide support from within as well as outside the theater of operations. In theater, contractors and DOD civilians perform specified supply support functions. Deploying and integrating forces in the theater are based on the combat commander's campaign plan. The operational level of supply encompasses that support which is required to sustain campaigns and major operations. It enables success at the tactical level of war.

The Tactical Level of Supply

Tactical-level supply focuses on readiness and supports the tactical commander's ability to fight battles and engagements. Successful support is anticipatory and provides the right supplies at the right time and place to supported units. Major emphasis is placed on fueling the force and supporting soldiers and their systems. Mobile, responsive capabilities are essential for accomplishing the supply mission.

I. Distribution

Ref: FM 4-93.52, chap. 4

A. Methods of Resupply

Distribution is moving supplies from one location to another or from one unit to another. The Army uses three methods of distribution: supply point, unit, and throughput.

1. Supply Point Distribution

Supply point distribution is the normal distribution method for units that receive direct support from DS supply and maintenance units. Supported units use their organic transportation assets to pick up supplies at supporting supply points or maintenance units.

2. Unit Distribution

Corps or theater transportation assets deliver supplies to customer units. The receiving unit is responsible for downloading transportation assets quickly. Unit distribution is the preferred method of distribution to using units and should be used whenever resources permit. It is also the standard method of distribution from GS to DS supply units.

3. Throughput

Throughput is a method of supply distribution wherein an intermediate supply source is bypassed to provide more efficient support. For example, EAC trucks bypass GS supply points to deliver directly to DS supply points. Engineer barrier material may be shipped directly from corps or theater Class IV GS points to the emplacing unit or engineer supply point (ESP). The receiving unit quickly downloads transportation assets. This method is not automatic. It must be specified in appropriate plans and coordinated through CMMC/CMCB.

B. Logistics Release Point (LRP)

A LRP is the point along the supply route where the supported unit meets the supporting unit to transfer supplies. Likely functions performed at the LRP are:

- Synchronization
- Load adjustment and cargo diversion
- Transfer of responsibility
- Updating battlefield intelligence
- Driver briefing/vehicle maintenance
- Decision making/C2 node
- Link-up point for convoy guides

Within a division's battlespace, one LRP is normally established in the vicinity of the BSA for each FSB, one for the DSB, and one for the DASB. Additional LRPs may be established based on METT-TC.

C. Flatrack Collection Point (FRCP)

Flatrack collection points are predetermined points conveniently located to facilitate the harvesting and management of common user flatracks. Flatrack employment, management, and retrograde operations are the responsibility of distribution managers integrated at each echelon of support throughout the distribution pipeline.

D. Techniques of Resupply

The tactical situation will dictate which technique of resupply the company will use: tailgate, service station, a variation of one type, or a combination of both types.

1. Tailgate Technique

In the tailgate technique, fuel and ammunition trucks, which have been handed off to the platoon sergeants (PSGs), are brought to individual vehicles. This method is used when routes leading to vehicle positions are available, and the company is not under direct enemy observation and fire. It is time-consuming, but it is useful in maintaining stealth during defensive missions because the vehicles do not have to move.

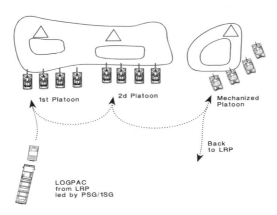

2. Service Station Technique

In the service station technique, vehicles move to a centrally located point for rearming and refueling, either by section, platoon, or an entire company. Service station resupply is inherently faster than the tailgate method, because vehicles must move and concentrate, however, it increases the security risk.

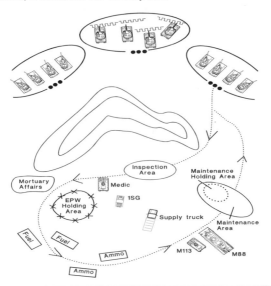

Sources of Supply

The unit maintains a sustaining level of supply that is formed from the UBL and PLL. The next higher source of supply, maybe the parent battalion or a DSU, continually replenishes this sustaining level. The DSU converts the unit's request into a requisition and either satisfies the demand or forwards it to the supporting MMC. Each intermediate MMC is a potential source of supply, and the TSC MMC overviews all of the command-controlled items throughout the theater of operations. Requisitions passed out of the theater are directed to the appropriate NICP for satisfaction.

Mobility of Supplies

Supplies (UBL and PLL) maintained in a unit should be 100 percent mobile. DSU forward elements supporting a brigade or regiment must be able to move 90 percent of their cube within 30 minutes. The remaining 10 percent should be moved within 4 hours. All DSU rear units supporting divisions or larger combat units must be 50 percent mobile, and they must be able to move their remaining ASL cube by shuttle. GSU activities have limited capability to move their ASLs. The preferred method of relocating GSU stocks is to establish a satellite operation at the new location, have replenishment stocks redirected to the new location, and draw down stocks from the existing location.

II. Flow of Supplies and Supply Requests

Requests for supplies generally flow from the user to the higher supply sources. Where possible, echelons are skipped to accelerate the rate of the request. As reporting procedures become faster and more reliable, it will be possible to better anticipate units' requirements and push the supplies to the units without the formality of requisitions and processing by intermediate management activities.

The CMMC receives requisitions from DMMCs, separate BMMCs, RMMCs, nondivision DSUs, and DSM units that issue their stockage items to customers to fill requests from supported units and to replace stockage items issued to customers. For line items available in corps GSUs, the CMMC prepares a MRO directing the COSCOM GSU to issue the items. If the items are not available or not stocked in COSCOM GSUs, the CMMC transmits the requisition to the appropriate CONUS NICP for fill. The CONUS NICP ships the items directly to the GS/DS supply unit or to the ALOC-designated DSM unit specified on the requisition. For theater command-controlled items, the CMMC transmits the requisition to the TSC MMC. The TSC MMC will either fill requisitions or transmit them to the appropriate CONUS NICP for fill. Supply distribution is through surface and ALOC shipment.

III. Field Services

The field services normally provided by division personnel include water purification and mortuary affairs (MA). Other field services, such as showers, laundry and textile renovation, are provided by the corps field services companies. The unit makes request for laundry and shower to the DSB, DASB and FSB support operations section. The requesting support operations section will make the appropriate coordination with DISCOM.

Field service support requires close coordination with those within and outside the division. The division support operations, DSB support operations, FSB support operations, DASB support operations, and commanders of the supply and services (S&S) and field services companies of the corps are all involved in providing field services to the division.

IV. Mortuary Affairs

All commanders are responsible for unit level search, recovery, and evacuation of remains to a mortuary affairs collection point (MACP). A well-organized mortuary affairs program in the division helps to ensure the following:

- Prompt and effective recovery of all remains from the division area of responsibility
- Prompt and accurate identification of the remains
- Prompt recovery, inventory, and security of personal effects found on remains
- Evacuation of remains, with their personal effects secured to them out of the division area to the corps MACP
- Prompt, accurate, and complete administrative recording and reporting
- Prompt and adequate care for deceased allied and threat personnel IAW current United Nations (UN) agreements
- Reverent handling of remains and adequate ceremonies and services for deceased
- Temporary interment of remains (when required and authorized)

All commanders are responsible for unit level search, recovery, and evacuation of remains to a MACP. Digital FBCB2, or per the TSOP, will be used to transmit the initial findings of the unit search and recovery teams to the MA team.

Upon deployment and transition to the concurrent return program, an MA forward collection platoon is detached from the corps' QM collection company and attached to the division. The MA forward collection platoon consists of a platoon headquarters and four forward collection teams. Functions include:

- Conduct limited search and recovery missions, as required
- Set up and operate collection points with refrigeration capability in the maneuver brigade area
- Set up and operate a division main collection point with refrigeration capability
- Conduct temporary interments and disinterments when directed by the geographic combatant commander. (Note: This mission is not resourced by the TOE and may require augmentation from the FSB Commander)
- Maintain essential records and reports
- Maintain security over collection points

Once the forward collection platoon is attached to the division, the platoon leader and platoon sergeant works with the division support operations or G4 as liaison officer and NCO technical representative. Forward collection teams establish MACPs at key locations within the division. Each forward collection section has seven personnel and can receive, process, and coordinate evacuation of about 20 remains and associated personal effects per day. The division commander has the flexibility to employ collection teams as the mission dictates, consolidating or shifting assets as needed. Normally one forward collection team is attached to the DSB (division collection point) and each FSB. These forward collection teams setup and operate MACPs.

Temporary interment of remains OCONUS is permitted as a last resort. Every effort should be made to return remains to CONUS as soon as possible. The geographic combatant commander may authorize temporary interments only when operational constraints prevent the evacuation of remains out of the AOR. Temporary interments are a last resort used for health, safety, sanitation, and morale reasons at unit levels and are conducted IAW joint publication 4-06 and FM 4-20.64 (10-64).

In extreme circumstances, when a unit is cut off and has no means to communicate with higher headquarters, the senior commander is responsible for deciding whether temporary interment will be utilized after all known support options have failed.

Class I Distribution

Ref: FM 4-93.52, fig. 5-8, p. 5-34.

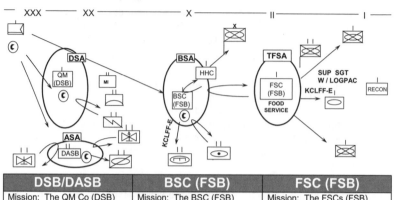

DSB/DASB	BSC (FSB)	FSC (FSB)
Mission: The QM Co (DSB) receives and issues Class I in support of Div Troops. DASB receives and issues Class I to the Cav Sqdn & Avn Bde.	Mission: The BSC (FSB) receives and issues Class I in support of the Brigade. Prepares rations for Engineers. HHC, FSB - prepare and issue rations to HHC BDE, Recon, FSB(-).	Mission: The FSCs (FSB) receive, prepare and issue rations to the maneuver Battalion and the FSC.

Class I consists of subsistence and gratuitous health and welfare items. Quantities are determined by the unit strength sent forward on digitized reports.

Food is one of the most important factors affecting a soldier's health, morale, and welfare. However, the acquisition, storage, transportation, distribution, preparation, and serving of food have always been a logistics challenge. The Army field feeding system (AFFS) is based on three basic rations. The MRE is the individual combat ration. The T ration is a group-feeding ration, and the B ration is also a group feeding ration but one that must be prepared. The requirement is to serve "three quality meals per day", with the capability to distribute, prepare, and serve a unitized group ration "A" (UGR-A), a "heat and serve" UGR meal, and a meal, ready to eat (MRE) individual ration" (Chapter 1, FM 4-20.2 (10-23)) after initial entry into the theater.

The DISCOM receives headcount data for Class I from the FSB, DSB, and DASB support operations sections from CSSCS, and in turn sends it to COSCOM support operations office. Corps or EAC will configure rations in BN/TF sets and push them forward to the FSB, DSB, and DASB field ration issue point IAW the ration cycle. The FSB, DSB, and DASB support operations sections coordinate with supported units for the location of ration issue point and pick-up schedule.

At the corps, the supply company (GS) provides Class I to the division using unit distribution. Some Class I may also be provided to the division via throughput distribution from theater GS supply companies. The Class I is normally shipped to the MSB S&S company in the DSA and the FSB supply company in the BSA. For nondivisional support, the GS supply company distributes Class I to the supply company (DS). The supply company (DS) provides Class I to area customers using supply point distribution.

At the division, the MSB S&S company and the FSB supply companies operate Class I distribution points in the DSA and BSA. The rations are distributed to units using supply point distribution.

Water Purification / Distribution

Ref: FM 4-93.52, fig. 5-9, p. 5-36.

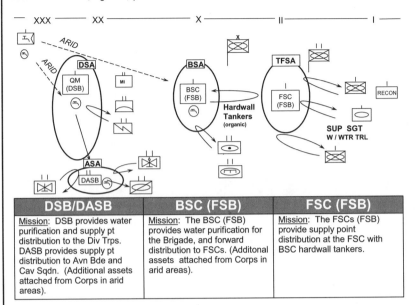

DSB/DASB	BSC (FSB)	FSC (FSB)
<u>Mission</u>: DSB provides water purification and supply pt distribution to the Div Trps. DASB provides supply pt distribution to Avn Bde and Cav Sqdn. (Additional assets attached from Corps in arid areas).	<u>Mission</u>: The BSC (FSB) provides water purification for the Brigade, and forward distribution to FSCs. (Additonal assets attached from Corps in arid areas).	<u>Mission</u>: The FSCs (FSB) provide supply point distribution at the FSC with BSC hardwall tankers.

The Class III and water supply branch of the division support operations will manage water distribution within the division. Water production and storage is provided to the division by an augmentation team from the modular water unit within the COSCOM. This water augmentation team is capable of establishing water points that produce, store and issue potable water. The augmentation team will establish water points in the DSB, DASB and each FSB. The team is dependent on the division for life support and force protection.

Water augmentation teams may produce, store, and issue or (without the availability of a suitable water source) simply store and issue potable water. In an arid environment, water points will receive additional storage capacity from the COSCOM. Within an arid environment or where there is no suitable water source, the COSCOM will deliver water as part of normal sustainment pushes. An adequate water source should be a consideration when selecting the division, aviation, and brigade support areas. Limited water sources may require massing production assets from the augmentation team and transporting the water to support area water points.

Water distribution within the DSA, ASA and BSA will be through supply point distribution at the water points. The HDC's hard-wall tankers will be used to distribute water to maneuver battalions. Maneuver company supply sergeants fill their water trailers at the TFSA according to an established schedule.

Bottled water may be locally procured or shipped from outside of the theater of operations. Bottled or packaged water is particularly well suited for RSOI and initial operation, however (situational dependent) may be routinely issued throughout an operation or conflict. It is normally distributed along with Class I. The Army Medical Command has the responsibility for quality surveillance and quality assurance for bottled water.

Supply Operations (II, III(P), IV, VII & IX)

Ref: FM 4-93.52, fig. 5-10, p. 5-38.

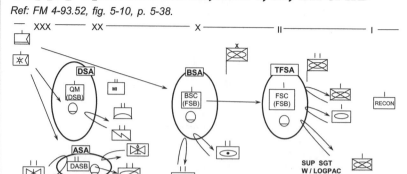

DSB/DASB	BSC (FSB)	FSC (FSB)
Mission: The QM Co (DSB) requests, receives, stores and issues Class II, IIIP, IV, & IX in support of the Division Trps. Class VII (receive & issue). The DASB supports the Avn Bde/Cav Sqdn.	Mission: The BSC (FSB) requests, receives, stores and issues Class II, IIIP, IV, and IX items in support of the Brigade. Class VII (receive & issue).	Mission: The FSCs (FSB) request, receive and issue Class II, IIIP, IV, & IX in support of the maneuver Battalion. Class VII (receive & issue).

Class II, III(P), and IV

Class II, III(P), and IV includes a wide variety of supplies and equipment from clothing to tools, to packaged petroleum products, to barrier materials. The FSC of the FSB issues Class II, III(P), and IV to units in the BN/TF. The HDC of the FSB will maintain limited stockage for support of the brigade supply point distribution to brigade troops. The QM company out of the DSB will issue Class II, III(P), and IV to division troops. Stockage for the support of division troops is kept in the supply platoon of the QM company. The HSC of the DASB will maintain stockage for support of the aviation brigade and division cavalry squadron.

Units in the brigade area submit their requests for Class II, III(P), and IV items through ULLS-S4, to their supporting FSC. The S&T platoon issues the item to the customer. Notification is then sent to the division support operations of the issue. If supplies are not on hand at the FSC, the request is sent to division support operations (SARSS-2A). Personnel in the Class II, III(P), and IV supply branch of division support operations check within SARSS2A. If they find the items are on hand in the SSAs, they will release it or forward the request to the corps SARSS-2A. The division support operations can also direct cross leveling of items within support battalions. The supporting COSCOM activity delivers the supplies to the respective SSA according to the DODAAC. Units in the division rear submit their Class II, III(P), and IV request through the ULLS S4 to their supporting QM company in the DSB. Units in the aviation brigade and division cavalry squadron submit their Class II, III(P), and IV request through the ULLS S4 to their supporting HSC in the DASB.

The QM company or, if appropriate, the gaining unit's supply element, re-equip soldiers returning to duty from medical treatment facilities (MTFs) in the division rear.

The brigade engineer officer is the one who determines and requests Class IV for upcoming counter-mobility operations. He passes the request to the brigade S4 and FSB support operations section, which in turn, passes it to HDC to be inputted into the SARSS-1 which is in the S&T platoon.

Class VII

Class VII items are intensively managed and are normally command controlled. Class VII replacement is based on combat losses reported through command channels to the division G3 and G4 via MCS & CSSCS. This permits the commander to remain apprised of the operational status of subordinate commands and to direct the distribution of items to those units having the most critical need. Weapon systems such as tanks are intensively managed by weapons system replacement operations (WSRO). If the item is a WSRO weapon system, the primary linkup points of the item with its crew may occur in the DSA, ASA, BSA, or in designated assembly areas.

Class VII requests will be accomplished by using the FBCB2 to submit combat loss reports from company level to the BN/TF S4. The CO/TM rollups will be consolidated by the BN/TF S4 and submitted to the brigade S4, with information copy provided to the FSC support operations. The brigade S4 will consolidate and submit battalion combat loss reports to the division support operations via CSSCS, with information copies provided to the division G4 and FSB support operations. The Class VII/PBO representative from the division support operations will enter the requests into the appropriate STAMIS (SPBS-R to SARSS-1). The DSB support operations will consolidate and submit division troops battle loss reports for Class VII to the division support operations, with copy provided to the G4. The DASB support operations will consolidate and submit aviation brigade and division cavalry squadron requests for Class VII to the division support operations, with a copy provided to the G4.

Class IX

As a result of the implementation of field maintenance (organizational and DS level maintenance) in FXXI, the maintenance control section (MCS) is now responsible for maintaining what we know as prescribed load lists (PLL) and shop supply items. For this reason we have designated the new term for these consolidated inventories as "combat spares." Both of these inventories have very different requirements for adding and maintaining parts on inventory. The MCS will manage the PLL using the ULLS-G and the shop stock using the SAMS-1. With the fielding of GCSS-Army, the maintenance module's consolidated ULLS-G and SAMS-1 functionality will have the ability to manage the combat spares. Combat spares are not meant to bring back the "iron mountains". Combat spares consist of a broad but shallow inventory of high use, combat essential parts that support a replace forward maintenance philosophy. Combat spares provide a buffer for the lead-time it takes the distribution system to deliver a required part and also acts as insurance against interruptions in the distribution pipeline. In FXXI parts can be stocked in several different ways. If there is a high use, combat essential part the support units believe needs to be stocked to support combat operations they can do it several different ways. If the part does not meet the stockage criteria for PLL it may be able to be carried on the shop stock. If an essential item fails to meet the criteria for both it may still be stocked at the MCS but will be centrally managed as ASL in the HDC .

Combat spares for the CO/TM are received, stored, and issued by the maintenance control section of the FSC. An operator identifies a fault and requests assistance from the CRT via FBCB2 (free text) or FM radio. The CRT will diagnose the fault and identify the required Class IX supplies. The DSU supporting the brigade troops is the HDC. The ASL for the brigade is maintained by the Class IX section in the HDC. The PLL for the HDC of the FSB, FSMC of the FSB, HHC brigade, engineer battalion, and the brigade reconnaissance troop may be managed by the MCS of the BSC. The Class IX supply section of the QM company, DSB, provides direct support to division troops. This section receives, stores, and issues Class IX (ground and missile) supplies. The section also maintains the division troop's ASL, and operates the reparable exchange service. The Class IX supply section of the HSC, DASB provides direct support to aviation brigade units and the division cavalry squadron. The section also maintains the aviation brigade/division cavalry's ground ASL, and operates the reparable exchange for ground equipment.

Class VIII Resupply at Echelon I

Ref: FM 4-93.52, fig. 5-12, p. 5-44.

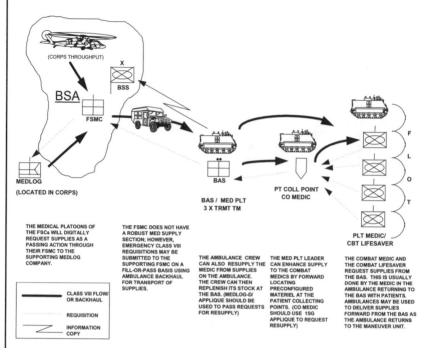

THE MEDICAL PLATOONS OF THE FSCs WILL DIGITALLY REQUEST SUPPLIES AS A PASSING ACTION THROUGH THEIR FSMC TO THE SUPPORTING MEDLOG COMPANY.

THE FSMC DOES NOT HAVE A ROBUST MED SUPPLY SECTION; HOWEVER, REQUISITIONS MAY BE SUBMITTED TO THE SUPPORTING FSMC ON A FILL-OR-PASS BASIS USING AMBULANCE BACKHAUL FOR TRANSPORT OF SUPPLIES.

THE AMBULANCE CREW CAN ALSO RESUPPLY THE MEDIC FROM SUPPLIES ON THE AMBULANCE. THE CREW CAN THEN REPLENISH ITS STOCK AT THE BAS. (MEDLOG-D/APPLIQUE SHOULD BE USED TO PASS REQUESTS FOR RESUPPLY)

THE MED PLT LEADER CAN ENHANCE SUPPLY TO THE COMBAT MEDICS BY FORWARD LOCATING PRECONFIGURED MATERIEL AT THE PATIENT COLLECTING POINTS. (CO MEDIC SHOULD USE 1SG APPLIQUE TO REQUEST RESUPPLY)

THE COMBAT MEDIC AND THE COMBAT LIFESAVER REQUEST SUPPLIES FROM THE BAS. THIS IS USUALLY DONE BY THE MEDIC IN THE AMBULANCE RETURNING TO THE BAS WITH PATIENTS. AMBULANCES MAY BE USED TO DELIVER SUPPLIES FORWARD FROM THE BAS AS THE AMBULANCE RETURNS TO THE MANEUVER UNIT.

- ——— CLASS VIII FLOW/ OR BACKHAUL
- .... REQUISITION
- ⟋ INFORMATION COPY

Typically, there are four Class VIII DSUs within the division (DSMC, 3-FSMCs). These DSUs will forward their requisitions to the DISCOM medical material management branch (MMMB). The MMMB will have asset visibility of on-hand quantities of Class VIII supplies. The MMMB can authorize and direct one DSU to fill another DSUs supported unit requisition. If the MMMB elects not to cross-level from one DSU to another DSU, then it forwards requisitions from the division to the supporting medical logistics company. Class VIII management in the Army's Force XXI division will be accomplished by medical units/elements using the combat health logistics (CHL) functional module of theater medical information program (TMIP)/medical communications for combat casualty care (MC4) system, when fielded. Currently the functional business system for Class VIII wholesale/retail management at echelons above division (EAD) is the theater Army medical management information system (TAMMIS) which is a legacy system. This system will be replaced in the future by the MC4/TMIP system. This system provides brigade medical elements a direct link with the FSMCs and division rear medical elements a direct link with the DSMC. Also, this system provides corps medical units/elements a direct link with the supporting MEDLOG battalion's units. The health service materiel officer (HSMO) of the division surgeon's section (DSS) and the DISCOM medical materiel management branch (MMMB) in the division support operations section, coordinates Class VIII resupply for division medical units/elements. Each medical unit maintains its own basic load of 3 to 5 days of medical supplies. The MEDLOG battalion assigns one MEDLOG company in direct support of each division. Once established, it provides Class VIII resupply for the division and corps medical elements operating in the division AO.

Class VIII Resupply at Echelon II

Ref: FM 4-93.52, fig. 5-13, p. 5-45.

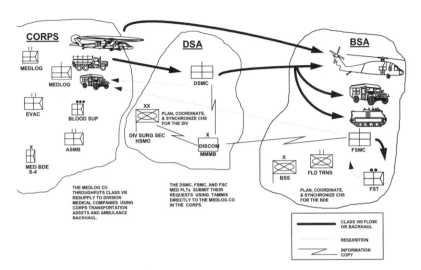

Routine Requisitions

Routine requisitions from maneuver battalion medical platoons for Class VIII resupply from their supporting FSMC will be via a digital request. An information copy of all requisitions within the brigade will be forwarded by the FSMC on-line to the DISCOM MMMB and also an information copy to the brigade surgeon's section (BSS). Routine requisitions submitted by FSMCs, division or corps medical elements operating in the BSAs are forwarded directly to the supporting MEDLOG company. An information copy goes to the DISCOM MMMB. The MMMB coordinates shortfalls in throughput distribution with the DSS and divisions support operations branch. The MMMB may update priorities with the MEDLOG company to correct deficiencies in the delivery system. If the requested items are available for issue, a materiel release order is printed and the requested supplies are prepared for shipment.

Immediate Requisitions

Immediate requisitions from maneuver battalion medical platoons are submitted to the supporting FSMC. When the supporting FSMC is unable to fill the request, the requisition is forwarded to the DISCOM MMMB. The DISCOM MMMB will expedite handling of this request to ensure tracking of critical Class VIII items and timely delivery. Cross-leveling in the division may be accomplished if it is the most expedient method of obtaining and shipping required items to the requesting unit/element. If the DISCOM MMMB is unable to locate requested item(s) in the division, the request is forwarded to the supporting MEDLOG company. Immediate requisitions from FSMCs are sent through the DISCOM MMMB for management and to ensure visibility of the requisitions. The DISCOM MMMB maintains a record of the requisition until it is filled. All immediate requests received by the MEDLOG company are processed for shipment by the most expedient transportation available. The MEDLOG company forwards all immediate requests not filled, to the MEDLOG battalion's logistics support company located in the corps rear. The DISCOM MMMB has the responsibility of monitoring all immediate requisitions not filled by the MEDLOG company. The DISCOM MMMB reports all immediate Class VIII requests to the DSS/CHS cell.

Material Management Centers (MMCs)

Ref: FM 4-93.4 Theater Support Command, chap. 5.

Material Management Centers (MMCs) are the materiel managers for the units they support. They manage materiel for weapon systems, control maintenance priorities, and coordinate and control supply functions to meet supported units' operational needs.

1. Division, Regimental and Separate Brigade MMCs

DMMCs, RMMCs, and separate BMMCs manage all materiel for which their support commands (i.e., DISCOM, regimental support squadron, or separate brigade support battalion) are responsible except Class VIII, COMSEC material, and classified maps. These centers receive and process requests for issue from the supported units' supply activities.

2. Corps MMC (CMMC)

This MMC is the central manager for the corps-level GS supply system (not to be confused with GSM that is not found in the corps but, rather, at the theater level). The philosophy of management is based on decentralized stockage locations with a centralized management process. The CMMC performs the functions of integrated materiel management for all corps classes of supply except Class VIII, COMSEC material, and classified maps. Integrated materiel management involves requirements computation, establishing stockage levels, procurement direction and distribution, disposal, and developing guidance for maintenance priorities. It also manages all of the COSCOM maintenance activities. The CMMC accepts requisitions from the DMMC and from nondivisional DSUs. The CMMC can cross-level assets within the corps AOR. If items are not available for issue within the corps, the CMMC transfers the requisition to the TSC MMC or to the CONUS NICP (also an MMC) that manages the requested item.

3. Theater Support Command MMC (TSC MMC)

The TSC MMC provides support and performs functions similar to those of the CMMC. This support is provided to units at the operational level. It provides inventory management functions for the entire theater. The TSC MMC's focus is on distributing war reserves and managing command-controlled items. Requisitions for noncommand-controlled items are transmitted directly to an NICP with information going to the TSC MMC.

The joint force commander has several organizational options for controlling distribution. To ensure total integration, he normally assigns responsibility for theater transportation movement control to a joint movement center. JP 4-01.3 covers the role of this center and of the entire joint movement control system, while FM 4-01.30 (FM 55-10) discusses Army movement control.

The TSC is a critical agent in the distribution-based CSS system. Its mission is to maximize throughput and follow-on sustainment of forces. The DMC along with the MMC, MCA, and the MEDCOM MLMC are critical to managing the system. The DMC is not a separate control center along the lines of the established control centers for materiel, transportation, and medical logistics. Rather, the DMC is the TSC staff agent for synchronizing the theater distribution system.

Note: See pp. 3-57 to 3-62 for information on the Theater Support Command.

Distribution Management Center

The distribution management center (DMC) is responsible for managing Army theater distribution by balancing the existing capabilities of the distribution infrastructure with the day-to-day and projected operational requirements.

VIII. Manning the Force

Ref: FM 12-6 Personnel Doctrine, FM 4-0 Combat Service Support, chap. 10 and FM 4-93.52 , chap. 5.

Note: See pp. 1-71to 1-74 for additional information on human resource support (FM 4-0) to include personnel readiness management, personnel accounting, personnel information management and replacement operations.

Soldiers are the focal point of Army operations. They are the foundation of the Army's will to win. Throughout the spectrum of operations, Human Resoure Support (HRS) is a critical element of successful operations. Soldiers and their spirit, initiative, discipline, courage, and competence are the basic building blocks of a successful Army. HRS provides an integrated system that is critical to the readiness of the fighting force and contributes to both national will and the will of the soldier in the fight.

Doctrinal references for HRS are FMs 3-0, 4-0, and 12-6. Human resource support (HRS) encompasses the following functions: manning the force, personnel support, and personnel services. These activities include personnel accounting, casualty management, essential services, postal operations, and morale, welfare, and recreation. They are provided to service members, their families, DA civilians, and contractors.

Military Personnel Manning

 A Personnel Readiness Management

 B Personnel Accounting and Strength Management (PASR)

 C Replacement Operations Management

 D Personnel Information Management

Ref: FM 4-0, chap. 10 (adds the new category of Personnel Information Mgmt).

Proper and effective manning is essential to the operational success of any military mission. Manning the force involves the uninterrupted flow of soldiers from mobilization and deployment through redeployment and demobilization.

The DISCOM S1 is responsible to the commander for all matters concerning human resources. Manning in the DISCOM remains the process of getting the right soldier at the right place and time with the right capabilities. Manning the force encompasses the tasks that current doctrine associates with personnel readiness management, replacement management, and casualty management.

I. Military Personnel Manning

Ref: FM 12-6 Personnel Doctrine.

Military personnel manning is comprised of three critical personnel systems/functions: personnel readiness management, replacement operations management, and personnel accounting and strength reporting. It is the planning and execution of the five critical manning tasks to predict, resource, monitor, assess, and adjust the personnel strength of the force. During operations, this core activity focuses on getting the right soldier at the right place and time. It is an activity that combines anticipation, movement, and skillful positioning of personnel assets. Additionally, it is further dependent upon the personnel information management system for providing essential personnel information.

A. Personnel Readiness Management

Personnel readiness management is the process of assigning soldiers to subordinate commands based on documented manpower authorizations and the commander's intent. Personnel readiness describes a state of operational preparedness. Personnel readiness management is a process for achieving and upholding that state. Personnel readiness management sub-tasks include casualty estimation, establishing manning priorities, projecting replacements, projecting return to duty soldiers, hasty strength reporting, and personnel accounting. These sub-tasks are performed during execution of the five critical manning tasks (predict, resource, monitor, assess, and adjust) with many of these tasks being performed simultaneously.

B. Personnel Accounting and Strength Reporting (PASR)

PASR is the process of accounting for soldiers, reporting other strength-related information, and updating command databases at all levels. Information gained through PASR provides readiness managers the details necessary to assess personnel strength as a component of combat power. Other elements of the staff use PASR information to plan and provide their services.

PASR

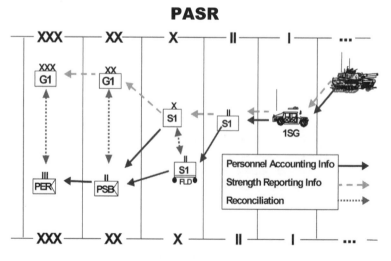

Ref: FM 63-1, fig. 10-1, p. 10-4.

- **Personnel accounting** is the deliberate reporting system for recording by-name data on soldiers when they arrive and depart units or when their status changes. Personnel accounting is accomplished by updating the personnel database to reflect these changes. Regardless of what method is being used to maintain personnel accountability during an operation, SIDPERS as the database of record must be updated to reflect changes in an individual's status.

- **Strength reporting** is a numerical end product of the hasty accounting process. Strength reporting is exception reporting only. Units should only report those changes to their personnel status as they occur or as soon as practical depending on the tactical situation.

C. Replacement Operations Management

Replacement management is a system that moves personnel from designated points of origin to ultimate destinations. Replacement management involves the physical reception, accounting, processing, support, and coordination with supporting units for re-equipping, training, and delivery of military personnel. This includes replacements, RTDs, and stragglers. The system provides primarily for individual replacements and groupings of individuals up through squad, crew, or team level as required by operations. Replacement management requires real-time access to information about all replacements, movement status from the point of selection, and personnel readiness management information to determine the final destination of replacements.

Replacement Operations

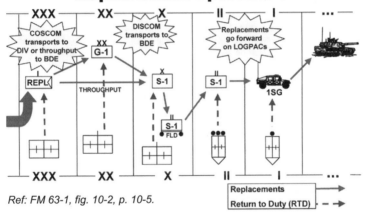

Ref: FM 63-1, fig. 10-2, p. 10-5.

- **Weapon system replacement operations (WSRO).** While the standard is individual soldiers, the replacement operations system must be able to provide squads, crews, or teams. It must also coordinate for their transportation to weapon system link-up and training locations.

- **Flow of replacements at corps.** Replacements arrive at the corps replacement company from theater and RTDs arrive from the corps support hospital. The corps replacement company coordinates with COSCOM for transportation to the division G1 replacement section or throughput to brigade level based upon personnel readiness management decisions. At the division level, the G1 coordinates with DISCOM for transportation from division to brigade level. The division G1 also receives RTD soldiers from the main support medical company. At brigade level, RTDs are received from the forward support medical company. Along with the replacements, they are taken to the battalion field trains co-located in the BSA where they will go forward to their units on LOGPACS. At bn and company levels, soldiers are RTD from the bn or company aid stations.

II. Critical Manning Tasks

Ref: FM 12-6 and FM 4-93.52.

The manning process includes the tasks of predicting personnel requirements, resourcing units with personnel assets in accordance with the commander's guidance, monitoring the personnel strength posture, assessing unit combat power, and adjusting personnel resources to provide the optimum combination of manpower and equipment to maximize combat power.

1. Predicting

Predicting is the process of anticipating the number, grade, and skill of personnel resources required to sustain the BOS of the DISCOM as they execute the operational patterns that destroy the enemy's will to fight. The S1 must complete a loss estimate based on threat and friendly force capabilities. This estimate provides planning parameters for replacements, medical facility/support rqmts and MA assets.

2. Resourcing

Resourcing is the process of bringing units to their required strength according to the commander's priorities. Although it occurs at every echelon of command, resourcing is the primary focus of the national provider. The Department of the Army deputy chief of staff for personnel (DA DCSPER) executes the task at the national level to structure, acquire, train, distribute, and separate the force. Individual replacements move to the central receiving center (CRC) under the direction of the DCSPER and CONUS major commands (MACOM)s to resource the force projection theater. At all levels personnel operators provide commanders combat power visibility by properly identifying the status of available personnel resources. The S1 then recommends the allocation of available resources to meet current and future requirements.

3. Monitoring

Monitoring is the process of gathering unit strength data on a real-time basis through digitized systems and communications. With digitization, we eliminate the requirement for unique personnel reporting systems by having the capability to absorb personnel information from tactical communications. The task of digitized strength monitoring begins with establishing the strength baseline. The S1s, under the direction of the G1, manifest all deploying personnel using TPS. Inbound or pre-positioned asset information is available through information systems of the manning the force automation architecture. It is transmitted to personnel operators performing manning tasks at the strategic and/or operational level and provided to the division.

4. Assessing

Assessing is the process of comparing current and projected unit strength data to personnel capabilities required to maintain OPTEMPO and achieve operational success. The S1 matches current assets with projected losses and replacements and recommends the method to properly resource units.

5. Adjusting

Adjusting is the process of packaging, positioning and dispatching replacements to deliver them when and where needed. The G1 notifies the DMC of movement requirements as commanders direct the proper adjustment of personnel assets to accomplish pending missions. Personnel operators both in the division and at EAD, in coordination with logisticians match personnel and equipment during the adjustment process by providing unit, squad, crew, team, or individual replacements according to the commander's operational requirements and the needs of the BOS. Movement time and distance factors influence the positioning of personnel replacement units which hold and process replacements until they are dispatched to the gaining unit.

Chap 3

IX. Theater Support Command

CSS Ops

Ref: FM 4-93.4 Theater Support Command.

The TSC is a multifunctional support headquarters that works at the operational level with links to strategic- and tactical-level support organizations and agencies. The ASCC commander supervises the TSC's peacetime contingency planning. When the TSC, or any part of it, deploys to an AO, it reports to the commander, Army forces. The ARFOR commander may be the ASCC commander or a lower-level commander depending on the scale of operations. During peacetime planning the ASCC commander provides guidance for the types of combat support (CS) and CSS capabilities that may be attached to the TSC for a given contingency. This is done in accordance with the Joint Operations Planning and Execution System (JOPES). (See Chairman of the Joint Chiefs of Staff Manual [CJCSM] 3122.03.)

The TSC has some permanently assigned major subordinate units. The ASCC commander may attach other units to the TSC for specific operations. Support requirements at the operational-level vary considerably depending on the type of operations and the scale of the deployment. The ASCC ommander has the flexibility to tailor the support presence in the AO appropriately.

TSC Mission

The mission of the TSC is to maximize throughput and follow-on sustainment of Army forces and other supported elements regardless of the scale of operations. Throughput in this sense means that the TSC ensures that unit personnel, unit equipment, and commodities move to their point of employment with a minimum number of intervening stops and transfers. For this reason the TSC establishes command of support operations and control of the distribution system before those elements arrive in the AO. The TSC provides area support to the operational-level units in the AOs and overall sustainment support to Army forces. This support may include interim tactical-level support to early deploying corps and divisional elements. The TSC also executes those lead service CUL support requirements that the ASCC commander assigns.

The TSC commander has a vital interest in the security and terrain management of the rear area. Depending on the joint force commander (JFC) and ARFOR commander decisions, the TSC responsibility may range from the inherent responsibility for the internal security of TSC elements to being formally designated as the joint rear area coordinator (JRAC).

Key Tasks

The UJTL contains guidance for developing the TSC's METL during the deliberate planning process. The ASCC commander approves the TSC's METL. The TSC develops its battle-focused mission essential task list (METL) as described in FM 7-0 (FM 25-100) based on guidance from its ASCC higher headquarters. The TSC's METL developers consider those specific UJTL tasks that support the Army's lead service responsibilities (CJCSM 3500.04C). These tasks are either stated or implied in the ASCC and geographic combatant command war plans. The TSC performs primarily UJTL tasks in its support operations. However, some tactical-level tasks covered in the Army Universal Task List (AUTL) (FM 7-15) may also apply because the TSC provides interim tactical support and the TSC's subordinate units will perform tactical-level support tasks. In addition, the TSC performs functions to support the Army's lead service responsibilities.

Universal Joint Task List (UJTL)

Sample UJTL tasks the TSC performs:

- **OP 1** Conduct Operational Movement and Maneuver. (Selected sub-tasks.)
  - **OP 1.1** Conduct Operational Movement.
  - **OP 1.3** Provide Operational Mobility. (Selected sub-tasks.)
  - **OP 1.5** Conduct Operationally Significant Areas. (Selected sub-tasks; for example, OP 1.5.5 Assist Host Nation in Populace and Resource Control.)
- **OP 4** Provide Operational Logistics and Personnel Support. (This is the primary area of interest for the TSC and the specialized commands.)
- **OP 5** Provide Operational Command and Control. (Selected sub-tasks.)
- **OP 6** Provide Operational Force Protection. (Selected sub-tasks in this area may apply to the TSC depending on the scope of rear area responsibilities given to the TSC.)
- **TA 4** Perform Logistics and Combat Support. (These tasks apply to the TSC when supporting tactical-level units during theater build-up.)
- **TA 6** Protect the Force. (Selected sub-tasks in this area may apply to the TSC depending on the scale of the operation and the scope of rear area responsibilities given to the TSC.)

Ref: FM 4-93.4, fig. 2-1, p. 2-3.

Area Support Groups (ASGs)

Area support groups (ASGs) are subordinate units assigned to the TSC. They are responsible for area support in the AO and may provide support to corps or other forces. The mission of the ASG is to provide DS logistic support to designated units and elements within its AO. This support typically includes DS supply (less ammunition, classified map supply, and medical supply and support), DS maintenance, and field services, as well as other support directed by the ARFOR commander through the TSC. ASGs can also provide GS supply and sustainment maintenance support to TSC and CZ DS supply organizations and sustainment maintenance to support the theater mission. If an operational-level ammunition group is not established, specialized battalions assigned to the ASG provide ammunition support. ASGs can support ISBs and RSO&I operations. EEMs of specialized units may be attached to an ASG headquarters EEM during the initial stages of an operation.

ASGs provide a variety of support to units stationed in or passing through their areas. An ASG area depends on the density of military units and materiel to support and on political boundaries and identifiable terrain features. One ASG is assigned to a TSC for every 15,000 to 30,000 troops supported in the AO. ASGs are located along the LOC to take advantage of the transportation network and provide responsive support to the units they support. FM 4-93.40 (FM 54-40) contains additional details on the composition and capabilities of ASGs.

I. TSC Command Relationships

Ref: FM 4-93.4 Theater Support Command.

In organizing the TSC, the ASCC commander may elect to reduce his span of C2 over these specialized commands. If he does, he has available to him the three command relationships spelled out in FM 5-0 (FM 101-5) and defined in FM 1-02 (FM 101-5-1)- attachment, OPCON, and TACON. In brief, these relationships are defined as follows:

1. Attachment

Attachment is the placement of units in an organization where such placement is relatively temporary. Subject to limitations imposed by the attachment order, the commander of the organization receiving the attachment has the responsibility to provide the attached units with sustainment support beyond their organic capabilities.

2. Operational Control (OPCON)

OPCON is the authority to perform those functions of command over subordinate forces involving organizing and employing commands and forces, assigning tasks, designating objectives, and giving authoritative direction of military operations and joint training necessary to accomplish missions assigned to the command. In the Army, a unit OPCONto a command/unit continues to receive logistics support from its parent unit.

3. Tactical Control (TACON)

TACON in the Army allows commanders to apply force and direct the tactical use of logistics assets but does not provide authority to change organizational structure or direct administrative and logistical support. As with OPCON, the parent unit retains responsibility for logistics support to a unit under the TACON of another unit.

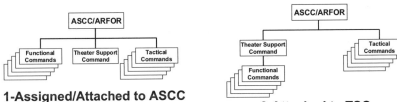

1-Assigned/Attached to ASCC

2-Attached to TSC

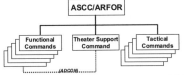

3-Attached for ADCON to TSC

Regardless of the option the ASCC commander chooses for the specialized commands, they retain technical linkages with their respective national provider-level command and ASCC staff principals in order to execute their ASCC special staff functions. The ASCC commander considers the effect on these links when specifying the command relationship. He may place any restriction on an attachment order that he believes is necessary to facilitate provision of support.

II. Operational-Level CSS

Ref: FM 4-93.4 Theater Support Command.

JP 4-0 and FM 4-0 (FM 100-10) identify three levels of CSS-strategic, operational, and tactical. Each level provides critical yet different types of support. Strategic- and operational-level CSS supports wars, contingencies, campaigns, and major operations. Tactical CSS supports battles and engagements. This section discusses the role of the TSC in force projection operations.

Given the range of responsibilities confronting the ARFOR commander, it is often necessary to consolidate and delegate selected responsibilities to subordinate commands. The TSC is uniquely designed to execute many of the CSS responsibilities for the ARFOR commander. During theater opening, the TSC focuses primarily on supporting RSO&I. As the AO matures, the TSC shifts focus to sustaining operations.

A. Deployment

The ARFOR commander receives deploying forces, stages them, moves them forward, and integrates them into the theater structure. RSO&I is critical to successful force projection. RSO&I is complete when deploying units are determined combat effective by the operational commander. The ARFOR commander, based on guidance from the geographic combatant commander/JFC, determines the necessary level of combat effectiveness and the indices for determining this level. The TSC and other units track the build-up of the force by providing appropriate reports. The operational commander retains responsibility to track and report through operational channels the build-up of combat capabilities. FM 4-01.8 (FM 100-17-3) contains a detailed description of the RSO&I process.

To meet requirements in this process, the Army developed a modular concept for opening theaters in which the TSC is a critical component. Modularity involves incrementally deploying only the minimum capabilities required to an AO. This is the basis of the theater force-opening package (TFOP) discussed in Chapter 7. The TSC early entry module (EEM) provides C2 for many of the elements initially conducting RSO&I as directed by the ARFOR commander.

B. Employment

Though the line between entry and decisive operations may not be clear-cut, once the ARFOR commander has sufficient forces integrated into the total force to meet the commander's requirements, the emphasis for the TSC shifts from RSO&I support to sustaining the force.

The ARFOR commander plans and conducts force sustainment operations throughout the AO. The TSC conducts operational-level force sustainment to support the ARFOR, and tactical-level sustainment to forces operating in or passing through the TSC's AO. The TSC may also support other services, multinational partners, and NGOs and/or OGAs in accordance with the ARFOR commander's lead service responsibilities. As the AO develops, the EEM matures into a TSC, with all required capabilities and other required commands (as determined by the ARFOR commander).

The TSC distribution system can provide DS and GS to all designated forces operating within the rear/sustainment area and to any forces requiring related sustainment support as they transit the TSC AO. The primary customers of tactical-level support in the rear and sustainment area are the elements of the TSC and any specialized CS and CSS commands in theater. However, the TSC through the distribution systems may also be involved in some direct support to tactical forces.

The TSC is also involved in reconstitution either as part of sustaining decisive operations or as preparing for redeployment. The ARFOR commander plans and directs reconstitution operations. However, the TSC is responsible for providing support as necessary. In a reorganization, the TSC is usually involved only when there is sufficient time for CSS beyond normal sustainment.

The TSC, typically through an area support group/area support battalion (ASG/ASB) is even more involved in regeneration. It usually establishes the regeneration site and provides most of the CSS elements of the regeneration task force. FM 4-100.9 (FM 100-9) provides details on reconstitution.

The goal during post conflict and post crisis operations is to attain the strategic end state. This means transitioning responsibilities to the HN or designated agency as smoothly as possible and supporting the other elements of national power. During this time, ARFOR may be conducting such support operations as handling refugees, decontaminating equipment, or clearing minefields while preparing for redeployment. Security remains a primary consideration during this period.

The TSC continues to provide selected sustainment support to the supported force during this stage. A key consideration is the continuously changing nature of the supported force, as well as changing support requirements as the force changes the nature of its operations. Reliance on contracted support to provide common supplies and services may increase, thus allowing Army CS and CSS forces to redeploy back to the home station or to subsequent operations in a different AO.

C. Redeployment

The TSC is actively involved in redeployment in a number of ways. It may help redeploying units move to assembly areas, and plays a major role in reconstitution. It also controls the movement of units to the port of embarkation (POE) and provides life support at all nodes in the TSC AO. (FM 3-35.5 [FM 100-17-5] contains more detailed redeployment information.)

Redeployment starts for forward units when they close into assembly areas (AAs) and continues at redeployment assembly areas (RAAs) activated and supported by the TSC. CSS activities are paramount during this period. Logistics functions include: identifying, separating, and reporting excess supplies and equipment to the appropriate materiel managers for disposing or redistributing as appropriate; initiating detailed equipment maintenance and cleaning; and canceling requisitions. Accounting for personnel and processing awards are two of the critical personnel activities under the responsibility of the PERSCOM. Combat health support (CHS) is an important factor throughout the redeployment process under the responsibility of the MEDCOM. Before redeployment, medical screening for clinical signs of disease and injuries and medical surveillance is required to ensure a fit and healthy force. If the ARFOR commander assigns the mission to the TSC cdr, the TSC may oversee these administrative activities.

In all anticipated cases, the TSC receives, identifies, and determines disposition; maintains accountability; and stores, prepares for shipment, and arranges for movement of Class I, II, III (packaged), IV, V, VI, VII, and IX items to the port or designated storage location. Carrying out these functions may require augmentation from other military elements and/or contractor personnel. Contracted support may be the preferred solution to support Army forces leaving the mission area by operating seaports and aerial ports of debarkation. This includes operating wash racks and providing life support for redeploying units. The USAMC LSE or contractors may also repair items in the theater or send them to designated forward stations or CONUS GS or depot maintenance activities. USAMC's LSE also has major responsibilities for retrograde of Army pre-positioned stocks (APS) in the theater.

The TSC staff plans to transfer its responsibilities to another organization as the theater draws down. This may be an organization of another service or multinational partner, the USAMC LSE, an host nation support (HNS) organization, or an international agency.

III. Support Operations

TSC support operations focus on establishing and maintaining the Army portion of the theater distribution system and sustaining the force in the AO consistent with the ARFOR commander and JFC strategic support priorities.

The TSC support structure responsible for support operations consists of three components —the support operations elements of the headquarters (in conjunction with the specialized commands), the control centers, and the operating units and organizations. The support operations staff with specialized commands and planning and coordination cells plan support operations, ensure plans are executed IAW the commander's intent, provide staff supervision over operating units, work to resolve support issues, and synchronize the operations of all TSC elements. The specialized control centers manage supply, transportation, and maintenance operations.

Support Operations Section

The support operations section supervises the provision of all TSC external mission support. It supervises supply, maintenance, field services, and movement control units and activities involved with external support. It also integrates transportation, aviation, medical, personnel, finance, and engineer mission support requirements into the overall support plan. In order to do this, the TSC support operations section requires planning and LNO cells from the specialized commands co-located with it. This is because the support operations section does not have organic specialized expertise to plan for and synchronize transportation, medical, personnel, finance, and engineer operations with other support operations. The theater-level specialized commands provide this expertise to the support operations section to ensure that their functions are integrated into the overall support plan. Specialized command representatives work most closely with the plans and policy office and the DMC. Planning considerations include the location of support activities, the use and maintenance of facilities, and the integration of distribution operations with other support operations. Examples include ensuring that Class IV supplies are available when and where required to provide engineer support, and ensuring that materiel handling equipment (MHE) and transportation are available for postal operations. Working together, planners ensure that all support providers have a common, relevant picture of support priorities and can execute those priorities at the operational and strategic levels.

IV. The TSC Role in Distribution Mgmt

Distribution is a critical component of support operations. Though many elements of the TSC are involved in distribution, and the entire support operations section— along with the specialized commands and modules—play key roles, this chapter focuses on the TSC DMC, MCA, MMC, and MLMC. Doctrine for the Army's role in theater distribution is explained in FM 4-01.4 (FM 100-10-1).

TSC elements involved in the distribution mission operate in a joint and often multinational environment. JP 4-01.4 discusses joint distribution, JP 4-0 addresses the joint boards and centers, and JP 4-08 covers multinational considerations.

Distribution Management Center (DMC)

The distribution management center (DMC) acts as the distribution management support element for the DCSO. It provides staff supervision to the TSC MMC and MCA, and coordinates with the MLMC. It synchronizes operations within the distribution system to maximize throughput and follow-on sustainment, and executes priorities in accordance with ARFOR commander directives. Specialized commands and organizations provide liaison personnel to integrate distribution aspects of other CSS functions (such as postal or replacement operations, Class IV and V support to engineer operations, Class VIII and medical materiel operations, and contracting activities) into the overall distribution operation.

The DMC has two branches—the distribution operations branch and the distribution plans branch. The distribution operations branch maintains situational awareness of the distribution system and is the "fusion center" for Army distribution-related information. It works closely with and synchronizes operations of the MMC and MCA. The distribution plans branch assimilates end-to-end information from the distribution pipeline to create a synchronized picture of the flow of units, personnel, and materiel into and throughout the AO concurrently.

Distribution Planning

Detailed planning for distribution operations is a key part of the environment of the distribution manager. The distribution plan is closely related to the LPT and is a part of the service support plan with its associated annexes and appendices. The ARFOR commander OPLAN/OPORD provides operational mission information essential for TSC planners, in coordination with the ASCC G1 and G4, to develop the LPT. The LPT provides the data required to prepare the logistics estimate. This estimate draws conclusions and makes recommendations concerning the logistics feasibility of various COAs and the effects of each COA on CSS operations. Once the commander selects a COA, the TSC staff coordinates with the specialized commands using both the logistics and personnel estimates to develop the service support plan and the distribution plan. The LPT, service support plan, and distribution plan are living documents within the CSS planning triad that are changed, refined, and updated as a result of continuing estimates and studies.

Force Tracking

Force tracking is the process of gathering and maintaining information on the location, status, and predicted movement of each element of a unit while in transit to the specified operational area. These elements include the unit's command element, personnel, and unit-related supplies and equipment The ARFOR G3 tracks readiness and location of all ARFOR. The TSC support operations sections support the ARFOR force tracking by monitoring the logistical readiness of ARFOR and responding to shifting support priorities IAW ARFOR commander intent.

Maneuver and Mobility Support (MMS)

Maneuver and mobility support (MMS), formerly known as battlefield circulation and control (BCC), refers to functions of MP forces to support movement control operations. MP forces support TSC operations in a variety of ways, from law and order to forming tactical response forces, as required, to meet JRA threats. However, MMS is perhaps the most direct MP contribution to the TSC's movement control role as well as its core distribution management function. MPs conduct MMS as described below. FM 3-19.1 (FM 19-1) and FM 3-19.4 (FM 19-4) describe MP functions in more detail. The highway traffic division (HTD) of the responsible road network controlling authority determines routes classification. In the TSC AO, the HTD is in the TSC MCA.

Movement Control Agency (MCA)

The Army executes movement control at the operational-level through a movement control agency (MCA). The MCA operates under the C2 of the TSC. The MCA helps develop and execute the Army portion of the joint movement program developed by the JMC. The MCA synchronizes its operations with those of the JMC, USTRANSCOM, and lower echelon movement control organizations, and follows the priorities established by the ARFOR commander.

Emerging Doctrine: The Army's theater MCA is pending a reorganization that incorporates its functions within transportation command elements (TCEs) that are subordinate to the Army theater TRANSCOM. One TCE supports each theater of operations and combines the functions of mode operations and movement control. Under this model, TSC staffs will interact with a single TCE rather than the separate elements of a TRANSCOM and an MCA.

V. The TSC Role in Force Protection

The TSC's role in force protection comes within the context of sustaining operations as discussed in the decisive-shaping-sustaining operations framework in FM 3-0. Sustaining operations elements include CSS, movement control, terrain management, and infrastructure development.

The Joint Rear Area (JRA)

The JFC is responsible to the geographic combatant commander for force protection at the operational level in a designated JOA. The ARFOR commander has responsibility for force protection of ARFOR, and receives resources from the ASCC to fulfill this mission. FM 3-93 (FM 100-7) discusses this topic in greater detail. The JRA is a specified land area within a JFC's operational area that the JFC designates to facilitate protection and operation of installations and forces supporting the joint force. In the context of the overall battlespace, the JRA is a and area near, or contiguous with, the CZ, where land component forces are conducting tactical operations. The JRA often shares borders with both sea and air battlespace areas. The JFC may assign responsibility for the JRA to a service component commander, such as the ARFOR commander. The ARFOR commander may then serve as the JRAC, or appoint a subordinate cdr or staff officer to serve as the JRAC. Designating the TSC as the JRAC implies a significant increase in the TSC's mission that requires staff augmentation and additional unit capabilities.

The TSC supports ARFOR operations primarily from within the JRA and executes Army lead service responsibilities to the joint force as assigned by the ARFOR commander. The TSC is normally the ARFOR commander's largest subordinate element in the JRA. Some TSC assets may be positioned in a sanctuary location, such as an ISB. However, the TSC's most critical facilities and base areas are in the JRA. These include SPODs; APODs; road, rail, and water networks; petroleum storage and distribution facilities; maintenance sites, and other critical facilities. The TSC commander, therefore, is a key player in security, terrain management, and movement control within the JRA. The TSC commander interacts closely with the JRAC, and TSC subordinate units interact closely with other services' security and support forces.

Joint Rear Area Coordinator (JRAC)

The joint rear area coordinator (JRAC) integrates the rear area security and intelligence efforts of all functional and service component commands. The JRAC also interfaces with the AADC and the NCWC functional elements that control security for the battlespace adjacent to the JRA.

VI. Theater Force Opening Package (TFOP)

Deploying U.S. forces requires an in-theater support infrastructure capable of executing RSO&I operations and sustaining and redeploying the force. Recent operations in Somalia, Haiti, and Bosnia demonstrate a need for establishing early adequate support infrastructures in places where they did not previously exist. The theater force opening package (TFOP) is the Army mechanism to do this.

The TFOP is a modularly configured, multifunctional support task force comprised of specialized CSS and related CS modules. A typical TFOP needed during the initial stages of deployment includes transportation, engineer, supply, contracting, maintenance, and medical modules. The JFC may also elect to include strategic CSS cells from the USAMC, USAMMA, DLA, MTMC, and DESC.

The composition of the TFOP varies throughout the stages of a force projection operation until it becomes a TSC. The TFOP's mission remains identical to that for the TSC: to maximize throughput and follow-on sustainment of Army forces and other designated supported elements.The only difference is scale. As the TSC (forward), the TFOP is also uniquely responsible for building the theater infrastructure from a combination of existing and deploying assets.

X. Rear Area & Base Security

Ref: FM 4-93.52, chap 6; FM 4-93.51, chap. 10; and FM 4-93.50, chap. 9.

I. Rear Area Defensive Operations

Rear area defensive operations are actions taken by all units to secure and sustain the force. These actions are taken in a concerted effort. They include those actions necessary to neutralize or defeat enemy operations in the rear area. They also ensure freedom of action in deep and close operations and include area damage control.

The division commander is responsible for rear operations within his boundaries. The ADC(S) through the rear operations center is responsible for the rear area defensive operations in the division rear. Within the maneuver brigade area, the brigade commander is responsible for rear operations. Threat activity may exceed the capability of a commander's assets. When this happens, the division commander may assume responsibility for defeating a Level III threat in the brigade rear area by restructuring the boundaries and providing additional forces.

The objectives of rear area defensive operations are:

- Secure the rear areas
- Prevent or minimize enemy interference with command, control, and communications
- Prevent or minimize disruption of combat support and CSS forward
- Provide unimpeded movement of friendly units throughout the rear area
- Provide continuous, unimpeded support to deep, close, and rear operations
- Provide area damage control before, during, and after an attack or incident

Rear Area Defensive Operation Considerations

The key considerations to rear area defensive operations are sound planning, early warning, continuous OPSEC, and the rapid deployment of sufficient forces and resources to counter the threat. Rear area defensive operations are a command responsibility. The division commander ensures battle planning includes consideration for deep, close, and rear operations. Rear operations are a vital part of the division's overall operations. They are part of the mission analysis, the threat assessment, and intelligence preparation of the battlefield (IPB). They are also part of resource allocation, and the base assessment process.

The DISCOM units must defend themselves against attempts to disrupt their operations. They must be able to minimize destruction and to reinforce their units. The DISCOM units must also be able to gain time until response forces arrive. As discussed below, units form base defense perimeters to defend against the threat. If enemy forces exceed base and base cluster defense capabilities, response forces are used. These forces will provide the initial force to close with and to destroy the enemy. If an enemy incursion exceeds the capability of response forces, tactical combat forces must be committed to neutralize the threat.

Responsiveness is a key to defeating enemy incursions in the rear area. Responsiveness requires the immediate reaction and rapid deployment of sufficient combat power and area damage control resources. These two forces destroy the enemy and ensure minimal damage to the area. Responsiveness is achieved through:

- Effective command relationships and supervision
- Reliable communications
- Accurate intelligence
- Centralized planning and decentralized execution
- Organic mobility of response force
- Training and rehearsals
- Prior assessment of the capabilities of bases and facilities to withstand enemy attack. This assessment is based on a unit's degree of exposure and that unit's importance to the division's ability to sustain operations. This mission-essential vulnerability analysis assists the DISCOM commander to allocate resources, to protect personnel, supplies, and facilities in consonance with their importance to the mission.

II. Security

Logistics traffic is a high priority interdiction target for threat aircraft, artillery, and unconventional warfare elements. In the offense, bypassed enemy forces will attempt to get supplies by force. Single vehicles, especially ones moving fuel and ammunition, may be ambushed by unconventional forces.

After assessing threat capabilities and intentions, the rear operations commander may decide to assign escorts to critical convoys such as those moving fuel and ammunition. Escort possibilities include ground escorts of military police (MP)s, combat engineers, or tactical forces. Also considered are aerial escorts or ADA systems such as Avengers and Stingers. When resources are scarce, dedicated escorts may not be practical or possible. In such cases, response forces, air defense, or fire support assets may be positioned along the MSR to provide general support.

Organization for Security

To enhance sustainment operations, DISCOM elements are often grouped together. Elements may be grouped into bases and base clusters for mutual support. The ROC is ultimately responsible for the composition of bases and base clusters in the division rear. In addition, the ROC must ensure units selected for collocation complement each other. A mix of weapon systems, planning and supervisory personnel, and varied communications assets are required to form a viable base.

The DISCOM S2/S3 and DSB S2/S3 sections coordinate with the ROC on grouping of DISCOM units in the division rear. In the maneuver brigade area, the FSB commander is responsible for BSA security. Through his S2/S3, he coordinates with the brigade rear CP for planning security operations.

Certain bases or base clusters are designated as critical by the ROC. This is done in coordination with the DISCOM staff. These critical bases may contain a majority of a class of supply or service. An example of a critical base might be ammunition or fuel storage sites. All command and control headquarters are considered critical, as are critical communications nodes. In addition to its criticality, each base is assessed for its vulnerability. Vulnerability is based on the base's location, composition, and relative target value. Since forces cannot be strong everywhere, resources must be used to protect the most critical and vulnerable assets first.

III. Base Cluster Operations

Ref: FM 4-93.52, chap. 6, pp. 6-4 to 6-6.

1. Base

A base is a unit or multi-unit position with a definite perimeter. For rear area units, the DISCOM commander determines the position of the base in conjunction with the ROC. Frequently, a DISCOM company constitutes a base. Normally, the base commander is the senior unit commander present. Selection of the base commander should take into consideration not only rank, but also branch and experience.

2. Base Clusters

Base clusters contain several bases grouped together to enhance security and mission accomplishment. A base cluster normally does not have a defined perimeter or established access points. Base clusters rely on mutual support among bases for protection. Mutual support is achieved through interlocking fires, integrated patrol and surveillance plans, and use of reaction forces. A base cluster reaction force also aids in mutual support.

3. Base Cluster Operations Center (BCOC)

Typically, the DSB commander is a base cluster commander. His base cluster will normally include units located in the DSA. Corps logistics units, such as ammunition supply points, may be located at isolated locations within the division rear. They either operate as separate bases or are assigned to a base cluster by the ADC(S). The FSB commander is normally the base cluster commander for units in the BSA. The base cluster commander establishes a base cluster operations center (BCOC) with assets primarily from the S2/S3 section. The BCOC provides the command and control to plan, coordinate, and supervise base cluster operations. It interfaces with the ROC on terrain management, movement's requirements, and security operations. The BCOC positions units assigned to the cluster into bases and designates the base commanders. The ROC assigns divisional and non-divisional units in the division rear to base clusters or independent bases. The base cluster commander is responsible for integrating base defense plans into a base cluster defense plan.

An effective base defense system must accomplish four tasks:

- **Security of the base.** The base and base cluster commanders must establish the necessary defensive measures to ensure the security of their units.

- **Detection.** Detection is the early warning of enemy infiltration attempts. Detection devices include day and night observation devices as well as communications, intelligence, radar, and sensor equipment. Chemical and radiological monitoring must also be used. Warning systems and procedures must be established and understood by all personnel. If an attack is unlikely, few people are involved in defensive operations.If a threat is probable, defensive requirements will disrupt support operations. The MPs may provide the base and base cluster commander's link for detection, early warning, and deployment against enemy attacks in the rear.

- **Delay.** The defense system must be able to hinder the threat's progress to permit defense forces to react. Obstacles covered by direct or indirect fires slow or canalize movement. The ROC can, with G3 approval, authorize mine emplacement in the division rear. However, he must ensure a proposed minefield is coordinated with adjacent, higher, and subordinate units.

- **Destruction.** DISCOM units should place machine guns and lightweight anti-armor weapons to cover obstacles and avenues of approach. Grenade launchers mounted on vehicles are effective fire suppression systems that can be quickly dispatched to threatened areas.

IV. Defense of the DSA/BSA (Base Cluster)

Ref: FM 4-93.51, chap. 10.

C4ISR

The commander is responsible for Division Support Area/Brigade Support Area (DSA/BSA) security and its protection. As such he has control of all elements in the DSA/BSA for defense and positioning. Normally, the DSA/BSA is a base cluster with the DSB/FSB commander as the base cluster commander. The major elements in the DSA/BSA (ASMC, DSMC, signal field trains etc...) become unit bases. The senior individual in each base is the base commander.

The S2/S3 section of the DSBFSB TOC is the base cluster operations center. Alternate BCOCs should also be designated. Possibilities include the DSMC and the DSMC in the DSA. In urban terrain, the DSB/FSB S2/S3 may have to establish subordinate base clusters and BCOCs within the DSA/BSA. One may be designated the alternate BCOC.

Base Cluster Operation Center (BCOC)

The DSB/FSB commander is responsible for integrating base defense plans into a base cluster defense plan. As discussed, this requires development of a rear operations communications system and coordination with field artillery, engineer, ADA, and MP units. As part of the terrain management function, the DSB/FSB S2/S3 assigns a defensive position and a sector to each base in the DSA/BSA. Bases on likely avenues of enemy approach are given a smaller sector. The S2/S3 ensures each base's sector of fire overlaps the adjacent base's sector. He does this by personally coordinating with base commanders, and confirming that tenant units are tied in at their respective boundaries. Infiltration routes for Level I threats, and main avenues of approach are covered by planning for fires, obstacles, patrols, OPs, or sensors. The DSB/FSB S2/S3 must carefully coordinate this planning with each base to avoid having troops engage friendly forces.

The DSA/BSA defense plan must be integrated into the plan for the entire division rear. This requires the BCOC to coordinate with the DISCOM S3 and ROC for the overall plan. It must also coordinate directly with other BCOCs in the division rear to plan mutually supporting fires and to prevent firing upon each other.

The S2/S3 keeps a sketch of the defensive plan. It shows base sectors of fire, locations of mines and obstacles, planned indirect fire coverage, OPs, patrol routes, and positions of automatic and anti-armor weapons. These weapons will include those in the DSA/BSA for repair. If the firing system is operable, these weapons should be included in the DSA/BSA defensive scheme.

Whenever possible, units should occupy the same location within the DSA/BSA relative to the other units every time the DSA/BSA moves. They should build a habitual relationship with the units on all sides of them. This will expedite coordination of sectors of fire. Since night vision devices are likely to be scarce, illumination plans must also be included in the overall DSA/BSA security plan. Details on sector defense planning are in FM 19-4.

In addition, the BCOC must plan for a quick reaction force (QRF) from assets in the DSB/FSB. This QRF will be called upon when a base's defenses cannot defeat the threat and MPs and combat forces from the division are not immediately available. As a minimum, the reaction force should include personnel equipped with machine guns, grenade launchers, rifles, FM radios, and vehicles.

The BCOC must ensure that all base commanders understand the different threat levels and the associated actions. The brigade staff must also be aware that the DSB/FSB is neither staffed nor equipped to continue support operations at normal levels while responding to increased levels of threat. Support will be degraded. How much it is degraded will depend on the level of the threat.

The BCOC determines the level of threat and issues prearranged alerts to all bases. The BCOC also determines the probability of an air attack and issues air defense warnings. The BCOC should also have planned in advance emergency move procedures. If the DSB/FSB is under imminent danger from a Level II or III threat, the BCOC will call for an emergency move of key DSA/BSA assets. Key elements should be identified in advance and prepared to move to a predesignated site with minimum notice.

Other duties of the BCOC are to identify primary and secondary entry points into the DSA/BSA and designating preplanned landing zones for division rear reaction forces to use when required. The BCOC will also conduct regular (preferably daily) meetings or shift change briefings with base representatives to update the defensive plan.

Communications

Communications for DSA/BSA security will be conducted by wire, radio, signals, and personal contact. The primary means will be wire. Each base will be required to establish a wire linkup to the BCOC. The BCOC will operate a switchboard 24 hours a day. Other elements located in the DSA/BSA are responsible for laying wire from their CPs to the BCOC. The ADA and FA units in the DSA/BSA will have direct wire comms with the BCOC to provide early warning of enemy aircraft and to facilitate calls for fire. Ideally, the DSB/FSB would also operate a separate rear operations radio net. If wire or BCOC FM communications are lost, units will monitor the DSB/FSB command net that will serve as the BCOC radio net. If communications by these means are lost, the tenant activities are responsible for sending a messenger to the BCOC to provide coordination.

In addition, units in the DSA/BSA cannot rely on wire and FM communications to relay alert status. Too much time would pass before every soldier received the message. The DSB/FSB should establish readily recognizable signals that are easy to initiate.

Maneuver

The only specific asset the DSB/FSB commander may have that is trained for and has the primary mission of rear area operations is the military police platoon. For details in planning for MP operations see FM 3-19.4 (19-4). With their ability to shoot, move, and communicate, MPs on the battlefield provide the commander both technical and tactical advantages.

MP elements are task-organized to accomplish their missions. Size and composition of a tasked element depend on mission needs and the tactical situation. MP teams have the experience, initiative, and ability to operate independently or as part of a larger unit.

The MP platoon carries out four basic missions in support of the cdr in the rear area:

- **Battlefield Circulation and Control (BCC).** Expediting forward and lateral movement of combat resources to ensure a way is open to move reinforcing troops, fuel, food, and ammunition across the battlefield.
- **Area Security.** Helping the commander to provide security and protection in the rear area.
- **EPW Operations.** Collecting, evacuating, and interning EPW to relieve the tactical commander of the responsibility.
- **Law and Order Operations.** Conducting these when necessary to extend the combat commander's discipline and control.

Movement

Maintaining security of the MSRs for swift and safe movement of units and resupplies is critical to combat mission success. To avoid locking too many MPs into this mission, the DSB/FSB must use the gun trucks (with caliber .50 weapons) and combat vehicles that are returning forward with supplies as security. If that is not possible, a good practice is to use no more than 50 percent of MP assets on BCC unless there is a major movement of forces.

CSS Ops

V. Threat Evaluation and Integration

Ref: FM 4-93.52, pp. 6-1 and 6-4.

CSS organizations are normally the units least capable of self-defense against a combat force. They are also often the targets of enemy action. Time and effort used to defend themselves degrade their ability to perform their primary support mission. Key support elements from the DSB/FSB are designated to evacuate the DSA/BSA to allow minimum support to the division troops should the enemy confront the DSA/BSA. The DSB/FSB should develop a displacement plan. However, all units must be able to defend against Level I activities (sniper or terrorist activities). They should be able to impede Level II attacks until assistance arrives. Assistance may come from an MP unit as a response force or a tactical combat force (TCF) located in the rear. No CSS unit can sustain a defense against a determined Level II or III attack, but it should plan and train to protect itself until a TCF arrives to repel the enemy attack.

DSB/FSB units must defend themselves against attempts to disrupt their operations. They must be able to minimize destruction and to reinforce their units. The DSB/FSB units must also be able to gain time until response forces arrive. Units form base defense perimeters to defend against the threat. If enemy forces exceed base and base cluster defense capabilities, response forces are used. These forces will provide the initial force to close with and to destroy the enemy. If and enemy incursion exceeds the capability of response forces, tactical combat forces must be committed to neutralize the threat.

Threat evaluation is a detailed study of the enemy forces. It considers threat organization, tactical doctrine, equipment, and support systems. The DISCOM passes any information it has on the threat to the ROC to assist in its evaluation. Supply vehicle drivers and customers coming into the division area are valuable sources of information.

Level I Threat

Level I threats are those which can be defeated by base or base cluster self-defense measures. They normally involve the activities of agents, saboteurs, and terrorists.

Level II Threat

Level II threats are those beyond base or base cluster selfdefense capabilities. Response forces, typically MPs with supporting fires, can defeat this threat. This threat normally involves sabotage, raid, ambush, and reconnaissance operations. Special purpose or unconventional forces and tactical reconnaissance units normally conduct these operations.

Level III Threat

A tactical combat force is required to defeat a Level III threat.

Level III threats normally involve:

- Heliborne operations
- Airborne operations
- Penetration by enemy forces from the main battle area
- Ground force deliberate operations (for example, operational maneuver groups with linkup of smaller airborne and assault units)
- Infiltration operations

XI. CSS Transformation

Ref: FM 4-0 Combat Service Support, chap. 1.

Today Army forces seek to dominate an expanded AO with a minimal number of deployed troops, through depth and simultaneous attack. Because future operations will often entail a nonlinear, noncontiguous AO, CSS personnel will face vast challenges. They will have to meet various simultaneous demands across a potentially large AO with a reduced CSS force presence. The Army can accomplish its mission with an agile system when the distribution flow suffers no breaks in the seams between levels. Its real success, however, will depend on fielding a force that consumes fewer resources.

To meet these challenges, the Army is transforming. As the Army transforms, it must continue to sustain the legacy force (Force XXI and Army of Excellence organizations) as it moves toward developing and fielding the Objective Force. The Stryker brigade combat team (SBCT) now being developed will consist of lethal and highly mobile Army units that will deploy to preclude large-scale aggression and shape the situation in the land AO for much earlier decisive operations.

CSS Ops

I. Directions in CSS Development

As the Army transforms, so must CSS. CSS transformation is much more than just putting new technology on top of old processes. It requires CSS forces to be able to deploy rapidly to support current and future forces, effectively sustain full spectrum operations, and synchronize Army with joint efforts. The CSS transformation charter has a three-fold goal:

CSS Transformation

 Enhance strategic responsiveness to meet deployment timelines

 Reduce CSS footprint in the AO

 Reduce logistics costs without reducing warfighting capability and readiness

Ref: FM 4-0, chap. 1.

A. Enhancing Strategic Responsiveness

Enhancing strategic responsiveness requires optimizing Army support organizations and streamlining support procedures. Establishing a national logistics provider could maximize effectiveness and efficiencies by providing not only deployment support but also sustainment support. Common unit designs will enhance flexibility by deploying unit modules based on METT-TC, instead of entire units. Standardizing loads when possible maximizes lift capabilities.

The Army is developing and maximizing the use of strategic mobility enablers. This effort includes:

- Developing and improving its information system capabilities and CONUS/theater infrastructure.
- Prepositioning required support to minimize lift requirements
- Leveraging technology to build high-speed/ultra-large sealift and airlift capabilities
- Improving support infrastructures; and leveraging future technologies to develop precision munitions, fuel-efficient engines, and built-in prognostic and diagnostic technology

B. Reducing the CSS Footprint

In the long term, minimizing the CSS footprint in the AO also requires a cultural change. The Army must leverage the use of contractors and host-nation support assets; develop procedures for split-based operations; and use ISBs when feasible. These are some of the key aspects of reducing the U.S. CSS footprint in the AO, and the cornerstones of CSS reach operations.

C. Reduce CSS Costs

The final goal of CSS transformation is to transform the institutional CSS components of the Army, reducing CSS costs without reducing warfighting capability and readiness. Some components of CSS cost reduction are the single stock fund, national maintenance program (NMP), and improved depots and arsenals.

Achieving the Army Transformation requires a cultural change in how the Army views CSS. It requires new approaches to such areas as database management and dependence on organizations outside the military for support. Traditional geographic-based CSS relationships, with wholesale and retail orientations and breaks between providers at various levels of war, must be transformed into a seamless CSS continuum. In a rapidly changing strategic environment with dramatic advances in technological applications to military operations, CSS doctrine must be flexible. CSS personnel must be willing and able to apply evolving principles and techniques to varying dynamic situations.

An enhanced COP and full synchronization of effort are critical to success. Support personnel must have an increased awareness of what is required and what is available. Understanding what is required relies on synchronizing CSS operations with operational activities through the Army battle command system (ABCS). Support will become more efficient and effective through improved anticipation, as CSS personnel are better able to foresee future operations and identify, accumulate, and maintain the assets, capabilities, and information required to support them.

Awareness of what is available and the ability to direct it to where it is needed at the required time requires total integration of all elements of the CSS system—including active and Reserve Component Army, joint, multinational, civilian, and other agencies. The system must network decision makers as well as those responsible for executing CSS operations. It must link combatant commanders, and service staff managers, personnel support managers, materiel managers, distribution managers, services managers, information managers, and CSS operators. This network will support continued CSS capability enhancements through initiatives such as telemedicine, total asset visibility, VM, and predictive anticipatory maintenance capability.

A number of future maintenance initiatives will also increase the agility and economy of the CSS force. The shift towards a low-level maintenance concept (field maintenance and sustainment maintenance) reduces the requirement for extensive repair facilities, tools, and personnel to push forward by providing units the capability to replace faulty equipment forward and repair in the rear. In addition, the multicapable maintainer, augmented by highly portable automated diagnostic aids and on-board weapon system prognostics/diagnostics will replace modules and line replaceable units more effectively, rapidly returning weapon systems and vehicles to mission-capable status. Battlefield computers will have built-in tests, built-in diagnostics, and eventually prognostics. Finally, combining organizational and direct support maintenance maximizes economy in fwd maintenance elements.

Information systems are the equipment and facilities that collect, process, store, display and disseminate information. These include computers—hardware and software—and communications, as well as policies and procedures for their use (FM 3-0). Objective Force information systems will greatly enhance the ability of CSS commanders and staffs to communicate status and near-term capabilities to force commanders, as well as to anticipate requirements. They will include, within weapon system platforms, a full set of sensors that report weapon status in terms of readiness, required maintenance, fuel, manning, and ammunition. This information will be transmitted to either GCSS-A or CSSCS or both, depending on the specific information. For example, fuel status would go to CSSCS for battalion supply officers and forward support battalion support operations personnel to track status and plan fueling operations, while maintenance prognostic information would go to GCSS-A for initiation of work order and parts requests. GCSS-A will update CSSCS as part of its next scheduled update. GCSS-A will be the main scheduled information feed to CSSCS.

II. Stryker Brigade Combat Team (SBCT)

One facet of the Army Transformation is the Stryker Brigade Combat Team (SBCT). This brigade contains an organic brigade support battalion (BSB) that provides direct support to the brigade. The BSB headquarters consolidates many of the CSS functions for command and control. The TSC support operations section may be required to synchronize tactical support to BSB operations. In the early stages of an SSC, the BSB may link directly into the TSC (Fwd) for direct support. The implies that the TSC (Fwd) may be required to provide temporary tactical-level sustainment, as well as operational-level support interface for the SBCT during early entry operations. Developers envisioned this potential for interim tactical-level sustainment from the beginning.

Brigade Support Battalion (BSB)

The SBCT has an organic brigade support battalion (BSB) that provides direct support to the brigade. The commander consolidates logistics functions under the C2 of the BSB headquarters. The BSB performs distribution-based, centralized support in accordance with Force XXI concepts, although the distribution capability is limited. Its effectiveness depends on employing the latest advances in CSS C2, enhanced CSS situational understanding, and exploiting available resources through joint, multinational, host-nation, or contract sources. The small size of the battalion significantly minimizes the CSS footprint in the SBCT AO, but also requires support from other organizations/sources for sustained operations. The BSB support operations section integrates into BSB operations the activities of the CSS assets required to support brigade augmentation slices. If the augmentation slice is large enough, a corps support battalion may have to deploy to provide the required C2.

The support provided by the BSB is austere; it does not provide the same level of support that FSBs provide to divisional maneuver brigades.

III. UEx Sustainment - Army Transformation

Sustainment for the UEx is supported and controlled by the Theater Sustainment Command (TSC) through sustainment brigades. These sustainment brigades work for the Theater Sustainment Command directly (operational logistics), work for a UEx (tactical logistics), or work for another component of the joint force (component logistics). The operational sustainment brigade(s) normally remains under the operational control of the TSC, and hence the UEy, while the tactical sustainment brigade is under the operational control of the UEx. Note that the brigade headquarters of the sustainment brigade is the same for any of the missions. The difference is the type and number of subordinate battalions assigned.

UEx and UEy

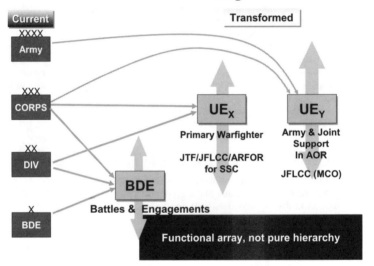

The sustainment brigades are assigned multifunctional combat service support (CSS) battalions and functional battalions, groups, and companies, tailored and task organized according to METT-TC. Sustainment brigades provide distribution-based logistics to the supported UEx, UEy, or other service element. Sustainment brigades also provide area support to forces not under the operational control of their supported headquarters. The operational-level sustainment brigade normally operates a theater level base in the JOA or on an intermediate staging base (ISB) near the JOA. The operational sustainment brigade provides area support to all units in the base, including units deploying or in route to the gaining tactical headquarters. The operational sustainment brigade also supports joint, interagency, and multinational forces as directed by the TSC and joint force cdr.

One or more tactical sustainment brigades move with the UEx and support it. The sustainment brigade OPCON to the UEx provides distribution-based replenishment to the brigades under the operational control of the UEx, and area support to any other unit located within the UEx area of operations. The sustainment brigade establishes temporary bases within the UEx area of operations to conduct mission-staging operations (MSO) and to provide replenishment to the brigades of the UEx.

Sustainment Brigade

Mission: Plan, prepare, execute and assess CSS operations within assigned AO.

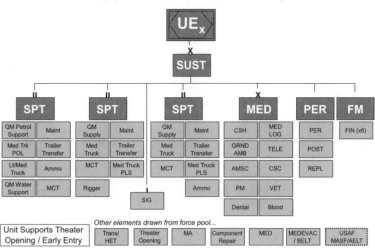

UEx

X

SUST

SPT		SPT		SPT		MED		PER	FM
QM Petrol Support	Maint	QM Supply	Maint	QM Supply	Maint	CSH	MED LOG	PER	FIN (x6)
Med Trk POL	Trailer Transfer	Med Truck	Trailer Transfer	Med Truck	Trailer Transfer	GRND AMB	TELE	POST	
Lt/Med Truck	Ammo	MCT	Med Truck PLS	MCT	Med Truck PLS	AMSC	CSC	REPL	
QM Water Support	MCT	Rigger			Ammo	PM	VET		
			SIG			Dental	Blood		

Other elements drawn from force pool...

Unit Supports Theater Opening / Early Entry	Trans/ HET	Theater Opening	MA	Component Repair	MED	MEDEVAC / BELT	USAF MASF/AELT

The UEx will cycle maneuver brigades in and out of offensive and defensive operations for mission staging. During mission staging operations, the maneuver brigade will refit, rearm, and replenish to enable it to operate three to four days at high tempo. Mission staging for a single brigade normally entails 24-48 hours.

Joint Sustainment

Joint capabilities extend the operational reach of the UEx

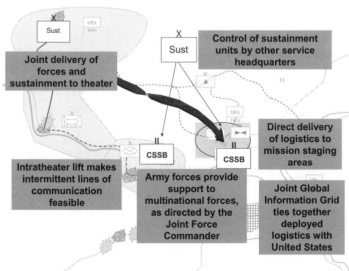

Joint delivery of forces and sustainment to theater

Control of sustainment units by other service headquarters

Direct delivery of logistics to mission staging areas

Intratheater lift makes intermittent lines of communication feasible

Army forces provide support to multinational forces, as directed by the Joint Force Commander

Joint Global Information Grid ties together deployed logistics with United States

In between mission staging, the logistics task force provides limited supplies to the brigade in the brigade area. These replenishment operations are intended to be rapid delivery of critical items and fuel and return. Joint capabilities, as illustrated above, extend the operational reach of the UEx.

CSS Ops

IV. UEy Sustainment - The TSC

Note: See pp. 3-57 to 3-64 for more information on Theater Support Commands.

Theater Support Command (TSC)

The TSC provides direct support to Army theater-level assets as well as common-user logistics and general support to other services, other governmental agencies, and multinational partners as directed. Its major subordinate organizations are modular, tailorable, and scalable transportation, Explosive Ordnance Disposal (EOD), and human resources units as well as tactical- and operational-level sustainment brigades The TSC provides a distribution management center capable of conducting materiel and transportation management functions for Army and joint forces. If required, the TSC functions as a multinational or joint logistic command, with suitable augmentation. For situations less than a full theater or for early entry, the TSC provides a tailored Army support element with a tailored sustainment brigade.

Modular Theater Sustainment Structure

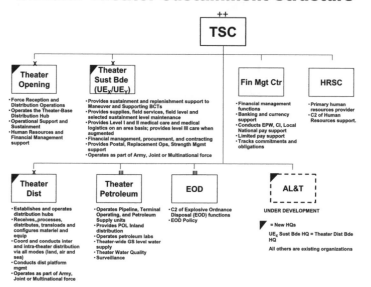

The TSC is a modular organization, that can be task organized based on the factors of the situation. It is a two-star command that includes units task organized to provide the required support.

Once the TSC commander determines the forces and capabilities for the TSC, the commander task organizes the TSC within the limits of the designated command and control authorities to accomplish the missions assigned by the UEy commander. Task organizing the TSC is dynamic in that it accounts for the order in which capabilities are made available to the ARFOR commander in the JOA, as well as aligning forces under the TSC. The TSC does this by designating portions or modules of its subordinate units that deploy in each phase of an operation. Subordinate units deploy in modular elements, as does the TSC headquarters, to optimize use of strategic transportation and minimize the CSS footprint in the AO. The TSC has the capability to support the theater and provide sustainment packages of other services.

I. CSS Planning & the MDMP

Ref: FM 4-0 Combat Service Support, chap. 5, FM 4-93.50 Tactics, Techniques, and Procedures for the FSB (Digitized), app. A.and FM 4-93.52 Tactics, Techniques, and Procedures for the DISCOM (Digitized), chap. 4.

CSS is vital to executing operations successfully. CSS planning, preparation, execution, and assessment must be versatile; they complement combat plans and operations, thus enhancing the ability of the supported commander to accomplish his mission. Commanders must anticipate their unit mission requirements and provide responsive support. They assess what resources and capabilities are available in theater and tailor follow-on forces accordingly. They ensure deploying/ deployed units are sustainable in the theater of operations until establishing lines of communication (LOC) or providing other support from within the area of operations (AO) (for example, through contracted support or host nation support [HNS]).

The combatant commander bases his CSS plan on the overall campaign plan. As he develops his strategic concept of operations, he concurrently develops, in coordination with his Army service component command (ASCC) and other service component commanders, a concept of support. They and their staffs consider the many support factors that affect the ability of forces to conduct operations. At operational level, CSS can be a dominant factor in determining the nature and tempo of operations.

CSS planning:

- Identifies significant time-phased materiel requirements, facilities, and other resources necessary to support the operation.
- Identifies the capabilities, vulnerabilities, and limitations of the aerial ports of debarkation (APODs), aerial ports of embarkation (APOEs), seaports of debarkation (SPODs), seaports of embarkation (SPOEs), and their reception and clearance capabilities.
- Identifies support methods and procedures required to meet the needs of the commander.
- Identifies vulnerabilities of certain types of systems and forces, including vulnerability to weapons of mass destruction.
- Provides coordinating and controlling onward movement of arriving forces and materiel.
- Includes reasonably assured joint, contracting, HNS, and multinational military sources.
- Includes coordinating with national providers to identify sustainment capabilities to fill materiel requirements.

The Military Decision Making Process - A Combat Service Support Perspective

Appendix A, FM 4-93.50 provides an overview of the military decision making process (MDMP) used by the CSS battle staff providing support to brigade and below echelons and is not intended as an all-inclusive description of the process. Refer to the appropriate tactical standard operating procedures for detailed information. Also, refer to FM 5-0 (101-5), Planning, Chapter 5, for more detailed information reference MDMP.

The MDMP must be integrated from top to bottom and from bottom to top in order to produce a synchronized concept of support that effectively supports the brigade tactical operation. The support battalion should have a CSS planner (liaison officer-LNO) who actively participates with the brigade S-1 and S-4 in the MDMP. Information must flow continuously between the brigade S-1/S-4, the support battalion, and the battalion task force S-1/S-4. At each level, the logistics estimate process should assess CSS capabilities, develop detailed requirements, and identify shortfalls as well as possible solutions. The logistics estimate process must be continuous and communication between the many CSS planners is essential. An integrated CSS concept of support must provide, at each level, the details of how a unit will both receive and provide support throughout an operation. It must provide enough detail so commanders know how they will be supported as well as how they and their subordinate units will execute the CSS

The CSS planners at all echelons must actively participate during each stage of the MDMP, and these planners must not only participate, but they must communicate with each other throughout the process.

The courses of action are compared, and one is recommended to the commander as the best option for providing support to the task force, support battalion, and the brigade. The commander selects the course of action which he feels best supports his concept of the operation. Throughout this stage of the MDMP, information must flow between the brigade, support battalion, and task force CSS planners. After the commander has made his decision, warning orders to subordinate units must be issued. Staffs at each echelon now produce a complete operations order. For brigade level CSS planners, this includes paragraph four (concept of support), a CSS annex/overlay and possibly a CSS matrix. For task force level CSS planners, this includes paragraph 4 (concept of support) and possibly a CSS annex/matrix with additional information on support arrangements. The support battalion should produce a full five-paragraph field order. Paragraph four for the support battalion should discuss the concept of internal CSS support. Additionally, this paragraph should be expanded upon in a CSS annex and possibly a CSS matrix. External CSS support to the brigade should be discussed in paragraph three of the support battalion base order, in an external CSS support annex, and possibly a CSS matrix. The support battalion order must also contain in the base order appropriate annexes on how the BSA and CSS assets will be supported by the battlefield operating systems (BOS) of fire support, air defense, intelligence (to include a reconnaissance and surveillance plan) and mobility/survivability (to include NBC).

I. CSS Considerations in Mission Analysis

Note: See pp. 4-8 to 4-11 for sample personnel/logistics estimates.

The MDMP begins when a mission is received from higher headquarters. Very rarely will this be in the form of a complete operations order. More likely it will begin after a verbal or written warning order is received. The commander, upon receiving a mission, should provide his staff with guidance as to how they should proceed with their analysis, and a warning order, in five-paragraph field order format, should be issued to subordinate units to allow them to begin to prepare for a new mission.

The staff begins mission analysis by developing their initial staff estimates based upon the higher headquarters order and their commander's guidance. Mission analysis also determines what the mission of higher headquarters is, what this equates to as a mission for their unit, and the situation/circumstances that may impact upon their unit's ability to execute a particular course of action that will be proposed to accomplish the mission. Each staff officer produces an estimate in his

The Military Decision-Making Process

Ref: FM 5-0 Army Planning & Orders Production, fig. 3-1, p. 3-3.

The military decision making process is a planning tool that establishes procedures for analyzing a mission, developing, analyzing, and comparing courses of action against criteria of success and each other, selecting the optimum course of action, and producing a plan or order. The MDMP applies across the spectrum of conflict and range of military operations. Commanders with an assigned staff use the MDMP to organize their planning activities, share a common understanding of the mission and commander's intent, and develop effective plans and orders.

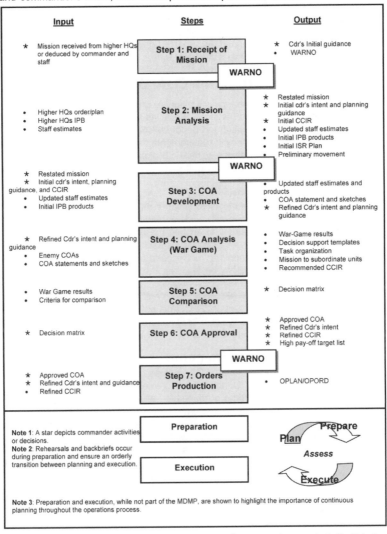

Input	Steps	Output
★ Mission received from higher HQs or deduced by commander and staff	**Step 1: Receipt of Mission**	★ Cdr's Initial guidance • WARNO
	WARNO	
• Higher HQs order/plan • Higher HQs IPB • Staff estimates	**Step 2: Mission Analysis**	★ Restated mission ★ Initial cdr's intent and planning guidance ★ Initial CCIR • Updated staff estimates • Initial IPB products • Initial ISR Plan • Preliminary movement
	WARNO	
★ Restated mission ★ Initial cdr's intent, planning guidance, and CCIR • Updated staff estimates • Initial IPB products	**Step 3: COA Development**	• Updated staff estimates and products • COA statement and sketches ★ Refined Cdr's intent and planning guidance
★ Refined Cdr's intent and planning guidance • Enemy COAs • COA statements and sketches	**Step 4: COA Analysis (War Game)**	• War-Game results • Decision support templates • Task organization • Mission to subordinate units • Recommended CCIR
• War Game results • Criteria for comparison	**Step 5: COA Comparison**	★ Decision matrix
★ Decision matrix	**Step 6: COA Approval**	★ Approved COA ★ Refined Cdr's intent ★ Refined CCIR ★ High pay-off target list
	WARNO	
★ Approved COA ★ Refined Cdr's intent and guidance • Refined CCIR	**Step 7: Orders Production**	• OPLAN/OPORD

Note 1: A star depicts commander activities or decisions.
Note 2: Rehearsals and backbriefs occur during preparation and ensure an orderly transition between planning and execution.

Preparation

Execution

Prepare
Plan
Assess
Execute

Note 3: Preparation and execution, while not part of the MDMP, are shown to highlight the importance of continuous planning throughout the operations process.

The MDMP helps organize the thought process of commanders and staffs. It helps them apply thoroughness, clarity, sound judgment, logic, and professional knowledge to reach decisions.

CSS Plans

or her area. The results of mission analysis should include completed staff estimates, including an initial intelligence preparation of the battlefield (IPB) by the S-2. The staff will also produce a proposed restated mission for their unit. These products will be presented to the commander and he will provide additional planning guidance to include: number of courses of action he wants the staff to develop, initial commander's critical information requirements (CCIR), timeline, risk guidance, and rehearsals to be conducted. Additionally, the commander will provide his initial intent that will include the method and end state for the operation. A second warning order should be issued to subordinate units no later than the end of mission analysis.

The Logistics Estimate

The logistician's input during mission analysis primarily comes from the logistics estimate. The logistics estimate is a continuous process that begins during mission analysis and is continually refined and updated through mission completion. The logistics estimate does not have a doctrinal format at the brigade level.

II. CSS Considerations in COA Development

During COA development, the logistics planners must refine the logistics estimate they developed during mission analysis. Facts and assumptions developed during mission analysis must be verified and updated. CSS planners must identify any significant CSS considerations and requirements that have a major impact on mission accomplishment. Additionally, the CSS planner must develop a draft concept of support during this phase of the MDMP.

COA Sustainment Feasibility

For each course of action, the logistics planner must access its sustainment feasibility. The sustainment feasibility is determined by whether or not the unit possesses the required resources to sustain the unit throughout the tactical operation. Tailoring your logistics estimate for each course of action can help make this determination. If requirements do not exceed capabilities, the sustainment of the course of action will generally be feasible. If any requirements do exceed capabilities you must again determine its significance and potential impact upon the mission. If the shortfall is a "WAR-STOPPER", and there are no workable solutions to the problem, then sustainment of the COA is not feasible. Ensure you have exhausted all possible means to solve the problem, to include support from higher headquarters, before you deem the COA not feasible.

Synchronization Requirements

The synchronization of CSS during COA analysis is critical to ensure continuous support during the operation. During the war game, the logistical planner will determine, based on the scheme of maneuver, what supplies and services must be where at a given time. This will generate critical CSS actions that must be accomplished to sustain the mission. He must consider time-distance factors and determine which support activity will be available to provide the required support. This is where the logistical planner begins to directly link the actions of task force logistics assets with the support battalion sustainment activities and division/corps resupply activities. He must ensure that all critical CSS activities are included in the synchronization matrix to successfully synchronize all levels of support.

Critical CSS Requirements

During this phase of MDMP, the courses of action are compared using the synchronization matrices and notes taken for each evaluation criteria used. A decision matrix with the evaluation criteria and some type of weighting factor (e.g., numbers, +/-, etc.) should be used to record the results of the course of action comparison. A decision matrix can be used as an aid to obtain a decision from the commander as to what course of action will be selected.

III. CSS Considerations in COA Comparison

In order to compare COAs and determine which is more supportable, logistical planners must calculate estimated attrition rates, project battle losses for critical weapons systems, and project personnel battle losses. The RSR for each COA must be refined and compared to any CSR that may be in effect. Quantities of supplies required, demands on transportation assets, and reconstitution requirements must be compared to determine which COA stresses the units' logistical system the most. An analysis of the risks to CSS assets and operations must be compared and considered.

IV. CSS Considerations in Orders Production

Note: See pp. 4-15 to 4-22 for sample paragraph 4, support concept and the CSS overlay.

The brigade logistic planners are responsible for paragraph 4 of the OPORD as well as the logistics annex (annex I). These products must be complete, concise and synchronize all levels of logistics support from top to bottom with the tactical plan.

Final Concept Of Support

The paragraph four consists of the final approved concept of support. Remember that this paragraph is written primarily to inform the commanders how they will be supported throughout the tactical operation, so do not include details on how the support elements are to execute the plan. Save all those details for the logistics annex. The concept of support should include a brief synopsis of the support command mission, support area locations to include the locations of the next higher logistics bases, the next higher levels support priorities, the commander's priority of support, significant or critical CSS activities, any significant risks, and the major support requirements in each tactical logistics function. If the tactical concept of operation is phased, the concept of support should also be phased to facilitate changes of priorities and logistics focus during each phase.

Complete/Concise

It is essential that the OPORD be complete, concise, and include all critical tasks that must be accomplished to support the tactical mission. Ensure you consider the command and support relationships of all units within your area of operation and ensure all elements receive support. Ensure you address all of the tactical logistics functions and properly phase the support concept if the tactical concept of operation is phased.

Synchronized Top To Bottom

To ensure proper synchronization, include all critical tasks and coordination requirements that were developed during the war gaming phase. Consider developing a logistics synchronization matrix, if possible. Ensure that all priorities of support are in agreement with the scheme of maneuver and weight the main effort. Coordinate with the other battlefield operating system elements to ensure that there are no inconsistencies in logistics information within the maneuver, engineer, artillery, and CSS annexes. As subordinate OPORDs are developed, you must ensure that their support plans are consistent and executable within your support framework. Synchronization of resupply operations from the corps/division, to the support battalion, to the task force level is critical.

Critical Commander's Information Requirements (CCIR)

Ref: FM 4-93.52, chap. 4.

The digital information system employed by the commander and staff is as sophisticated as the weapon systems they employ. The information available to the commander is only valuable if it can be focused to a manageable level. Information that the battle staff generates focuses on and is driven by the CCIR. It is prepared by the commander and his staff. They are based upon the commander's continuously evolving vision for the concept of support (current, future, and sequel to the future) and the commander's continuing, independent estimate of the situation. The staff supports the commander's development of CCIR, develops the common relevant picture in response to the CCIR and other parameters the commander identifies. The battle staff manages the type and volume of information fed to the commander based upon satisfying the commander's CCIR. In response to the CCIR, information systems focus on getting the right information to the commander or decision-maker as soon as possible.

The use of CCIR focuses the information gathering process for the staff. It is that information which the staff will notify the commander of, regardless of his location or time. CCIR allows the commander to define information needs and, in turn, focus the battle staff (and subordinate commanders) on information acquisition, fusion, and analysis. They vary with each phase of an operation and consist of only those essential information requirements that the commander must know to make a decision concerning logistical support of a particular phase of a battle. The battle staff must continuously update the CCIR so that they are current with the ongoing operation. The following sources normally feed the CCIR:

- **Priority Intelligence Requirements (PIR)** - What we want to know about the enemy?

- **Essential Elements of Information (EEI)** - Crucial information on enemy and environment needed by commander by a specific time.

- **Essential Elements of Friendly Information (EEFI)** - How the enemy sees the friendly unit?

- **Friendly Forces Information Requirements (FFIR)** Information commander needs on forces available for the operations such as personnel, maintenance, supply, ammunition, POL, experience and leadership capability.

How can the commander anticipate logistics requirements to best support the combat mission? CCIR allows the commander to define information needs and in turn, focus the staff (and subordinate commanders) on information acquisition, fusion, and analysis. The CCIR can be further described as being:

- Dependent upon the situation

- Specified by the commander for each operation or phase

- Generally time-sensitive in terms of the decision point on a decision support template or the event requirements of the synchronization matrix driving their collection

- Applicable only to the commander, who specifies and publishes them; normally published in the applicable operations plan/order; and transmitted via specified means

- A link between current, future, and sequel to the future operations

- Logistics preparation of the battle field (LPB) process

CSS Plans

Chap 4

II. Logistics Preparation of the Theater/Battlefield (LPT/LPB)

Ref: FM 4-0 Combat Service Support, chap. 5 and FM 4-93.52, chap. 5. See pp. 2-11 to 2-18 for additional information on planning Joint and Theater Logistics.

I. Logistics Preparation of the Theater (LPT)

Logistics preparation of the theater (LPT) is a key conceptual tool available to personnel in building a flexible strategic/operational support plan. Logistics preparation of the theater consists of the actions taken by combat service support personnel at all echelons to optimize means (force structure, resources, and strategic lift) of supporting the joint force commander's plan. These actions include identifying and preparing ISBs and forward operating bases; selecting and improving LOC; projecting and preparing forward CSS bases; and forecasting and building operational stock assets forward and afloat. They focus on identifying the resources currently available in the theater for use by friendly forces and ensuring access to those resources. A detailed estimate of requirements, tempered with logistics preparation of the theater, allows support personnel to advise the JTF/ASCC/ARFOR commander of the most effective method of providing adequate, responsive support while minimizing the CSS footprint.

A. Relevant Information

Relevant information is all information of importance to commanders and staffs in the exercise of command and control (FM 3-0). Relevant information provides the answers commanders and staffs need to conduct operations successfully, that is, all elements necessary to address the factors of METT-TC. Once CSS planners know a contingency country or geographic region, they begin to build a CSS relevant information database. They develop this CSS relevant information in close coordination with the intelligence and operations community's intelligence preparation of the battlefield effort. When completed, they can use the information in the database to develop a comprehensive plan for LPT.

Planning must provide for the timely arrival of CSS assets balanced according to the mission. Strategic lift assets are extremely limited, and commanders cannot afford to squander even one sortie on movement of unnecessary supplies, equipment, or personnel. A detailed LPT plan covers the following areas:

1. Geography

Planners collect information on climate, terrain, and endemic diseases in the AO to determine when and what types of equipment are needed. For example, water information determines the need for such things as early deployment of well-digging assets and water production and distribution units.

2. Supplies

Planners collect information on supply items that are readily available in the AO and can support U.S. forces. Subsistence items, bulk petroleum, and barrier materials are the most common. Planners must answer several questions, such as:

- Can any of these items be purchased locally?
- What supply systems are the Allies/coalition partners using? Are they compatible?
- Are major equipment items compatible?
- Does the host nation have repair parts that support current U.S. systems?

CSS Plans

3. Facilities

Planners collect information on the availability of such things as warehousing, cold-storage facilities, production and manufacturing plants, reservoirs, administrative facilities, hospitals, sanitation capabilities, and hotels. Availability of such facilities could reduce the requirement for deployment. For example, force provider can house approximately 3,300 personnel. However, if space is available in a complex of hotels with the requisite support in the required location, deploying the force provider, with its strategic lift requirements, could be eliminated or deferred.

4. Transportation

Planners collect information on such things as road and rail nets, truck availability, bridges, ports, cargo handlers, petroleum pipelines, MHE, traffic flow, choke points, and control problems.

5. Maintenance

Planners examine the multinational partners' armed forces and answer such questions as:

- Can they supplement the Army capability?
- Does a commonality exist in such things as equipment and repair parts?
- Does the host nation have adequate machine works for possible fabrication of repair parts?
- Are there theater support contract maintenance capabilities available?

6. General Skills

Planners collect information on the general population of the AO. They get answers to such questions as:

- Is English commonly spoken?
- Are interpreters available?
- Will a general labor pool be available?
- What skills are available (drivers, clerks, MHE operators, food service personnel, guards, mechanics, and longshoremen available)?

B. Negotiations

The LPT should be the basis for negotiating HNS and theater support contracting agreements. Considerations may include prepositioning of supplies and equipment, civilian support contracts, OCONUS training programs, and humanitarian and civic assistance programs designed to enhance the development and cooperative solidarity of the host nation, and provide infrastructure compensation should deployment of forces to the target country be required.

C. Time-Phased Force & Deployment Data (TPFDD)

The LPT should be synchronized on a regular basis with the TPFDD to ensure that only the CSS capabilities that cannot be met with assurance from another source are phased into the AO. This synchronization takes place, at a minimum, each time the commander updates the LPT to ensure that only the minimum necessary strategic lift is committed to CSS assets.

The ASCC commander identifies the number of Army units, including CS and CSS organizations, required to support the combatant commander's campaign plan. This force tailoring becomes the basis for resourcing decisions concerning the various force compositions active component, U.S. Army Reserve, Army National Guard, and stationing plans. (FM 3-0 discusses force tailoring.) A current, well-developed LPT enables the ASCC commander to make sound force tailoring and resourcing decisions.

General LPT Information Sources

Ref: FM 4-0 Combat Service Support, chap. 5.

Collectors routinely provide an abundance of information on targeted theaters or likely contingency areas. Also, agencies can assist CSS personnel in building the information file. The CSS planner must not underestimate the time and resources required for these actions. The LPT is a living document that is in a continual state of review, refinement, and use. Forces should use it as the basis for negotiations, preparing the TPFDD, and the Total Army analysis process.

The following sources of information are only a few; this list is not all-inclusive.

Department of State
Department of State embassy staffs routinely do country studies. They also produce information on foreign countries, including unclassified pamphlets. These pamphlets focus on political and economic issues, not military or CSS matters.

Intelligence Preparation of the Battlefield (IPB) Data
The weather and terrain databases in the IPB, with its overlays, provide current information for preselecting LOC and sites for CSS facilities. The IPB event analysis matrix and template can determine the need for route improvements and bridge reinforcements. FM 34-130 has more details.

Special Operations Forces, to Include Civil Affairs Units
Whether in country or targeted on a specific country, SOF can provide a wealth of CSS information. They include functional specialists who focus on particular areas (such as civilian supply, public health, public safety, and transportation). Civil affairs (CA) units also can provide vital assistance when coordinating theater contract support and CUL support to NGOs.

Culturegrams
Culturegrams are a series of unclassified pamphlets published by Brigham Young University that provide general/social information on specific countries. Though not focused on governmental or military interests, they provide a variety of useful information that can be used by deploying forces.

Army Country Profiles
Army country profiles (ACPs) are produced by the Army Intelligence Threat Analysis Center. ACPs are classified country profiles providing information on logistics, military capabilities, intelligence and security, medical intelligence, and military geography. They include photos, maps, and charts.

Country Contingency Support Studies
Country contingency support studies are produced by the Defense Intelligence Agency (DIA). These classified documents contain extensive information on railways, highways, bridges, and tunnels within a given country.

Other assets or tools the CSS planner may want to consider as the LPT plan is developed include:

• Army prepositioned stocks

• Use of containerization to limit handling

• HNS agreements

• ISSAs and ACSAs

• Prearranged contracts to provide support

CSS Plans

II. Logistics Prep of the Battlefield (LPB)

Ref: FM 4-93.52, chap. 5.

Logistics preparation of the battlefield is the process of gathering data against pertinent battlefield components, analyzing their impact on sustainment, and integrating them into tactical planning so that support actions are synchronized with maneuver. It is a conscious effort to identify and assess those factors, which facilitate, inhibit, or deny support to combat forces. Just as intelligence preparation of the battlefield is important to the conduct of actual combat operations, logistics preparation of the battlefield is equally important to sustaining the combat power of the force.

The process requires tacticians to understand the data needed by logisticians to plan and provide timely, effective support. It requires TF logisticians to understand the mission, the tactical plan, and the battlefield's time and space implications for support. It is a coordinated effort to prepare the battlefield logistically. The basic steps in systematizing the process are:

- Determine battlefield data pertinent to support actions

- Determine sources from which raw data can be derived

- Gather pertinent data

- Analyze collected data elements and translate them into decision information by assessing their impact on the mission and the competing courses of action

- Integrate decision information into tactical planning by incorporating it in CSS estimates and TF plans and orders

When determining what battlefield data are relevant to sustainment, it's helpful to break down CSS operations into certain key elements against which data can be collected for study and analysis. These data elements are called the components of tactical CSS. The following descriptions of the components of tactical CSS are not intended to be all-inclusive. They are offered here, however, to stimulate thought and to facilitate an understanding of those factors which impact on tactical CSS support:

- Logistics resources are the wherewithal to effect support, including CSS organizational structures, command and control, task organizing for support, communications, information automation systems, medical facilities, and materiel such as transportation assets and supply, maintenance and field services equipment.

- Logistics capabilities include soldier and leader skills and the personnel staffing which, collectively, activate CSS resources and bring to life the required support.

- Logistics capacities include reception and clearance capacities, carrying capacities of transportation assets, volumes of storage facilities, maintenance production output rates, and supply route characteristics such as surface composition, tunnels, overhead obstructions, bridge weight limits and traffic circulation rates.

- Materiel stocks include the quantity and status of weapon systems, ancillary equipment, ammunition, repair parts and consumable supplies required or available to sustain or reconstitute combat power of deployed units. Also included are CSS status reports and known or projected shortfalls.

- Consumption and attrition rates include experienced or expected usages of consumable supplies and weapon systems, which must be considered to anticipate support requirements.

- Time and space factors are those requirements and restrictions of the battlefield, which influence whether logistic support is provided to deployed forces at the right place and time. Included here are plans, orders, rehearsals, priority of support, positioning for support, tempo of support (intensity of demand), security, risk assessment, the effects of terrain, weather, contaminated areas, minefields, night time enemy threat on CSS operations, and the battlefield signatures of logistic resources. Time and space factors, especially, impact on the synchronization and integration of CSS on the battlefield.

Sources from which relevant battlefield data are derived include:

- Higher headquarters briefs, plans and orders
- The commander's planning guidance
- The commander's intent (or concept)
- Operations and intelligence briefings and overlays
- Modified table of equipment (MTOE) of task force units
- CSS status reports
- Scouts
- Engineer route reconnaissance overlays
- Traffic circulation and highway regulating plans
- Personal reconnaissance

Logisticians should treat the components of tactical CSS as essential factors that should be assessed for each plan. By doing so, they bring a professional approach to the contributions they make in the planning process. The components are variables. Some are dynamic and change with METT-TC so they should be validated daily, even hourly, if necessary. Commanders should appreciate the unique contributions their logisticians make in the planning process and when they've done a thorough job of collecting and analyzing pertinent battlefield data. Commanders must not accept less.

The commander and staff conduct LPB. Successful LPB contributes immeasurably to the favorable outcome of battle. Logistics preparation of the battlefield is an on-going process by which logisticians analyze:

- Tactical commander's plan/concept of operation
- Tactical commander's intents
- Supported force CSS requirements
- Available CSS resources
- Combat service support shortfalls
- The enemy (intentions, capabilities, weaknesses, doctrine)
- Terrain and weather
- Intelligence preparation of the battlefield (IPB) products
- Transportation infrastructure
- Host nation support available
- ·• Time/distance factors

Logistics preparation of the battlefield (LPB) products are:

- A logistics estimate
- A visualization of the pending battle and logistics activity required by phase
- Anticipated logistics challenges and shortfalls
- Solutions to logistics challenges and shortfalls
- How, when, and where to position logistics units to best support the tactical commander's plan
- A synchronized tactical and logistical effort

Tactical Level Logistics (Div Level & Below) Needs & Considerations Checklist

Ref: FM 4-93.52, app. D.

Appendix D, FM 4-93.52 provides a checklist of the primary logistics information needs and considerations required by the DISCOM battle staff and is not intended as an all-inclusive description or identification of each. Refer to the appropriate field manuals and standard operating procedures for detailed information. The logistics information needs and considerations required by the DISCOM battle staff are:

2ND and 3RD order effects of decisions
Acquisition law
Advance echelon (ADVON)
Aerial refueling operations status
Aerial/seaport throughput capacity
Air defense umbrella
Airfields/airstrips in area of operations
Air line of communications rqmts and status
Air force prime beef/red horse/prime rib eng tms
Air force war readiness spares kit (WRSK)
Allied/coalition support provided and required
Area damage control and fire fighting resources
Area of responsibility/operations (AOR/AO)
Armed services blood program status
Army and Air Force Exchange service (AAFES)
Base development
Battle losses
Battlefield damage assmt.& repair (BDAR)
Battlefield distribution scheme
Boundaries
Bridge and road classifications
Calibration support for theater
Campaign plan
Campaign plan assumptions
Casualty rates (expected and actual)
Civil-military operations (CMO) posture (current and projected)
Civil reserve air fleet (CRAF) support
Combat health logistics
Commander's priorities
COMMZ development
Concept of support develop. w/campaign plan
Concept of support coordination
Conflict termination arrangements
Consumption factors (current and projected)
Consumption rates (estimated and actual)
Containerization and container handling equipment
Contingency contracting support
Contractor support
Convoy tracking
Courses of action analyses

Cross-leveling of stocks with theater
Current mission(s)
Defense Logistics Agency (DLA) coordination/assistance
Disease, a non-battle injury (DNBI) rates
Echelon above corps (EAC) logistics unit
Emergency force modernization efforts
Emergency modification work orders (MWOs)
Emergency resupply
Enemy prisoner of war (EPW) logistics support
Engineering and construction standards/policies
Executive agents for joint force
Explosive ordnance disposal assets
Fast sealift ship (FSS) availability/status
Food service support
Force provider; harvest bare/eagle/falcon status
Force tracking
Funding
Health service support posture
Heavy equipment transport (HET) asset posture
High mortality item stockage criteria
Host nation support (HNS) arrangements
Humanitarian support missions
Identification, friend or foe (IFF) arrangements
Imagery of area of operations
In-transit visibility (ITV) of logistics resources
Intermediate staging/support bases (ISBs)
International laws and customs
Interoperability
Intra-theater airlift and sealift
Labor sources
Law enforcement capability, Law of land warfare
Liaison officer (LNO) exchange program
Linguists
Local purchase procedures and theater policy
Logistics force integration and task organization
Logistics situational awareness at all levels
Logistics preparation of the battlefield
Logistics capabilities (current and projected)
Logistics shortfalls/challenges
Logistics work-arounds (current and projected)

Logistics infrastructure maturation
Logistics force adequacy
Logistics lessons learned
Logistics over the shore (LOTS) operations
Logistics resources in occupied territory
Long-lead procurement items
Maintenance force adequacy
Maintenance trends
Maintenance operational readiness float (ORF)
Major subordinate command missions
Major subordinate commands' situation reports
Major weapon systems status
Maneuver control system (MCS) information
Map production and distribution
Marine force service support group (FSSG)
Master DoD activity address code (DODAAC)
Unit identification code (UIC) directory for force
Material management
Maturation of logistics C4I system
Media coverage
Combat health logistics status
Mission branches and sequels
Mortuary affairs
Movements management status
Nuclear, biological, and chemical protection arrangements
New equipment training activities
Non-developmental item (NDI) maint/supply
Non-governmental organizations in theater
Offshore petroleum distribution system availability
On-going staff actions and suspenses
Order-ship-times
Out- of-sector logistics support
Overflight and basing rights
Personnel status (current and projected)
Personnel stop-loss policy
Petroleum lab testing
Political sensitivities
Port opening and operations
Port clearance posture
Post support activity (PSA) requirements
Postal support
Post-conflict battlefield clean up
Preferred munitions stockages
Private volunteer organizations in theater
Property disposal process
Provisional logistics unit activations
Ready reserve force (RRF) vessels
Real estate management
Reception, staging, onward mvmt & integration

Reconstitution of forces
Redeployment arrangements reporting
Resource conservation
Retrograde operations (logistics)
Risk management and risk assessment
Rules of engagement (ROE)
Safety issues
Security for modes & lines of communications
Senior logistician's concept of support
Senior logistician's intent
Single fuel or multiple fuel concept for theater
Specialized repair activity (SRA) support
Stockage levels in days of supply
Storage facility requirements/availability
Supply trends
Support for civilian/non-combatant population
Support for special operations forces (SOF)
Support planning by phase of operations
Support for airborne operations
Support for deception operations
Support for train-ups
Support relationship lash-up
Support unit/activity/vessel locations
Support for rehearsals
Supporting combatant commander
Tactical assembly areas (TAAs)
Technical intelligence
Theater aircraft maintenance program (TAMP) status
Theater ammunition status
Theater command and control arrangements
Theater depot level maintenance support
Theater medical evacuation policy and process
Theater war reserve stocks
Threat equipment
Threat capabilities and intentions
Threat logistics shortfalls
Threat logistics support bases
Time duration (expected and actual) of ops
Time phased force and deployment list (TPFDL)
Total asset visibility (TAV)
Trafficability study of area of operations
Transportation network status (current and projected).
Unique characteristics of area of operations
U.S. Customs Service during redeployment
USTRANSCOM coordination
Wargaming
Water production, supply, and distribution
Weather conditions
Wholesale level augmentation in-theater

CSS Considerations in the Offense and Defense

Note: See pp. 1-15 to 1-17 for additional information on CSS support to offensive, defensive, stability and support operations (FM 4-0).

Offense	Defense
Supply	
• **Responsiveness** • Coordinate w/ deception plan (mask CSS prep) • Stage supplies fwd to shorten LOC • Echelon support forward • Uploaded/mobile supply stocks • Use captured supplies • Attach CSS to maneuver units • Arrive on OBJ w/sufficient CSS for further ops • Transition to defense	• **Activity greatest during preparation** • Night ops for resupply • WSRO (crew/wpn) • SPT facilities positioned out of the flow of battle • CSS for corps units • Use prepositioned stocks for security force • Sustainment of deep operations • Transition to offense
Fuel	
• CL III most important – high fuel consumption • Higher fuel consumption in Offense	
Arm	
• Ammo close to user • ASP/ATP displacement plan • Replenish UBL	• **High Use in Defense** • ASP/ATP located for responsive support • Stockpile CL V in excess of basic load; far fwd/successive defensive positions
Move	
• Requirements increase • LOC lengths • Replacements increase • CL III, V, VII • Movement of supply bases fwd • Traffic control (rearward evac of casualties) • Primary modes motor/air • Throughput distribution	• Critical in the prep stage of Def (stockpiling; shifting of personnel, wpn sys & supplies laterally or in depth) • Priorities established/enforces • Movement control
Fix	
• Fix fwd/recover fwd • Maint timelines shortened • MSTs (properly configured) • Minimize evacuation – leave equip at UMCP for follow and support units • BDAR • CL VII replacements	• Max # wpn sys ready for battle • MSTs fwd; consolidated • Consideration given to augment maint to covering force elements when they return to MBA so they may rapidly be returned to fighting condition • Maint timelines extended • CL VII (gun tubes, tracks) positioned fwd
CSS C2	
• Mobile CSS, Move by echelon	• Terrain management
Medical	
• High casualty rates • Echeloned fwd • Corps hospitals displace fwd • Increase requirements for evacuation assets • Short MEDEVAC policy	• Priority for evacuation based on location of the probable enemy main effort – weight main effort • Clearing facilities away from possible points of penetration • AXP established • Longer MEDEVAC policy • Patient evacuation preplanned & routes
Field Service	
• Suspended except: • GRREG • Airdrop	• CEB, bakeries, renovation, PX operates when tactical situation permits
Supply (CL I, II, IV, VI, VII)	
• Requirements for obstacle breaching & bridging material	• CL IV/V barrier heaviest in prep for defense • Increased use of chemical equipment • Use CCLs on a scheduled basis

This is intended only as a guide. Actual requirements depend on terrain and the enemy (METT-TC dependent).

CSS Plans

Combat Service Support Planning
III. Mission Analysis and the Logistics/Personnel Estimate

Ref: ST 101-6, chap. 2; FM 4-93.52, app. B; FM 4-93.50, app. A.

The logistician's input during mission analysis primarily comes from the logistics estimate. The logistics estimate is a continuous process that begins during mission analysis and is continually refined and updated through mission completion. The logistics estimate does not have a doctrinal format at the brigade level.

The mission analysis process and personnel/logistics estimate are logical and systematic processes staff officers use to analyze the influence CSS factors have on a contemplated course of action (COA).

Mission analysis considerations feed information into the estimate process. The estimates are as thorough as time permits. At division level, estimates are not normally written. At echelons above division, the estimate is written and follows the format outlined on the following pages. Personnel/logistics staff officers coordinate with other staff officers when preparing their estimates. They may incorporate material from other staff estimates, but they are still responsible for the validity of all data included in their estimate.

Personnel/logistics estimates are kept current. As factors that influence operations change, new facts are developed and assumptions become facts or become invalid. The estimates are an integral part of any commander's decision-making process. The following CSS mission analysis considerations and personnel/ logistics estimates contain guidance and information for completing the estimate process.

I. CSS Mission Analysis Considerations - The Logistics Estimate

The following is a methodology for logistics planners as they go through the decision-making process. As part of the process, the five basic questions logistics planners and operators should always be able to answer are:

- Where are we on the battlefield?
- Why are we here?
- How do we support from here?
- How do we get support from here?
- When, to where, and in what sequence do we displace to ensure continuous operations?

This methodology is based on the customer and the customer's needs. In short, there are five areas that must be addressed: requirement, capability, shortfall, analysis, and solution model. This methodology can be used throughout the decision-making process. The level of detail at which each question can be answered is a reflection of the planner's position and organization.

The logistician's input during mission analysis primarily comes from the logistics estimate. The logistics estimate is a continuous process that begins during mission analysis and is continually refined and updated through mission completion. The logistics estimate does not have a doctrinal format at the brigade level.

II. The Logistics Estimate (Sample)

Ref: ST 101-6, Jul 04, pp. 2-11 to 2-14.

See p. 4-22 for an outline of the logistics estimate process.

The G4 prepares the logistics estimate, which provides an accurate and current assessment of the CSS situation of the organization, its subordinate units, and any attached or supporting elements. The logistics estimate is an analysis of how service support factors can affect mission accomplishment. It contains the G4's (S4's) conclusions and recommendations about the feasibility of supporting major operational and tactical missions with respect to the proposed COAs.

(Classification)

> Headquarters
> Place
> Date, time, and zone
> Msg ref no.

LOGISTICS (LOG) ESTIMATE NO

References: Maps, charts, or other documents.

Time Zone Used Throughout the Estimate:

1. MISSION

This paragraph lists the command's restated mission.

2. SITUATION AND CONSIDERATIONS

a. Characteristics of the Area of Operations.

(1) Weather. Describe effects.

(2) Terrain. Describe effects.

(3) Other pertinent facts.

b. Enemy Forces. Enemy dispositions, composition, strength, capabilities, and COAs as they affect specific staff areas of concern.

c. Friendly Forces.

(1) Friendly COAs.

(2) CSS situation. This subparagraph should reflect the current status. (Use appropriate subheadings.) In the case of detailed information at higher levels of command, a summary may appear under the subheading with reference to an annex to the estimate. You may use an overlay to show all CSS units and installations, current and proposed. Include current status, capability, and any enhanced or reduced capability attached, detached, or supporting units may cause.

(a) Maintenance. Provide a general statement about the present capability [such as repair time factors, posture of maintenance units, some reference to Class VII and Class IX status if it affects maintenance capability, status of Class VII end items (such as repair parts, vans, wreckers) that may affect maintenance, and so forth].

(b) Supply. Provide overall status of controlled items and POL allocations, including pertinent comments on resupply availability and so forth. Provide information under subheadings of classes of supply; list them in the most meaningful measure [days of supply (DOS), total line items, equipment shortages—Class VII] by unit.

(c) Services. Provide present status; include both capabilities and problems.

(d) Transportation. Provide present capabilities of mode-operating units to support transportation requirements. Detail adequacy of routes, facilities, and terminals to support distribution requirements. Discuss capability of movement control and battlefield circulation control (BCC) to provide intransit visibility of movements and to assure sustained flow. Address time and distance factors that would influence the capability to provide support at the right place and time. Consider factors such as facilities and terminals, airlift/drop, and intransit visibility.

(e) Labor. Provide present situation, status, restrictions on use of civilians, and so forth.

(f) Facilities and construction. Provide availability of host nation facilities to serve as headquarters and support facilities. Provide status of construction to upgrade existing facilities and create facilities where needed.

(g) Combat health support (CHS). Provide present status of medical treatment and evacuation resources, projected location of patient-collecting points and ambulance exchange points (AXPs), and status of combat health logistics (including blood, medical regulating, and any anticipated increase in casualty rates or EPW workloads).

(h) EPW operations. Provide facilities, construction, and sustainment functions.

(i) Other factors that may adversely affect CSS operations such as refugee/humanitarian relief operations and support to United Nations (UN), nongovernmental organization (NGO), or private volunteer organization (PVO) operations.

(3) Status of other areas affecting CSS.

(a) CMO situation. Information for this subparagraph comes from the CMO officer. Include present dispositions of CA units and installations that affect the personnel situation. Show any projected developments within the CMO field that might influence personnel operations.

(b) Personnel situation. Include information you obtain from the personnel officer. Include total strength; strengths of units; and factors for casualties, replacements, hospital returnees, and so forth. Present dispositions of personnel and administration units and installations that would affect the CSS situation. Show any projected developments within the personnel field likely to influence CSS operations.

(c) Present disposition of forces. Describe the effects.

(4) Comparison of requirements versus capabilities. Show comparison for each element affecting personnel. Determine whether a shortfall or excess capability exists. If a shortfall exists, discuss ways to overcome it.

(5) Key considerations for COA supportability. List your evaluative criteria.

d. Assumptions. Until the commander provides specific planning guidance, you may need assumptions for initiating planning or for preparing the estimate. Modify assumptions as factual data becomes available.

3. ANALYSIS. Analyze all CSS factors for each subheading (paragraph 2e) for each COA, indicating problems and deficiencies. This paragraph, and any subparagraphs, should contain narrative analysis statements explaining mathematical calculations and applied logic. (Mathematical calculations you perform to assess status of any class of supply, maintenance attrition rates, tonnage lift capacity, and so forth, are solely a means to obtain information for full analysis.) The result of your analysis for subheadings for each COA should provide both CSS and tactical impact.

a. Sufficiency of Area. Determine if the area under control will be adequate for CSS operations. Will it be cleared of enemy units? Will other units be sharing the same area (units passing through one another)? Will boundaries remain unchanged?

b. Materiel and Services. Include the following subparagraphs if appropriate:

(1) Maintenance	(7) Human Resources Support
(2) Transportation	(8) Financial Management
(3) Supply	(9) Religious
(4) Combat Health Support	(10) Legal and Band
(5) Field Services	(11) Contract Services
(6) EOD	(12) Other

4. COMPARISON

a. Evaluate CSS deficiencies. List the advantages and disadvantages of accomplishing the mission.

b. Discuss the advantages and disadvantages of each COA you consider. Include methods of overcoming any deficiencies or modifications each COA requires.

5. RECOMMENDATION AND CONCLUSIONS

a. Indicate which COA or COAs CSS can best support.

b. List the major CSS deficiencies the cdr must consider. Include specific recommendations concerning the methods of eliminating or reducing the effect of these deficiencies.

/s/_____
Combat Service Support Officer—G4

ANNEXES: (as required)

(Classification)

III. The Personnel Estimate (Sample)

Ref: ST 101-6, Jul 04, pp. 2-6 to 2-11. Note: Alternate (macro) format for the Personnel Estimate can also be found in App. A, Joint Pub 1.

PERSONNEL ESTIMATE NO.　　　　　　　　　　　　　DTG:

References. Maps, charts, or other documents.

1. Mission.

The restated mission as determined by the commander.

　a. Intelligence situation. This consists of information obtained from the intelligence officer. When the details make it appropriate and the estimate is written, a brief summary and reference to the appropriate intelligence document or an annex of the estimate may be used.

　　(1) Characteristics of the area of operations ⁻ discuss how it may affect personnel.

　　(2) Enemy strength and dispositions.

　　(3) Enemy capabilities.

　　　(a) Discuss those capabilities that affect the mission.

　　　(b) Discuss capabilities that affect personnel activities. Example: Enemy air superiority may affect the movement of replacements.

　b. Tactical situation. This consists of information obtained from the commander's planning guidance and from the operations officer.

　　(1) Present dispositions of major tactical elements.

　　(2) Possible courses of action to accomplish the mission. (These are carried forward through the remainder of the estimate.)

　　(3) Projected operations, if known, and other planning factors as required for coordination and integration of staff estimate.

　c. Logistics situation. This is comprised of information obtained from the logistics officer.

　　(1) Present dispositions of logistic units and installations that have an effect on the personnel situation.

　　(2) Projected developments within the logistic field likely to influence personnel operations.

　d. Civil-military operations situation. This information obtained from the civil-military operations officer.

　　(1) Present dispositions of civil-military operations, units, and installations that have an effect on the personnel situation.

　　(2) Projected developments within the civil-military operations field likely to influence personnel operations.

　e. Troop preparedness situation. In this subparagraph, the status is shown under appropriate subheadings. In the case of detailed information at higher levels of command, a summary may appear under the subheading with reference to an annex to the estimate.

　　(1) Unit strength maintenance. Indicate authorized, assigned, and attached strengths. Include the effects of deployability, losses (combat/noncombat), critical shortages, projections (gains and losses), and any local situations effecting strength, for example, restrictions on the number of soldiers allowed in an area by treaty.

　　(2) Replacements.

　　(3) Noncombat matters. Indicate, as appropriate, personnel other than unit soldiers whose presence affects the unit mission. Included in this paragraph are prisoners of war, third country nationals, augmentees (non-U.S. forces), civilian internees and detainees, Department of the Army civilians, and others depending on local circumstances; indicate availability for labor requirements.

　　(4) Soldier personnel readiness. Report the status of morale, esprit de corps, and any current factors of major significance, which influences the morale of units.

　　　(a) Indicate factors affecting stability and human potential of individual soldiers, teams, and crews to accomplish the mission.

　　　(b) Include factors that might affect organizational climate, commitment, and cohesion, if appropriate.

(5) Services support.

(a) Indicate changes or problem areas in support services to the soldier that affect the combat mission and require new policy or programs to maintain troop preparedness and that affect individual soldier's morale and welfare.

(b) Report problems in personnel service support which include — awards; assignments/ reassignments; finance services; health services; leaves; legal services; morale supportactivities; orders; pay; personal affairs; personnel services; postal services; promotions; public affairs services; records; religious activities.

(6) Organizational climate. This includes indicators affecting personnel readiness.

(a) Communication w/i the chain of command.   (d) Supervision.

(b) Performance and discipline standards.   (e) Physical combat stress.

(c) Human relations.   (f) Other.

(7) Commitment. Indicate the relative strength of the soldier's identification with and involvement in the unit.

(a) Morale.   (c) Confidence.

(b) Motivation.   (d) Trust.

(8) Cohesion. Indicate factors that attract and bind soldiers together to produce commitment to the unit to accomplish the mission.

(a) Esprit.   (b) Teamwork.

f. Assumptions. Any assumptions required as a basis for initiating, planning, or preparing the estimate (modified as factual data when specific planning guidance becomes available).

2. Analysis. For each course of action, when appropriate, analyze cause, effect, outcome, and relationships, indicating problems and deficiencies.

3. Comparison.

a. Evaluate deficiencies from a personnel standpoint (list advantages/disadvantages).

b. Discuss the advantages and disadvantages of each course of action under consideration. Include methods of overcoming deficiencies or modifications required in each course of action.

4. Conclusions.

a. Indicate whether the mission set forth in paragraph 1 above can be supported from the personnel standpoint.

b. Indicate which course(s) of action can best be supported from the personnel standpoint.

c. List the major personnel deficiencies that must be brought to the cdr's attention. Include specific recommendations on ways to reduce or eliminate the effect of these deficiencies.

d. The format for an estimate of the situation helps the estimator apply thoroughness, clarity, judgment, logic, and professional knowledge to the situation and helps reach a sound decision.

e. The format is a logical and useful tool that is not rigid. You do not have to complete one paragraph before you go to the next.

f. Review the following points:

(1) Paragraphs of the estimate format do not have to be completed in a fixed sequence, and information, conclusions, and recommendations from other pertinent estimates may be used.

(2) The personnel estimate of the situation is a continuous process for the commander and staff. Estimates are revised continuously as factors that affect operations change, as new facts are recognized, as assumptions are replaced by facts or rendered invalid, or as changes to the mission are received or indicated.

(3) The S1/G1 uses information, conclusions, and recommendations from other pertinent estimates to analyze his problem.

(4) Sound decisions result only from a thorough, clear, unemotional analysis of all data pertinent to the situation. In further projecting the human dimension during combat, providing input to the unit health services plan is crucial. You may have a medical platoon leader, surgeon or a PA to assist. Areas to examine include medical supplies, personnel, evacuation capabilities, and any others that may have an impact on mission accomplishment. To keep the folks at home informed of the status of their loved ones, a hometown news release program must continue to be implemented during periods of crisis. Additionally, you may find yourself involved with reporters and camera crews that are providing coverage in your unit area of operation. Try to establish a line of communication with the PAO representative to track the news reporters in your area.

IV. Mission Analysis Briefing Format

Ref: FM ST 101-6, app. J.

1. Mission and commander's intent two levels up.

2. Higher HQ mission and commander's intent.

3. Higher HQ concept.

4. Higher HQ deception plan.

5. Commander's initial guidance.

6. Initial intelligence preparation of the battlefield (IPB) products.

7. Determine specified, implied, and essential tasks (logistics tasks would be briefed here along with other staff areas).

8. Constraints (logistic constraints such as CSR, shortfalls in capability, LOCs, host nation support, etc., would be briefed here).

9. Forces available (vital information about CSS forces' availability would be briefed here).

10. Hazards/risks (logistics hazards and risks would be briefed here).

11. Recommended initial commander's critical information requirements (CCIR). (CCIR essential to

logistics operations could be pointed out here.)

12. Recommended time line (logistics time-line information would be combined with other staff recommendations).

13. Proposed restated mission.

NOTE: The level of detail the G1/G4 or logistics staff officer provides during the briefing will depend on the target audience and the time available. Obviously, the DISCOM commander would receive a significantly more detailed briefing than the division commander.

If time permits or the target audience requires greater detail, supplement the briefing format with the following outline. This outline could be placed under the heading of Forces Available or under separate headings.

CSS FUNCTIONS

1. Maintenance.

  a. Facts.

    (1) Maintenance status (equipment readiness).

    (2) Class IX status.

    (3) Repair times, evacuation policy, and assets.

    (4) Critical shortages.

  b. Assumptions.

    (1) Host nation support.

    (2) Other.

  c. Conclusions.

    (1) Projected maintenance status on D-day.

    (2) Shortfalls and critical CSS risks/events.

    (3) Recommendations.

2. Transporation

  a. Facts.

    (1) Status of transportation assets.

    (2) Critical LOC and MSR status (air, water, rail, road, and transfer point).

    (3) Critical shortages.

  b. Assumptions.

    (1) Host nation support.

    (2) Other.

  c. Conclusions.

    (1) Projected status of transportation assets on D-day.

    (2) Projected status of LOCs and MSRs.

    (3) Shortfalls and critical CSS risks/events.

    (4) Recommendations.

CSS Plans

3. Supply

a. **Facts.**

(1) Classes I, II, III(p), IV, VI, VII, X, and water status.

(2) Critical shortages.

b. **Assumptions.**

(1) Resupply rates.

(2) Host nation support.

(3) Other.

c. **Conclusions.**

(1) Projected supply levels and field services status on D-day.

(2) Shortfalls and critical CSS risks/events.

(3) Projected treatment capability.

(4) Recommendations.

d. **Class III (B).**

(1) Facts.

(a) Class III(b) status.

(b) Distribution system (FSSP, ROM, rail to tanker, pipeline, and air).

(c) Restrictions.

(d) Critical shortages.

(2) Assumptions.

(a) Resupply rates.

(b) Host nation support.

(c) Other.

(3) Conclusions.

(a) Projected supply status on D-day.

(b) Projected distribution system.

(c) Shortfalls and critical CSS risks/events.

(4) Recommendations.

e. **Class V.**

(1) Facts.

(a) Class V status.

(b) Distribution system.

(c) Restrictions.

(d) Critical shortages.

(2) Assumptions.

(a) Resupply rates.

(b) Host nation support.

(c) Other.

(3) Conclusions.

(a) Projected supply status on D-day.

(b) Projected distribution system.

(c) Shortfalls and critical CSS risks/events.

(4) Recommendations.

4. Combat Health Support/Human Resources

a. **Facts.**

(1) Personnel strengths and morale.

(2) Replacements and medical RTD.

(3) Critical shortages.

b. **Assumptions.**

(1) Replacements.

(2) Host nation support.

(3) Other.

c. **Conclusions.**

(1) Projected strengths on D-day.

(2) Projected critical MOS status on D-day.

(3) Shortfalls and critical CSS risks/events.

(4) Recommendations.

5. Field Services

a. **Facts.** Location of corps field service units and personnel operating in division AO.

b. **Assumptions.** Availability of corps field services capability to divisional units

c. **Conclusions.** Field service shortfalls.

6. Explosive Ordnance Disposal

a. **Facts.** Location of corps EOD units and personnel operating in division AO.

b. **Assumptions.** Availability of EOD capability to divisional units.

c. **Conclusions.** Shortfalls in EOD capability.

7. Finance/Legal/Religious and Band

a. **Facts.** Location of finance/legal/religious and band units and personnel operating in division AO.

b. **Assumptions.** Availability of finance/legal/religious and band capability to divisional units.

c. **Conclusions.** Shortfalls in finance/legal/religious and band capability.

8. Other.

a. **Political analysis.**

b. **Economic analysis.**

c. **Sociological analysis.**

d. **Foreign nation support.**

e. **Assumptions.**

(1) Host nation support.

(2) Other.

f. **Conclusions.**

(1) Proj. foreign nation support on D-day.

(2) Projected host nation spt on D-day.

g. **Shortfalls & critical CSS risks/events.**

h. **Recommendations.**

The Logistics Estimate Process

Ref: FM 4-93.50, app. A.

1. Requirements

The first step in the log estimate process is to determine the logistical requirements for the mission. To determine the requirements, you may use a number or combination of methods. Automated systems such as OPLOG PLANNER, LEW or the SURE program are good tools to use to estimate requirements. If you prefer to do the number crunching yourself, planning factors from the CGSC ST 101-6 (G1/G4 BATTLEBOOK) or the FM 101-10-1/2 may be used to determine your own estimates. Historical data from previous missions should also be used.

2. Capabilities

To correctly determine the logistics capability of your unit, you must consider the capabilities of all the available CSS assets at your disposal. This includes all available CSS units assigned, attached, or OPCON, and the CSS capability organic to the maneuver units themselves. Be sure to consider the unit's current status in terms of personnel and equipment, as well as the projected status at mission execution.

3. Comparison/Shortfall

Once you have determined your estimated requirements and the unit's CSS capability, compare them to determine any logistical shortfalls. If there are no shortfalls, go to the analysis step of this methodology. Shortfalls may occur in terms of storage, distribution, and transportation capability or may be caused by personnel or equipment shortfalls based on current on hand shortages or maintenance status. A shortfall may also occur if required facilities or terrain are not available or the plan does not provide enough time to prepare. If there is a shortfall, determine what the shortfall is in terms of short tons, gallons, or other units of measurement and when or where during the operation the shortfall occurs.

4. Analysis

Whether or not there is a shortfall, the analysis process must occur for all support operations. The CSS planner must determine: when the support operation must begin, how much time there is to prepare for the mission, the purpose of the support mission, the duration of the mission, and whether the mission can be supported from a fixed location or whether to echelon support forward in some way. If there is a shortfall identified in the comparison of requirements and capabilities, you must also determine its cause, its significance and its potential impact on the tactical operation.

5. Solutions

Determine the most workable solutions based on your analysis. Ensure that all solutions are integrated into the MDMP to enhance continuity between the tactical decision making and logistical planning.

During course of action development, the CSS planners within the brigade must begin to draft possible ways to provide the brigade's concept of the operation with CSS. This is challenging because, at this stage of planning, the brigade probably has not selected a specific course of action for the upcoming operation. However, CSS planners should have the restated mission, commander's guidance and intent, and continuously updated staff estimates. This input should come from both the brigade and battalion levels. With this information, the CSS planners at various echelons (i.e. brigade S-1/S-4, support battalion and task force S-1/ S-4) can begin to develop several options to support the brigade. Concept of support options for the support battalion include: supply point distribution from the BSA, using a forward logistics element (FLE) during fast paced offensive operations, or using a logistics release point that stages outside the BSA for short periods of time to resupply the task force.

CSS Plans

IV. Support Concept (para 4a) and the CSS Overlay

Ref: ST 101-6, chap. 3 and app. C-G.

After the commander selects a specific COA, the staff communicates this decision by publishing the operation plan/operation order (OPLAN/OPORD). The G4, with input from the other logistic staff elements (G1, G5, surgeon, finance and personnel officers, and the support command), will prepare paragraph 4 of the plan. This paragraph contains CSS information as follows:

Paragraph 4a is the support concept. This concise, but comprehensive, paragraph tells the maneuver commander and his primary staff those critical or unusual logistic actions that will occur by phase or before, during, and after the battle to support the concept of the operation.

Additional subparagraphs can be used to provide more detailed CSS information by functional area. Usually, these subparagraphs are omitted, and this detailed information is published as part of the service support annex to the plan. The G4 prepares this order with input from the other logistic staff elements. The G4 can also prepare a CSS overlay to show supported units' supply route locations and supporting logistic organizations. Finally, routine, doctrinal, or constant information is incorporated into the unit tactical standing operating procedures (TSOP) to avoid repetition.

I. Developing the Support Concept

The logistician actively participating in the decisionmaking process facilitates the support concept's development. Specifically, during mission analysis, the CSS planner determines the units' current materiel and personnel posture before the operation begins. This, with the commander's priorities, determines which units and items of equipment should receive priority before the operation.

The wargaming and quantitative analysis portions of COA analysis highlight critical and/or unusual logistic requirements and determine support priorities during each phase of the operation. By its very nature, wargaming facilitates logistic synchronization with the concept of the operation.

There are numerous other information sources for the support concept:
- Commander's guidance and intent
- Concept of the operation
- Higher HQ support concept, service support order or plan (if applicable), and CSS overlay
- Maneuver control system screens and/or other locally generated status charts
- Lessons learned data and historical perspectives to view how others successfully, or unsuccessfully, supported other similar operations
- The unit's battle book

II. The CSS Overlay

The CSS overlay is a graphic representation of the tactical array of support areas and units. Ideally, it accompanies copies of the OPLAN and/or OPORD distributed to subordinate HQ and is used as a graphic backdrop to the support concept briefing.

The CSS overlay should include (as a minimum)—
- Locations of current and proposed support areas.
- Boundaries for CSS responsibilities.
- MSRs.
- Locations of major HQ.
- Locations of CSS installations and units.
- Locations of critical resources [potable water, maintenance collection points, ATPs, mortuary affairs (MA) collection points, ambulance exchange points (AXPs), etc.].

The CSS overlay will not only depict the tactical array of CSS units/nodes, but it is also an integral part of the overall OPLAN/OPORD graphics and must be synchronized with the operations overlays.

The **BRIGADE CSS overlay** would include (as a minimum)—
- The brigade support area (BSA) location and, using type unit symbols, the CSS units and HQ located therein.
- Locations of alternate/proposed BSAs.
- Locations of forward logistics elements (FLEs)
- The supply routes from the BSA to the logistic release points and/or maintenance collection points.
- The MSR from the division support area (DSA) to the BSA.

The **DIVISION CSS overlay** would include (as a minimum)—
- The division support area (DSA) location and using type unit symbols, the CSS units and HQ contained there-in, whether they are divisional or nondivisional.
- Locations of alternate and/or proposed DSAs.
- The MSRs from the corps rear area to the DSA and from the DSA to each BSA.

The **CORPS CSS overlay** may have to encompass the entire corps area of operation (AO) as well as a part of the communication zone (COMMZ) and, as a minimum, would depict—
- The logistic support areas (LSAs) and, using type unit symbols, the CSS units and HQ located therein, and the locations of any other critical CSS nodes not located in an LSA.
- The MSRs leading into the corps rear area from the COMMZ and the MSRs leading from the corps rear area to each DSA (or, as a minimum, to the division rear boundary) and to other critical logistic nodes.
- Locations of alternate and/or proposed LSAs.
- Locations of corps CSS units operating forward of the divisional rear boundaries.

III. The CSS Matrix

The oral support concept briefing will allow the commander and his subordinates to visualize how the operation will be logistically sustained. The CSS planners' oral briefing, using the CSS overlay, is useful in communicating the support concept to the commander. In addition, a support concept matrix can be used to make complex logistic concepts more easily understood.

The support concept matrix's design is aligned with the support concept format. The logistic functions are in the "by phase" context. The matrix can also be modified to reflect before, during, and after phases. The matrix will highlight those critical aspects of each CSS function. It can also depict other critical information such as priorities, shifts in priorities, problem areas, critical events, and other critical action. The matrix is not intended to stand alone or to replace the support concept briefing. It should complement and supplement the support concept briefing.

Support Concept Format & Briefing

Ref: ST 101-6, chap. 3, pp. 3-5 to 3-7. See following pages for sample format.

The logistician's role in the overall OPLAN/OPORD briefing is to brief the support concept, but he must first understand the general concept of the operation and the commander's intent.

The support concept briefing should address the critical, non-SOP, or unusual aspects of logistic support by phase of an operation by critical CSS functions. Doctrinal, usual, or SOP matters should not be addressed unless there is a deviation in support relationships or normal methods.

4. SERVICE SUPPORT (Paragraph 4a)

a. Support Concept. Paragraph 4a will provide an overall view of the support concept. Its intent is to provide the non-CSS commanders and their primary staffs an image of how the operation will be logistically supported. If the information pertains to the entire operation, or if it pertains to more than one unit, include it in the introductory portion of paragraph 4a. Change it in the ensuing subparagraphs when needed. This could include: a brief synopsis of the support command mission; support command headquarters and/or support area locations, including locations of next higher logistics bases if not clearly conveyed in the CSS overlay; the next higher level's support priorities and where the unit fits into those priorities; priorities that remain unchanged throughout the operation; units in the next higher CSS organization supporting the unit; significant and/or unusual CSS issues that might impact the overall operation; the use of host nation support; and any significant sustainment risks

   (1) PHASE I (repeat for each phase)
- Logistics focus.
- Priorities: By unit; for personnel replacements; maintenance and/or recovery and evacuation priorities (by unit and equipment type); mvmt; class of supply.
- Critical events. Use the CSS functions for information.
- CSS risks.

   (4) Paragraphs 4b through 4e are normally more detailed and are included in the service support annex. They are not part of the support concept.

   (5) Concept of support written before, during, and after format. Follow the same guidance as by phase.

Support Concept Briefing Format

1. Introduction (overview of the support concept and orientation to the map, if required). Orientation to the map is not required if another briefer has done so previously. Do not assume the commander totally knows the terrain. Focus on locating critical CSS nodes, MSRs, etc.

2. Brief the support concept starting with critical actions that must be accomplished in the first phase of the operation and concluding with critical actions to be accomplished in the last phase. This will prepare for future operations using the CSS functions as a guide.

3. Identify which units have priorities for each critical CSS function (this should correlate with the commander's priorities; e.g., main effort).

4. Identify the next higher echelon unit providing support and/or backup support.

5. Identify any critical shortages/problem areas for each CSS function and solution. For example, this can be supported, but ____ , or it can be done, but not without risk in____ .

6. Identify any other CSS problem areas, arrangements, special requirements, or any other critical aspects addressed elsewhere in the briefing.

CSS Plans

Brigade Support Concept (Sample)

Ref: ST 101-6, app. C & F.

1. SERVICE SUPPORT

a. Support Concept. O/O, 202d FSB establishes BSA DEUCE vicinity GUTENBERG (NU3010) and provides DS to 2d Bde operations. 52d ID (M) DISCOM(-) establishes DSA LAMP vicinity FREIDHAUSEN (NU0917) and provides reinforcing DS to 202d FSB. 211th Pers and 212th Fin Dets provide support from the BSA. Division initial priority of support is to 52d Avn Bde, DIVARTY, 2d Bde, 3d Bde, and 1st Bde, in order. 843d FST collocates with 202d FSB to provide urgent surgery capability. 825th Med Co (Air Ambulance) positions a forward support MEDEVAC teams in the BSA; aeromedical evacuation authorized as far forward as battalion aid station locations. CSR of 2 TOW-2B per BFV and 10 APFSDS-T per M1 is in effect for duration of this operation. No Class VII replacement items expected to be available until units reach PL DESK. Cannibalization authorized at DS level. Brigade units transport all KIAs to brigade MA collection point vicinity NUTZEN (NU295185) in the BSA. MSR CARDINAL is designated as the division chemical contamination route. MSR CARDINAL remains under division control throughout the operation. Brigade SRs are designated as SR GREEN and SR BLUE. All refugee flow and traffic to be passed along MSR EAGLE to the refugee holding area vicinity the DSA at OBERFRIEDHAUSEN (NU0818). No host nation support available in BSA. Risk throughout the operation exists in enemy direct action against lines of communications and support areas. Convoys and supply points of Class III(B) and V are at particular risk.

(1) PHASE I. Movement from TAA BOOK to ATK POSs INK, PAPER, and PEN. This phase begins when TF 4-5 departs TAA BOOK and ends when all units have closed in ATK POSs. Initial logistics focus is improving unit combat power, then supporting brigade movement to attack positions. Priority of support and replacements is to TF 4-5, TF 3-32, and TF 2-32. Priority of maintenance and evacuation is to M1s, recovery vehicles, M2/3s, M109s, and M978 fuelers. Priority of movement forward is to maneuver units (TF 4-5, 3-32, 2-32), DS artillery and HEMTTs. Elements of 202d FSB will be integrated with the maneuver units for movement forward to begin establishing BSA DEUCE. Priority of movement rearward is to casualty evacuation, refugees, and maintenance evacuation. Priority of supply is replenishing Class V UBLs. 843d FST establishes operations vicinity TAA BOOK. Brigade accepts risk of resupply of Class III(B) on MSR ROBIN between PL TERAPIN and PL TIGER

(2) PHASE IIa Support. Attack to destroy lead MIBRs. This phase begins when TF 4-5, attacks in zone to seize OBJ WHEELER and ends when lead MIBRs are destroyed Logistics focus is forward support of units in contact while echeloning remaining CSS assets forward from TAA BOOK to BSA DEUCE. Priority of brigade support by unit–no change. Priority of support will shift to TF 2-32 upon commitment of the brigade reserve. Priority of maintenance and evacuation is to M1s, M2/3, M978 fuelers, and recovery vehicles. No change to forward movement priorities. Priority of movement rearward is to casualty evacuation, maintenance evacuation, EPWs, and refugees. Priority of supply shifts to Class III (B). Personnel replacement, finance support, and field services (except MA) operations are discontinued until units secure OBJ WHEELER. 202d FSB will establish a forward maintenance collection point vicinity GEVERWEG (NU5025) after units clear to PL HORNETS. AXPs will be established generally along the 45 N-S gridline but no farther east than PL HORNETS. No aeromedical evacuation authorized east of PL Terapin. EPW holding area to be operational vicinity NUTZEN (NU295185). By-passed enemy forces continue to threaten CSS resupply convoys.

(3) PHASE IIb Support. Counterattack. This phase begins when TF 2-32, brigade reserve, is committed and occupies AA PENCIL, and ends when enemy forces are blocked north of PL TILE. Logistics focus is supporting committed units and preparing to reconstitute TF 4-5 and TF 3-32. Brigade priority of support and personnel replacement is to TF 2-32, TF 4-5 and TF 3-23. Priority of CGSC/ST101-6/APC/JUL03 C-1 maintenance, movements, and supply—no change. Risk to CSS operations is enemy direct action against support areas and convoys.

(4) PHASE III Support. Prepare for offensive operations. This phase begins when TF 4-5 moves to and occupies AA ERASER and ends when TF 3-32 occupies OBJ WHEELER. Logistics focus is reconstituting combat units. Priority of support and replacements is to TF 4-5, TF 3-32, and TF 2-32. TF 2-32 reorganizes to a minimum combat level of 85 percent; all others, 75 percent. Priority of maintenance is to M1s, M2/3, 5K tankers and PLS Systems. Priority of movement forward is to replacements, Classes IX, VII, III, and V. Priority of movement rearward remains the same. Personnel services, finance support, and field services resume. 202d FSB remains in BSA DEUCE until the brigade continues attack east across PL TIGER, then begins displacement to establish BSA COFFEE vicinity KAISENDORF (NU7524). AXPs move to OBJ WHEELER; aeromedical evacuation authorized from as far forward as AAs ERASER and LEAD. MA collection point collocates with maintenance collection point vicinity GEVERWEG. Risk—no change.

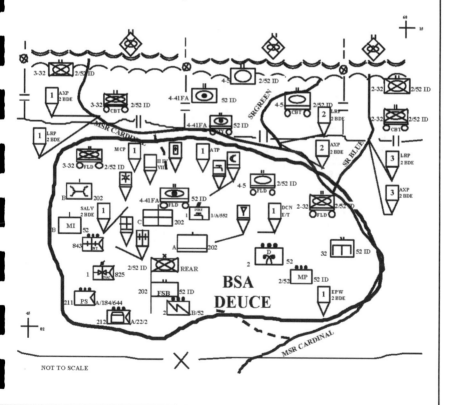

NOT TO SCALE

Support Concept Matrix (Sample)

Ref: ST 101-6, app. I.

CSS ANNEX _____ TO OPORD _____

CSS Functions	PHASE I (Move from TAA to ATK POS)	PHASE IIa (ATK to Defeat Lead Divisions)	PHASE IIb (Counterattack)	PHASE III (Hasty Defense)
Priority of Support	52: AVN, ARTY, 2 BDE, 3 BDE, 1 BDE	2 BDE, 3 BDE, 52 AVN, ARTY, 1 BDE	3 BDE, 2 BDE, 52 AVN, 1 BDE, ARTY	1 BDE, 2 BDE, AVN, 3 BDE, ARTY
Human Resources Support	PRI REPL: AVN, ARTY, 2 BDE, 3 BDE, 1 BDE	PRI REPL: 2 BDE, 3 BDE, AVN, ARTY, 1 BDE. SHIFT TO 1 BDE IF COMMITTED. REPL OPS SUSPENDED UNTIL PL DESK	PRI REPL: 3 BDE, 2 BDE, AVN, 1st BDE, ARTY	PRI REPL: 1 BDE, 2 BDE, AVN, 3 BDE, ARTY. REPL OPS RESUME.
Supply (CL I, II, III(p), III(B), IV, V, VI, AND VII)	PRI CL III: AVN, 3 BDE, 2 BDE, 1 BDE PRI CL V: HELLFIRE, 25MM, TANK ATGM, 155 DPICM	PRI (LESS CL V): 2 BDE, 3 BDE, 52 AVN, ARTY, 1 BDE. PRI CL V: 120MM HEAT, TOW, 155 DPICM	PRI (LESS CL V): 3 BDE, 2 BDE, AVN, 1 BDE, ARTY. REPLENISH CL III UBLs. PRI CL V:155 DPICM, HELLFIRE, TOW, TANK. REPLENISH UBLS	PRI ALL CLASSES: 1 BDE, 2 BDE, AVN, 3 BDE, ARTY.
Maintenance	PRI MAINT: M109, M1, M2/3, 5K TANKERS, PLS, AND M88 PRI MAINT AVN: AH-64, OH-58D, AND UH-60	PRI MAINT: M1, M2/3, M109, MHE. PRI AVN MAINT: UNCHANGED	PRI – NO CHANGE	PRI MAINT: M1, M109; M2/3, M88 PRI AVN MAINT: UNCHANGED
Transportation	PRI FWD: DS ARTY, MNV UNITS, III, V PRI REAR: MED, EQUIP EVAC, REFUGEES.	PRI FWD: MNV UNITS, DS ARTY, III, V PRI REARWARD: MED, MAINT EVAC, EPWs, REFUGEES	PRI FWD AND REARWARD UNCHANGED.	PRI FWD: IX, VI, III, V. PRI REARWARD: UNCHANGED
Field Services	FS PROVIDED BY 13th CSB IN DSA LAMP.	FS OPERATIONS SUSPENDED UNTIL PL DESK KIA EVAC TO MA	FS – NO CHANGE	FS OPS RESUME IN DSA.
CHS	842d FST & 1FSMT DS TO 303D FSB, 843D FST & 1 FSMT DS TO 202D FSB, 1FSMT W/ 404TH FSB, MSMT AREA COVERAGE DREAR. ASMT W/ DASB	2XCH-47 AVAIL FOR MASS CAL CSH LOCATED IN LSA BELL	2XCH-47 AVAIL FOR MASS CAL CSH LOCATED IN LSA BELL	
EOD	EOD SPT AVAIL IN DSA LAMP	NO CHANGE	NO CHANGE	NO CHANGE
Financial MGT Support	CORPS PROVIDES IN UNIT SPT AREAS	FIN OPS SUSPENDED UNTIL PL DESK	NO CHANGE	FIN OPS RESUMED
Religious, Legal and Band Support	DIV BAND SPT AVAIL UPON REQUEST TO G3	DIV BAND PROVIDES FORCE PROTECTION TO DMAIN	NO CHANGE	NO CHANGE

V. CSS Rehearsals

Ref: ST 101-6, app.K.

FM 101-5-1, Operational Terms and Graphics, defines rehearsals as "the process of practicing a plan before actual execution." Regardless of the type of operation (high intensity, support or stability), the CSS rehearsal is the tactical logistician's validation of the concept of support. Most units in the Army have CSS rehearsal SOPs or TTPs (tactics, techniques, and procedures). The CSS rehearsal is a process used to articulate the sustainment results of wargaming. The rehearsal is structured, rehearsed, timed, and provides both active and AC/RC units an opportunity to express their understanding of CSS execution to their respective mission. The purpose of this article is to provide the tactical logistician a 5-step CSS rehearsal framework that if tailored, may support any military operation.

I. Identify the Briefers and Audience

The CSS rehearsal audience is critical to the execution of the logistics plan. The most effective CSS rehearsal occurs when commanders, executive officers and primary staff of each BOS attend. Unfortunately, as we know, this is difficult to achieve. At a minimum, the success of the rehearsal hinges on identifying those briefers who provide CSS command and control and are responsible for executing a specific CSS mission.

Commanders will typically delegate his or her CSS rehearsal responsibilities to executive officers, ADCs, or deputy commanders (depending on the tactical level). This occurs due to CSS being one of their primary responsibilities. Alternatively, if designated representatives are chosen to replace primary briefers, they should be competent on the plan. Failure to prepare designated representatives will result in unproductive rehearsals. Briefers should arrive prepared and ready to discuss respective actions during the rehearsal.

II. Determine the Location

The location of the CSS rehearsal is largely dependent on METT-TC. The ideal location is with the maneuver rehearsal. If CSS rehearsals occur at different locations other than maneuver rehearsals, rarely will the right players attend. The advantages of CSS rehearsals following maneuver rehearsals is audience availability, use of maneuver terrain models, and attendees sharing a common view of the battlefield.

The CSS rehearsal location should be centrally located to support the majority of participants. It should provide adequate space and support for the number of attendees. CSS rehearsals, along with maneuver rehearsals, should be included in the mission analysis timeline. While backwards planning, sufficient time should be allocated to CSS rehearsal planning, preparation, and execution. The amount of time required for the execution of the rehearsal is typically METT-T driven. Additionally, due to lack of planning, turning away participants due to lack of space only degrades the rehearsal's effectiveness. Units must plan in advance for security measures, parking, TOC passes and ration support.

CSS Plans

CSS Rehearsals

Ref: ST 101-6, app. K.

CSS Rehearsal Audiences

Brigade CSS Rehearsals	
Audience (not inclusive)	Bde Cdr, Bde XO, Bde S1, Bde S2, Bde S3, Bde S4, BRT Cdr, TCF Cdr, Reserve Cdr, TF Cdrs or XOs, Bn S4s, Med Plt Ldrs, BMOs, HHC Cdr, FSB Cdr, FSB Spt Ops, FSB CO Cdrs (supply, maintenance, medical).
Remarks	The brigade XO facilitates the brigade CSS rehearsal and assigns a recorder.

Division CSS Rehearsals	
Audience (not inclusive)	ADC(S), COS, G1, G2 Rep, G3 Rep, G4, DTO, G4 Planner, Bde XOs, COSCOM liaison officer (LNO), CSG(F) Cdr with Log Ops Off, CSB(F) Cdr with Log Ops Off, DISCOM Cdr, DISCOM Spt Ops, DISCOM MMC Chief, movement control officer (MCO), FSB Cdrs with Spt Ops, MSB Cdr with Spt Ops, DASB Cdr with Spt Ops, Div Surgeon, division medical operation center (DMOC), TCF Cdr, Cav Cdr and XO, Cav SMO and Med Plt Ldr.
Remarks	The ADC(S) oversees the division CSS rehearsal with the chief of staff and the division G4 as facilitators.

Corps CSS Rehearsals	
Audience (not inclusive)	Deputy Corps Cdr, Corps G1, G2 Rep, G3 Rep, G4, Corps Surgeon, COSCOM Cdr, COSCOM Log Ops Off, CMCC, CMMC, CSG Cdrs, CSB and Functional Bn Cdrs, ADC(S) of Divisions, Reg Cav Cdr and XO, Corps FA Bde Cdrs, Corps ENG Bde Cdrs, Corps Avn Cdr, DISCOM Cdrs with staff, Div G4s with planners, DTO, LNOs, CGS(F) Cdr with Log Ops Off, CSB(F) Cdr with Log Ops Off, DISCOM Cdr, DISCOM Spt Ops, DISCOM MMC Chief, FSB Cdrs with Spt Ops, MSB Cdr with Spt Ops, DASB Cdr with Spt Ops, Div Surgeon, DMOC, TCF Cdr, Cav Cdr and XO, Cav SMO and Med Plt Ldr.
Remarks	The deputy corps commander chairs the corps CSS rehearsal with the corps G4 as the facilitator.

CSS Terrain Model Control Features

	Brigade	Division	Corps
Terrain Model Control Features	• Boundaries (bde and bn – includes rear boundaries). • Phase lines. • Objectives. • Eas. • Div MSRs (clean and dirty). • Bde SRs (primary and alt). • DSA location. • BSA (primary and alt). • FSB (supply points and ATP). • FST and AXPs. • Decontamination sites. • Bn CPs & fld TNS. • Bn cbt trains. • Corps MEDEVAC and support assets in bde AO.	Boundaries (div and bde – includes rear boundaries). • Phase lines. • Objectives. • Eas. • Corps MSRs (clean and dirty). • Div MSRs (& alt). • CSG(F) location. • DSA location. • BSA locations. • Div CPs. • ROM locations. • Avn FARPs. • Cav Sqdn HQ. • CSH location bde CP locations.	• Boundaries (corps and div – includes rear boundaries). • Phase lines. • Objectives. • Eas. • Corps MSRs (clean and dirty). • Div MSRs (& alt). • LSA locations (pri/alt). • CSG HQs location. • CSG Bn locations. • COSCOM HQ. • DSA locations. • BSA locations. • Div CPs. • CSH locations. • Bulk fuel locations. • ASP locations. • Personnel service

CSS Plans

Sample Brigade CSS Rehearsal Format

Sequence/ Speaker	Areas Covered	Remarks	Responsibilities
1. BDE XO	Conducts roll call.	Verifies attendees.	Facilitator of rehearsal. Timeline manager.
2. BDE CDR	Opening remarks.	Provides commander's guidance for CSS rehearsal.	
3. BDE S3	Provides overview of terrain model/states task organization, friendly situation, mission, concept of operation and commander's intent.	Overview of terrain model includes: division/brigade boundaries, and location of friendly forces (in AAs and ATK POS).	Responsible for terrain Model set up. Responsible for coordination with bde S4 and FSB spt ops on CSS terrain model control measures.
4. BDE S2	Provides overview of enemy situation.	Focuses on enemy threats pertaining to logistics (MSRs, to rear areas, refugees, civilians, terrorists).	Displays enemy symbols on terrain model.
5. BDE S4	Provides overview of logistics.	Includes brigade support unit locations, MSRs (primary and alternate) – TF support infrastructure.	The S4 provides a snapshot of Paragraph 4a (concept of support) to the bde order.
6. BDE S1	Provides personnel status by unit.	Includes critical shortages and replacements.	
7. FSB SPT OPS	Covers all DS actions BEFORE Phase I.	Includes task org for support, location of DS CSS units in BSA, status of O/H stocks, & CSS force protection.	CSS actions BEFORE combat operations set the conditions for success. Information covered here is critical.
8. BDE S3	Covers concept of operation – by phase, beginning with Phase I.	Sets the stage for the rehearsal by reading when each phase begins and ends.	Turns over to next briefer.
9. BRT, TF1, TF2, TF3, ENG, FA, TCF	TF XOs cover maneuver actions during Phase I, while S4s cover battalion level logistics supporting to Phase I.	The key to these briefings is ensuring the TF/battalion has synchronized CSS within the unit. S4s brief locations of battalion level CSS assets.	BRT, TF, ENG, and FA XOs with S4s should come prepared to discuss organizational CSS support.
10. FSB SPT OPS	Covers DS actions during Phase I.	Focuses on DS support during Phase I. Specific actions include priorities of support (by unit), supply and movement forward and rearward.	Includes any other specific CSS area, as required by Bde XO, such as current combat power status and status of DS stocks.
11. BDE S3	Covers actions during Phase II-IV.	Reads when each phase begins and ends.	
12. BRT, TFs, ENG, FA	Covers actions in each phase. Refer to sequence #9.		
13. FSB SPT OPS	Covers DS actions during each Phase. Refer to sequence #10.		
14. BDE XO	Has scribe review support issues, then concludes	Tasks respective units.	

CSS Plans

III.Maximize the Use of the Terrain Model

As mentioned earlier, the CSS rehearsal should normally follow the maneuver rehearsal. This allows for maximizing the use of pre-made terrain models and equipment, thus reinforcing the current battlefield as viewed by most players. An effective terrain model technique is the sand table. It provides a 3-dimentional picture of the area of operation and includes cities, major terrain features, and pre-made unit icons.

IV. Conduct the CSS Rehearsal

Conducting the CSS rehearsal is an art. The most effective rehearsals result from prior planning, coordination, and integration with maneuver units. The CSS rehearsal format is similar to the maneuver rehearsal format, but integrates CSS into all aspects of the operation. The rehearsal format should be approved, and training conducted at homestation prior to deployments. All players/briefers should arrive at the rehearsal fully prepared.

V.Adjust/Execute

At the conclusion of the rehearsal, the facilitator reviews all outstanding issues from the recorder. Outstanding issues are either resolved or given back to units as taskings with suspenses. Once issues are resolved, units make necessary adjustments to concepts of support and begin execution. Proactive logisticians anticipate changes to the plan and immediately adjust to outcomes from the rehearsal. Time is of the essence and responsiveness to change is critical.

Chap 5

I. Unit Mvmt Overview

Ref: FM 4-01.011 Unit Movement Operations, chap I.

A unit move is the relocation of a force and its materiel to a desired area of operations. To accomplish a unit move, movement plans are developed and unit movement operations are conducted.

Unit Movement Operations Overview

A unit movement operation is the movement of unit equipment, personnel, and accompanying supplies from one location to another. Unit movement operations are conducted during training exercises, mobilization, and deployment. Unit movement operations are planned, coordinated, and executed by four principal modes: rail, motor, air, and sea. The mode of movement determines tactics, techniques and procedures for preparation, planning, coordination and execution of unit movements.

Every movement is unique. These operations seldom begin with a clear idea of the entire package or purpose. Often, they develop by bits and pieces, with a few false starts and subsequent large adjustments. They follow a general sequence, although the stages often overlap in space and time, and can happen simultaneously. The process is flexible and can be abbreviated and adjusted as required. However, the fundamental processes of moving units do not change to support a deployment. They become more complex because of the need to coordinate on a broad scale with other Services and organizations (outside the US Army).

I. Unit Movement Roles and Responsibilities

Unit movement operations involve the command's staff expertise in personnel, intelligence, operations, and logistics. At the battalion and brigade level, staff proponency for movement operations resides with the S3 and is executed in coordination with the S4. Higher headquarters operations and intelligence staff conduct mission analysis and receive the commander's intent for accomplishing the mission. The next step is to produce several courses of action to accomplish the mission. These courses of action may involve several task organizations and usually address limitations in transportation capability to support the mission. A course of action and task organization are selected which starts the unit movement planning sequence. Staff planners need to translate operational mission requirements into detailed and realistic unit movement plans. This translation must occur in a short time frame and must be able to capture continuous changes based on the current tactical situation. This process involves task organizing, echeloning, tailoring and movement.

Brigade level, battalion level, and separate company level organizations select soldiers to be trained in unit movement operations. These tasks are performed as additional duties in support of the unit mission. These soldiers are then appointed on additional duty orders to be responsible for these functions for their units. Unit movement training includes hazardous material certification, aircraft load planning, and unit loading teams. Unit loading teams that execute the load plans by physically loading, blocking, bracing, and tying down the load on the truck, aircraft, or railcar. Additional training is required on automated information systems such as Automated Air Load Planning System (AALPS) and Transportation Coordinators' Automated Information for Movement Planning System (TC-AIMS II). Additionally, the staffs in these organizations play an integral part in the unit movement process.

Unit Mvmt

Unit Movement Responsibilities

Ref: FM 4-01.011, chap 1.

Unit movement operations involve the command's staff expertise in personnel, intelligence, operations, and logistics. At the battalion and brigade level, staff proponency for movement operations resides with the S3 and is executed in coordination with the S4.

1. Unit Commanders

Commanders responsibilities include: ensuring adequate movement plans are prepared; ensuring proper execution of movements; appointing a unit movement officer (UMO) and providing proper training; ensuring that load teams are appointed and trained, ensuring that hazardous materials (HAZMAT) personnel are properly certified, trained, and equipped; ensuring that personnel responsible for movements receive the required training; ensuring that the proper equipment and supplies are available for movements; ensuring that the unit follows required regulatory and higher command guidance for unit movements; maintaining the morale of the unit; and ensuring that unit responsibilities outlined are performed

2. Executive Officers

XOs assist the unit commander in meeting the commander's movement responsibilities and supervises the unit staff in all matters dealing with unit movements.

3. Brigade and Battalion S1

Brigade and battalion S1 and personnel administrative specialists have responsibility for maintaining the personnel and medical readiness information on all soldiers assigned to the unit. The battalion S1 coordinates the soldier readiness processing program. Unit commanders must have a formal review process in place to ensure soldiers meet deployment readiness requirements IAW AR 600-8-101. Soldier readiness is a continuous process that involves unit commanders and staff and the installation staff agencies. Unit commanders are responsible for ensuring their soldiers are prepared for deployment. To assist the unit commander in performing this task, the battalion S-1 and admin specialist must provide current information concerning an individual soldier's completion of the following requirements prior to deployment.

4. Brigade and Battalion S3

Brigade and battalion S3 and training officer and NCO have the responsibility for maintaining the training readiness information on the unit and the individual soldiers assigned to the unit. Unit movement training is also required to support unit movement operations. Unit movement missions can occur rapidly, leaving the moving unit with little or no time to correct training deficiencies. Unit commanders are responsible for unit movement training of soldiers and units to support movement operations. The battalion S3 and training officer and NCO supports the commanders by scheduling required training, maintaining individual soldier training records, and providing soldier's current training status.

5. Brigade and Battalion S4

Brigade and battalion S4 and supply sergeant has the responsibility for maintaining the equipment and supply information on the unit. The S4 and supply sergeant maintains updated equipment on hand, unit basic load and equipment status information. The supply sergeant maintains updated supply information such as supplies and equipment assigned to individual soldiers in the unit. The battalion S4 is responsible for coordinating support requirements for unit movement operations. The S4 uses TC-AIMS II to plan, manage, and execute the movement.

6. Unit Movement Officer

The unit movement officer (UMO) is appointed at the company and battalion levels. The UMO represents the company or battalion commander in attending to the details of getting the unit ready for movement and maintaining that readiness when it is achieved. Commanders appoint in writing an officer or senior NCO (E6 or above), with an alternate (E5 or above), to serve as the UMO at the battalion, company, or detachment level. The UMO is trained in a school or in the unit (on-the-job training).

7. Unit Movement Coordinator (UMC)

The UMC is the command technical movements expert. As such, the UMC provides advice to those in both superior and subordinate positions. When reviewing plans, the UMC ensures that they adequately address all aspects of logistics and are designed to meet the needs of the unit. The UMC is usually found in the installation transportation office (ITO) in CONUS, and OCONUS, in the MCT. The UMC coordinates strategic movements and assists units in developing and executing unit movement plans.

8. Brigade Movement Coordinator (BMC)

The brigade movement coordinator (BMC) coordinates the movement of personnel and equipment beyond the capability of organic unit assets with the installation transportation officer or UMC. The BMC is the liaison between the UMO (at battalion and company) and the ITO in CONUS locations, the MCT in OCONUS locations; and in both locations, the UMC. BMCs are appointed to coordinate and support Bde mvmt activities and to assist in the development, maintenance, & evaluation of subordinate units' mvmt plans.

9. Mobility Warrant Officer (MWO)

The mobility warrant officer (MWO) program (MOS 882A) is designed to provide the combat commander a soldier with proven expertise who can work through the specific unit movement challenges. The MWO is the commander's key staff officer for movement operations planning, execution, advice, coordinating, and training.

The brigade mobility warrant officer and transportation logistics NCO provide the brigade with deployment training and execution expertise. The mobility officer is a movement technician who manages and controls the flow of Army Transportation during unit movement operations.

10. Hazardous Cargo Certifying Official

Each unit (company or detachment) requires at least one individual trained to certify hazardous cargo. This individual should not be the UMO. Hazardous cargo certifiers must be trained at a DOD approved school on applicable regulations for all modes. Once trained and appointed by the unit commander in writing, these individuals can certify documentation for all commercial and military modes of shipment. The hazardous cargo certifying official is responsible for ensuring shipments are properly prepared, packaged, labeled, and segregated. Appendix D of FM 4-01.011 provides general HAZMAT guidance for commanders and UMOs.

11. Air Load Planners

Air load planners are appointed and trained to prepare and update unit aircraft load plans. The UMO uses the AALPS to supervise the development of aircraft load plans and manifests for both equipment and personnel. TC-AIMS II through its air load planner module allows the UMO to develop aircraft loading plans and manifests for both equipment and personnel.

12. Unit Loading Teams

Each unit requires an appropriate number of personnel trained in vehicle preparation, and aircraft and rail loading and unloading techniques formed into loading teams. Composition of each loading team is tailored to the type and quantity of equipment for which it is responsible and for the time available for loading it.

II. Intratheater/Intertheater Unit Mvmt

Ref: FM 4-01.011, chap. 1.

A. Intratheater Unit Movement

Intratheater unit movements normally involve units moving from an origin location to a tactical assembly area (TAA). Based on the transportation assets available and the unit movement plan, any available mode may be used for intratheater movements. How the unit moves from the origin to the TAA depends on the modes selected (e.g., a unit may move by highway directly by from its motor pool to the TAA). Some of the functions depicted below may occur at the same geographical location. For instance, if there are rail ramps in or near the motor pool, a unit moving by rail may find the origin and rail marshalling areas collocated.

Intratheater Unit Movement

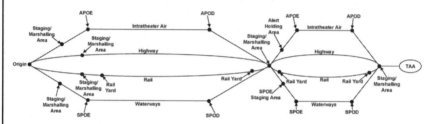

Ref: FM 4-01.011, fig. 1-1, p. 1-8.

B. Intertheater Unit Movement

Intertheater unit movements normally involve units moving from an origin location to a TAA. The strategic lift portion of intertheater unit movements is by air or sea. As in intratheater moves, all available modes can be used for intertheater moves. And depending on the facilities available and activities to be performed, staging and marshaling area functions may be collocated.

Intertheater Unit Movement

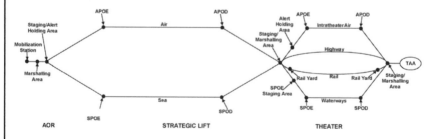

Ref: FM 4-01.011, fig. 1-2, p. 1-9.

Future intertheater unit movements may occur in the absence of reception, staging, onward movement, and integration (RSOI) capabilities. Future movements of Army forces will not have traditional RSOI in the area of operations. The reception function and preparation for onward movement and integration will take place at an intermodal transfer point (this could be as simple as the unit home station) as depicted below, or the unit may deploy directly into the theater as depicted in the second illustration.

Intertheater Unit Movement

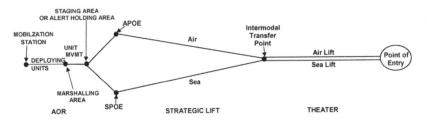

Ref: FM 4-01.011, fig. 1-3, p. 1-10.

Future organizational and materiel designs are going to enhance our ability to arrive in the AO in a much more "ready to fight" configuration than is possible today.

Intertheater Unit Movement

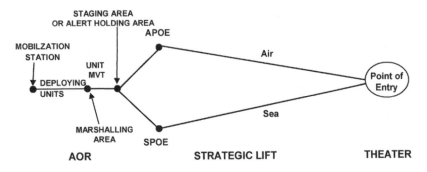

Ref: FM 4-01.011, fig. 1-4, p. 1-10.

III. Deployment Training

Ref: FM 4-01.011, app. J.

Deployment planning and preparation is a critical unit level activity. At the battalion and brigade level, staff proponency for movements normally resides with the S4. Battalions and companies, depending on local regulations or standard operating procedures (SOPs), normally require a number of soldiers be appointed and trained in unit movement operations, hazardous material (HAZMAT) certification, aircraft and rail loading, and air load planning. These personnel need to be trained.

Unit Movement Officer Deployment Planning Course

The purpose of the UMODPC is to serve as both an orientation tool and a refresher tool. As an orientation tool, this course introduces critical transportation functions and responsibilities to personnel who do not have a transportation background. The target is personnel serving in deploying units or in units that support deployments.

Air Deployment Planning Course (ADPC)

The Air Deployment Planning Course instructs soldiers in air movements and qualifies them to sign Air Force load plans.

Transportation Coordinators Automated Information For Movements System II (TC-AIMS II)

To provide selected personnel with a working knowledge of how TC-AIMS II, an information management and data communication system, automates unit, and installation Transportation Coordinators (TC) functions. It assists unit and installation personnel in preparing for and expediting unit movements and supporting unit actions.

HAZMAT Certification Training

Hazardous cargo certifiers must be trained by a DOD approved school, or by DOD approved instructors at the unit location, on applicable regulations for all modes within the past 24 months. These personnel must also receive refresher training every two years to continue to certify shipments of HAZMAT for transport.

Hazardous Cargo Handlers, Packers And Vehicle Drivers

HAZMAT training is required for personnel who offer, accept, handle, prepare, mark, placard, or label HAZMAT packages; prepare HAZMAT shipping papers; or operate or crew any transport mode carrying HAZMAT. Training instruction can be locally conducted and tailored to meet the needs of the unit based on the tasks performed. It is also available through contractors, commercial training kits, and through the schools listed above for certification training. DOD personnel must be trained and pass a written test every two years (DOD 4500.9-R chapter 204 section E).

Unit Loading Teams

Units are required to have an appropriate number of personnel trained in vehicle preparation and aircraft and rail loading/unloading techniques. Training can be arranged through the installation UMC or DTO. Load team composition is tailored to the type and quantity of equipment being loaded and time available for loading:

- **For rail movements**, a well trained team of five operators, using prefabricated tiedown devices, can complete loading and lashing of equipment on a chain equipped flatcar. Units are normally provided 72 hours for loading once the cars are spotted.

- **For air movement**, a six person team can provide efficient loading and tie down of equipment. United States Air Force Mobility Command offers the Equipment Preparation Course to train unit load teams to prepare, load and tie down unit equipment on military aircraft.

Ref: FM 4-01.011 Unit Movement Operations, chap 2.

Army units are required to move globally in support of force projection operations. Units prepare in peacetime to conduct operations supporting contingency plans. Deployments supporting a major theater war and some smaller scale contingencies are planned using the Joint Operations Planning and Execution System (JOPES) deliberate planning process. These plans result in operation plans (OPLAN) with time-phased force deployment data (TPFDD). Deployment planning is based on these OPLANs and related TPFDD, other contingency plans, and exercise plans.

Units prepare detailed movement standing operating procedures (SOPs) to support unit movement planning. The SOP should define the roles and responsibilities of all unit personnel from Brigade to Company level. The SOP should outline preparations for all modes of movement: air, rail, sea and convoy. Functions addressed in SOPs could include unit property disposition, supply issue, equipment maintenance, vehicle and container loading, security, marshaling procedures, purchasing authorities, unit briefings, risk assessment and other applicable deployment activities.

To meet their responsibilities to support operational, exercise, and contingency plans, units develop movement plans. Normally divisions, brigades, and battalions create movement plans and companies use extracts from battalion movement plans in company operation orders. Unit movement plans are tailored to the requirements for mobilization, deployments, and exercises, which have specific goals and missions. The plans are written in operation order format and are usually an annex to an operation order. The unit plans the move using the movement plan and executes the move under an operation order.

Joint Operational Planning & Execution System (JOPES)

The JOPES is the system used to conduct joint planning and operations. Each combatant commander conducts deliberate planning to produce a series of OPLANS that provide detail on how to execute potential operations in their area of responsibility (AOR). Source movement data from TC-AIMS II is produced by units to maintain accurate movement data in JOPES. This source data provides the warfighters visibility of personnel, equipment, and supplies available to support his OPLAN. During a crisis, each combatant commander conducts crisis action planning (CAP).

Unit movement plans are the result of either deliberate planning, which occurs as a matter of course in peacetime, and CAP, which is the reaction to an occurring crisis. Both plans are parallel processes in terms of how they are accomplished.

Note: Detailed information on JOPES can be found in The Joint Forces & Operational Warfighting SMARTbook.

TC-AIMS II Movement Plan

The TC-AIMS II System creates a product called a movement plan. In it is a wealth of information and data that is both useful and crucial to the formulation of unit movement plans to support a JOPES OPORD or OPLAN and exercises. (Much of the information in the TC-AIMS II movement plan can be used as attachments in the unit movement plan.) However, a TC-AIMS II movement plan, while defined as a movement plan within the system, is not a unit movement plan as envisioned in this FM. TC-AIMS II contributes much to the creation of unit movement plans, but does not produce them.

I. Developing a Unit Movement Plan

Ref: FM 4-01.011, chap 2.

Note: See FM 4-01.011 Unit Movement Operations, Appendix L for guidance on developing a movement plan. See FM 4-01.011, Appendix B for a sample Unit Movement SOP.

1. Identify what needs to be moved

Based upon mission requirements (mission, enemy, terrain and weather, troops and support available, time available, civil considerations [METT-TC]) and command guidance, deployment planning must reflect personnel, equipment, supplies, and how the unit will accomplish the move. In the absence of guidance, units plan to deploy with assigned personnel and on-hand equipment. Upon execution, the plan may need to be modified if additional personnel are assigned or equipment cross-leveled to bring the unit to the required readiness level. Units should plan to move their basic load of supplies to sustain their operations upon arrival in the AO. The days of supply, by supply class to be deployed, are normally directed in OPLANs, unit SOPs or MACOM instructions. The UMO must have a detailed listing of each piece of equipment to be deployed. This listing is based on the OEL produced by TC-AIMS II. All outsize, oversize, overweight, or hazardous equipment or cargo must be identified as it will require special considerations.

NOTE: If the deploying unit is authorized to draw Army Prepositioned Sets (APS), the UMO and other appropriate unit personnel should review the battlebook within the Automated Battlebook System (ABS) for the site(s) involved in the operation. The ABS provides reference information and real-time visibility of the afloat and land based APS. Each site may require a different mix of advanced party and main body personnel. Within APS, unit prescribed load list (PLL) and authorized stockage list (ASL) items are often prepositioned with unit equipment sets and must be considered when determining deployment requirements.

2. Identify equipment to accompany troops (yellow TAT), equipment needed immediately upon arrival (red TAT), and equipment which does not have to accompany troops (NTAT)

Yellow TAT must accompany troops and be accessible enroute. Examples include Class I basic load items and individual carry on baggage and weapons. For personnel traveling via commercial air, this is generally the baggage that will fit under the seat. Red TAT must be available at the destination before or upon unit arrival. This equipment may be sensitive cargo that requires special security or handling at the POE or POD. Red TAT must be unitized/palletized and reported on the OEL/UDL. Examples include CBRNE (chemical, biological, radiological, nuclear explosive) equipment, mechanics tools and generators. NTAT equipment is normally shipped by surface and does not accompany the troops. It consists of all other equipment required by the unit to perform its mission.

3. Identify what needs to move by air

Items to move by air could include personnel, advance parties, baggage, and some equipment. The balance of equipment normally moves by sea. For deployments supporting OPLANs and OPORDs, the TPFDD stipulates the movement mode. This TPFDD mode stipulation is provided to the unit by TC-AIMS II.

Appendix D, FM 4-01.011 provides general guidelines for commanders and UMOs concerning general HAZMAT procedures and documentation requirements. Appendix D also provides guidelines for classified and sensitive cargo movement. TC-AIMS II identifies HAZMAT equipment.

4. Identify bulk cargo and develop packing lists

All consolidated cargo (boxed, crated, etc.) loaded in vehicles, containers, and on 463L pallets must display a separate packing list that shows complete contents. Packing lists are not required for items that do not need identification such as empty vehicles, nested cans, or bundled shovels. These items must, however, be listed on the load diagram if loaded in a truck or container. Packing lists are usually distributed based on unit commander or MACOM guidance.

5. Develop vehicle load plans for unit equipment

Vehicle load plans are created for organic vehicles and trailers carrying secondary loads. Equipment that cannot be loaded on organic vehicles should be planned for movement by other means (container, commercial rail or highway, other military assets). Additional guidance for preparing vehicles for movement is contained in Appendices E and F of FM 4-01.011. Unit cargo (vehicles and equipment) is prepared for shipment according to the mode of transportation and the type of move. Preparing vehicles for shipment requires that unit personnel ensure that equipment conforms to clearance and space restrictions. Vehicle modifications (e.g., shelters, bumper modifications, etc.) made by the unit which change the vehicle configuration, dimensions, or weight must be approved by the unit's MACOM and ultimately by MTMC Transportation Engineering Agency (TEA). Modified vehicles cannot be deployed without this approval. Vehicle modifications must be reflected on the OEL and UDL.

6. Identify Blocking, Bracing, Packing, Crating & Tie-Down (BBPCT) requirements

All crates, containers, boxes, barrels, and loose equipment on a vehicle must be blocked, braced, and tied-down to prevent shifting during transit.

7. Translate into transportation terms

Personnel and equipment data are translated into meaningful transportation terms as unit movement data and recorded on the OEL. An OEL is a computerized listing (in printed and data file formats) of on-hand equipment, personnel and supplies in a unit. The OEL supports cargo manifesting for movements and provides input to transportation managers to identify movement requirements. The UDL has evolved to mean an OEL tailored for a specific move. The UDL shows the equipment, personnel, and supplies that will actually deploy. Both the OEL and UDL are created in TC-AIMS II.

8. Determine how personnel & equip will move to POEs

In CONUS, wheeled vehicles normally move to the POE in convoy when distances are less than a one day drive (< 400 miles), with tracked vehicles going via military heavy equipment transporters or commercial rail, motor, or inland waterway. Unit personnel usually move to the POE by organic vehicles or by military or commercial buses.

9. Prepare the unit movement plan

The administrative, logistical, and coordination requirements for the plan must be determined. Items such as enroute medical, messing, and maintenance for movement to POEs must be coordinated and documented. · Appendix L provides a sample movement plan that can be tailored to a deploying unit's requirements.

10. Maintain the movement plan

Keep the OEL current with changes in unit equipment, personnel, and supplies. Update the UDL as changes occur in the OPLAN, CONPLAN, and commander's intent. The importance of maintaining the OEL, which is updated to produce the UDL, cannot be overemphasized. This is the data used to produce the unit's equipment, supplies, and personnel manifests and military shipping labels (MSLs) and radio frequency-automatic identification technology (RF-AIT) tags.

II. Movement Activities
Ref: FM 4-01.011, chap 2.

Preparation for movement is an ongoing unit activity in peacetime that continues after the unit receives a warning or alert for movement. Units normally identify deployment as a mission essential task and annotate it on their mission essential task list (METL). Predeployment activities are those tasks accomplished by Army units and installations prior to movement to POEs. During normal peacetime operations, predeployment activities involve preparation for force projection, crisis response missions, and field exercises. Units conduct routine movement training to ensure they can meet the Joint Force Commander's mission requirements.

I. Peacetime Movement Preparation

1. Unit Alert Procedures
Division and higher level headquarters are normally alerted for missions through the JOPES procedures. Procedures for alerting subordinate units for movement are contained in higher headquarters SOPs, deployment regulations, and unit movement or deployment SOPs. These SOPs normally contain unit alert reporting requirements. Units maintain alert rosters for contacting unit personnel. Alert procedures are validated and tested according to unit SOP or other direction.

2. Identifying Support Requirements
Units generally require extensive support to prepare for movements. This support can include assistance related to equipment inspection, maintenance, property transfer and loading. It also can include assistance in the marshaling and staging areas, and help with predeployment and life support activities. These support requirements are usually identified in division and installation SOPs. Installation and non-deploying units are normally tasked to provide this support to deploying units. Additional support is available from MTMC which dispatches deployment support teams where needed.

3. Soldier Readiness Processing (SRP)
The goal of the SRP program is that all soldiers are maintained administratively ready for deployment at all times. Soldier readiness is a continuous process that involves both the unit commander and the installation staff. Headquarters, Department of the Army requires that specific administrative deployment processing requirements be checked and updated prior to individual soldier or unit movement [SRP requirements are categorized by levels ranging from Level 1 (basic movement SRP requirements) to level 4 (deployment area and mission unique SRP)]. Prior to soldier or unit movement in support of combat or contingency operations, commanders with the assistance of a soldier readiness processing team (SRP Team) physically review on-site processing requirements in levels 1 through 4 within the 30 days prior to departure. AR 600-8-101, Personnel Processing, establishes readiness requirements for each of the levels, and MACOMs and installations ensure they are met.

4. Movement Training
Units are required to have an appropriate number of personnel trained to perform special movement duties previously discussed in chapter one. These special duties include the UMO, the unit loading teams, the hazardous cargo certifying officials, and the air load planners. Each MACOM has specific requirements and policies for appointing and training personnel in these positions. Many commands and installations maintain a local capability to provide deployment training because all deployable units require personnel trained to perform these duties.

II. Predeployment Activities

Predeployment activities are those that units accomplish based on initial notification, warning orders, and alert orders for operations. These activities may overlap in the deployment process or occur in a different order than presented here, depending on time available between initial notification and actual deployment execution.

1. Initial Notification Activities

Following warning order receipt, the deploying unit headquarters evaluates the ability of its subordinate units to meet mission requirements. If a unit needs reorganization or augmentation, a plan is developed to meet established requirements through cross-leveling or outside augmentation. Using TC-AIMS II, personnel adjustments are made to the OEL, then the UDL and equipment and supplies adjustments are made directly to the UDL.

The deploying unit creates a UDL by identifying items from the OEL for deployment. It verifies the shipping information (size, weight, line identification number [LIN], model, and configuration) of the equipment selected for the UDL. The deploying unit also begins preparing other required deployment documentation such as HAZMAT certification.

Upon notification of a potential deployment, the unit reviews its deployment readiness status. The deploying unit's higher headquarters confirms readiness status of all its units and identifies actions needed to raise deficient units to standard. The deploying unit also begins gathering information to identify any special needs (e.g., clothing, equipment) based upon climate, location, or current unit configuration.

2. Movement Order Activities

Receipt of the movement order causes the unit to refine its movement plan based on information provided in the alert order and verifies or updates the following:

- Maintenance lead times and maintenance priorities for deploying equipment
- Requisition and personnel fill times
- Train-up completion time (if required) for unit movement personnel
- Container availability (pack, load, certify, and transport to POE) time

If the deploying unit is drawing APS, the unit deploys or prepares to deploy the APS advance party and unit representatives to the survey, liaison, reconnaissance party, and the off-load preparation party. These soldiers coordinate with the gaining command and act as liaison in preparing for reception and staging.

During warning order activities, the deploying unit continues cross-leveling equipment and submits requisitions for needed supplies that were not identified earlier. As in the initial notification, supply levels may be directed in the alert order or by the deploying unit's higher headquarters. Requisitions may be filled at point of origin and incorporated into the UDL, received at the POE and added to the UDL, or shipped separately to arrive at the POD.

Refinement of the UDL is a continuing process with the deploying unit based on unit status and changes imposed as a result of force tailoring or higher headquarters guidance. The unit verifies equipment status compared to the UDL and updates load plans, equipment dimensions and weight, and HAZMAT shipping declarations. Once corrections are made, the unit prints and applies military shipping labels (MSLs; DD Form 1387) to supplies and equipment. Additionally, the red and yellow TAT, and NTAT equipment are identified.

Unit equipment must be safeguarded IAW governing regulations and SOPs, while it is being transported to and staged at installations, marshalling areas, and POEs. Beyond usual unit safeguarding provisions, certain cargo categories require care while in transit and some special cargo categories require extraordinary protection and monitoring while in transit.

Unit Movement Dates

Ref: FM 4-01.011, chap 2.

To meet their responsibilities to support operational, exercise, and contingency plans, units develop movement plans. Normally divisions, brigades, and battalions create movement plans and companies use extracts from battalion movement plans in company operation orders. Unit movement plans are tailored to the requirements for mobilization, deployments, and exercises, which have specific goals and missions. The plans are written in operation order format and are usually an annex to an operation order. The unit plans the move using the movement plan and executes the move under an operation order.

ULNs on JOPES OPLAN reports divide the unit by transportation mode, ports of embarkation or debarkation, and movement dates. Dates correspond to the established commence movement from origin day (C-day) for the designated plan TPFDD.

The unit movement is phased by the following dates relative to C-day:

1. Ready-to-Load Date (RLD)

The RLD is the TPFDD date when the unit must be prepared to depart its origin. For AC (Active Component) units, origin is the installation and for RC units origin is the mobilization station or site.

2. Available-to-Load Date (ALD)

The ALD is the TPFDD date when the unit must be ready to load on an aircraft or ship at the POE.

3. Earliest Arrival Date (EAD)

The EAD is the earliest date that a unit, a resupply shipment, or replacement personnel can be accepted at a POD during a deployment. It is used with the latest arrival date to describe a delivery window for transportation planning. The supported combatant commander specifies the EAD.

4. Latest Arrival Date (LAD)

The LAD is the latest date when a unit, a resupply shipment, or replacement personnel can be accepted at a POD to support the concept of operations. It is used with the EAD to describe a delivery window for transportation planning. The supported combatant commander specifies the LAD.

5. Required Delivery Date (RDD)

The RDD is the date when a unit, a resupply shipment, or replacement personnel must arrive at a POD and complete off-loading to support the concept of operations. The supported combatant commander specifies the RDD.

6. Schedules

Air Mobility Command publishes airflow schedules to call forward personnel and equipment from the APOE. The call-forward schedules are movement directives that specify when units must have their equipment at the POE to meet ALDs. Based on these schedules, deploying units and intermediate command levels backward-plan movements to the POE. Movement directives (if published) provide windows by mode for cargo arrival at the POE. MTMC performs the same functions for sealift.

Chap 5

III. Movement by Mode

Ref: FM 4-01.011 Unit Movement Operations, chap 3.

This section provides general planning and coordination guidance for unit movements within Continental United States (CONUS) and Outside Continental United States (OCONUS) by rail, highway, and air.

Mode Operations

Note: See pp. 1-54 to 1-55 for additional information on terminal and mode operations (FM 4-0).

The Army can move personnel, cargo, and equipment by motor, rail, air, and water with organic, host nation, or contract assets. While each situation may not be conducive to using a particular mode, the Army must prepare to operate, or supervise, the operation of all these modes of transport. Mode platforms include trucks, trains, containers, flatracks, watercraft, aircraft and commercial delivery, when permitted by METT-TC. Mode operations include intratheater air (C-130 and CH-47); local and linehaul motor transport; heavy equipment transport; and rail, coastal and inland waterway transport. Mode operations and movement control elements working together match up the correct asset capability, cargo characteristics, and required delivery time.

A. Motor

Tactical vehicles are the backbone of the support structure. They are mobile, flexible, and reliable. The motor transportation unit and equipment mix for an operation depend on METT-TC. Motor transport provides the connecting links between the PODs and the receiving units. FM 55-10 has detailed information on motor transport units and operations.

B. Rail

Rail is potentially the most efficient method of hauling large tonnages of materiel by ground transportation; the Army normally depends on the host nation to provide this mode of transportation. The Army has limited railway operating, construction, and repair capability. Information on rail transport units and ops is in FM 55-20.

C. Air

Air is the most flexible transportation mode. Air Force and Army airlift assets provide airlift within a theater. Army cargo and utility helicopters provide support at the operational and tactical levels through movement control channels in response to mission requirements and the commander's priorities.

D. Water

Army watercraft is an essential component of theater transportation. They may augment capabilities of other modes when integrated with appropriate terminal operations. Army watercraft move materiel and equipment along inland waterways, along theater coastlines, and within water terminals. Their primary role is to support cargo discharge and onward movement from the SPOD to inland terminals or to retrograde from inland terminals. Army watercrafts have a role in joint operations along with Navy and Marine Corps lighterage, or in conjunction with HNS assets. FM 55-80 has details on Army watercraft units and operations.

Unit Mvmt

I. CONUS Unit Movements

Ref: FM 4-01.011, chap 3.

A. Convoy Movements

Within the United States, each state establishes rules, procedures, and laws that govern the use of public highways. Counties, cities, and municipalities establish and add restrictions for the use of their respective county or city routes. No vehicular movement that exceeds these legal limitations, or that subjects highway users to unusual hazards (including movement of explosives or other dangerous cargo), is made over public highways without the permission of the appropriate authority. Military convoys require approved convoy clearances and special hauling permits to travel on public highways and roads.

A military convoy is defined as any group of six or more vehicles temporarily organized to operate as a column, with or without escort, proceeding together under a single commander. Ten or more vehicles, dispatched in less than groups of six, traveling the same route to the same destination, in an hour, are also a convoy. During mobilization or deployment, vehicle infiltration (movement of vehicles in units of less than convoy size on a public highway) is prohibited, therefore all movement through a mobilization station(MS) or power projection platform (PPP) or port is considered a convoy. Local policy may be more restrictive.

Note: For more information, see FM 4-01.011 Appendix C, Convoy Operations.

B. Rail Movements

Responsibility for planning and executing rail movements is split between the unit and the ITO. The unit determines movement requirements and submits them to the BMC. The brigade movement officer (BMC) validates and consolidates the movement require-ments prior to forwarding them to the supporting UMC.

The UMC creates rail load plans, using the rail load planning tool within TC-AIMS II, to identify the amount and type of rail assets needed to move unit equipment from the installation. After reviewing these plans, the ITO makes arrangements to have rail equipment spotted for loading to meet scheduled arrival dates in the TPFDD (based on dates specified by the unit). For those items of equipment designated to move by commercial rail, the ITO designates a load-out staging area on the installation. The unit utilizes fixed or hand-held bar code readers or RF-Tag readers to identify unit equip-ment that is being staged for rail loading. This information is then up-loaded to TC-AIMS II and sent to the In-transit Visibility (ITV) regional server, which provides it to the Global Transportation Network (GTN).

The ITO is the official liaison with MTMC and the railway agent. ITO personnel inspect all railcars for serviceability before units begin loading, and provide technical advice to units on blocking, bracing and tie down materiel. The unit provides the ITO with all required HAZMAT documentation.

Note: For more information, see FM 4-01.011, App. A, Railguards and Supercargoes.

C. Air Movement

A key air movement planning consideration is whether the movement is tactical (combat) or nontactical (administrative). A nontactical movement is a movement of troops and equipment that is organized, loaded, and transported to expedite movement and conserve time and energy when no hostile interference is anticipated. It empha-sizes economical use of the aircraft cabin space and maximum use of the allowable cabin load. Tactical movements are organized, loaded, and transported to aid accom-plishment of a tactical mission. The unit arranges personnel, equipment, and supplies to support the tactical operation. Proper use of the aircraft allowable cabin load is still an important factor, but the commander's sequence of employment has priority. Army units plan for nontactical movements unless they are conducting operations that anticipate hostile reception.

For movements conducted under Joint Operations Planning and Execution System (JOPES), the TPFDD identifies the movement mode. It can plan movement for personnel and equipment by air, or the majority of personnel could move by air with the equipment moving by sea. In the latter case, the TPFDD synchronizes the air movement with equipment arrival at sea port of debarkation (SPOD).

USTRANSCOM, using its air component, the Air Mobility Command, is responsible for strategic airlift. Airlift assets can be military, commercial, or a combination of both. For JOPES moves, units may not be notified of the specific type of aircraft being used until after the unit line number (ULN) has been validated for movement. For non-JOPES moves, units request military airlift by submitting a SAAM request and/or other required documentation to the installation UMC.

For Joint Chief of Staff (JCS) directed unit movements, airlift requirements are registered and validated in the JOPES. A unit air movement requires careful load planning, selection of equipment, and personnel processing. It requires transported units to be convoyed, marshaled, received and inspected at APOE; and finally, outloaded to the aircraft. It is a complex process requiring careful planning, prudent execution, and attention to detail at every step.

The parent organization (or home station commander) from which units moving originate, is responsible for assigning, equipping, and training personnel to establish and operate the A/DACG. In CONUS, installations tasked in AR 5-9 and FORSCOM/ARNG Reg 55-1 are responsible for providing A/DACG support.

Using AALPS, the UMO prepares initial air load plans to identify the amount and type of strategic airlift assets required to execute the plan. The deploying unit (as coordinated by its UMO) is also responsible for:

- Preparing cargo (weigh, mark, measure, load, secure, manifest, and compute and mark center of balance)
- Preparing passenger manifest
- Assuring proper preparation and certification of hazardous cargo
- Preparing and certifying load plans
- Providing load teams
- Loading, securing, and off-loading cargo
- Providing shoring, dunnage, and vehicle operators

D. Commercial Truck Movement

When a unit does not have enough organic assets to move its equipment, it coordinates with the installation UMC for movement of unit assets by commercial truck. The unit ensures cargo and equipment is properly marked and prepared for commercial transport.

When the shipment departs, the ITO scans the equipment and inputs the information into TC-AIMS II which provides the information to the local ITV server. The local ITV server provides the information to GTN.

When requested by the moving unit, the ITO arranges for commercial trucks to move the unit equipment to the POE. The unit ensures cargo and equipment is properly marked and prepared for transport.

The UMC coordinates with the ITO to make arrangements for commercial trucks. These services include shipment of sensitive items and hazardous materials.

II. OCONUS Unit Movements

Ref: FM 4-01.011, chap 3.

A. Convoy Movements

Responsibility for highway regulation rests with commanders having area jurisdiction. The highway regulation mission is performed OCONUS by:

- The senior movement control element (MCE) in the theater
- The transportation battalion in the corps rear area
- The division transportation officer in the division rear area
- The brigade S4 in the brigade rear area

The commander who controls the area through which convoys move exercises highway regulation authority with its movement control elements. Each organization at corps and above includes a highway traffic headquarters that prioritizes and schedules convoy traffic on the road network within its area of operation. The division transportation officer, augmented by a division support movement control team (MCT), executes this mission for the division. Unit commanders request permission to use the division road space in accordance with the division highway regulation plan. Units use TC-AIMS II to create clearance and special hauling requests and forward them to an MCT. The MCT forwards the request to the appropriate authority. The approving authority takes action and returns the clearance to the unit.

Using TC-AIMS II to Plan Convoy Movements

Convoy clearance requests are a form of message that details the itinerary of the move, the number and types of vehicles, and movement planning information. TC-AIMS II provides a convoy-planning tool that the S3, S4, or UMO uses to develop convoy movement schedules for unit vehicles. The TC AIMS tool provides for organizing vehicles into convoys, serials, and march units using standard command parameters for vehicle spacing and number of vehicles per march unit/serial. (The standard parameters identify convoy speeds (minimum and maximum) for the type vehicle and area of operation.)

March tables and convoy vehicle listings for the proposed convoy are an output of TC-AIMS II. If the convoy requires clearance to use the route selected, TC-AIMS II prepares a convoy clearance request. The unit sends the requests to the area highway regulation authority at the movement control headquarters. The movement control headquarters coordinates with host nation authorities to secure the route clearance. At OCONUS locations, a movement regulating team equipped with TC-AIMS II and AIT interrogators track convoy movements. During the convoy movement, convoy vehicles equipped with the Movement Tracking System (MTS) can transmit the convoy coordinates to the MTS control station.

Note: For more information, see FM 4-01.011 Appendix C, Convoy Operations.

B. Rail Movements

Responsibility for planning and executing OCONUS rail movements is split between the units and the MCT. The units determine movement requirements and submit them to the BMC. The BMC consolidates and validates the movement requirements and forwards them to the supporting MCT.

The MCT obtains railcars based on unit movement requirements. MCT personnel compute railcar requirements based on the shipping configuration of the items being shipped. Accurate UDL data is essential. The unit provides required HAZMAT

Unit Mvmt

documentation, and based on data from the UDL, the MCT prepares the bill of lading or the freight warrant. Alternatively, the MCT can scan the MSLs on the equipment to prepare the bill of lading or the freight warrant.

The MCT is the official liaison with the HN railway agent. MCT personnel inspect all railcars for serviceability before units begin loading, and provide technical advice to units on blocking, bracing and tie down materiel. The area support group (ASG) or base support battalion (BSB) is normally responsible for providing units blocking and bracing materials needed to load military equipment on railcars. Units request these materials as far in advance as possible. The ASG or BSB also provides tools and assistance as required.

Units are responsible for preparing their equipment for OCONUS rail loading. This includes packing, crating, banding, and blocking and bracing secondary loads. Units load railcars under the technical supervision of the MCT. (In extraordinary circumstances, TOE rail teams assist in loading railcars.) Units can generate automated rail load plans using TC-AIMS II. The MCT and the HN railway agent are ultimately responsible for approving all rail loads.

Note: For more information, see FM 4-01.011, App. A, Railguards and Supercargoes.

C. Air Movement

When moving from OCONUS to CONUS the UMO is responsible to have customs officials observe the packing process and attach a seal of approval. UMOs ensure that all equipment meets air shipment standards.

A key planning consideration is whether the movement is tactical (combat) or nontactical (administrative). This depends on the unit's mission in the theater. A nontactical movement is a movement of troops and equipment that is organized, loaded, and transported to expedite movement and conserve time and energy when no hostile interference is anticipated. It emphasizes economical use of the aircraft cabin space and maximum use of the allowable cabin load. Tactical movements are organized, loaded, and transported to aid accomplishment of a tactical mission. The unit arranges personnel, equipment, and supplies to support the tactical operation. Proper use of the aircraft allowable cabin load is still an important factor, but the commander's sequence of employment has priority. Army units plan for nontactical movements unless they are conducting operations that anticipate hostile reception.

D. Using Host Nation (HN) Assets

Using HN Assets

The United States has agreements with some countries that provide for coordinated tasking of HN transportation assets when US Army assets are not available to handle military cargo. When Army assets are not available, the MCT requests the senior movement control element to task HN assets under the provisions of these agreements.

Using Theater Support Contractor Assets

MTMC is responsible for contracting for and coordinating use of HN theater support contractor assets until a theater headquarters can assume the mission. The MCT identifies a commercial operator identified in the origin MCT's geographic area. Commitments flow through predetermined channels developed between the senior movement control element and the commercial carrier. If the commercial carrier cannot support the transportation request for any reason, it notifies the MCT immediately. The MCT attempts to establish an alternate delivery date that satisfies the consignee; selects another mode; requests HN assets; delays lower priority shipments; or requests assistance from its headquarters.

Hazardous, Classified, and Protected Sensitive Cargo

Ref: FM 4-01.011, app. D.

1. Hazardous Material (HAZMAT)

Packaging, shipping, handling, and inspecting of HAZMAT is mandated by US and international laws. These laws also apply to the use of intermodal containers and container equipment. This appendix provides an overview of doctrinal guidance and tactics, techniques, and procedures that are common to Department of Defense (DOD) and other US government agencies and organizations. This appendix also applies to the selection of standard American National Standards Institute/International Standards Organization (ANSI/ISO) commercial- or military-owned intermodal containers that meet the standards for shipment of Class I explosives and other HAZMAT. (See MIL-HDBK 138 for compliance with container standards criteria.)

HAZMAT must be properly prepared and documented IAW DOD Regulation 4500.9-R, Volume II and III; TM 38-250; and other service or command regulations. Documentation must include the total HAZMAT quantity and a certification statement stating that the HAZMAT is properly classified, described, packaged, marked, and labeled. Only specially trained individuals have authority to certify HAZMAT for transportation. Contact the Installation Transportation Officer (ITO) or Movement Control Team (MCT) for assistance in determining what certification requirements apply to each HAZMAT item being prepared for shipment.

Ammunition

Ammunition shipments are usually scheduled through military ammunition ports. Designated military ammunition ports serve the strategic purpose of routinely handling shipments of ammunition. To meet deployment requirements, ammunition may be moved through a commercial port. If the unit is deployed through a commercial seaport and must carry basic load ammunition with them, the MTMC manager for the port must first be notified of the intent to ship ammunition. The Joint Munitions Transportation Coordinating Activity (JMTCA) consolidates all containerized munitions movement requests for OCONUS shipment aboard common-use sealift.

2. Classified Cargo

Classified cargo is cargo that requires protection in the interest of national security. The nature of classified cargo requires that shippers and transporters handle it in a way that it be identified, accounted for, secured, segregated, or handled in a special way to safeguard it. Detailed instructions are included in DTR 4500.9R. Do not identify classified cargo on the outside of the shipping containers.

When transporting classified material, enclose it in two sealed containers, such as boxes or heavy wrappings. Detailed instructions for packing classified material are contained in AR 380-5.

When traveling by motor convoy, escorts must ensure constant surveillance of classified material. Classified material must stay within the escort's personal possession and observation at all times. Larger pieces of secret shipments, such as missiles, may require outside storage. If so, take special protective measures to include constant and continuous surveillance by at least one or more escorts in the area.

3. Sensitive Cargo

Sensitive cargo is cargo that could threaten public safety if compromised. Sensitive cargo must be properly secured and identified to port personnel so sufficient security can be provided. Do not identify security cargo on the outside of the shipping containers. Detailed instructions are included in DTR 4500.9R.

IV. POE Operations

Ref: FM 4-01.011 Unit Movement Operations, chap 4 and FM 3-35.4 Deployment Fort-to-Port, chap. 4.

Note: Aerial Ports of Debarkation (APODs) and Sea Ports of Debarkation (SPODs) are covered on pp. 6-18 to 6-22.

Units normally deploy via airports and seaports of embarkation. Each power projection platform has an associated strategic seaport and airport. The proximity of the port facilities to the platform determines the type of movement to the port required. At some ports, the distance is short, so units can convoy; at others, commercial support is required. In the overall global deployment scheme, each point at which a unit changes the type of transportation platform (that is, air, ship, rail, commercial and military truck) is a node. Nodes are, by their nature, friction points. Friction slows the deployment time line. Therefore, throughput, the amount of cargo that can move through a node, becomes a principal concern. This is particularly true at the POEs. The objective is to maximize quickly the throughput capability by moving transportation assets, units, and enablers into position for immediate execution of the plan. Any time lost in this pursuit is lost forever and, if ports are used at less than capacity, the unused portion is irrecoverable.

Fort-to-Port Movement

Convoy Movements

Most units conduct convoy operations to get to the ports of embarkation. A convoy is a group of vehicles organized for the purpose of control and orderly movement under the control of a single commander. Theater policy (OCONUS unit), standardization agreement, or the HN directs the minimum number of vehicles in a convoy. In the absence of policies to the contrary, convoys consist of six or more vehicles. Vehicles in a convoy are organized into groups to facilitate command and control, and normally move at the same rate. To assist in centralized convoy management, FORSCOM has developed and implemented a computerized mobilization movement control system/program known as MOBCON. The MOBCON software uses the national highway transportation network (NHTN) in conjunction with a system of nodes (road junctions, critical points) and links (road segments between nodes).

Rail Operations

Although most units conduct convoy operations to get to the POE, not all units or power projection platforms are located within driving distance to seaports, and not all cargo, particularly for heavy forces, is transportable by military or commercial truck. In these cases, rail travel is used. The railroad facilities serving the POE may be at the head of a pier or at an inland transfer point. The transfer point may be truck-to-rail or amphibian-to-rail. Terminal service units will load or unload rail equipment during cargo-handling operations. These units must plan rail-loading procedures and secure cargo on rail cars. They must also know the type of equipment required at destination to load and unload cargo to minimize the amount of rail equipment used and to make the loading/unloading as simple and quick as possible. See FMs 4-01.41 (55-20 and 55-21), FM 4-01.50 (55-17), and FM 3-35.4, Appendix H for more information on rail operations.

I. Aerial Port of Embarkation (APOE)

Ref: FM 4-01.011, chap 4.

Battalion and companies deploy personnel, supplies, and equipment by air through an aerial port of embarkation (APOE) that is generally operated by the Air Force. It may be on an Air Force Base or a commercial airfield. All ports must have communications and be able to provide ITV of unit equipment during this phase of movement. This capability must extend to providing advance arrival information to the APOD. There are distinct differences between a SPOE and an APOE. Most notably is that the APOE uses four separate areas of movement preparation. Personnel, supplies, and equipment go from the marshaling area to an alert holding area, to a call forward area, and finally to a loading ramp area. These latter three areas, the alert holding area, call forward Area, and loading ramp area, are used at an APOE instead of the single staging area of an SPOE.

Aerial Port of Embarkation (APOE)

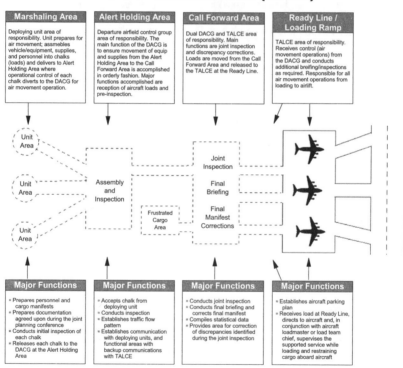

Marshaling Area	Alert Holding Area	Call Forward Area	Ready Line / Loading Ramp
Deploying unit area of responsibility. Unit prepares for air movement; assembles vehicle/equipment, supplies, and personnel into chalks (loads) and delivers to Alert Holding Area where operational control of each chalk diverts to the DACG for air movement operation.	Departure airfield control group area of responsibility. The main function of the DACG is to ensure movement of equip and supplies from the Alert Holding Area to the Call Forward Area is accomplished in orderly fashion. Major functions accomplished are reception of aircraft loads and pre-inspection.	Dual DACG and TALCE area of responsibility. Main functions are joint inspection and discrepancy corrections. Loads are moved from the Call Forward Area and released to the TALCE at the Ready Line.	TALCE area of responsibility. Receives control (air movement operations) from the DACG and conducts additional briefing/inspections as required. Responsible for all air movement operations from loading to airlift.

Major Functions	Major Functions	Major Functions	Major Functions
▪ Prepares personnel and cargo manifests ▪ Prepares documentation agreed upon during the joint planning conference ▪ Conducts initial inspection of each chalk ▪ Releases each chalk to the DACG at the Alert Holding Area	▪ Accepts chalk from deploying unit ▪ Conducts inspection ▪ Establishes traffic flow pattern ▪ Establishes communication with deploying units, and functional areas with backup communications with TALCE	▪ Conducts joint inspection ▪ Conducts final briefing and corrects final manifest ▪ Compiles statistical data ▪ Provides area for correction of discrepancies identified during the joint inspection	▪ Establishes aircraft parking plan ▪ Receives load at Ready Line, directs to aircraft and, in conjunction with aircraft loadmaster or load team chief, supervises the supported service while loading and restraining cargo aboard aircraft

Ref: FM 4-01.011, fig. 4-3, p. 4-9.

The Arrival/Departure Airfield Control Group (A/DACG) is an Army organization established to control and support departure preparation and facilitate Army deployments at the APOE. The A/DACG is normally run by a CTC or can be an ad hoc organization provided by an Army organization (installation, ASG, etc.) tasked to support the deploying forces and the APOE with the A/DACG mission. Its size and capabilities are mission dependent. The A/DACG is task organized with personnel and equipment not associated with the deploying units. Cargo transfer companies are well-suited to perform this mission. Its organizational structure provides, as a minimum, command, administration, operations, joint inspection, and loading/unloading capabilities.

The aerial port complex is under the control of a Tanker Airlift Control Element (TALCE). The TALCE is a deployed Air Mobility Command organization established at fixed, en route, and deployed locations where AMC operational support is non-existent or insufficient. A TALCE is composed of mission support elements from various units and deploys in support of contingency/emergency relief operations on both a planned and "no-notice" basis. The TALCE provides continuing on-site management of Air Mobility Command airfield operations including command and control, communications, aerial port services, maintenance, security, weather, and intelligence — those critical elements needed to ensure a safe and efficient air base for airlift operations.

The four distinct port complex areas are:

1. The Marshaling Area

The Marshaling Area activities are the responsibility of the deploying commander. . It is the area where units start, continue, or complete preparation for loading. (The deploying unit should not be required to perform support functions, thus permitting its concentration on preparation for the deployment.) the marshaling area is normally located at or in the vicinity of the airfield, but may be located in any location to ease movement and control. in any case, the marshaling area activities should take place as lose as possible to the departure airfield. Its location should not cause unnecessary congestion to airfield operations or undue hardship to the deploying unit.

2. Alert Holding Area

The Alert Holding Area is the equipment, vehicle, and passenger control area, and is the responsibility of the A/DACG. It is normally located in the vicinity of the departure airfield. It is used to assemble, inspect, hold, and service aircraft loads. Control of the load is transferred from the individual unit to the A/DACG at this point.

3. Call Forward Area

The Call Forward Area is that portion of the departure airfield where the joint inspection is conducted. It is the dual responsibilityof the A/DACG and the TALCE. A final briefing is provided to deploying troops and all manifests are reviewed for accuracy. The deploying unit corrects all discrepancies found by the A/DACG and TALCE joint inspection. Control of the load moves from the A/DACG to the TALCE when the load moves from the call forward area to the loading ramp.

4. Ready Line / Loading Ramp Area

The Loading Ramp Area is that portion of the departure airfield beyond which aircraft operations are conducted. It is the responsibility of the TALCE who receives sole control of the load from the A/DACG when the load or "chalk" moves from the call forward area to the loading ramp area. Additional briefings and inspections may be conducted in this area. Here the aircraft parking plan is executed and loads directed to the parked aircraft. Actual loading of the aircraft is accomplished in this area under the supervision of loadmasters or load team chiefs.

II. Sea Port of Embarkation (SPOE)

Ref: FM 4-01.011, chap 4.

Battalions and companies deploy unit personnel, supplies, and equipment by sea through a port that is commanded or contracted by the Military Traffic Management Command (MTMC). Before being loaded on vessels, unit personnel, supplies, and equipment are held in the port staging area to prepare for shipment. Before moving to the port staging area, the unit, its supplies and equipment may be assembled in a marshaling area. There is a distinction between the two areas, although they serve much the same purpose. In a marshaling area, the owning command retains responsibility and accountability for the shipment. Once in the staging area, the port commander assumes custody of equipment and supplies. Both marshaling and staging areas are discussed in the paragraphs following.

A. Marshaling Area

When port call instructions are received from MTMC Operations Center, units are notified when and where to move their personnel, supplies, and equipment. This destination may be a port marshaling area or a port staging area. Support installations (SI), area support groups (ASG), or other organizations may be tasked to operate the marshaling area.

When deemed necessary, support installations, area support groups, or other organizations are tasked to establish a marshaling area near the port staging area. The primary purpose of a marshaling area is to provide a location to receive unit personnel, equipment and supplies, and configure them for overseas movement by sea, prior to entering the staging area. Accountability for personnel, equipment, and supplies remains with the deploying unit in the marshaling area. The following activities take place in the marshaling area:

Marshaling Area

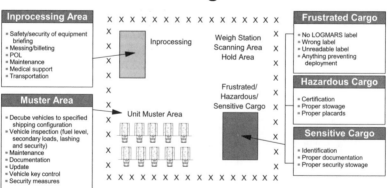

In many cases, there is not enough room at the ocean terminal to stage the entire unit or large numbers of units scheduled to move at the same time. If required, a marshaling area will be operated by a designated FORSCOM supporting installation in close proximity to the port, if possible. At the marshaling area, units make final Preparation for Overseas Movement (POM), and are called forward to the terminal as ships are positioned for loading. Supercargoes accompany the unit's cargo on the ship as it sails to the designated Sea Port of Debarkation (SPOD). These personnel periodically start the vehicles and perform minor maintenance to ensure vehicles are ready upon arrival in the theater.

Ref: FM 4-01.011, fig. 4-1, p. 4-4.

Sea Port of Embarkation (SPOE)

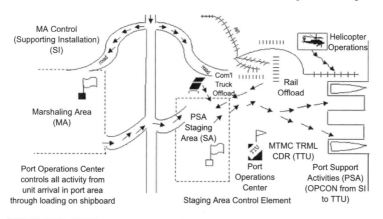

MA Control (Supporting Installation) (SI)	Helicopter Operations

Com'l Truck Offload · Rail Offload

Marshaling Area (MA)

PSA Staging Area (SA)

MTMC TRML CDR (TTU)

Port Operations Center controls all activity from unit arrival in port area through loading on shipboard

Port Operations Center

Staging Area Control Element

Port Support Activities (PSA) (OPCON from SI to TTU)

Military Ocean Terminal (MOT)	Designated Supporting Installation
• Command and operate SPOE • Provide traffic management and terminal support • Coordinate security • TML Cdr has OPCON of PSA and will provide PSA chief	• Establish and operate MA • Provide PSA Provide the following to deploying units: • Coordination and control • Billeting • Messing • Transportation back to MS (by exception) • Security of unit classified cargo • Vehicle wash facilities • Parking • Fueling • Emergency maintenance • Local transportation
Deploying Unit	
• Establish liaison with MA control • Indentify personnel and equipment to be moved • Identify cargo requiring special handling • Secure unit equipment with MA • Provide unit load teams	

Ref: FM 4-01.011, fig. 4-2, p. 4-7.

B. Staging Area

The MTMC port commander has responsibility for the staging area. The staging area is the final location where unit personnel, supplies, and equipment are assembled prior to boarding the vessel. As the vessel readies for loading, the port commander calls forward supplies and equipment from the marshaling area to the staging area based on a call forward plan. The port commander assumes custody and accountability of the equipment and supplies in the staging area. Units usually arrange equipment and supplies in the staging area in the order that it is to move onto the ship.

Unit movement teams (UMT) transportation terminal brigades (TTBs), port support activities (PSAs), cargo transfer companies, freight consolidation and distribution teams (FCDT), and cargo documentation teams may be assigned to operate staging areas under MTMC control. (The MTMC UMT is an ad hoc organization that opens and temporarily operates a SPOE until the transportation terminal brigade (TTB) is operational. When alerted, a UMT is formed and immediately deploys to the SPOE to coordinate contracts, set up operations, and begin to receive cargo. The team also plans for traffic flow, obtains waivers and clearances, establishes liaison with the deploying unit, develop pre-stow plans, and provides reports. Liaison with the deploying unit is especially critical to establish the flow into the port based on the priority of load. The team's composition is determined by the team chief based on mission requirements. Command authority remains with the team until the TTB commander arrives and assumes command.) (Note: See FM 3-35.4.)

SPOE Responsibilities
Ref: FM 4-01.011, chap 4.

In organizing for reception of personnel, equipment, and supplies at its SPOEs, MTMC may be assigned any of the following to assist in the deployment mission: UMT, a TTB, a PSA, cargo transfer companies, FCDTs, and cargo documentation teams.

Transportation Terminal Brigade (TTB)
TTBs are Reserve Component (RC) units that allow the MTMC to expand the number and capability of seaports. TTBs conduct ocean terminal operations at established ports where existing manpower, equipment, and infrastructure are available. They may be deployed Outside Continental United States (OCONUS) to expand the number and capability of ports for sustainment or redeployment purposes.

A typical TTB operates two or three berths simultaneously (four or five berths for limited surge periods), provides traffic management, and supervises contracts. It employs Army information systems such as Integrated Computerized Deployment System (ICODES) and Worldwide Port System (WPS), and uses automated identification technology (AIT) to maintain in-transit visibility. (See new FM 3-35.4.)

Port Support Activity (PSA)
The PSA is a temporary military augmentation organization (or contracted organization) comprised of personnel with specific skills that aid the port commander in receiving, processing, and clearing cargo at the SPOE. It is under the operational control of the port commander. CONUS installations are tasked by FORSCOM to provide PSAs to specific ports. This includes the PSA and associated logistic support for deploying units. The PSA establishes the necessary communications to ensure the proper flow of cargo. It provides daily operational reports of cargo received, maintenance performed, and operational problems to the port commander. In an OCONUS area of operation (AO), the ASG provides the PSA and associated logistic support for deploying units. (See FM 3-35.4.)

Cargo Transfer Company (CTC)
A CTC is organized with four cargo transfer platoons and a documentation section. The four platoons have material handling equipment (MHE) to support transshipping cargo, containers, and unit equipment to ships and aircraft. Each platoon can operate independently at a remote site to support transshipment operations. The company assists in loading ships and operating a staging area. The small CTC Documentation Section, equipped with TC-AIMS II, cannot support each of the four Platoons simultaneously when they operate at remote terminals. When operating remote terminals, the CTC is augmented with one or more cargo documentation teams. (See FM 55-1; new FM 4-01.)

Cargo Documentation Team (CDT)
A cargo documentation team is staffed with 88N Documentation Specialists. The cargo documentation team has no MHE. The team is normally assigned to augment a cargo transfer company to prepare documentation for cargo and equipment being loaded on vessels. (See FM 55-1; new FM 4-01.)

Freight Consolidation and Distribution Team (FCDT)
The FCDT is staffed to operate its forklifts, loading ramps, and a TC-AIMS II computer with AIT devices and printers. The FCDT can be located at small terminals to provide independent loading and documentation services or at larger port complexes as a tailored augmentation to the TTB. The FCDT prepares documentation for cargo and equipment being loaded on vessels. (See FM 55-1; new FM 4-01.)

I. RSO&I Overview

Ref: FM 100-17-3; Reception, Staging, Onward Movement & Integration, chap. 1.

I. The Power Projection Challenge

US military strategy rests on the twin concepts of forward presence and power projection to facilitate accomplishment of military objectives. Complementing overseas presence, power projection is the ability of the US to apply all necessary elements of national power (military, economic, diplomatic, and informational) at the place and time necessary to achieve national security objectives.

Processes of RSO&I

 Reception

The process of unloading personnel and materiel from strategic transport, marshaling the deploying units, transporting them to staging areas, if required, and providing life support to deploying personnel.

 Staging

The process of assembling, holding, and organizing arriving personnel and equipment into units and forces, incrementally building combat power and preparing units for onward movement, and providing life support for the personnel until the unit becomes self-sustaining.

 Onward Movement

The process of moving units and accompanying materiel from reception facilities and staging areas to TAAs or other theater destinations, moving arriving non-unit personnel to gaining commands, and moving arriving sustainment materiel from reception facilities to distribution sites.

 Integration

The synchronized transfer of authority over units and forces to a designated component or functional commander for employment in the theater of ops.

Ref: FM 100-17-3, chap. 1.

RSO&I

During major contingencies, forces deploy from power projection platforms within the United States, or from forward bases. The first forces to deploy secure the lodgment for the receipt of follow-on forces. Initial forces generally arrive by air in tactical configuration. They may be followed by personnel transported by air, who draw prepositioned equipment. Most troops are transported by air, but the majority of equipment travels by sea. Historically, 90 percent of all cargo by weight has been transported by sea, with the remaining 10 percent transported by air.

II. RSO&I in a Contingency Environment

A contingency environment has two entries-Opposed and Unopposed.

A. Opposed Entry

Deployments may be either opposed or unopposed. In opposed operations, units must have sufficient combat capability to fight immediately upon arrival in-theater. Units are configured tactically, and are under command and control of the force commander, from origin to destination. In cases where objectives are limited or AO is small, it may be possible for early entry forces to accomplish missions with limited support of follow-on forces. In most cases, the immediate focus of early entry forces will be seizure of a lodgment area to expedite unopposed entry of follow-on forces. Critical planning considerations are the time and force needed to secure lodgment, and the speed of subsequent transition to unopposed entry. The challenge is balancing the competing requirements of force protection and force projection.

B. Unopposed Entry

In unopposed deployments, personnel routinely move by air, while most unit equipment moves by surface transport. Units are divided into separate groups of passengers and cargo; commanders retain command, but no longer exercise control over multiple parts of units moving by different modes. Various elements of deploying force arriving in-theater must reach specific locations and reassemble into tactical units before unit commanders can reestablish control. RSO&I maximizes this process.

In contingency operations, early and simultaneous deployment of tactical and operational headquarters, including both combat and logistical command structures, is necessary to meet force closure timelines. Planning and coordination with host nation, allied, and other Service early entry forces ensure adequate allocation of resources to the JFC's priority. Reception and employment of both combat and CSS forces must be monitored to establish and sustain the maximum level of combat power. Throughout deployment, Army forces must maintain flexibility to reconfigure units and adjust deployment sequencing to accommodate the theater commander's requirements.

III. Force Projection

Note: See pp. 1-20 to 1-23 for additional information on force projection processes.

Combat power is built incrementally throughout RSO&I, which often involves multiple iterations of staging and onward movement. Thus, when an armored company is combat ready at the TSB, the ground force commander must have visibility of this potential capability and be able to impact subsequent decisions on onward movement. This visibility requires standing reporting procedures and adequate communication

Reporting incremental build of combat power begins with well-understood standards for readiness. Assessments of combat power are based on unit capability, rather than simple tallies of numbers of vehicles and weapon systems on hand. Readiness and reporting are inherently operational matters, normally handled through operational channels; however, the theater movement control organization may be an appropriate channel for readiness reporting until headquarters units become operational in-theater.

IV. Deployment Segments

Ref: FM 100-17-3, chap. 1 and FM 4-0, chap. 3.

Deployment encompasses all activities from origin or home station through destination, specifically including intra-continental United States, intertheater, and intratheater movement legs, staging, and holding areas (JP 4-0). The deployment process includes all planning, preparation, execution, and assessment activities beginning with a mission requiring deployment of U.S. forces. Deployment operations support the initial projection of forces and, once deployed, link the deployed forces with their home station and the strategic-level sustainment base.

FM 100-17-3, RSO&I, lists three distinct and interrelated deployment segments: fort to port, port to port, and port to foxhole. The newer FM 4-0, CSS Operations, lists four segments, outlined below *(see pp. 1-22 to 1-23 for additonal information)*:

1. Predeployment Activities

Predeployment activities are actions taken to prepare forces for deployment. They are essentially constant and on-going activities performed at home station before and continuing after warning or alert notification. Predeployment activities include training validation; deployment planning, to include force protection plans (see detailed discussion in paragraph 3-52); task organization; equipment maintenance; and soldier readiness processing (SRP). During normal peacetime operations, pre-deployment activities involve preparation for crisis response and force projection missions, always considering the operational requirements of the supported force commander.

2. Fort to Port

Activities at POEs focus on staging, marshaling, and loading personnel, units, equipment, and supplies on designated transportation assets prior to movement to ports of debarkation (PODs). Load planning is driven by the deployment concept and lift assets supporting deployment, the anticipated operational environment, and the anticipated situation at the POD to receive, offload, and reassemble mission capable organizations.The TPFDD synchronizes arriving personnel, equipment, and supplies with mission needs during deployment, and echelons, configures, and schedules units for movement. Time phasing allows for rapid theater reception and onward movement of arriving personnel, equipment, and supplies.

3. Port to Port

Movement to PODs can be conducted using common-user and organic or assigned/attached lift assets. PODs include seaports of debarkation (SPODs) and aerial ports of debarkation (APODs). USTRANSCOM conducts movement to PODs on common-user transportation in consultation with the supported and supporting combatant commanders. USTRANSCOM's primary responsibility is ensuring operational effectiveness in support of the JFC's deployment requirements while striving to attain the most efficient use of transportation resources. Alternatively, movement to PODs on organic or assigned/attached lift is the responsibility of the deploying unit commander in response to mission guidance from the supported JFC.

4. Port to Destination

The last phase of deployment (joint reception, staging, onward movement, and integration (JRSOI)) is the responsibility of the supported combatant commander and subordinate JFC. Joint Reception Staging Onward movement and Integration comprises the essential processes required to transition arriving personnel, equipment, and materiel into forces capable of meeting operational requirements (JP 4-01.8). The Army refers to these same processes as RSO&I. Deployment is not complete until the deploying unit is a functioning part of the in-theater force.

V. Building Combat Power
Ref: FM 100-17-3, chap. 1.

RSO&I is the means by which commanders shape and expedite force closure in the theater of operations. Effective, well conceived RSO&I operations greatly speed force closure; conversely, ineffective RSO&I delays force closure and compromises the CINC's ability to implement his concept of operations.

By examining flows of major units into the theater, and the required times of force closure, planners can define the infrastructure required to meet the overall C+75 day force closure requirement. Note that early entry forces and their support all arrive by air (unless forward-based forces and/or equipment prepositioned ashore or afloat are already in-theater).

A. Theater Infrastructure

Understanding capabilities and limitations of the theater infrastructure, and times at which various infrastructure assets must become available, is essential to developing a successful RSO&I operation. Theater RSO&I infrastructure is divided into two general categories-organizational capabilities of the theater, for example, military units, host nation support, and so forth; and physical capabilities of the theater, for example, ports, road networks, inland waterway, and so forth.

The theater CINC has five sources available to provide RSO&I organizational infrastructure, the relative mix of which will vary according to the operation: forward-deployed forces, Army prepositioned stocks, deploying RSO&I units, host nation/allied support, LOGCAP and other contractor support.

The RSO&I physical infrastructure consists of the theater's nodes and available modes of transportation. The two major modes of transportation are surface and air. Surface is further subdivided into sea, inland waterways, coastal waterways, highway, and rail.

B. Operational Dilemma

The commander's operational dilemma is balancing the need for early deployment of combat forces against the requirement to deploy tailored logistical units that maximize throughput of sustainable combat forces. To resolve this dilemma, the commander must have the ability to see, understand, and balance the flow.

The JFC's Strategic Concept defines force requirements in terms of size, location, and time. The TPFDD defines the force flow needed to meet these requirements. Building the TPFDD requires reverse planning, with the concept identifying the requirements against which the tactical, operational, and strategic plans are developed. The JFC must see what forces have arrived in the theater, their combat capability, and schedule for integration. In addition to in-theater information, the JFC requires a forecast of units scheduled to arrive in-theater and projected integration dates.

C. Understand the Flow

Knowledge of the RSO&I infrastructure present in the theater, coupled with assets arriving via the TPFDD, is critical to understanding the flow. The IPB process of defining and describing the battlefield, the enemy, and developing enemy courses of action are crucial to understanding the flow. The IPB process provides an awareness of other demands on the infrastructure that may impact our use. Understanding the flow includes the recognition that change is inevitable.

Unfortunately, the impacts of TPFDD changes are not usually readily apparent; sometimes the effects on the rest of the flow may not be worth the change. Modeling and simulation can provide the means of determining the impact of TPFDD changes.

Deployment is the relocation of forces and materiel to desired operational areas. Deployments must be planned based on the JFC's requirements. It is the JFC who defines success in deployment, establishing what, where, and when force is needed. The force projection challenge is to balance these requirements with the theater's ability to conduct RSO&I operations by properly scheduling the arrival of RSO&I assets in the TPFDD flow.

The Strategic Mobility Triad

The Army has designated CONUS bases from which earmarked forces deploy as "Power Projection Platforms." These key bases are equipped with expanded and modernized loading and cargo handling facilities for rapid transport of military forces and equipment to designated ports of embarkation, that is, seaports and airfields. These modern, capable power projection platforms enable our strategic mobility triad-strategic airlift, strategic sealift, and prepositioned equipment to operate at peak efficiency.

1. Airlift

Airlift can move forces rapidly from CONUS to any theater, but is an expensive and inefficient means of moving bulk goods and heavy equipment. It is best suited for the transport of light, early-entry forces, or for the movement of troops falling in on prepositioned stocks or equipment transported by sea.

2. Sealift

Sealift is the most economical means of moving bulk goods and heavy equipment, but in comparison with air transport, it is extremely slow. Even fast transport ships can require two or three weeks to transit from CONUS to conflict sites in Asia or the Middle East.

3. Prepositioning

There are two types of prepositioning in the triad-prepositioning ashore (APS-2/4/5) and prepositioning afloat (APS-3). Prepositioning ashore allows heavy equipment to be kept in-theater, near the point at which it will be needed. However, the prepositioned stockpiles are expensive to maintain, require host nation cooperation, may generate international tensions, and can be a security risk. Prepositioning afloat also allows for forward prepositioning of sustainment stocks, unit equipment, and port opening capabilities on Military Sealift Command vessels home based in Diego Garcia and Guam. The vessels can be sailed worldwide in response to any contingency. Prepositioning afloat is limited by cost, loss of capability during periodic maintenance, reception port capabilities, and sailing time. Both prepositioning types rely on strategic airlift to rapidly transport troops to the equipment.

The prepositioning leg of the triad includes equipment prepositioned at selected contingency sites worldwide, as well as materiel prepositioned afloat. Together, these assets enhance force projection by allowing CONUS-deployed personnel to be equipped with in-theater stockpiles. This reduces the need for heavy lift assets during the critical "Early Entry" phase. Floating prepositioned assets provide critical sustained combat power in-theaters lacking a forward presence or prepositioned stockpiles ashore. They allow rapid buildup of heavy forces to demonstrate US resolve, reduce risk of open conflict, and counter hostile actions before arrival of the CONUS or OCONUS-based heavy divisions. Assets afloat include TOFMs, which are modular theater-opening packages designed to provide theater commanders the ability to open, operate, and clear sea and air ports; to onward move; to sustain; and to conduct LOTS operation.

RSO&I

VI. Principles of RSO&I

Ref: FM 100-17-3, chap. 1.

The functions of RSO&I apply to the entire spectrum of military operations, at all levels of war-strategic, operational, and tactical. Reception is often the interface between the strategic and the operational levels. Staging and onward movement are normally within the operational level. Integration represents the interface between the operational and tactical levels of war.

RSO&I Principles

Four principles guide the development and execution of RSO&I:

- Unity of Command
- Unit Integrity
- Optimum Logistical Footprint
- Unity of Effort

A. Unity of Command

The employment of military forces in a manner that masses combat power toward a common objective is essential to success at all levels of war. The same principle applies to RSO&I. Only one organization should control and operate the RSO&I process. It must be able to adjust resources based upon deployment flows, control movements in the area of operations, and provide life support to arriving personnel.

B. Unit Integrity

Moving unit cargo and personnel by the same strategic/operational transportation asset provides distinct advantages for units and the force closure process. It leverages the strength of the chain of command, simplifies force tracking, and increases training opportunities. While it is impossible to put an armored battalion's cargo and personnel in one airplane, theincreased sealift of the LMSR allows movement of all battalion equipment on a single ship. Maintaining unit integrity while in strategic transport can simplify the RSO&I challenge of incrementally building combat power.

C. Optimum Logistical Footprint

Defining the logistic structure required and sizing the logistics footprint to deploying forces are essential to effectiveness. The goal is to avoid burdening strategic lift, infrastructure, and the commander with more support than is necessary, yet deploy minimum assets necessary to optimize throughput of units and materiel. Supporting assets must be deployed in a properly timed sequence to leverage their capabilities. Sizes of logistical footprints may be increased to reduce vulnerability of the overall force. Increasing the RSO&I capability to clear backlogs in ports and staging areas can be a tool to reduce force vulnerability.

D. Unity of Effort

All RSO&I must be directed towards, and measured against, the degree to which it achieves the JFC's force closure objectives. Each RSO&I process must be orchestrated as part of the whole to achieve this objective.

II. Planning RSO&I Ops

Ref: FM 100-17-3; Reception, Staging, Onward Movement & Integration, chap. 2.

In all force projection operations, the focus is on bringing the proper force to the right location at the appropriate time. RSO&I is a means by which this is achieved. Successful RSO&I is fully integrated into the campaign plan. This chapter examines general planning considerations and procedures essential to permit a quick transition from RSO&I to combat operations.

The Campaign Plan

A campaign is a series of related military operations designed to achieve strategic or operational objectives within a given time and space. A campaign plan describes how these operations are connected in time, space, and purpose. While campaign planning is done in crisis or conflict, the framework for a successful campaign is laid in peacetime analysis, planning, and exercises.

Campaigns consist of major operations; RSO&I is one such major operation within a campaign, and consequently must be as well planned and clearly understood as any other major operation. Moreover, RSO&I must be synchronized with the other phases to achieve designated objectives.

Theater Structure

Theater structure is a product of the JFC's strategic objective; the forces allocated for the theater, the strategy for employment, the factors of METT-TC, and the presence of alliance and coalition structures.

In developing the campaign, the JFC imposes structure on the theater environment and the full range of military operations. Inherent in the structure is a clear picture of the potential theater organization and command relationships-factors that assist the JFC in determining priorities and assigning tasks.

There are obvious advantages of designating one organization as the RSO&I command and control element. It avoids duplication of effort, waste of resources, and competition for critical facilities. It optimizes use of valuable strategic lift. It allows integrated and specific reporting of activities related to incremental buildup of combat forces. Although the specific responsible organization may change from one phase to another or between different contingencies, the principle of unity of command must be maintained. One organization needs to be able to control and operate the entire RSO&I process to maximize the throughput of forces and materiel. The organization must be able to adjust resources based upon the deployment flows into the air and seaports, control movements in the area of operations, and provide life support to personnel arriving in-theater.

The JFC will routinely designate the ASCC as executive agent for RSO&I. The ASCC will designate the senior support commander to provide unity of command to execute RSO&I and specific units will be assigned or OPCON to the senior support command.

The largest support command is the TSC. It is a major subordinate command of the ASCC. It may, at the option of the ASCC Commander, centralize control of CSS and some CS functions dependent on theater requirements. It is modularly deployable.

I. The RSO&I Operation

Planning for RSO&I operations requires application of operational art-for by its nature, RSO&I helps the commander fight when and where he wants. Properly planned, it ensures the effective use of soldiers, materiel, and time. RSO&I also requires a simultaneous awareness of everything that affects the operation, such as theater infrastructure elements, development of a sequenced TPFDD, and integrated, timely, and reliable communication.

To develop an effective deployment plan, "reverse planning" techniques are used. First, tactical plans and timetables are developed, and the RSO&I timetable needed to meet force closure objectives is worked out. Next, strategic lift required to move the force is determined, and then timetables needed to move forces from "fort to port" are calculated.

The JFC commander evaluates the geographical area to determine whether it is adequate for efficient employment of assets, forces, facilities, and supporting systems. In cases where the geographical area is inadequate, the JFC has the following options:

- Increase RSO&I infrastructure
- Reduce deployment flow
- Extend allowable force closure times

The JFC sees the RSO&I operation-with its availability of ports, roads, host nation support capabilities, in-theater stockage, communications, and so forth-affecting the tempo of his operation, and manages it to build combat power needed to achieve strategic objectives.

In a mature theater, RSO&I forces must balance demands for deployment of reinforcement or follow-on forces, with the demands of sustainment flow for the engaged force. In a contingency theater, the focus is on building the necessary force capability while simultaneously building the necessary physical infrastructure.

Time-Phased Force Deployment Data (TPFDD)

The TPFDD prioritizes arrival of forces in-theater. RSO&I effectiveness is dependent upon proper TPFDD development. For example, the JFC places rapid port clearance capabilities early in the TPFDD, as well as coordinating personnel and equipment flows on the TPFDD, so they can be united without delay at ports or staging areas. Decisions on force mix and sequence are critical, because adjustments after deployments begin become difficult to implement. Moreover, changes cause ripple effects and may seriously disrupt the flow to the battlefield.

The JFC also ensures the TPFDD prioritizes joint rather than individual component RSO&I needs. Components normally build their portion of the TPFDD based on their Service requirements, rather than on the needs of the entire force. This results in duplication of capabilities, wastes valuable lift, and siphons support from the main effort. The TPFDD must contain the required capability and nothing more.

II. Procedures and Relationships

The Army operates in diverse environments and conducts a variety of operations as part of joint, multinational, or interagency teams. This fact increases the difficulty of RSO&I and reaffirms the need for established procedures, mutually understood relationships, and robust liaison. Army commanders need to understand how best to integrate their forces into the various organizations under which they will operate (for example, joint commands, UN, NATO, and so forth). This understanding, and appropriate planning, can improve the immense RSO&I difficulties inherent in joint and multinational operations, as well as allow the best use of the complementary features of each nation and Service to maximize RSO&I.

RSO&I

A. Joint RSO&I

Joint integration of planning and execution is key to successful RSO&I. Even though logistics is a Service responsibility, the JFC may direct that certain logistics functions be performed by a particular Service, based on the dominant-user or most-capable-Service concept. For example, if the Army provides all transportation and movement control for RSO"&"I, the Army component commander must be intimately familiar with the total transportation and movement control requirements of the other Services and SOF, to permit optimum resource allocation necessary to address their needs.

B. Multinational RSO&I

As compared with joint operations, multinational RSO&I presents a greater challenge. Major differences in logistics doctrine, mobility, resources, interoperability, and language all create problems in coordinating use of highways, rail lines, seaports, and airfields, as well as providing support and services to RSO&I operations. Considerable planning is required to optimize use of multinational land, naval and air forces, space management, ship berthing and unloading facilities, transportation, labor, and construction materials-all critical elements of RSO&I.

While logistics is ordinarily a national responsibility, it frequently falls to the United States to provide strategic lift and logistics support. Where appropriate and possible, coalition commanders may combine staffs of two or more nations to better coordinate complementary RSO&I capabilities, facilitate exchange of vital information, and reduce friction, congestion, and duplication associated with multiple use of limited assets and capacities.

C. Host Nation Support

Host nation support is civil and military assistance rendered by a nation to foreign forces within its territory during peacetime, crises or emergencies, or war based on agreements mutually concluded between nations. In many cases, US forces must rely on host nation support to supplement or provide services, supplies, and facilities. This is especially significant when the JFC tries to minimize the number of CS/CSS forces and equipment early in the TPFDD.

Host nation support, by providing a variety of services and facilities, relieves US forces from the task of establishing and maintaining equivalent capabilities, thereby reducing the US logistical footprint and RSO&I "overhead." Additional lift becomes available for transport of combat forces, expediting force closure.

D. Liaison

Liaison with forces of each Service, nation, and the next higher headquarters is a prerequisite for smooth operation of RSO&I. It is indispensable for understanding each participant's operating procedures, and for timely transfer of critical information. Whenever possible, liaison personnel should be familiar with operational organizations, doctrine, and procedures of the force with which they will work.

E. Interagency Support

In the course of joint and multinational operations, the Army operates alongside US and non-US government agencies, non-governmental agencies, and private voluntary organizations. In most cases, these organizations and agencies will compete for space at ports, airfields, and facilities used for military operations. They will travel over the same LOCs and require a variety of support from the military. They may disrupt RSO&I and siphon resources away from military tasks.

III. Deployment Operating Tools

Ref: FM 100-17-3; App. B.

This section discusses the many different systems used as deployment operating tools.

1. Global Command and Control System-Army (GCCS-A)

GCCS-A provides a single seamless command and control system built around a common operating environment and is being integrated with the GCCS. Integration will be partially achieved from the "best of breed" process as GCCS-A and GCCS share and reuse software modules. The Joint Service/Agency GCCS engineering team, sponsored by the Defense Information Systems Agency is identifying these software modules. GCCS-A is fundamentally GCCS with additional Army functionality.

2. Joint Operations Planning and Execution System (JOPES)

JOPES is the integrated, joint, conventional command and control system used by JPEC to conduct joint planning, execution and monitoring activities. JOPES supports senior-level decision-makers and their staffs at the NCA level and throughout the JPEC. It is a combination of joint policies, procedures, personnel, training and a reporting structure supported by automated data processing systems, reporting systems, and the GCCS. JOPES is a GCCS application.

3. Army Mobilization and Operations Planning and Execution System (AMOPES)

AMOPES is the Army supplement to JOPES. Army components plan Army forces and resources to meet combatant commanders' needs using JOPES. AMOPES provides the interface between unified plans for deployment and Army plans for mobilizing forces and resources. AMOPES identifies active and reserve component major Army combat forces available to execute operational plans. It sets priorities for the apportionment of CS and CSS units in conjunction with OPLANs. AMOPES provides mobilization and deployment definitions and guidance for planning and execution along with a detailed description of the Army's Crisis-Action System.

4. Computerized Movement Planning and Status System (COMPASS)

COMPASS is a FORSCOM system that provides deployment planning systems with accurate Army unit movement requirements. COMPASS describes unit property and equipment in transportation terms. It converts UMD into a COMPASS AUEL and maintains UMD for use in mobilization and deployment planning. This data originates from the UMD provided by Army units. The preferred system to transmit UMD to COMPASS is TC-ACCIS. ITOs (UMCs) validate and transmit the data to FORSCOM COMPASS. COMPASS then reformats the data and updates JOPES. Detailed guidance on how to prepare and submit UMD is in FORSCOM Regulation 55-2.

5. Transportation Coordinator-Automated Command and Control Information System (TC-ACCIS)

The TC-ACCIS is an information management and data communications system that Army units (active and reserve) use to plan and execute deployments. System capability includes the ability to create and maintain unit movement data, prepare convoy requests, create military shipping labels and other movement documentation, and prepare vehicle load cards and vehicle/container packing lists.

Units maintain their AUEL and develop their DEL using TC-ACCIS. TC-ACCIS software resides on computers at the ITOs of CONUS installations and ITOs or movement control units in overseas theaters. The ITO, using the central computer, will consolidate requirements and transmit equipment lists and transportation requests to systems outside TC-ACCIS. For example, CONUS ITOs transmit AUEL and DEL to FORSCOM's COMPASS database. The information can then be used to update JOPES. Through TC-ACCIS, the ITO also provides MTMC the deployment requirements (such as DEL), domestic routing requests, export traffic release requests, and passenger transportation requirements.

6. Dept of Army Movements Management System-Redesigned (DAMMS-R)

DAMMS-R provides an automated movement information management capability to movement managers involved in providing movement control and allocation of common user land transportation in a theater. It also provides theater mode operators with a tool to assist in the management of their assets, including personnel, equipment, and terminal/trailer transfer points. The system has a financial management capability to assist in maintaining records and payment for commercial movements. DAMMS-R consists of six separate but interrelated subsystems used by transportation planners, movement managers, mode operators, traffic controllers, transshippers, and unit movement personnel. These subsystems are the shipment management module, movement control team operations module, mode operations module, convoy planning module, highway regulation module and transportation addressing module.

Currently, DAMMS-R is fielded in two Blocks. Block 1 includes the shipment management, movement control team operations, mode operations and transportation addressing modules; and block 2 contains the highway regulation and convoy planning modules. DAMMS-R Block 3 will replace Block 1. Selected DAMMS-R functionality will migrate to TC-AIMS-II.

7. Global Transportation Network (GTN)

GTN is an automated command and control information system that provides the family of transportation users and providers with an integrated view of transportation information. It provides USTRANSCOM the ability to perform command and control operations, planning and analysis, and business operations to meet customer requirements. GTN also provides ITV for the DTS. GTN collects and integrates transportation information from selected DOD systems for use by transportation data customers-the NCA, CINCs, USTRANSCOM, and the Services. The system provides these users the ability to monitor movement of forces, cargo, passengers, and patients and movement of military and commercial airlift, sealift and surface assets.

8. Joint Total Asset Visibility (JTAV)

JTAV is being developed as a joint task force logistics management AIS to provide an in-theater TAV capability. JTAV provides the capability to fuse information from selected AISs into one picture. Through JTAV, theater logisticians will access in-transit, in-storage, and in-process information in GTN, the inventory control point AIS, and the LIPS. Additionally, JTAV will interface with Services' logistics databases to capture visibility of assets held by theater forces and with the theater transportation information system to provide visibility of shipments within the theater. JTAV will merge this information with in-theater unit information and other in-theater-related logistics information for both inbound and outbound assets. The JFC will use the logistics information in JTAV to enhance planning for the deployment of forces and materiel, the diversion of forces and materiel in-transit, and, if required, to meet changing contingency requirements. Also for the management of in-theater assets, cross leveling and distribution, and for the redeployment of forces and retrograde of materiel.

RSO&I

IV. RSO&I Resources/Enablers

Ref: FM 100-17-3; chap. 2.

The RSO&I planner has access to a number of RSO&I resources or enablers. They include organizations, personnel and equipment supporting these organizations, contract or based support, and the information management systems used by these organizations. FM 100-17-3 Appendix E lists key Army units and their functions that support RSO&I operations. Examples are as follows:

LOGCAP

LOGCAP is contractor based support arrangement made in peacetime designed to support Army forces in contingency operations worldwide. The concept is to maintain, based on regional needs, a worldwide umbrella contract. The program includes the contracting equivalent of contingency plans for various regions. It allows for the swift acquisition of contract logistic support required in crisis. The JTF commander may choose to execute elements of the plan to increase flexibility and to fill shortfalls in the force as he evaluates the TPFDD. He must decide where to use force structure to accomplish the mission and where contract support can be used.

Corps Transportation Group (CTG)

CTG is able to operate all theater ports (aerial and sea), other nodes (railheads, trailer transfer points, and so forth), inland transportation (road and water), and assorted life support. It can perform harbor operations, terminal and terminal service operations, cargo transfer operations, cargo documentation, A/DACG and railhead operations, movements control and surface transportation operations (truck). The CTG is assigned Army watercraft and lighterage and is capable of conducting instream off-load operations. The CTG provides the supported JFC with RSO&I capability throughout the theater of operations.

Corps Transportation Company (CTC)

CTC are units within the CTG and are able to load, discharge, and transload cargo at air, rail, truck terminals, and water terminals located in fixed ports or LOTS operations. They also supplement cargo/supply-handling operations at corps and division areas to alleviate cargo backlogs.

Corps Support Group (CSG)

CSG provides command and control, CSS functional support, and life support capabilities. Specific capabilities are tailored to the commander's needs. It provides the logistics resources to support corps soldiers and to arm, fuel, fix, and move the corps force. See FM 54-30 for more information on the Corps Support Group.

Area Support Group (ASG)

ASG provides support to forces in power projection roles. Selected ASG elements may augment the COSCOM or DISCOM when support requirements exceed their support capabilities. They may deploy from a forward presence site in response to a crisis or remain at that forward site to receive and process follow-on forces. ASGs may tailor a slice of support to set up a forward support base or provide support at a staging area. An ASG is a tailored CSS organization in the COMMZ. It has area responsibility for supply (including petroleum support), field service support (including water purification and mortuary affairs), and maintenance (including aviation intermediate maintenance). It may also have area responsibility for real property maintenance activity. The ASG may include other capabilities to fulfill designated theater support responsibilities. Though it has no fixed structure, it may include civil affairs, supply and service, petroleum supply, and maintenance battalions. See FM 54-40 for more information on ASGs.

MTMC Advance Party

The MTMC Advance Party is the MTMC port manager's advance party and provides technical support to the port operator and the CTG. The advance party's mission includes liaison with port authorities, assessment of port capabilities, initial recommendations for size and type port operations required, assessment of contracting capabilities, and initial contract coordination.

MTMC Port Management Cell

The MTMC Port Management Cell provides a port management cell or reinforces an existing cell to support the JFC. The cell will workload the port operator based on the theater commander's priorities and intent. The cell will assist with OPLAN development and analysis, conduct assessment of ports, and recommend the size and type of port operations required. The cell will establish liaison with host nation port authorities and develop statements of work for contracting facilities and stevedore labor, if available. The cell will provide ADP and communication capabilities in support of water terminal operations. It will provide common-user container management services.

Army Movement Control Organizations

Army Movement Control Organizations contribute to the joint theater movement control plan. In the COMMZ, the MCA supports echelons above corps; in the corps AOR, MCBs provide support; and in division AORs, the DTO is responsible for movement control.

Allied and Host Nation Support (HNS)

Allied and HNS provide civil and/or military assistance to US forces during peacetime, crises or emergencies, or war, based on mutual agreements. If available, Allied and HNS can be a significant military force multiplier. Properly planned for and utilized, it can augment deployment shortfalls or requirements and assist deploying and deployed units and, therefore, reduce the requirement for strategic lift assets.

Local Contracting

Local Contracting provides use of local resources, such as truck drivers, warehousing, stevedores, and so forth, which can reduce the RSO&I footprint by offsetting the requirement for US forces.

Theater Support Command (TSC)

The TSC is a major subordinate command of the ASCC. It may, at the option of the ASCC Commander, centralize control of CSS and some CS functions dependent on theater requirements. It is modularly deployable. Elements can deploy early as part of a Major Theater War to establish the COMMZ or may augment with required functionality the primary logistical organization in smaller operations. Additional information on the Theater Support Command will be available in FM 100-10-1, Theater Distribution.

Medical Command (MEDCOM)

MEDCOM is the single medical manager for combat health support in the theater.

Theater Opening Force Module (TOFM)

TOFM are modules of selected logistics functions designed to provide the deploying force the capability to open air and seaports and establish RSO&I capability in-theater. They are available for employment across the full spectrum of military operations. Additional information on the TOFMs is available in FM 100-17-1, Army Pre-positioned Afloat Operations.

See also p. 3-64, TSC Theater Force Opening Package (TFOP).

RSO&I

V. Intermediate Staging Bases (ISB)

Ref: FM 100-17-3, chap. 2.

In an ideal situation, secure bases are available in the AO for RSO&I and continued support of the deploying force. Unfortunately, the very situation that compels deployment of US forces may negate the advantage of basing within the AO. The JFC weighs requirements against the risk of basing within the AO. The theater operational situation may constrain the joint commander to select and prepare an ISB. The ISB is located within the theater of operations and outside of the combat zone and area of operations.

Intermediate Staging Base

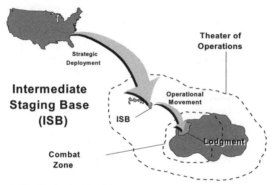

Ref: FM 100-17-3, fig. 2-2, p. 2-14.

If established, the ISB may be the initial theater reception and staging facility. Deploying forces debark from strategic lift, reassemble, and prepare for missions in the AO.

Onward movement from the ISB to the combat zone may be multimodal and require some level of reassembly in the AO. Transportation assets employed in onward movement will normally include strategic and theater assets including truck, rail, sea, and airlift. These movements are a part of deployment and should be included in the TPFDD.

The location of the ISB is dependent on a number of variables including distance to combat zone, host nation access, ports, and tempo of operations. Coordination with the host nation for use of an ISB is a State Department responsibility.

The selection of an ISB is a JFC decision. However, if the Army is tasked to operate the ISB, it should have a primary role in the selection process. The ISB should include properly sequenced and sufficient Army C2, CS, CSS, and joint support to enable projecting the force into the combat zone. The ISB should be shielded from long-range engagement systems, including missile, SOF, and terrorists.

The ISB may serve as the principle staging base for entry operations, which allows the joint commander to project the maximum number of forces into the combat zone. For example, armored forces arrive at the ISB by strategic air and sealift. They reassemble, prepare for combat operations, and conduct a joint entry operation using Army watercraft.

The longevity of the ISB varies according to the circumstance. The ISB may function throughout the operation serving as a secure facility for split-based operations which include selected logistic management functions that can be accomplished from home station or from a forward based location, deploying only those functional capabilities absolutely necessary into the AO.

III. Reception

Ref: FM 100-17-3; Reception, Staging, Onward Movement & Integration, chap. 3.

Reception is the process of unloading personnel and materiel from strategic transport, marshaling the deploying units, transporting them to staging areas if required, and providing life support to deploying personnel

As the initial step in introducing combat power, reception can determine success or failure of an entire operation. Reception from strategic lift is implemented at or near designated air and seaports of debarkation, under control of the JTF commander. While the reception plan for each theater may vary, reception capacity should, at a minimum, equal planned strategic lift delivery capability.

I. Reception Functions

Reception functions are activities facilitating throughput at the ports of debarkation. They include C2, movement control, and port operations.

Reception Functions

 A Command and Control

 B Movement Control

 C Port Operations

 D Port Security

Ref: FM 100-17-3, chap. 3, pp. 3-10 to 3-11.

A. Command and Control

Like any other in-theater activity, reception is under command and control of the JFC. Reception planning and execution, however, is the responsibility of the commander assigned the overall RSO&I mission. This designation can require an augmentation of functional units capable of conducting RSO&I and an early presence on the TPFDD.

The TSC is organized to conduct RSO&I for large deployments while the TOFM are designed specifically to perform RSO&I for smaller deployments. If the JFC determines a TSC or TOFM is needed, it should be positioned early in the TPFDD flow. TOFMs are configured according to the size of the deploying force.

The arrival of strategic air and sealift will be controlled by the JFC through the USTRANSCOM element attached to his staff. Strategic lift assets remain under command of USTRANSCOM and cannot be retained or diverted by the JFC without concurrence of USTRANSCOM. The APOD and SPOD will normally be managed by AMC and MTMC respectively, and operated by the designated logistics command under C2 of the JFC. Movement control in-theater is the responsibility of the JFC, and should not be delegated below that level.

It should be noted that reception activities continue after force closure is achieved, in order to facilitate arrival and processing of sustainment stocks and unit replacements. These sustainment activities do not have as strong operational emphasis (hands-on participation of the operational commander) as do RSO&I.

B. Movement Control

Movement control is a subset of command and control. Efficient movement control allows commanders to redirect forces and rapidly compensate for disruptions in the LOC. A movement control element must be positioned at each reception node, and remain in constant communication with USTRANSCOM elements on-site, and with other movement control elements in-theater.

C. Port Operations

As outlined in the Unified Command Plan, USTRANSCOM has the mission to provide worldwide common-user air and seaport terminal services. To ensure consistency in common user ports worldwide, USTRANSCOM, through its components AMC and MTMC, will normally manage common-user air and sea POEs and PODs and workload the port operator based on the JFC's priorities and intent. The port management function remains a military responsibility through all phases of a theater port operation continuum. Conversely, the port operator can be military, host nation, contractor, or a combination thereof.

D. Port Security

Seaports represent lucrative targets and must be secured. Efficiency of operations can reduce the threat to forces and equipment being processed through the port but the port's physical facilities remain vulnerable. Security for the port complex is normally provided pier side and waterside. The naval component is normally responsible for the waterside of the port, with the USCG providing that security. Pier side security is provided through port security units and their linkage to the rear area protection organization and the base cluster defense plan.

II. Force Flow

Combat operations generally have three distinctive phases. Initial forces are deployed to the theater to conduct a halt operation. They secure an area to conduct buildup operations in preparation for a counterattack. Reception occurs during the halt, buildup and counterattack phases of a force flow. The force flow is initially light in the halt phase and dramatically increases to a peak during the buildup phase.

A. Halt

During the halt phase the lodgment is secured and expanded in preparation for the increase of the force flow. At this time, reception assets required for meeting crucial increases in force flow for the buildup phase must arrive in-theater. The first ship arriving from the US begins closing the heavy force in-theater. This event is called "Sea LOC closure," and it starts a dramatic increase in the amount of tonnage flowing into the theater. Although airlift continues to be a critical element of the force flow, the volume of tonnage is shifted to sealift. While the reception of sustainment stocks begins during the halt phase and continues throughout the deployment, the peak for the sustainment flow normally occurs after force closure is achieved.

Secure the Lodgment

If the tactical situation dictates, airborne or light forces arrive and secure an aerial port so that the brigade drawing the land prepositioned equipment can arrive into the theater. Prior to the arrival of this brigade the selected theater opening force module arrives and becomes operational. This module includes elements of the composite transportation group and the supporting headquarters. Force projection timeline requirements call for the initial brigade to be in-theater at C+4, draw the prepositioned equipment, and be operational within 96 hours.

Expand the Lodgment

By C+8, Army Prepositioned Stocks-3 vessels arrive. Concurrently, troops fly in, draw the equipment, become operational, and move to the TAA by C+15.

During this time, they expand the lodgment to ensure sufficient capability to receive the massive flow of equipment and personnel. These flows generate a requirement for multiple seaports. Arriving personnel depart the airfield for the theater staging base rather than the seaport to marry-up with their equipment because of insufficient physical space in the seaport to accommodate them.

The first heavy division must be operational by C+24. To meet this timeline, equipment or personnel must clear the aerial port in 2 hours after arrival, while ships must be discharged in 2 or 3 days.

B. Buildup

Experience in Operation Desert Storm and lesser contingency operations has shown the need to rapidly expand and improve port reception capability, regardless of the nature of ports being used.

As the buildup of combat forces begins, capability for rapid expansion depends on well-synchronized arrival of personnel and equipment. The JFC must, therefore, control the deployment flow. Communication between supported and supporting commanders is key to adjusting priorities so that reception capabilities are not overwhelmed.

APOD and SPODs should, in most cases, be considered integral parts of a single reception complex, unless the distance separating them precludes mutual support. Reception capacity depends on:

- Harbor, port, and airfield characteristics
- Availability of labor and port services
- Off-loading and holding space
- Condition and capacity of exit routes
- Efficiency of movement control systems

Port Clearance

Two factors determine reception throughput: reception capacity and clearance capability. All ports have finite processing and storage space, and unless personnel and equipment are cleared quickly, the port will become congested and unable to receive forces at the required rate of delivery. Three factors contributing to efficient port clearance are documentation, movement control, and adequate container handling equipment and personnel. Port operators need timely and accurate documentation including information on forces and equipment arriving in-theater. Efficient movement control assures smooth flow of those forces and equipment according to operational priorities.

RSO&I

III. Aerial Port of Debarkation (APOD)

Ref: FM 4-01.011, chap 5.

An APOD is an airfield that has been designated for the sustained air movement of personnel and materiel, to serve as an authorized port for entrance into or departure from the country in which it is located. It is designated an APOD by the supported combatant commander in coordination with USTRANSCOM. Reception at the APOD is coordinated by the senior logistics commander and executed by (an Air Force) tanker airlift control element (TALCE), a port movement control team (port MCT), an arrival/departure airfield control group (A/DACG), or both, depending upon the magnitude of the operations. The port MCT and/or A/DACG must be in the lead elements of the transported force. Augmentation with cargo transfer companies, cargo documentation teams, theater support contractor, and host nation support (HNS) is desired to rapidly clear the port. The port MCT has the mission of coordinating transport services for the APOD and ensuring quick clearance of cargo movements into and out of the APOD. Both Air Force and Army have responsibilities at an APOD

Maximum on Ground (MOG)

There are two constraining factors for airfields. The first is the parking MOG, the number of aircraft that can fit on the ground. The second constraining factor is the working MOG, how many of the parked aircraft can be worked simultaneously. Optimally, working MOG should equal parking MOG. In Dhahran there were 114 acres of 463L pallets on the ground when the ground war kicked off. The inability to clear the pallets reduced the working MOG and, therefore, reduced the throughput capability of the airfield.

Joint Aerial Port Complex

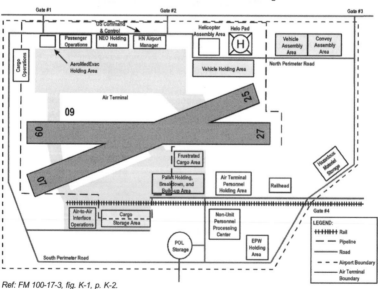

Ref: FM 100-17-3, fig. K-1, p. K-2.

Note: Normally, the majority of personnel, unit equipment, and materiel will enter a theater through two types of reception complexes, the Joint Aerial Port or the Joint Water Port. See p. 6-22.

The main areas of the APOD are the off-load ramp, the holding area, and the unit marshaling area. The TALCE supervises off-loading arriving aircraft. The A/DACG escorts loads to the holding area and assists the unit in assembling and moving to the marshaling area.

A. Off-Load Ramp Area

The TALCE controls the off-load ramp area activities. The off-load ramp area is where the aircraft are off-loaded. Each load is released to the A/DACG for return to unit control at the holding area. Unit responsibilities in the off-load ramp area are:

- Provide assistance to the loadmaster
- Comply with instructions from the off-load team chief when unlashing and off-loading the aircraft
- Ensure that all aircraft tie-down equipment is returned to the TALCE
- Retain all shoring and dunnage for further use
- Provide passenger and cargo manifests to the A/DACG

B. Holding Area

In the holding area, arriving units locate their equipment, prepare it for movement to the marshalling area, and generally begin the process of "marrying-up" with organic supplies and equipment. Arriving units perform the following:

- Provide unit liaison personnel to the A/DACG
- Assist the A/DACG as required
- Assume custody of equipment and supplies
- Move equipment and supplies to the marshaling area outside the terminal

Note: If marshaling areas are not available, units should be prepared to move directly from the holding area to their TAAs, to an APS site to draw equipment, or to the SPOD to receive unit equipment off-loaded from vessels. When this is necessary, marshaling area functions are performed in the staging areas.

C. Marshaling Area

The marshaling area is a location next to the port where units reconfigure their equipment and prepare for onward movement. Prompt clearance of cargo from the APOD is essential to the efficiency and success of the total theater logistics system. It is also necessary to avoid serious congestion in the port holding area.

Marshaling areas are established to allow units to complete the process of restoring their equipment and supplies from shipment configuration to operational configuration, as well as to clear the port area. The marshalling area is where the unit prepares for onward movement. In this area the unit is responsible to:

- Breakdown pallets
- Ensure that all aircraft pallets and nets are returned to the TALCE or A/DACG
- Perform required maintenance checks and refuel equipment
- Configure secondary loads for onward movement
- Use TC-AIMS II to plan convoys
- Mark convoy vehicles properly
- Use TC-AIMS II to create requests for convoy clearance and special hauling permits
- Use TC-AIMS II to create support requests

RSO&I

IV. Sea Port of Debarkation (SPOD)

Ref: FM 4-01.011, chap 5.

An SPOD is a port designated by the theater commander in coordination with USTRANSCOM. When vessels arrive at the SPOD, the port commander is responsible for discharging the unit equipment, staging the equipment, maintaining control and ITV, and releasing it to the unit. The port commander remains responsible for unit equipment and supplies until they reach the staging area where arriving units assume responsibility for their supplies and equipment. The port MCT coordinate, plan, control, and manage the processing of the units' equipment for onward movement. Their actions are based on advanced manifests received via Worldwide Port System (WPS), available transportation, theater priorities, tactical situation, and throughput capacity.

Vulnerability of the force during discharge operations is a significant concern. The volume of cargo arriving in the theater in a small window of time can drive the need for multiple seaports to meet deployment timelines. The physical size of the LMSR and the draft requirement to bring the vessel pier side may also present a challenge. If world class port facilities are available, off-loading can be rapidly accomplished. If facilities are less than world class or limited, then multiple ports and slower in-stream operations may be required.

Types of Seaports

There are three categories of ports that commanders must plan for: improved, world class ports; unimproved or degraded ports; and bare beach or no port environment, LOTS operations are necessary.

Joint Water Port Complex

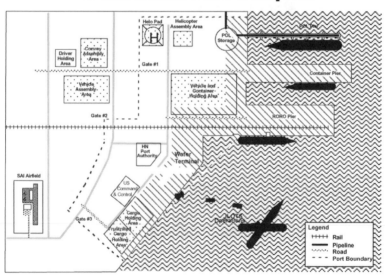

Ref: FM 100-17-3, fig. K-3, p. K-8.

Note: Normally, the majority of personnel, unit equipment, and materiel will enter a theater through two types of reception complexes, the Joint Aerial Port or the Joint Water Port. See p. 6-22.

A. Staging Area

As the vessel readies for off-loading, the Military Traffic Management Command (MTMC) port commander establishes a staging area for the transshipment and accounting of equipment. The port commander determines discharge priorities based on the supported combatant commander's guidance and assigns missions to terminal service units that discharge vessels. The port commander assumes custody of the cargo from the vessel master upon discharge. Equipment offloaded is then staged by support elements based on theater onward movement requirements. Transportation terminal brigades (TTB), PSAs, cargo transfer companies, and cargo documentation teams may be assigned to operate staging areas under MTMC control. As unit personnel arrive in the theater, support units transport them to the staging area to assume custody of their equipment. Units assemble their equipment and supplies, assume custody, and move it to the marshaling area outside the terminal.

Generally, arriving units are recipients of support in the staging area. Unit responsibilities in this area are very basic. Staging area responsibilities of units are shown below.

- Assume custody of equipment and supplies from the port commander
- Assemble equipment and supplies for movement to the marshaling area
- Move equipment and supplies to the marshaling area outside the terminal

NOTE: If marshaling areas are not available, as may be the case OCONUS, units should be prepared to move directly to their tactical assembly area (TAA) or to an Army prepositioned stock (APS) site to draw equipment from the staging area. When this is necessary, marshaling area functions have to be performed in the staging area.

B. Marshaling Area

Prompt clearance of cargo from the terminal is essential to the efficiency and success of the total theater logistics system. It is also necessary to avoid serious congestion in the terminal staging area. To clear the port efficiently, marshaling areas are established. The marshaling area is a location next to the port where units their equipment and supplies to assemble, reconfigure them, and prepare for onward movement.

While arriving units are recipients of support in the staging area, they assume custody and responsibility for equipment and supplies there and move to the marshaling area. Unit responsibilities in the marshaling area are the usual responsibilities for its equipment and supplies.

Marshaling area responsibilities of units include:

- Ensure all personnel, cargo, and equipment is accounted
- Conduct necessary maintenance and reconfigure equipment for onward movement
- Fuel equipment for onward movement
- Unpack containers and repack cargo as secondary loads
- Reconfigure secondary loads as necessary for onward movement
- Ensure HAZMAT is correctly packed and segregated for onward movement
- Provide security for sensitive items
- Provide movement requests to the supporting ITO or MCT using TC-AIMS II
- Prepare to conduct operations (OCONUS)

Note. The arrival/unloading processes that occur at a motor transport or rail intratheater terminal are similar to those that take place at a SPOD. Though there is more flexibility with motor transportation, both motor transport and rail arrival terminals have a similar organization to their terminal operations to include staging and marshaling areas.

RSO&I

V. Reception Complexes

Ref: FM 100-17-3; app. K.

Appendix K of FM 100-17-3 discusses the different ways personnel, unit equipment, and materiel will enter a theater. Normally, the majority of personnel, unit equipment, and materiel will enter a theater through two types of reception complexes, the Joint Aerial Port and the Joint Water Port.

1. Joint Aerial Port Complex

The Joint Aerial Port Complex containing an Air Terminal is a key node in any reception and deployment operation. During deployment operations the Aerial Port Complex handles flows in both directions, inbound as well as outbound movement.

The operation of a Joint Aerial Port Complex can be divided into two parts, the air terminal operations run by the Air Mobility Command and the air terminal support functions which are, in most cases, the responsibility of the Army Component Command. However, other Service Component Commands may be responsible for operating some functions. These support operations may include port clearance, movement control, onward movement, liaison, operation of holding areas, postal operations, and personnel replacement processing.

In the Joint Aerial Port Complex various organizations establish sites to carry out these functions. These sites are designated by the Joint Aerial Port Complex Commander in coordination with the host nation and other Allied commands which may be using the facility. Many of these functions are performed at supporting nodes. Some of these supporting nodes include Holding Areas (Enemy Prisoner of War, NEO, Frustrated Cargo, and so forth), Assembly Areas (Convoy, Helicopter, Vehicle, and so forth), and Railheads.

2. Joint Water Port Complexes

Another key node in any reception and deployment operation is the Joint Water Port Complex containing a water terminal. As with the Joint Aerial Port Complex, the Joint Water Port Complex may handle flows in both directions including the reception of unit materiel and non-unit cargo, as well as the outbound movement of equipment requiring repair, empty containers, and possibly captured enemy equipment.

As with the Joint Aerial Port Complex, a number of US and host nation support organizations are responsible for performing the many functions associated with the operation of a Joint Water Port Complex. Some of the US organizations are provided by the JFC's component commands while others are provided by components of USTRANSCOM. USCINCTRANS has established standing agreements with each of the unified commanders. These agreements are CAA and delineate command relationships for USTRANSCOM elements located in the unified commander's AOR under peace and wartime conditions. The unified commander is the ultimate authority for command relationship within the theater and delineates them via OPLANs and orders.

The JFC may designate MTMC as the port manager and a Service component (normally the Army as the primary user) as the port operator.

Sea-Air Interface Site

The units located at the facility will accomplish the following functions: receive the materiel; validate theater air clearance for onward movement; arrange theater airlift; coordinate aircraft operations and servicing at the facility; prepare loads and load them on the aircraft; prepare the necessary documentation and render reports, necessary to maintain visibility of the materiel and personnel moved through the site.

Chap 6

IV. Staging

Ref: FM 100-17-3; Reception, Staging, Onward Movement & Integration, chap. 4.

Staging is the process of assembling, holding, and organizing arriving personnel and equipment into units and forces, incrementally building combat power and preparing units for onward movement; providing life support for the personnel until the unit becomes self-sustaining.

Staging is that part of the RSO&I operation which:
- Reassembles and reunites units with their equipment and schedules their movement to the TAA
- Uploads unit basic loads
- Provides life support to personnel

I. Theater Staging Bases (TSBs)

Staging activities occur at multiple sites in controlled areas called Theater Staging Bases (TSBs). TSBs are required because space limitations normally preclude reassembly of combat units at seaports of debarkation. In general, there will be at least one TSB for each SPOD/APOD pairing.

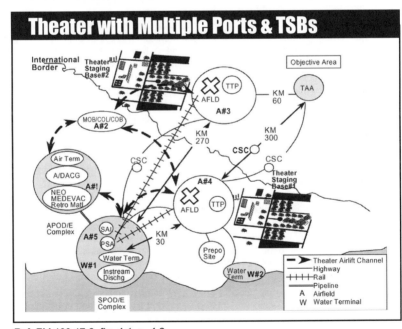

Theater with Multiple Ports & TSBs

Ref: FM 100-17-3, fig. 4-1, p. 4-3.

RSO&I

The Impact of Staging on Force Closure

In order to meet the force closure requirements, time units spend staging through the TSB must be minimized. In Desert Storm, staging was extended by inefficiencies such as: personnel arriving before their equipment, equipment arriving before its personnel, and delays in matching troops with proper equipment. As a result, time required to reach force closure exceeded 200 days. Units were still staging through TSBs even after the ground campaign commenced. Now, the Army standard for force closure of a similar size force is only 75 days. To achieve this, a battalion-sized unit should spend no more than two days staging in the TSB.

TSBs should be located in areas convenient to both the SPOD and APOD, with good lines of communication back to ports of debarkation and forward to designated TAAs. In addition, the TSB should have sufficient space to accommodate the largest force scheduled to stage through it, together with facilities for vehicle marshaling, materiel handling, equipment maintenance and calibration, and possibly boresighting and test firing weapons. All of these are needed if the TSB is to fulfill its function of converting personnel and equipment into mission-ready combat units.

Other factors affecting selection of a TSB include geography and terrain (for example, water supply may be a factor in desert operations, land space in urban setting), and availability of organic and host nation assets. These factors, together with the size of the deploying force, may often necessitate multiple TSBs. The requirement for multiple staging bases is most evident in the urban sprawl of Europe and Korea particularly around seaport facilities. In many cases, it is tremendously difficult to find even one square mile of open terrain much less the total space requirement for a TSB.

The requirement for multiple theater staging bases, in turn, multiplies support requirements. Movement control and communication are especially important, due to the increased complexity of synchronization between the ports of debarkation and the theater staging bases, between the theater staging bases themselves, and between the theater staging bases and the tactical assembly areas.

The Army Prepositioned Stocks Afloat equipment (APS-3), which supports a 2x2 heavy brigade, requires 47 acres of staging area for its cyclic maintenance, as well as two million square feet of storage on ships.

TPFDD Considerations

Under normal circumstances, troops deploy by air, while equipment deploys by sea. The speed differential between air and sea transportation is the fundamental cause of complexity and potential difficulties in the staging process. Troops and equipment must be sequenced in the TPFDD so that both arrive (nearly) simultaneously, expeditiously unite, and ready themselves for onward movement.

Troops arriving too early must wait an extended time for their equipment to arrive. Sustenance, housing, and sanitation then become serious problems. Moreover, the mass of immobile, unprotected troops presents an inviting and vulnerable target. On the other hand, if equipment arrives much earlier than the troops, ports of debarkation can become congested, and space management becomes critical.

Notwithstanding the duration of a unit's stay in the staging area, support remains a necessity. Units and supplies required to support the troops and equipment in the staging area must be sequenced early in the TPFDD flow. The commander must ensure availability of rations, billeting, showers, toilets, medical care, and so forth, in addition to materiel handling equipment.

METT-TC considerations may effect the location of TSBs. In Desert Storm the original TSB was augmented with another TSB much farther forward. Soldiers were flown to the forward TSB, while theater assets transported their equipment from the seaport to the forward TSB.

Early deployment of essential support units may reduce the number of early-entry combat units in-theater, but pays dividends later by speeding the flow of the entire force, enhancing the JFC's operational flexibility. Conversely, front loading the TPFDD with combat forces may hurt the JFC's ability to build up forces as rapidly as required and thus reduce flexibility.

II. Theater Staging Base (TSB) Functions

The key to success in staging is understanding the role of the TSB in the RSO&I process, and of functions performed at the TSB to support force closure.

TSB Functions

- Communication
- Command and Control
- Force Tracking
- Life Support
- Arming, Fueling, Fixing
- Preparation for Onward Movement
- Security
- Conversion to Sustainment Operations

Ref: FM 100-17-3, pp. 4-4 to 4-7.

Theater Staging Base Responsibilities

Ref: FM 100-17-3; App. M.

Appendix M of FM 110-17-3 discusses the factors involved in the planning of staging operations. It also discusses the factors to consider in selecting a TSB and the TSB Commander's responsibilities:

Command, Control, and Communications
- Area Selection-selects staging area based on guidance received from the JFC, space available for unit dispersion, transportation network to and from the port, and transportation network to support onward movement
- Automatic Data Processing
- Command and Control
- Terrain and facilities management
- Communications (internal and external)
- Reports Procedures-processes reports on staging units
- Security-coordinates area security and the internal security requirements

Host Nation Support
- Host Nation Support- coordinates host nation support to support TSB operations
- Linguists - linguistic support for contract, local purchases, and so forth

Onward Movement
- Blocking, bracing, and tie-downs
- Movement Control
- Railhead Operations- plans and operates railhead as required

Security
- OPSEC
- Security- plans TSB defensive operations

Services and Supply Support
- Contracting Support
- Food Service Operations and Water/Ice Supply
- Latrines, Laundry and Shower Support; Trash Disposal
- Material Handling Equipment (MHE)
- Combat Health Support and Mortuary Affairs
- Refueling, Transportation (local), and Traffic Control
- Religious Support
- Maintenance Support as required
- SSSC and Class II items/CIF/Clothing Exchange/Individual Equipment

Other Support
- Engineer Support
- EOD-coordinates countermines measures, explosive ordnance disposal
- Maps
- NBC-develops and implements NBC defense plan
- Power (generators, and so forth)-provides/coordinates power sources
- Public Affairs-plans and coordinates public affairs/news releases
- Tents-provides tents (for office, billeting, and storage)

V. Onward Movement

Ref: FM 100-17-3; Reception, Staging, Onward Movement & Integration, chap. 5.

Onward movement is the process of moving units and accompanying materiels from reception facilities and staging areas to the TAA or other theater destinations; moving arriving non-unit personnel to gaining commands and moving sustainment materiel from reception facilities to distribution sites.

Factors Affecting Onward Movement

Personnel and equipment reassembled as combat-ready units must be onward moved to TAAs based on the JFC's priorities. Onward movement is a joint/multinational effort using capabilities and organizational structures of other Services, Allies, Host Nation and other governmental entities. It is an iterative activity in which units advance from one LOC node to another. Onward movement occurs when units move from ports to theater staging bases or forward to TAAs.

Primary Factors Affecting Onward Mvmt

 A Movement Control

 B Transportation Infrastructure

 C Security and Enemy Interdiction

Ref: FM 100-17-3, chap. 5.

Improving Onward Movement

Enhancing speed and efficiency of onward movement requires development of three capabilities:

- Robust communications to allow ITV and communications with units in transit
- Joint/Multinational procedures to ensure unity of effort and uninterrupted flow
- Movement control to allow the most effective routes and modes

A. Movement Control

Movement control is defined as planning, routing, scheduling, and control of personnel (units) and cargo over lines of communication, while maintaining in-transit visibility and force tracking. This is not a passive activity. Successful movement control requires continual analysis of requirements, capabilities, shortfalls, alternatives, and enhancements. Bottlenecks within the theater must be identified and possible interruptions to the flow minimized. One of the biggest challenges of movement control is rapidly adjusting to changes in battlefield conditions and the commander's priorities.

B. Transportation Infrastructure

The total transportation infrastructure-modes, routes, control factors, host nation assistance, and specialized handling requirements-must be coordinated to maximize speed of movement. Capabilities of the transportation network must be balanced against movement requirements, so that modes and routes are neither saturated nor underused.

During onward movement, mode selection (rail, HET, barge, and so forth) is an operational issue, as it determines whether the commander of the unit in transit maintains control or whether control is lost and further staging required. Ideally, rail HET should transport tracked vehicles and wheeled vehicles should convoy.

C. Security and Enemy Interdiction

Establishment of CSC and TTP along MSRs and other support centers at temporary airfields, rail sites and waterway drop off points, further aids onward movement. These allow units and line haul drivers to rest, eat, perform vehicle maintenance, and contact unit/movement control personnel to receive updates in operational priorities and diversions.

Loading unit containers and other sustainment cargo on theater trailers for movement into corps and division areas is an efficient method of onward movement. There is, however, a twofold challenge: have MHE forward to download containers and getting the trailers back into the transportation system.

The onward movement phase can provide the enemy with numerous opportunities to inflict serious losses and delay the build-up of combat power by exploiting vulnerability of units in transit from the TSB to the TAA. Planners should assume that interdiction of lines of communication will form an integral part of enemy strategy.

Enemy interdiction of onward movement, with an asymmetrical threat or with weapons of mass destruction, presents special challenges to the commander. To minimize disruption, commanders should plan using multiple LOCs. Alternative routing and mode substitution must be integrated into operational plans; air, sea, and inland waterway LOCs may supplement ground LOCs.

Security of all LOCs should be established at a minimum cost to committed combat units, through exploitation of geography, host nation and allied civil and military security forces, uncommitted combat units, as well as assets of other Services. It may be necessary to conduct a major operation to secure the LOCs over which onward movement is conducted, to guarantee incremental build of combat power.

Due to proliferation of ballistic and cruise missiles among potential US adversaries, it may be necessary to establish air defense sites around critical choke points, such as bridges, tunnels, ferries, and rail yards. Because these missiles may be armed with weapons of mass destruction, they represent a potential source of massive casualties.

Enemy special operations forces represent yet another threat to onward movement. The ability of small forces exploiting surprise along extended lines of communication cannot be underestimated. Convoy escort may be required whenever the enemy has a credible special operations capability, especially if the units must travel on transporters (or by rail), rather than in a tactical mode. This may, in turn, require the commitment of other combat units, thereby delaying the build-up of combat power at the TAAs. Tradeoff analyses must be conducted to determine the appropriate size of the security force, given the potential for long-term disruption of LOCs.

Security measures such as minesweeping and clearing (tasks requiring cooperation with US/allied naval forces) may be needed before smaller ports can open.

VI. Integration

Ref: FM 100-17-3; Reception, Staging, Onward Movement & Integration, chap. 6.

Integration is the synchronized transfer of authority over units and forces to a designated component or functional commander for employment in the theater of operations

During integration combat-ready units are merged into the operational plan. Consequently, integration planning and coordination must occur early in the force projection process, continuing until force closure. Integration is complete when the receiving commander establishes positive command and control over the arriving unit, usually in the tactical assembly area.

I. Integration Process

There are two prerequisites for unit integration:

- The unit must become operational and mission-ready. It must be able to move, fight and communicate at nominal levels of capability. Internal command and control must be re-established, and the unit must meet the readiness standard formulated by the tactical commander.
- The unit must be absorbed into the joint force, be able to communicate, and receive command and control from its higher headquarters.

The time required for integration may vary, depending upon the size of the total force, contingency conditions, and amount of predeployment and ongoing planning and coordination. Rapid integration, however, is critical to the success of combat operations, and adequate planning and coordination can reduce integration time.

Accurate prediction of the time of unit integration is critical to the commander's ability to operate in accordance with the five basic tenets of Army operations. In order to accomplish this, the JFC and component staffs must be able to build a TPFDD which meets the commander's intent, usually expressed in the unit's CINC's required date or required delivery date. Transportation feasibility is conducted throughout the military decision making process as a means of checking course of action feasibility. Once the TPFDD is executed, the JFC, through subordinate and its links to the ITV system, monitors the TPFDD. Changes are analyzed for their impact on integration of mission essential capabilities and the TPFDD revalidated by the JFC to adjust these changes.

II. Coordination and Planning

Predeployment planning establishes force structure for the contingency, and identifies units that must integrate. Once identified, units establish predeployment liaison and plan for theater integration. Coordination measures, ITV, and force tracking are used to predict the start of force integration, and the time required for its completion. Unit mission readiness criteria are an essential element of integration and must be included in the integration plan. Integration requirements are best defined using end-state analyses based on the JFC's force requirements. The analysis identifies milestones for deploying units.

No plan survives first contact with the enemy. Plans must be open and flexible enough to adapt to reality on the ground. Technical problems, natural conditions, land space constraints, and enemy action all conspire to alter the commander's initial plan. The concept of operations should be broad enough to accommodate changes in strategic, operational, and tactical situations as they occur.

III. Command and Control

Battle command is a combination of equipment (mainly communications, but also information management), organizations (unit staff) and procedures (SOP, OPLANs, and so forth). Each command echelon will have its own unique battle command structure, but all battle command systems must be compatible with the theater command.

Problems of battle command are exacerbated by the non-linear nature of the future combat environment. As opposed to past operations, with well-defined front lines and areas of responsibility, future Army forces may deploy into fluid, non-contiguous battle spaces. Relative positions of friendly and enemy forces may change on a daily or hourly basis, requiring a high degree of coordination and situational awareness. This applies as much to deployment activities as actual combat operations.

Deployment operations are time sensitive; compressed planning timelines and furious activity are the norm. Commanders need timely, accurate information to execute or modify initial plans in response to rapidly changing operational and tactical conditions. Confusion inherent to deployment often results in conflicting guidance, frequent planning changes, and inefficient task execution, all of which delay the build-up of combat power and the force closure.

Control measures, such as LOs or movement control teams can reduce confusion by coordinating between integrating units, RSO&I forces, and receiving headquarters. These measures act as guardians of the Commander's Intent and focus effort on force integration. These measures should be established immediately as part of the planning process and be maintained throughout the RSO&I process.

IV. Force Closure

The objective of RSO&I operations is force closure, the point at which the JFC determines that adequate, combat-ready force is available to implement the concept of operations. Force closure requires well-defined criteria by which unit commanders can judge readiness.

Thus, RSO&I operations must also be particularly flexible regarding force closure. Commander's may accelerate rates of force integration or change the sequence of unit integration.

Due to both limitations of strategic lift, and time delays inherent in intercontinental deployments, many decisions made at the beginning of the deployment process are practically irrevocable. Initial deployment plans should be flexible enough to ensure that unit integration is able to meet "real," as opposed to "planned" force closure requirements.

V. Improving Integration

Integration flexibility depends on three specific capabilities:

- Standardized procedures for transfer of authority
- Standardized reporting
- Nonlinear decision support tools

Combat Service Support Resources

I. CSS Symbology

The following represents a partial listing of commonly-used joint doctrinal CSS graphics and symbols.

I. CSS Maneuver Graphics

Ambulance Exchange Point *(Point #3 serviced by 2nd BDE)*

Logistics Release Point (LRP)

Ammunition Points: ASP & ATP

Maintenance Collection Point (MCP)

Canibalization Point

Refugee Holding Area

Casualty Collection Point

Rearm, Refuel, and Resupply Point (R3P)

Civilian Collection Point

Refuel on the Move (ROM) Point

Convoy:
Moving

Support Area: *BSA, DSA, RSA*

Halted

Supply Point: *Unspecified and Multiple Classes*

Detainee Holding Area

Supply Route: *Main (MSR) and Alternate (ASR) One-Way Traffic; Two-Way Traffic; Alternating Traffic*

Detainee Collection Point

Enemy Prisoner of War (EPW) Collection Point

Traffic Control Point (TCP)

Enemy Prisoner of War (EPW) Holding Area

Trailer Transfer Point (TTP)

Forward Arming and Refueling Point (FARP)

Unit Maintenance Collection Point (UCMP)

II. Supply Points

Supply Point:
Class I

Supply Point:
Class VI

Supply Point:
Class II

Supply Point:
Class VII

Supply Point:
Class III

Supply Point:
Class VIII

Supply Point:
Class IV

Supply Point:
Class IX

Supply Point:
Class V

Supply Point:
Class X

Supply Point:
*Unspecified and
Multiple Classes*

III. Classes of Supply

Class I
(Food)

Class VI
(Personal demand)

Class II
(Clothing, indiv. equip,
tents)

Class VII
(Major assemblies)

Class III
(Petroleum supply)

Class VIII
(Medical supplies)

Class IV
(Construction/ barrier)

Class IX
(Repair parts)

Class V
(Ammunition)

Class X
(Agricultural &
nonmilitary material)

Note: See pp. 1-45 to 1-47 for a description of the classes of supply.

IV. Multifunctional CSS Unit Symbols

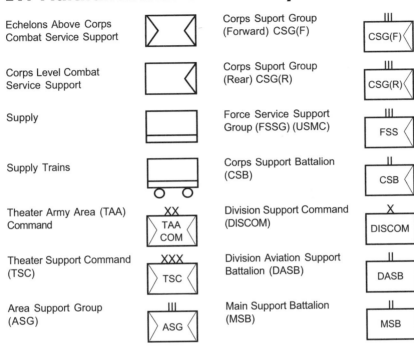

Echelons Above Corps Combat Service Support		Corps Suport Group (Forward) CSG(F)	CSG(F)
Corps Level Combat Service Support		Corps Suport Group (Rear) CSG(R)	CSG(R)
Supply		Force Service Support Group (FSSG) (USMC)	FSS
Supply Trains		Corps Support Battalion (CSB)	CSB
Theater Army Area (TAA) Command	TAA COM	Division Support Command (DISCOM)	DISCOM
Theater Support Command (TSC)	TSC	Division Aviation Support Battalion (DASB)	DASB
Area Support Group (ASG)	ASG	Main Support Battalion (MSB)	MSB
Corps Support Command (COSCOM)	COSCOM	Forward Support Battalion (FSB)	FSB

V. Functional CSS Unit Symbols

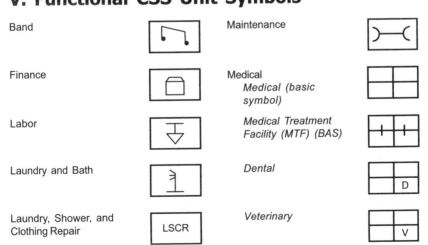

Band		Maintenance	
Finance		Medical Medical (basic symbol)	
Labor		Medical Treatment Facility (MTF) (BAS)	
Laundry and Bath		Dental	D
Laundry, Shower, and Clothing Repair	LSCR	Veterinary	V

Resources

Morale, Welfare, and Recreation (MWR)	MWR	Service	SVC
Mortuary Affairs	✝	Supply (Basic Symbol)	
Personnel Services	PS	Support	SPT
Postal or Courrier		Transportation *(Basic Symbol)*	⊕
Public Affairs	PA	*Railhead*	⊕
Broadcast Public Affairs Detachment	BPAD	*Seaport (SPOD or SPOE)*	⊕
Corps Media Center	PRESS	*Airfield/Airport (APOD or APOE)*	⊕
Joint Information Bureau (JIB) - EAC	JIB	Water *Distribution*	
Replacement Holding Unit	RHU	*Purification*	PURE
Salvage	SALV		

Resources

Combat Service Support Resources
II. CSS Bibliography

The following represents a partial listing of commonly-used Army and joint doctrinal CSS publications.

Field Manuals (Dept of Army)
Ref: www.train.army.mil

FM 3-35.4   Deployment Fort-to-Port,18 JUN 2002

FM 3-100.21   Contractors on the Battlefield, SS FM 100-21, 03 JAN 2003

FM 4-0   Combat Service Support, 29 AUG 2003
SS FM 100-10

FM 4-01.011   Unit Movement Operations, 31 OCT 2002
SS FM 55-65 & FM 55-9

FM 4-01.30   Movement Control, SS FM 55-10, 01 SEP 2003

FM 4-01.41   Army Rail Operations, SS FM 55-20, 12 DEC 2003

FM 4-20.41   Aerial Delivery Distribution in the Theater of Operations, SS FM 10-500-1, 29 AUG 2003

FM 4-20.102   Airdrop of Supplies and Equipment: Rigging Airdrop Platforms, SS FM 10-500-2, 22 AUG 2001

FM 4-20.105   Airdrop of Supplies and Equipment: Dual Row Airdrop Systems, Change 1, 3 SEP 2003 01 APR 2002

FM 4-20.107   Airdrop Derigging and Recovery Procedures, SS FM 10-500-7 07 OCT 2004

FM 4-20.108   Airdrop of Supplies and Equipment: Rigging Military Utility Vehicle (M-GATOR), Change 1, 7 MAY 2004; SS FM 10-508 29 JUN 2001

FM 4-20.112   Airdrop of Supplies and Equipment: Rigging Typical Supply Loads, SS FM 10-512 07 MAY 2004

FM 4-20.113   Airdrop of Supplies and Equipment: Rigging 3/4-Ton Cargo Trailers, SS FM 10-513 08 JUL 2003

FM 4-20.116   Airdrop of Supplies and Equipment: Reference Data for Airdrop Platform Loads, Change 1, 1 OCT 2004 20 AUG 2001

FM 4-20.117   Airdrop of Supplies and Equipment: Rigging High-Mobility Multipurpose Wheeled Vehicles, SS FM 10-517 01 OCT 2001

FM 4-20.121   Airdrop of Supplies and Equipment: Rigging of Tractors and Tractor-Dozers, SS FM 10-521 20 MAR 2003

FM 4-20.127   Airdrop of Supplies and Equipment: Rigging M198, 155-MM Howitzer, SS FM 10-527 29 JUN 2004

FM 4-20.137   Airdrop of Supplies and Equipment: Rigging Forward Area Refueling Equipment (FARE) and Advanced Aviation Forward Area Refueling System (AAFARS), SS FM 10-537 10 JUN 2003

FM 4-20.147   Airdrop of Supplies and Equipment: Humanitarian Airdrop, SS FM 10-547
              28 NOV 2003

FM 4-20.153   Airdrop of Supplies and Equipment: Rigging Ammunition, SS FM 10-500-53
              01 MAY 2004

FM 4-30.1   Munitions Distribution in the Theater of Operations, 16 DEC 2003
              SS FM 9-6

FM 4-30.3   Maintenance Operations and Procedures, 28 JUL 2004

FM 4-30.13   Ammunition Handbook: Tactics, Techniques, and Procedures for Munition
              Handlers, 01 MAR 2001
              SS FM 9-13 (1986) & FM 9-38 (1993)

FM 4-93.4   Theater Support Command (SS FM 63-4); 15 APR 2003

FM 4-93.50   Tactics, Techniques, and Procedures for the Forward Support Battalion
              (Digitized); 02 MAY 2002

FM 4-93.51   Tactics, Techniques, and Procedures for the Division Support Battalion
              (Digitized); 26 MAY 2002

FM 4-93.52   Tactics, Techniques, and Procedures for the Division Support Command
              (Digitized); 02 MAY 2002

FM 4-93.53   Tactics, Techniques, and Procedures for the Division Aviation Support
              Battalion (Digitized); 02 MAY 2002

FM 9-15   Explosive Ordnance Disposal Service and Unit Operations, 08 MAY 1996

FM 9-207   Operations and Maintenance of Ordnance Material in Cold Weather, 20
              MAR 1998

FM 10-1   Quartermaster Principles, Supersedes FM 10-1, 24 Sep 91, 11 AUG 1994

FM 10-15   Basic Doctrine Manual for Supply and Storage, Change 1, 30 Sep 93, 12
              DEC 1990

FM 10-16   General Fabric Repair, 24 MAY 2000

FM 10-23   Basic Doctrine for Army Field Feeding and Class I Operations Management,
              18 APR 1996

FM 10-23-2   Tactics, Techniques, and Procedures for Garrison Food Preparation and
              Class I Operations Management, 30 SEP 1993

FM 10-27   General Supply in Theaters in Operations, 20 APR 1993

FM 10-27-1   Tactics, Techniques, and Procedures for Quartermaster General Support
              Supply Operations, 20 APR 1993

FM 10-27-2   Tactics, Techniques, and Procedures for Quartermaster Direct Support
              Supply and Field Service Operations, 18 JUN 1991

FM 10-27-3   Tactics, Techniques, and Procedures for Quartermaster Headquarters
              Operations, Ch 1, 20 Sep 94, 30 OCT 1990

FM 10-27-4   Organizational Supply and Services for Unit Leaders, 14 APR 2000

FM 10-52   Water Supply in Theaters of Operations, 11 JUL 1990

FM 10-52-1   Water Supply Point Equipment and Operations, 18 JUN 1991

FM 10-64   Mortuary Affairs Operations, 16 FEB 1999

FM 10-67   Petroleum Supply in Theaters of Operations, Ch 1, 10 Oct 85, 18 FEB 1983

FM 10-67-1   Concepts and Equipment of Petroleum Operations, 02 APR 1998

FM 10-67-2   Petroleum Laboratory Testing Operations, 02 APR 1997

FM 10-115   Quartermaster Water Units, 15 FEB 1989

FM 10-286   Identification of Deceased Personnel, 30 JUN 1976

FM 10-416   Petroleum Pipeline and Terminal Operating Units, 12 MAY 1998

FM 10-426   Petroleum Supply Units, 12 JUL 1997

FM 10-450-3   Multiservice Helicopter Sling Load: Basic Operations and Equipment, 10 APR 1997

FM 10-450-4   Multiservice Helicopter Sling Load: Single-Point Rigging Procedures, Change 2, 1 APR 2002, 30 MAY 1998

FM 10-450-5   Multiservice Helicopter Sling Load: Dual-Point Rigging Procedures, Change 3, 3 DEC 2003, 30 AUG 1999

FM 10-500-3 - Airdrop of Supplies and Equipment
FM 10-591   *(Range of related-subject publications)*

FM 10-602   Headquarters and Headquarters Units, Petroleum and Water Distribution Organization, 12 SEP 1996

FM 21-16   Unexploded Ordnance (UXO) Procedures, 30 AUG 1994

FM 21-305   Manual for the Wheeled Vehicle Driver, 27 AUG 1993

FM 38-700   Packaging of Material - Preservation, 01 DEC 1999

FM 38-701   Packaging of Material: Packing, 01 DEC 1999

FM 42-414   Tactics, Techniques, and Procedures for Quartermaster Field Service Company, Direct Support, 03 JUL 1998

FM 42-424   Quartermaster Force Provider Company, 06 AUG 1999

FM 54-40   Area Support Group, 03 OCT 1995

FM 55-1   Transportation Operations, 03 OCT 1995

FM 55-15   Transportation Reference Data, 27 OCT 1997

FM 55-17   Cargo Specialist's Handbook, 16 FEB 1999

FM 55-21   Railway Operating and Safety Rules, 17 JUL 1989

FM 55-30   Army Motor Transport Units and Operations, Change 1, 15 September 1999, 27 JUN 1997

FM 55-50   Army Water Transport Operations, 30 SEP 1993

FM 55-60   Army Terminal Operations, 15 APR 1996

FM 55-80   Army Container Operations, 13 AUG 1997

FM 55-450-2   Army Helicopter Internal Load Operations, 05 JUN 1992

FM 55-501   Marine Crewman's Handbook, 01 DEC 1999

FM 55-502   Army Watercraft Safety, 23 DEC 1996

FM 55-509-1   Introduction to Marine Electricity, 01 SEP 1994

FM 55-511   Operation of Floating Cranes, 12 DEC 1985

FM 63-2   Division Support Command, Armored, Infantry, and Mechanized Infantry Divisions; 20 MAY 1991

FM 63-11   Logistics Support Element Tactics, Techniques, and Procedures; 08 OCT 1996

FM 63-20   Forward Support Battalion (SS FM 63-20, 17 May 85); 26 FEB 1990

FM 63-21   Main Support Battalion; 07 AUG 1990

FM 63-23   Aviation Support Battalion; 06 JUN 1996

FM 100-9   Reconstitution, 13 JAN 1992

FM 100-10-1   Theater Distribution, 01 OCT 1999

FM 100-10-2   Contracting Support on the Battlefield, 04 AUG 1999

FM 100-17-2   Army Pre-Positioned Land, 16 FEB 1999

FM 100-17-3   Reception, Staging, Onward Movement, and Integration, 17 MAR 1999

FM 100-17-5   Redeployment, 29 SEP 1999

Joint Publications

Ref: http://www.dtic.mil/doctrine/index.html

JP 4-0   Doctrine for Logistic Support of Joint Operations, 06 April 2000

JP 4-01   Joint Doctrine for the Defense Transportation System, 19 March 2003

JP 4-01.2   JTTP for Sealift Support to Joint Operations, 9 October 1996

JP 4-01.3   Joint Tactics, Techniques, and Procedures for Movement Control, 09 April 2002

JP 4-01.4   Joint Tactics, Techniques, and Procedures for Joint Theater Distribution, 22 August 2000

JP 4-01.5   Joint Tactics, Techniques, and Procedures for Transportation Terminal Operations, 9 April 2002

JP 4-01.6   Joint Tactics, Techniques, and Procedures for Joint Logistics Over the Shore, 12 November 1998

JP 4-01.7   JTTP for Use of Intermodal Containers in Joint Operations, 7 January 1997

JP 4-01.8   Joint Tactics, Techniques, and Procedures for Joint Reception, Staging, Onward Movement, and Integration, 13 June 2000

JP 4-02   Doctrine for Health Service Support in Joint Operations, 30 July 2001

JP 4-02.1   JTTP for Health Service Logistic Support in Joint Operations, 6 October 1997

Ref: ST 101-6 CGSC Combat Service Support Battle Book, app. M.

The following lists acronyms or abbreviations frequently used in combat service support operations. Acronym Finder http://www.acronymfinder.com/

A

AA assembly area
AAFES Army and Air Force Exchange Service
AASLT air assault
abn, Abn airborne
ACE Army casualty estimator
acft aircraft
ACR armored cavalry regiment
AD airdrop
ADA air defense artillery
ADAM area denial artillery munitions
ADC(S) assistant division commander (support)
ADP automatic data processing
AG adjutant general
AHB attack helicopter battalion
ALOC air lines of communication
alt alternate
AMB aviation maintenance battalion
AMC aircraft maintenance company
AMCO aviation maintenance company
AMEDD Army Medical Department
AO area of operations
AOE Army of Excellence
AP armor-piercing
APC armored personnel carrier
APDS-T armor-piercing discarding sabot—tracer
APERS antipersonnel
APFSDS-T armor-piercing, fin-stabilized, discarding sabot—tracer
API armor-piercing incendiary
APOD aerial port of debarkation
APOE aerial port of embarkation
AR armor
armd armored
arty, ARTY artillery
ASB aviation support battalion (division)
ASL authorized stockage list

ASMB area support medical battalion
ASMC area support medical company
ASP ammunition supply point
assy assembly
AT antitank
ATCOM Aviation Troop Command
ATGM antitank guided missile
atk, ATK attack
ATLAS all-terrain lifter articulated system
ATP ammunition transfer point
aug augmentation
autmv automotive
AVIM aviation intermediate maintenance
Avn aviation
AVUM aviation unit maintenance
AXP ambulance exchange point

B

BAS battalion aid station
B/B breakbulk
BCC battlefield circulation control
BCT brigade combat team
BDAR battle damage assessment and repair
bde, Bde brigade
BDO battle dress overgarment
BFV Bradley fighting vehicle
BMSO brigade medical supply office
bn, Bn battalion
BOS battlefield operating system
BRT brigade reconnaissance troop
BSA brigade support area
BSTF base shop test facility
btry battery

C

C2SRS command and control strength reporting system
CA civil affairs
CAB combat aviation brigade
CAC combat aviation company
CAPS II consolidated aerial port system

CAS close air support

CASCOM US Army Combined Arms Support Command

CASEVAC casualty evacuation

cav, CAV cavalry

cbt, Cbt, CBT combat

CCIR commander's critical information requirements

CCL combat-configured load

CCP casualty collection point

CCSS commodity command standard system

CDE chemical defense equipment

cdr, Cdr, CDR commander

CE communications-electronics

CERL construction equipment requirements list

CEV combat engineer vehicle

CEWI communications electronic warfare intelligence

CFM CONUS freight management

CFV combat fighting vehicle

cgo cargo

chg charge

CHS combat health support

CI civilian internees

civ civilian

CLGP cannon-launched guided projectile

CMCB corps movement control battalion

cmd command

CMMC corps materiel management center

CMO civil-militaryoperations

CMOC civil-military operations center

co, Co company

COA course of action

CofS chief of staff

COMMZ communications zone

compt comptroller

COMSEC communications security

COSCOM corps support command

CP command post, check point

CPHD Copperhead

CSA corps storage area

CSB corps support battalion

CSC combat stress control

CSG corps support group

CSH combat support hospital

CSR controlled supply rate

CSS combat service support

CSSCS combat service support control system

ctg cartridge

D

DA Department of the Army

DAG division artillery group (enemy)

DAMMS-R Department of the Army Movement Management System-Redesign

DAO division ammunition officer; division ammunition office

DAS3 Decentralized Automated Service Support System

DASB division aviation support battalion

DCAS database commitment accounting system

DD disability discharge (from CONUS hospital)

det, Det detachment, detainee

DIH died in hospital

DISCOM division support command

distr distribution

division

DIVARTY division artillery

DLRO Department of Logistics and Resource Management

DMMC division materiel management center

DMOC division medical operation center

DMSO division medical supply office

DNBI disease and nonbattle injuries

DOD Department of Defense

DOS days of supply

DPICM dual-purpose improved conventional munition

DS direct support

DSA division support area

DSB division support battalion

DTO division transportation officer

DZ drop zone

E

EA engagement area

EAB echelons above brigade

EAC echelons above corps

ech, Ech echelons

EMS emergency medical service

EMT emergency medical treatment

ENCOM engineer command

Eng, ENG engineer

EO equal opportunity

EOD explosive ordnance disposal

EOD BN explosive ordnance disposal battalion (replaces EOD control team - EODCT)

EPW enemy prisoner of war
evac evacuation
EXTAL extra time allowance
F&E fuel and electronic

F

FAAR forward area alerting radar
FARE forward area refueling equipment
FARP forward arming and refueling point
FASCAM family of scatterable mines
FAWPSS forward area water point supply system
FB finance battalion
FC finance command
FD finance detachment
FDRP first destination reporting point
FG finance group
FINCOM finance command
FL forklift
FM field manual
FPOL forward passage of lines
FSB forward support battalion
FSC forward support company, field supply company
FSMC forward support medical company
FSSP fuel system supply point
FST forward surgical team
FSU finance support unit
fwd, Fwd forward
fz fuze

G

G G stands for general's staff (vs. S, staff for brigade and below)
G1 personnel
G2 intelligence
G3 operations and training
G4 logistics
G5 civil-military operations
G6 signal operations
Gal/Man/Day gallons per man per day
GB green bag
GMC ground maintenance company
gp, Gp group
GP general purpose
GPH gallons per hour
GPM gallons per minute
GS general support
GSE ground support equipment
GTN global transportation network

H

HCP health and comfort pack

hdlr handler
HE high explosive
HEAT high-explosive antitank
HEDP high-explosive dual-purpose
HEI high-explosive incendiary
HEIT high-explosive incendiary—tracer
HELLFIRE helicopter launched fire and forget missile system
HEMAT heavy expanded, mobility, ammunition trailer
HEMTT hvy expanded mobility tact. truck
HEP high-explosive plastic
HERA high-explosive, rocket-assisted
HET heavy-equipment transporter
HHC headquarters and headquarters company
HHD headquarters and headquarters detachment
HHT headquarters and headquarters troop
hlth health
HMMWV high-mobility multipurpose wheeled vehicle
HNS host nation support
HOGE hover out of ground effect
how howitzer
HQ headquarters
HSC headquarters and supply company
HUB hospital unit base
HUS hospital unit surgical
HUSF hospital unit, surgical, forward
HUSM hospital unit, surgical, main
hvy, Hvy heavy

I

IAW in accordance with
ICE individual chemical equipment
ICM improved conventional missile
ICP incremental change package
IDA Institute of Defense Analysis
IED improvised explosive device
IFTE Integrated Family of Test Equipment
IFV infantry fighting vehicle
IG inspector general
ILAP integrated logistics analysis program
IPB intelligence preparation of the battlefield
IR infrared
ISO International Standards Organization
ITV improved TOW vehicle

J

J J stands for JOINT staff
J1 manpower and personnel

J2 intelligence
J3 operations
J4 logistics
J5 plans and operations
J6 command, control, communications and computers (C4I)
JA judge advocate
JIB joint information bureau
JTF joint task force

K

kg, KG kilogram
KIA killed in action
km, KM kilometer
KMPH kilometers per hour
kw kilowatt

L

LADS laundry advanced system
LAWS light, anti-tank weapon system
lb, lbs pound(s)
LC load center
LCD limited conversion division pounds
LCMS land combat missile system
LCSS land combat support system
ldr, Ldr leader
LID light infantry division
LMTV light medium tactical vehicle
LNO liaison officer
LOC lines of communication
log, Log, LOG logistics
LOGPAC logistics package
LOTS logistics-over-the-shore operations
LP/C launch platform container
LRP long-range reconnaissance pack, logistics release point
LRU line replaceable unit
LSA logistic support area
LZ landing zone

M

MA mortuary affairs
MACOM major Army command
MAFFMS man, arm, fuel, fix, move, sustain
maint maintenance
MANPADS man-portable air defense system
MASF mobile aeromedical staging facility
mat materiel
MCO movement control officer
MCT movement control team

MCTNS man-portable common thermal night sight
mdm medium
mech mechanized
med, Med medical
MEDCOM medical command
MEDEVAC medical evacuation
MEF Marine expeditionary force
METT-TC mission, enemy, terrain, troops, and time available, civilians
MHE materials handling equipment
MI military intelligence
MIA missing in action
MIBR mechanized infantry brigade
MICLIC mine-clearing line charge
MID mechanized infantry division
MILSTAMP military standard transportation and movement procedures
MILVAN military-owned demountable container
MLRS multiple-launch rocket system
MMC materiel management center
MOADS maneuver-oriented ammunition distribution system
MOGAS motor gasoline
MOPP mission-oriented protection posture
MORT mortuary
MOS military occupational specialty
MP military police
MPAD mobile public affairs detachment
MPH miles per hour
MPSM multipurpose submunition
MRI Medical Reengineering Initiative
MRS medical resupply sets
MSB main support battalion
MSBMC main support battalion medical company
MSC major subordinate command
MSE mobile subscriber equipment
MSF mobile strike force
MSR main supply route
MST maintenance support team
MTF maintenance test flight
MTOE modified table of organization and equipment
MTSQ mechanical time, superquick
MTV medium tactical vehicle
MTW major theater of war
MU march unit
MWR morale, welfare, and recreation

MODULAR INTEGRATED
  COMMUNICATIONS HELMET (MICH)

MARITIME LOAD CARRIAGE System
                    (mLCS)

CUSTODY TRACKING SUBSYSTEM
                    (CTS)

PERSONAL ENVIRONMENTAL   PEASE
PROTECTION SURVINAC
   EQUIPMENY

N

NATO North Atlantic Treaty Organization
NBC nuclear, biological, and chemical
NDI nondestructive inspection
NEO noncombatant evacuation order
NGO nongovernment organization
NMC not mission-capable

O

obj, Obj, OBJ objective
OCONUS outside the Continental United States
O/H on hand
O/O on order
OPLAN operation plan
OPORD operation order
op(s), OP(S) operating/operation(s)
opt optometry
OPTEMPO operating/operational tempo

P

PAC personnel and administration center
Pam pamphlet
PAO public affairs officer, public affairs office
PAOC public affairs operations center
PAR population at risk
PASR personnel accounting and strength reporting
PAX passengers
PD point designating; personnel detachment
PDY present for duty
PERSCOM personnel command
petrl petroleum
PG personnel group
pl pipeline
PL phase line
plt, Plt platoon
PLL prescribed load list
PLS palletized loading system
PM preventive medicine
PMC personnel management center
PMD pounds per man per day
POL petroleum, oils, and lubricants
POM program objective memorandum
pos position
PPD pounds/person/day
PPL petroleum pipeline
prop propelling
prox proximity
PSB personnel services battalion

PSR personnel status report
PST pass times
Pts, PTS patients
PVO private volunteer organization
PX post exchange (Army)

Q

QA quality assurance
QC quality control
QM quartermaster
QSS quick supply store
QSTAG Quadripartite Standardization Agreement

R

R3P rearm, refuel, and resupply point
R/CW ration/cold weather
RAMMS remote antiarmor mine system
RAOC rear area operations center
RAP rocket-assisted projectile
RB red bag
regt regiment
rep, Rep representative
repl replacement
rkt rocket
ROM refuel on the move
RORO roll on/roll off
ROWPU reverse osmosis water purification unit
RP release point
RSA regimental support area
RSR required supply rate
RSS regimental support squadron
RSSP ration supplement sundries pack
RT rough terrain
RTCC rough-terrain container crane
RTCH rough terrain container handler
RTD returned to duty
RTFL rough-terrain forklift
RX repairable exchange

S

S&P stake and platform
S&S supply and service
SAAS Standard Army Ammunition System
SAMS Standard Army Maintenance System
SARSS-1 Standard Army Retail Supply System-Level 1
SATCOM satellite communications
SB supply bulletin
SDS standard depot system
sec section

sep separate
SFV Stinger fighting vehicle
SHORAD short-range air defense
SIB separate infantry brigade
SIDPERS Standard Installation/Division Personnel System
sig signal
SJA staff judge advocate
SLCR shower, laundry, and clothing repair
SOP standing operating procedure
SP self-propelled; start point
SPBS Standard Property Book System
SPOD seaport of debarkation
SPOE seaport of embarkation
spt, Spt support
SRC standard requirement code
sqd, Sqd squad
sqdn, Sqdn squadron
SRP soldier readiness processing
SRU shop replaceable unit
SST system support team
ST student text
STANAG standardization agreement
STGR Stinger
STON short tons
SVCS services

T

TA theater army
TAA tactical assembly area
TACAIR tactical air
TACCS Tactical Army Combat Service Support (CSS) Computer System
TACFIRE tactical fire-direction system
TACSAT tactical satellite communications set
TADDS target alert data display set
TAMMIS Theater Army Medical Management Information System
TB technical bulletin
TBP to be published
TCACCIS transportation coordinator automated command and control information system
TCF tactical combat force
TCP tactical control point
TDA table(s) of distribution and allowances
TDIS time distance
TEMPER tent, expandable, modular, personnel
TF task force

TFE tactical field exchange
TLAT TOW, light antitank (bn)
tm, Tm team
TMDE test, measurement, and diagnostic equipment
tml terminal
TMT transportation motor transport
TOE tables of organization and equipment
TPT tactical petroleum terminal
TRANSCOM transportation command
trmt treatment
TRP target reference point
TSA theater storage area
TSC theater support command
TSOP tactical standing operating procedures
TTP trailer transfer point; tactics, techniques, and procedures
TTS transportation terminal service
TWPS tactical water purification system

U

UBL unit basic load
UDP unit defense pack
UGR unitized group rations
ULLS unit level logistics system
UMCP unit maintenance collection point
UMT unit maintenance team
UN United Nations
UO urban operations
USAF US Air Force
USPW US prisoners of war
UXO unexploded ordnance

V

veh, Veh vehicle
VPK vehicles per kilometer

W

w with
w/o without
WB white bag
whl wheeled
WHNS wartime host nation support
WIA wounded in action
WP white phosphorus
WPS worldwide port system
WSM weapon system manager
WSRO weapon system replacement operations

X

XO executive officer

The Combat Service Support & Deployment SMARTbook

Index

Resources

Resources

Resources

Resources

Speak the Language of Your Profession

Military SMARTbooks

The Leader's SMARTbook
Step-by-Step Guide to Training, Leadership, Team Building & Counseling (2nd Revised Ed.)
Updated with the the new FM 7-0! Covers the complete doctrinal series on training management, team building, leadership and developmental counseling. Topics include FM 7-0 Training the Army, Company-Level Training Management (TC 25-30), After Action Reviews (TC 25-20), The Army Leader (FM 22-100) and Levels of Leadership (FM 22-100), Combat-Ready Teams (FM 22-102) and Developmental Counseling.

The Battle Staff SMARTbook
Step-by-Step Visual Guide to Military Decision Making & Tactical Operations
Covers the entire spectrum of planning and conducting military operations. Topics include the military decision making process (mission planning), intelligence preparation of the battlefield, plans and orders (WARNOs/OPORDs/FRAGOs), rehearsals, after-action reviews (AARs), tactical operations center (TOC), information management, and operational terms and graphics (FM 101-5-1).

The Operations SMARTbook
FM 3-0 Full Spectrum Operations and the Battlefield Operating Systems (3rd Revised Ed.)
Fully updated! Guide to FM 3-0 Full Spectrum Operations and the battlefield operating systems (BOSs): intelligence, surveillance & reconnaissance (ISR); maneuver and U.S. Army organization; fire support; air defense and Army airspace command and control (A2C2); mobility, countermobility & survivability (MCS) to include NBC operations; combat service support (CSS); and command & control (C2).

The Joint Forces & Operational Warfighting SMARTbook
Guide to Joint Doctrine, Operational Warfighting and Theater/Campaign Planning
Applicable to ALL Services plus the Dept of Defense and Joint Staff. Covers fundamentals of joint ops; joint structure and org; joint strategy & resource development (DPS, NSC, JSPS, PPBS); Joint Operations Planning & Execution System (JOPES); campaign/theater planning; joint task forces (JTFs); log spt to joint ops; and joint doctrine resources.

The Combat Service Support & Deployment SMARTbook
Doctrinal Guide to Combat Service Support, RSO&I and Unit Movement Operations
Complete guide to FM 4-0 Combat Service Support; joint force logistics (JP 4-0); CSS operations (FSB, DSB, DASB, DISCOM, TSC, rear area defensive ops, transformation); CSS planning; unit movement ops (FM 4-01.011); reception, staging, onward movement and integration (RSO&I - FM 100-17-3); and combat service support resources.

www.TheLightningPress.com
Purchase/Order Form

Indicate quantity desired ($29.95 each + shipping):

_____ The Battle Staff SMARTbook

_____ The Operations SMARTbook (3rd Ed.)

_____ The Leader's SMARTbook (2nd Ed.)

_____ The Joint Forces & Operational
Warfighting SMARTbook

_____ The Combat Service Support &
Deployment SMARTbook

Order SECURE Online:
Place your order online at **www.TheLightningPress.com**

24-hour Voicemail/Fax/Order:
Record your order by voicemail at 1-800-997-8827

Business Fax:
Fax your completed order to 1-800-997-8827

Mail:
Mail this order form to 2227 Arrowhead Blvd., Lakeland, FL 33813

For up-to-date pricing and ordering details, visit www.TheLightningPress.com

Shipping Information

Name————————————————

Address——————————————

Address——————————————

City ———————————— State ————— Zip —————

Phone————————— E-mail ——————————

If ordering by credit card (Mastercard, Visa, American Express)

Card Holder's Name ———————————— Card Type —————

Card Number ———————————— Expiration Date —————

Card Holder's Signature ————————————

Billing Address (if different from above) ————————————

In addition to Mastercard, Visa and American Express, we also accept qualified purchase orders, government IMPAC cards, personal checks and money orders.

Shipping

___ Standard ($5.00 first book, +$1.50 each additional book). Allow 2-3 weeks.

___ APO ($5.50 first book, +$1.50 each additional book). Allow 2-4 weeks.

All published prices (to include postage), specifications and services are subject to change without notice. This includes preprinted order forms included in books.